Catalan Narrative 1875–2015

LEGENDA

LEGENDA is the Modern Humanities Research Association's book imprint for new research in the Humanities. Founded in 1995 by Malcolm Bowie and others within the University of Oxford, Legenda has always been a collaborative publishing enterprise, directly governed by scholars. The Modern Humanities Research Association (MHRA) joined this collaboration in 1998, became half-owner in 2004, in partnership with Maney Publishing and then Routledge, and has since 2016 been sole owner. Titles range from medieval texts to contemporary cinema and form a widely comparative view of the modern humanities, including works on Arabic, Catalan, English, French, German, Greek, Italian, Portuguese, Russian, Spanish, and Yiddish literature. Editorial boards and committees of more than 60 leading academic specialists work in collaboration with bodies such as the Society for French Studies, the British Comparative Literature Association and the Association of Hispanists of Great Britain & Ireland.

The MHRA encourages and promotes advanced study and research in the field of the modern humanities, especially modern European languages and literature, including English, and also cinema. It aims to break down the barriers between scholars working in different disciplines and to maintain the unity of humanistic scholarship. The Association fulfils this purpose through the publication of journals, bibliographies, monographs, critical editions, and the MHRA Style Guide, and by making grants in support of research. Membership is open to all who work in the Humanities, whether independent or in a University post, and the participation of younger colleagues entering the field is especially welcomed.

ALSO PUBLISHED BY THE ASSOCIATION

Critical Texts
Tudor and Stuart Translations • *New Translations* • *European Translations*
MHRA Library of Medieval Welsh Literature

MHRA Bibliographies
Publications of the Modern Humanities Research Association

The Annual Bibliography of English Language & Literature
Austrian Studies
Modern Language Review
Portuguese Studies
The Slavonic and East European Review
Working Papers in the Humanities
The Yearbook of English Studies

www.mhra.org.uk
www.legendabooks.com

STUDIES IN HISPANIC AND LUSOPHONE CULTURES

Studies in Hispanic and Lusophone Cultures are selected and edited by the Association of Hispanists of Great Britain & Ireland. The series seeks to publish the best new research in all areas of the literature, thought, history, culture, film, and languages of Spain, Spanish America, and the Portuguese-speaking world.

The Association of Hispanists of Great Britain & Ireland is a professional association which represents a very diverse discipline, in terms of both geographical coverage and objects of study. Its website showcases new work by members, and publicises jobs, conferences and grants in the field.

STUDIES IN HISPANIC AND LUSOPHONE CULTURES

Catalan Narrative 1875–2015

EDITED BY
JORDI LARIOS AND MONTSERRAT LUNATI

LEGENDA
Studies in Hispanic and Lusophone Cultures 16
Modern Humanities Research Association
2020

Published by Legenda
an imprint of the Modern Humanities Research Association
Salisbury House, Station Road, Cambridge CB1 2LA

ISBN 978-1-78188-710-3

First published 2020

Copy-Editor: Richard Correll

CONTENTS

ACKNOWLEDGEMENTS

The co-editors would like to thank the late Prof. Trevor Dadson, our series editor, and Dr Graham Nelson, from Legenda, for commissioning this volume and for their patience and unfailing courtesy; Prof. Alan Yates for translating from Catalan into English several of the contributions to the volume as well as his example and his friendship over the years; and Prof. Will Fowler, Head of the School of Modern Languages at the University of St Andrews when the conference 'Catalan Narrative 1870–2015' was held, for his moral support and for making the gathering financially viable. We would also like to express our gratitude to Dr Abraham Davies, Roger Maimí and Dr Rhiannon McGlade for lending a hand with preparing this volume, and Richard Correll for his copy-editing.

J.L. & M.L., March 2020

NOTES ON THE CONTRIBUTORS

Enric Bou is Professor of Iberian Studies at the Università Ca' Foscari Venezia. Previously, he taught at Brown University (1996–2011). His research interests include Spanish Peninsular and Catalan literature, autobiography, city and literature, space and film. His latest books are *Invention of Space: City, Travel and Literature* (2013) and *Irradiaciones: estudios de literatura y cine* (2018).

Helena Buffery teaches and researches at University College Cork, where she is currently Vice Head (Research) of the College of Arts, Celtic Studies and Social Sciences. Her main teaching and research interests are in contemporary Hispanic Theatre and Performance, Translation Studies and Catalan Studies, and her work on Catalan culture is characterized by a focus on processes of intercultural translation and performativity. Key publications include *Shakespeare in Catalan: Translating Imperialism* (2007), *Stages of Exile: Spanish Republican Exile Theatre and Performance* (2011), and *Barcelona: Visual Culture, Space and Power* (2012, with Carlota Caulfield).

Jordi Cornellà-Detrell is Senior Lecturer in Hispanic Studies at the University of Glasgow. His research interests are the post-war publishing industry; censorship and translation during Franco's regime; twentieth-century Catalan and Spanish literature; and multilingual literature. He has published *Literature as a Response to Cultural and Political Repression in Franco's Catalonia* (2011), and *El plurilingüisme en la literatura catalana* (2014, with Albert Rossich). He has co-edited the volume *Translation and Global Spaces of Power* (2018) and guest-edited a special issue of *Target* with Stefan Baumgarten ('Rethinking Hegemony and Domination in Translation', 2017).

Kathryn Crameri is Emeritus Professor at the University of Glasgow, having formerly been Head of the School of Modern Languages and Cultures, and Stevenson Chair of Hispanic Studies. She is the author of *Goodbye, Spain? The Question of Independence for Catalonia* (2014) as well as numerous other publications on Catalan politics, culture and literature.

P. Louise Johnson is Reader in Catalan and Spanish at the University of Sheffield. She works broadly across modern and contemporary Catalan and Peninsular Hispanic Studies, with a dual focus on literature, specifically the novel, and on intellectual engagements with physical culture and sport. Cross-cutting these areas are issues of gender, sexuality, identity, nation and inclusion. She has published on Llorenç Villalonga, Manuel de Pedrolo, Maria Aurèlia Capmany, Miquel López Crespí, Eduardo Mendicutti, Guillem Viladot, and on 1930s' Catalan and Spanish sporting culture, the tradition of Catalan Olympism, and the emergence of mass sporting culture in twentieth-century Spain. Her most recent publications on Viladot include 'Art at the Biomedical Interface: Trans/Sculptural Discourses in Guillem Viladot's *Ruth*' (*Hispanic Research Journal*) and 'The Lyrical Taboos of Guillem Viladot' (*Barcelona: Visual Culture, Space and Power*, ed. by Helena Buffery and Carlota Caulfield).

Dominic Keown is Professor of Catalan Studies at the University of Cambridge. He specializes in contemporary Iberian culture and has published widely on the ideological dimension of Catalan literature: *Sobre la poesia catalana contemporània* (1996), *Polifonia de la subversió: la veu col·lectiva de Vicent Andrés Estellés* (2000), *A Companion to Catalan Culture* (2011), and *After the Classics: The Selected Verse of Vicent Andrés Estellés* (2013). He also writes on cinema from Spain with special reference to Buñuel, Berlanga, Monleón and Bigas Luna. His current interests extend to the interface between Catalan and Spanish creativity, transnational issues in the cultural production of Catalonia, and the metacritical divide between Hispanism and Iberian Studies. He is the editor of the Anglo-Catalan Society's Occasional Papers, the *Journal of Catalan Studies* (1998–2019) and the editor/translator of Joan Salvat-Papasseit (1982; 2005), Ausiàs March (3 vols: 1986; 1989; 1993), Valle-Inclán (1991) and Joan Fuster (1992; 2006).

Jordi Larios is Professor of Spanish at the University of St Andrews. Previously, he taught at Cardiff University and Queen Mary University of London, where he was the Director of the Centre for Catalan Studies. He has written on twentieth-century Catalan literature and culture (Joan Miró, Josep Pla, Llorenç Villalonga) as well as twentieth-century Spanish literature (Luis Cernuda, Benjamín Jarnés, Pedro Salinas). He has published four collections of poetry and has translated into Catalan works by Robert Coover, Henry James, Dorothy Parker, Anthony Powell, Saki and Oscar Wilde, among others. He co-founded *Tesserae: Journal of Iberian and Latin-American Studies*, which he co-edited for twenty years.

Montserrat Lunati is Honorary Reader at the University of St Andrews, and Honorary Senior Research Fellow at Cardiff University, having taken early retirement from Cardiff University in 2016 as Reader in Catalan and Spanish Studies. She was Visiting Professor at the University of Chicago in 2012, and at Stanford University in 2018. She has published extensively on Catalan ironists, narratives of illness and contemporary women's writing. She is the author of *Imma Monsó: la narrativa de la diferència i la ironia* (2008) and has edited several anthologies of contemporary Spanish short stories. She co-founded *Tesserae: Journal of Iberian and Latin-American Studies*, which she co-edited for twenty years. She is currently working on a book on narratives of mourning and memory in contemporary Catalan culture.

Elisa Martí-López is Associate Professor Emerita of Spanish at Northwestern University. She is the author of several articles and a book (*Borrowed Words: Translation, Imitation, and the Making of the Novel in Nineteenth-Century Spain*, 2002) on the processes of cultural production and consumption in mid-nineteenth century. As part of her project 'The Urban Spaces of Death: Cemeteries as Narratives of the Modern City, 1780–1918', she has published 'It's All about Location: The Space of Death in Barcelona, 1819–1972' (2012), 'Memory and the City in Barcelona's Cemeteries' (2017), and 'Death and the Crisis of Representation in Narcís Oller's *La febre d'or* (and Pérez Galdós's *La de Bringas*)' (2017).

Sílvia Mas Sañé has a degree in Literary Theory and Comparative Literature (Universitat Autònoma de Barcelona), and a PhD in Hispanic Studies (University of Birmingham). She received the Mercè Rodoreda Foundation Prize in 2007 for her study *Les novel·les d'exili d'Avel·lí Artís-Gener* (2008). She has worked as a lecturer at the Universitat de Girona and the Universitat Oberta de Catalunya. She is a member of the research group TEXLICO and has written on the work of Avel·lí Artís-Gener and Catalan literature in exile. She is currently the Pro-Vice Chancellor of the UVic-UCC Manresa Campus, and the Dean of the School of Social Sciences at Manresa.

Rhiannon McGlade is Affiliated Lecturer at the University of Cambridge, having previously held roles including Research Associate as part of the AHRC-funded project, 'Multilingualism: Empowering Individuals, Transforming Societies' (MEITS) and Lecturer of Catalan Studies at Queen Mary University of London, where she was also the Director of the Centre for Catalan Studies. Her research considers the implications and nature of humour in visual print media, literature, theatre and the press within a Hispanic context. She has authored *Catalan Cartoons: A Cultural and Political History* (2016). Recent major projects include: the co-edited special issue 'Between the Frames: Visual Print Media in Spain since 1975', with Dr Bryan Cameron; and the current book-length investigation 'Humour, Gender and Sexual Dissidence in the Visual Print Media of Spain's Transition'.

Josep Murgades is Professor of Catalan Philology at the Universitat de Barcelona. He specializes in the Catalan literary and cultural movement from the early twentieth century known as *Noucentisme*. He has been the philological editor of the works of *noucentista* writer Eugeni d'Ors, and the philologist Pompeu Fabra. He is co-editor of the language and literature sections of the academic journal *Els Marges*, and has translated into Catalan writers such as Johann Wolfgang von Goethe, Frank Kafka, Hermann Hesse, Thomas Mann and Thomas Bernhard.

Joan Ramon Resina is Professor of Comparative Literature and of Iberian Cultures at Stanford University. His latest books are *Josep Pla: The World Seen in the Form of Articles* (2017) and *The Ghost in the Constitution: Historical Memory and Denial in Spanish Society* (2017). He has edited eleven volumes, most recently *Inscribed Identities: Writing as Self-Realization and Repetition, Recurrence, Returns* (2019). Awards include the Donald Andrews Whittier Fellowship at the Stanford Humanities Center, the Internationales Kolleg Morphomata fellowship at the Center for Advanced Studies of the University of Cologne, the Fulbright scholarship, the Alexander von Humboldt fellowship, and the *Serra d'Or* award for literary criticism.

Mario Santana is Associate Professor of Spanish and Deputy Dean of Humanities at the University of Chicago, where he is also the faculty coordinator for the programs in Basque and Catalan Studies. His most recent publications include essays on the media and memory in Catalan television, the institutionalization of Iberian Studies in the United States, translation and Iberian interliterary relations, among them 'Screening History: Television, Memory, and the Nostalgia of National Community' (2015), 'Translation and Literatures in Spain, 2003–2012' (2015), 'La memorialització de la Història en la ficció contemporània' (2017), and 'Iberian Studies: The Transatlantic Dimension' (2019).

Alan Yates was Illes Balears Professor of Catalan Studies at the University of Sheffield from 1980 until retirement in 1999. His research centred on nineteenth- and twentieth-century Catalan literature, especially narrative. Language studies were always a complementary interest and he published various contributions on that front (*Teach Yourself Catalan* [1975], *A Catalan Handbook* [1993] and (with Max Wheeler and Nicolau Dols) the *Routledge Catalan: A Comprehensive Grammar* [1999]). This activity was complemented by a deeply ingrained interest in, and enthusiasm for, literary translation which he has recently been pursuing with great satisfaction. His English version of Ferran Soldevila's *Hores angleses* is scheduled for publication in 2020.

INTRODUCTION

Jordi Larios and Montserrat Lunati

This volume gathers a selection of papers presented at the conference 'Catalan Narrative, 1875–2015' held at the University of St Andrews on 14–16 December 2015. Despite its title, it does not seek to provide a comprehensive survey of the last one hundred and fifty years of Catalan narrative practice across the genres of novel, short story and parable — a quite impossible task for a volume of this length, and anyway one more appropriate for a textbook of Catalan literary history. Nor does it issue a verdict on the current state of narrative form in Catalan literature, a task ably undertaken in other books.[1] Rather, the collection's enquiries are directed by the specific interests of its contributors, and thus focus on the authors, texts, literary periods, and philosophical and cultural strategies that seem of especial significance to those scholars. There is a thread that runs through many of the essays, however, which is the conviction that a cultural studies approach, mobilizing intertextual, interdisciplinary, and translation-related perspectives and methodologies, has much to offer to literary studies.

These chapters engage with canonical and younger authors alike,[2] sometimes comparing one novelist or short-story writer (even, occasionally, a poet) to another by identifying thematic and intertextual connections between them, and in doing so bringing to bear a wide variety of philosophical and theoretical frameworks. In *A Companion to Catalan Literature*, Arthur Terry observes that 'contradictions and alternatives' should be taken into consideration when viewing literary production from a historical perspective, as many 'writers [...] positively refuse to be fitted into the neat schemes of conventional histories of literature' (2003: 151). This is to say that traditional critical approaches may work well for many writers, but cannot do so for all: they often leave female authors in a no-man's-land, to take one example, reading them in terms of the supposedly dominant characteristics of their period while ignoring the very aspects of their work that defy convention. The variousness of the approaches adopted in this volume endorses and reflects Terry's view. Some of its chapters study particular aspects of well-codified literary and cultural movements, such as the *modernista* crisis of representation, the *modernista* rural linguistic register, or the nuances of the *noucentista* narrative genre of the parable. Some address single authors by thinking about interests and methods that feature throughout their works: humour applied to identity issues and post-colonial concerns; malaise, or madness, in historical figures; Catalonia's imperial history; translation; the transmission of historical and personal memory; or writing under political repression. Other contributions concentrate on one theme across the work of several authors, such as the concept of national family in historical novels, or multilingualism. Another cluster of essays ranges across time and aesthetic boundaries to relate writers and texts according to transhistorical criteria such as death and mourning, or cultural memory, by highlighting connections between women authors. In general, all the contributions to the volume are underpinned by philosophical and literary historical concerns, and there are some that adopt one philosophical or theoretical perspective as their point of departure: Siobhan Carroll's *atopia*, Schopenhauer's *genius* and Paul Virilio's *picnolepsy* are all examples of specific concepts instrumental in critical analyses undertaken here.

Joan Ramon Resina reflects on the work of five canonical figures — Joan Maragall, Salvador Espriu, Josep Pla, Pere Quart and Mercè Rodoreda — in terms of their representation of death and colour, prompted by Albert Camus's assertion that Mediterranean people are not inclined to discuss such matters. Resina moves from Maragall, a classicist poet with a soft spot for Nietzschean ideas not far from Camus's, to Pere Quart half a century later, who, in dialogue with Maragall's Catholic poetry and view of death as a 'greater birth' or 'eternal peace', declares in 1960 that his 'fe en un Cel ulterior' [faith in an ulterior Heaven] fails him, and wishes for a continuity of material reality. Resina considers Pere Quart's 'disinclination to engage in speculative thought' and quotes him to the effect that 'és més urgent viure que filosofar' [it is more important to live than to philosophize], yet notes also that for Pere Quart the opposition 'to live/to think' is in itself metaphysical because 'it conceives philosophy as a variant of nothingness, insofar as it relates to the "non-existing" or to an "after life"'. Resina explains that Pere Quart, in a radical gesture, asks God to put a stop to everything, to 'disown His creation', and links this gesture to Salvador Espriu's *Llibre de Sinera* [Book of Sinera] (1963). Espriu sees 'Death as a relentless power' and claims to conceive nothing beyond the world around him, a world constrained by death and perceived 'against the background of eternity'. Therefore, Espriu's poetry and theatre cannot but be sad: 'Hi ha tristesa darrera les paraules' [Sadness lies behind words], he writes, and, as Resina puts it, 'Sinera cemetery [...] anchors the poet's existential anguish'. The essay then turns to Josep Pla's interest in funerary culture in the Mediterranean islands, detecting Heidegger's *Dasein* in his thinking about Corsican and Sicilian attitudes towards death and mourning. Pla's descriptions of lost Catalonian death rituals then bring Resina back to the poets discussed earlier in his essay and he finally focuses on Mercè Rodoreda's *La mort i la primavera* [Death in Spring] (1997). Resina ponders the considerable complexities of this multi-layered novel, from the characters' Oedipal drives to the symbolical meaning of life and death, and the influence on Rodoreda's dystopia of Teilhard de Chardin's contention that 'cosmic matter has evolved into forms of life in a process leading to a final point of absolute consciousness called the Omega point, [...] the teleological motor of evolution'. In closing, Resina distinguishes his five authors' views of death — 'mystical in Maragall, sceptical in Pere Quart, sarcastic in Josep Pla, existential in Espriu and initiatic in Rodoreda' — but stresses also what they all have in common: their belief in the importance of the body and the senses when it comes to 'imagining a life for which death is not a metaphysical abstraction but a presence that must be eliminated'.

Josep Murgades starts by revisiting his own previous work on Catalan *Noucentisme*, a movement which he sees as primarily the product of two figures: Prat de la Riba, who provided its political and ideological leadership, and its literary leader Eugeni d'Ors. Accordingly, for him *Noucentisme* comprises two key dimensions: 'anagogy', or 'the ambition of influencing and transforming' the values and behaviours of a society, in the case of *Noucentisme* through the 'bourgeois revolution' of political Catalanism that resisted the Spanish state in the first decades of the twentieth century; and 'analogy', or 'the discourse of myth', the 'deliberately literary fashion of language', which was foundational to the movement's faith in the power of the arts and culture to bring about fundamental social changes. In analysing *noucentista* narrative, Murgades takes as his examples a number of parables, the narrative subgenre that best represents 'the postulation — and exercising — of containment and renunciation, elusion and metalepsis, limitation and ellipsis' that is so characteristic of this litotic literary movement that constantly displays an 'ironic awareness of its own limitations'. In Eugeni d'Ors's paradigmatic analogical discourse in *La Ben Plantada* (1911); in parables principally by Josep Carner but also Josep Maria López-Picó, Carles Soldevila, Joan Sacs, Martínez Ferrando and Duran Reynals; and in a novel by Manuel Brunet, Murgades analyses the use of irony as a rhetorical tool that helps to diffuse conflicts, quite often bourgeois conflicts, 'be they at the individual or the collective level'. Besides paying attention to *noucentista* narrative procedures, Murgades also considers some matters that were of significant concern to the movement, such as *déclassement*, or its endorsement of a work ethics of enterprise and professionalism.

Enric Bou brings to bear the concept of *picnolepsy*, defined by Paul Virilio as momentary absences of consciousness, on issues of cultural memory in Josep Carner, Marta Rojals and Joan Todó. Bou's examples are instances of writing that register the everyday disappearance of objects, urban buildings and even entire districts, as well as of attitudes and tastes, and he relates these to a slight redefinition of *picnolepsy* as 'the unremitting alternation between tiny moments of consciousness and diminutive "deaths" of unconsciousness'. Carner's quasi-elegies for Barcelona characters from a period that is about to recede into oblivion are here compared to the observations made from a plane by the female protagonist of Rojals's *Primavera, estiu, etcètera* [Spring, Summer, Etcetera] as she tries to identify the rural places she left behind in order to move to the unfamiliar urban space where she experiences the loneliness of the immigrant. Her feelings in this regard, as Bou illustrates, are not unlike those of Todó's male protagonist in *L'horitzó primer* [The First Horizon], who finds that after having lived abroad he needs to guess how to establish basic communication with his fellow villagers, and who like Carner is acutely aware of the passing of time. Bou ends by figuring these writers' practices as forensic examinations, 'treating reality almost as if it were a cadaver' — yet one with an indispensable cultural memory.

Jordi Cornellà-Detrell's chapter examines the role of multilingualism in contemporary Catalan literature, arguing that Ramon Solsona, Joan-Daniel Bezsonoff and Marta Rojals are the novelists who mix languages in 'more provocative and imaginative' ways. Cornellà notes how attitudes to language have shifted: from a monolingual Romantic one which regards language as an expression of national identity, to a more flexible contemporary acceptance of code-mixing in creative writing. This transgressive practice does not 'present tongues as separate identities which exist in isolation, but as an amalgam of correlations and interdependencies'. He takes as examples the complex though not necessarily conflictive cohabitation of Catalan and Spanish in Solsona's and Rojals's work, and contrasts it with the more multifaceted, albeit less coherent, multilingualism in Bezsonoff's writing. Bezsonoff is a French national from Perpignan, of Russian descent, who has chosen to write mainly in Catalan. In one way or another, he incorporates several languages into his novels and autobiographical texts, including Catalan, French, Russian, German, Romanian, Latin, Italian and Vietnamese. Cornellà points out that in these authors' works 'languages appear in flux, freeing the text from conventional constraints, enhancing the metalinguistic and metafictional possibilities of the narrative, and highlighting the ethical and political dimension of communication'. He also addresses claims that multilingualism in contemporary Catalan literature threatens to undermine further a language already struggling to survive, arguing convincingly that Catalan readers, firstly, are alert to multilingualism as an ironic strategy and, secondly, are perfectly able to distinguish between languages and between standard and non-standard varieties.

The notion of the Catalan national family is a central element in the several historical novels discussed by Kathryn Crameri, all of which are set during the War of Spanish Succession and deal specifically with the Siege of Barcelona in 1714 and the city's surrender to Philip V's Bourbon Army. The significance of this landmark in Catalan history cannot be overestimated: on 11 September each year Catalonia's National Day remembers the last day of the Siege and huge pro-independence demonstrations take place. The novels Crameri investigates, all published between 2008 and 2012, are by Alfred Bosch, Víctor Jurado Riba, Jaume Clotet and David de Montserrat, all in Catalan, and Albert Sánchez Piñol, whose bestseller *Victus* appeared first in Spanish. Crameri follows and simultaneously takes issue with Lauenstein, Murer, Boss and Reicher's claim that the concept of the 'imagined family' is a more useful tool in considering how the nation is conceived than Benedict Anderson's more widely accepted 'imagined community'. If these scholars affirm that the ethnic model of the imagined family 'reifies social relations as biologically determined', Crameri argues, in the novels she analyses the opposite is true, since they 'are trying to imagine what Anderson calls "a deep horizontal comradeship"' and family ties and loyalties are not necessarily biologically determined. Nevertheless, the essay concludes that even though the 'nature of the ties that create the Catalan national family may have shifted, [...] they are still assumed to bind'.

Montserrat Lunati studies how novelist and short-story writer Mercè Ibarz leaves in her own work overt intertextual traces of the twentieth-century author Mercè

Rodoreda and of the contemporary (though late) poet Maria-Mercè Marçal — the second of whom, in turn, did the same with some of her predecessors, including the Majorcan poet Maria-Antònia Salvà. Without advocating the essentialist project of establishing an 'impossible' female genealogy, Lunati stresses the significance of women's writing in literary history, and how the canon, despite the inclusion of some 'token' women authors, has always been hegemonically male. She reads Ibarz's intertextual inclusions of Rodoreda and Marçal as a feminist political enterprise that follows what Derrida thinks we ought to be doing: granting the ghosts of the past hospitable accommodation in our discourse as a way of repairing injustices. Particularly innovative for Lunati, and certainly Derridean, is Ibarz's literary transformation of Marçal into a ghost that accompanies the narrator and lives in the rafters of her house in *No parlis de mi quan me'n vagi* [Don't Talk about Me When I'm Gone], a novel that also engages with the lives of former anti-Franco fighters in the post-Franco years. Apropos of Ibarz's multi-layered and postmemory-oriented short story 'Kilimanjaro', with its references to Rodoreda's *La plaça del Diamant* [In Diamond Square] and other works, Lunati suggests as a metaphor for intertextuality the architect Gaudí's use of discarded material (*trencadís*), which similarly generates utility, beauty and meaning out of old things. It is a trope that she applies to Ibarz's vindication of Marçal's poetry as 'una veu que acull altres veus' [a voice that includes other voices], as well as to Ibarz's own literary practice.

Translation Studies and other translation-inflected methodologies have in recent years become increasingly influential in the study of literature. In Helena Buffery's essay on Maria-Mercè Marçal's novel *La passió segons Renée Vivien* [The Passion according to Renée Vivien] (1994), we find both Translation Studies' 'cultural turn' and Cultural Studies' 'translation turn' in conjunction. This blurring of disciplinary borders is an apposite strategy in approaching Marçal, since in her work her poetic legacy becomes indistinguishable from her theoretical, methodological and narrative practices, as pointed out by Meri Torras in the epigraph to Buffery's essay. The novel 'tells the story of an incomplete intermedial translation undertaken by the fictional documentary film-maker Sara T. [...] of the lives and works and passion(s) of hybrid Anglo-French Parisian-based cross-dressing *fin-de-siècle* writer and female *flâneuse* Pauline Tarn, the body behind the pseudonym Renée Vivien'. Buffery has herself translated Marçal's novel into English, and has a particular interest in the processual and translational aspects of this highly intertextual novel with its different narrative layers, voices and combinations of history and fiction. The essay throws light on how the novel parades the author's 'self-consciously performative and embodied narrative practice', and links this to Marçal's much shorter reflection from 1989 on her spatiotemporal relationship with Barcelona. Written while Marçal was working on Renée Vivien, the latter piece renders a vision of a city 'shaped by bodily encounters in and between public and private spaces', and of a female protagonist 'shuttling between centre and margins'. For Buffery, this illustrates how interaction 'with other readings, writings, memories, experiences and tactics' takes place in Marçal's narrative discourse in *La passió*, as the shorter text mirrors the novel's 'processual mode of composition'. Mirroring is a powerful, disturbing motif in *La passió*, and the essay covers this aspect of its construction as well, following the mobile and meandering paths the novel lays out between different literary, cultural, geographical and societal discourses and spaces. Translation is a complex cultural process and, inevitably, a political one, and *La passió* offers a vision of it as a creative and transformational mode of rewriting. Buffery reflects on how Marçal's process in translating the work of other writers, similar to Vivien's within *La passió*, can help us in reading the novel itself, parts of which Buffery understands as articulating the conflict between the lesbian voice and the accepted norm, and others as evoking the Catalan nation's struggle for 'visibility'. The essay ends with a reminder that translating such a novel presents a considerable challenge, and of the inevitable 'triangle between I/you/world' in which the translator is compelled to ' "triar" [to choose] yet in doing so to "trair" ' [to betray]. Above all, Buffery reveals the ethical and aesthetic power of Marçal's pioneering novel as a model for renegotiating and rewor(l)ding world literature from the margins, never settling for the illusory comforts of identification, but attending to, articulating and celebrating the multiple traces of difference, the elusive pleasures — and pain — of singularity.

Alan Yates's essay also deals with translation, this time within the framework of Catalan *Modernisme*, and conveys his own experience translating one of the crucial novels of that epoch, *Els sots feréstecs* (1901), by Raimon Casellas, as *Dark Vales* (2014). Yates begins by professing that literary translation — for him 'the ideal complement of linguistic and literary studies' — has been 'the most satisfying if not the most remunerative facet' of his professional life. The body of his essay exemplifies his view that sensitive translation is in itself an elevated mode of close reading and exegesis, as is evidenced in his meticulous opening focus on adequately rendering the title itself of Casellas's novel. In a broader focus, Yates's interpretation of his source text relates it to an international corpus of classic fictions that explore the 'landscape of the mind', as in the English canon from *Wuthering Heights* to Graham Swift's *Waterland*. More microscopically, Yates pays attention to the notoriously perplexing opening sentence, with its extreme dialectal texture, which he sets alongside other canonical first-sentence examples in the Western tradition, from Cervantes's *Don Quixote* through to Joyce's *Ulysses*, Camus's *L'Étranger*, etc. Regarding the stylized earthiness cultivated in the 'ruralist' strain of *modernista* writing, Yates deploys a broad intertextual perspective and experience. In justifying his personal *modus operandi* in the translation process, he celebrates having had in mind an 'amalgam of canonical voices from the English tradition of ruralist/working-class fiction from the nineteenth and early twenty centuries'. Representative samples of his translation are commented on, and Casellas's innovations in style and narrative strategy are examined in some detail, from the punctuation, influenced by post-Symbolism, to the 'earthy vocabulary and rough-edged diction', as well as his replacement of the omniscient narrator of the nineteenth century 'by inserting another consciousness in the narrative as a presence operating in the text close to the level of a character's mind'. In true literary-translator's fashion, Yates concludes that rendering such a challenging text into English has done nothing but to increase his admiration for a novel which he has been re-reading for over half a century.

Jordi Larios engages in his chapter with *modernista* writer Caterina Albert, who signed her works with the male pseudonym Víctor Català — a poet and playwright, and the celebrated author of two novels and several collections of short stories and novellas. He begins by piecing together from various forewords and press interviews statements made by Albert about her own poetics. What these make clear is that she was inclined to see the world through a dark prism; that what she termed 'the voluptuousness of sorrow' was no less real and attractive than the voluptuousness of pleasure. Noting that Albert's themes are '[d]estitution, greed, jealousy, as well as all kinds of physical and psychological violence, from assassination to rape', Larios sets out to identify the philosophical underpinning to her poetics. He provides a close reading of Gaietà, one of the male characters in *Solitud* [Solitude] (1905), 'the first significant modern Catalan novel written by a woman and which has a woman as its main character': Larios takes stock of existing interpretations of Gaietà, who has been associated by critics with Joan Maragall's romantic theory of the 'paraula viva' [living word], and presents him as a fictionalization of Arthur Schopenhauer's notion of *genius*. Recently, documentary evidence that the young Caterina Albert intended to acquaint herself with Schopenhauer's work has come to light. Larios's reading of Gaietà as an individual who experiences, in Schopenhauer's words, 'a complete silencing of the will which leaves the person as pure subject of knowing', shows that the German philosopher had a major impact on Albert's best-known novel, and that the dark tones that pervade her entire *oeuvre* are also informed by his philosophical pessimism.

Elisa Martí's essay takes as its focus Narcís Oller's novel *La febre d'or* [Gold Fever] (1890–92), which explores the thirst for money that devours Gil Foix, a self-made man who becomes rich through shrewd financial activities in 1880–82. These were two of the most intense years of the period 1876–86, 'when the bullish stock market [...] had the greatest impact on [Barcelona]', which was going through a rapid process of modernization. In her analysis, Martí closely follows critic Joan Ramon Resina's understanding of the novel as 'the first attempt in Catalan literature to produce a bourgeois epic', but one which 'falls short of its goal', a view that itself continues a long tradition in Oller studies of regarding *La febre d'or* as a flawed work. Martí acknowledges the novel's alleged 'reduction' from social to domestic drama and goes on 'to articulate a different way of approaching [it] in order to address both the perceived shortcomings in the author's artistry and his "faulty" naturalism as he struggles with realism or, more precisely, with the limits of realist writing'. She accepts Resina's suggestion that 'the crisis of "dependable objectivity" [is] the novel's main theme' and contends that its 'limitations as an intimate drama should be read in relation to the work's exploration, and struggle with, the crisis of representation both in society and art that characterized the 1890s'. Thus, she interprets the novel more constructively than other critics as a great modern work of literature, irrespective of its flaws. Martí discusses how the 'crisis of dependable objectivity' is represented in it through objects, especially paintings, and metaphors such as the titles of its two sections: 'Pujada' [Ascent] and 'Cayguda' ('Estimbada', in later editions) [Fall], a title change that the essay relates to the etymology of the word 'timba' [precipice, gambling house]. According to Martí, in *La febre d'or* Barcelona has become a 'modern metropolis where money no longer bears any marks of its origin in labor', a booming marketplace under the control of speculators. Wealth is described as chaotic: the protagonist's apartment is cluttered with an 'incongruous accumulation of composite objects', 'a metonymic confusion of monstrous things' that are useless to their occupants. Martí also focuses on secondary characters trapped in the workings of this speculative society, whose 'brightness [...] creates [a] perceptual blur'. One is Gil Foix's brother Peret, 'a manual labourer working in a forge' who troubles the protagonist's conscience to the point that he prefers to see Peret as a ghost. Another is Blanche, 'the paid-companion of Gil Foix's daughter', who has to leave his house (and her place of work) due to Gil's sexual advances, and ends up in a Bovarian carriage with dishonest broker Eladi Balanyà, in a 'ride [which] initiates Blanche's social mobility, a rootlessness that she will not be able to escape'. Yet another is the cynical Pauleta, Eladi's mother, who lives off the wealth provided by her unscrupulous son and despises Blanche's lowly origins. Martí concludes that Oller struggled with the representation of Barcelona's libidinal and inflationary economy during the *febre d'or* years. This struggle was 'to undermine his search for dependable objectivity' and his attempts at realist writing.

P. Louise Johnson studies two novels by Guillem Viladot that depict historical figures: *Joana* (1991) and *Carles* (1994). The first tells the story of the character known as 'Juana la loca', daughter of Isabel and Ferdinand and the queen of Castile 'who never ruled Castile or Aragon'. The protagonist of the second is Juana's great-grandson, Don Carlos of Austria. Viladot does not consider these to be historical novels and likewise Johnson's reading does not treat them as instances of that genre, even though it does not ignore, nor does Viladot, the historical reality of both characters and the relevance of their historical contexts. The essay looks into how Juana and Carlos have appeared in various forms in many works of literature, art, opera and so on, fictive incarnations that have added in different ways to the construction of their legends, particularly as key figures in the construction of Spain's Black Legend. Despite the 'relative success' of both novels, the essay shows how misunderstood they have been, how 'simplistically' they have been interpreted, and how the 'historicist understanding' of them has been reductive. Johnson reminds her readers that, for Viladot, writing was tantamount to dissidence, and particularly that he mocked the dictum, attributed to Bishop Josep Torras i Bages towards the end of the nineteenth century, that 'Catalunya serà cristiana o no serà' [Catalonia will be Christian or not at all]. For her, 'these "historical" novels need to be read from the perspective of resistance to male-gendered authoritarianism and oppressive structures of power in a psychoanalytic sense'. Indeed, reflecting that abandonment is suffered by 'each protagonist [...] at the hands of their literal or figurative fathers', Johnson argues that Viladot's main concern is 'power, however constituted'. She draws attention to the fact that psychoanalytic elements, mostly Freudian and Lacanian, and a subversive focus on the materiality of the body, especially its abject components, are crucial in both novels, where the body is 'both literal — as are its torments — and metaphorical, a *corpus mysticum* aligned with a sense of nationhood, or state, which is decomposed by the very existence of the uncrowned queen (Juana) and the errant, malformed prince (Don Carlos)'. Dissidence is at the heart of Viladot's treatment of his subjects' embodiment, including that of Carlos's servant Sòcrates, 'the archetypal court dwarf', and the essay reflects it by refusing to shy away from the erotic and the scatological in its thinking about issues of corporeality, and by connecting them to the unfortunate personal and historical circumstances of the characters as well as to their responses to adversity.

In his chapter, Mario Santana concentrates on the poetics and the ethics of contemporary Catalan fiction by referring to the novels and short stories published by Jaume Cabré since the turn of the century, particularly *Jo confesso* [Confessions] (2011), a long novel already translated into twenty-three languages. Cabré is one of the most celebrated contemporary Catalan writers, to a significant degree on the basis of his highly innovative narrative strategies, which often rely on 'sentences that [...] change focalization, grammatical subjects, and spatial and temporal locations with astonishing ease'. Santana's main preoccupation, however, is Cabré's sophisticated way of dealing with how historical and personal memory are transmitted, how the past weighs on the present. In *Jo confesso*, this involves weaving 'several plots within one larger story' in order 'to represent the dynamism of history'. Love, friendship, family relations, religion — all are tainted by greed, envy, cowardice, frustration and, most importantly, by how evil actions go unpunished throughout history, something Cabré underlines in his narrative strategies by according the past the urgency of the present and by emphasizing '[the] *presentness* of the past, the fact that history, and especially the crimes of history, do not disappear or fade away'. *Jo confesso* also offers fertile ground for thinking about the political relevance of objects, and in doing so Santana draws in particular upon Remo Bodei's theoretical approach to the importance of materiality in processes of memory. Among the many objects to which the novel pays close attention is a violin: its history is followed across centuries, from the seeds of the tree out of whose wood the luthier fashions it, to the different owners of the instrument, and the often illegitimate or even horrific circumstances in which they acquire it. With a Benjaminian slant, Santana suggests that 'the result of Cabré's experimentation with time and materiality [...] is not so much the memorialization of the past, but rather the permanent reopening of the past onto the present. His is not a poetics of forgiveness, but one of redemption'.

The early novels of Albert Sánchez Piñol are the subject of Dominic Keown's essay, which begins by contrasting different ways of conceiving Catalonia: as a small country presented in mostly positive terms (the view, for example, of Salvador Espriu, Josep Pla, Pere Quart and Lluís Llach), or alternatively as complicit in the ambitions and conflictive history of an imperial country which, like many other Western nations, participated in, and benefited from, the 'execrable trade' of slavery in the nineteenth century. The novels upon which Keown focuses — *La pell freda* [Cold Skin] (2002) and *Pandora al Congo* [Pandora in Congo] (2005) — take the latter view and, in order to deal with 'the inhumanity of colonialism', they contextualize Catalonia 'within the alien but more global configuration of British expansionism'. Keown believes that this strategy is 'hugely enriching' because it 'internationalizes the speculation in geopolitical terms' and 'facilitates an intertextual dialogue on the subject, outside the Hispanic context, with the most popular and influential writers of world literature'. He also uses Siobhan Carroll's concept of *atopia* to think about 'inhospitable or mutable regions', spaces that Carroll sees as 'presumed to lie at or beyond the fringes of everyday life', the kind of *terra nullius* that constituted 'a challenge to territorial appropriation and state control'. These are the settings of Sánchez Piñol's novels, whether polar regions or the jungle, which provide the context for the 'dissenting anti-imperialist line' that Keown explores in them. As he also argues, the presence of Irish characters in *La pell freda* allows for historical parallels to be drawn between Ireland and Catalonia, locating the book's representation of Catalan politics in a global context. Similarly, the essay sees broad as well as specific political significance in *Pandora al Congo*, particularly in the way the novel relates its pathetic fallacies to 'the ontological threat of dehumanization posed by capitalism [...]: the conversion of human beings into produce whose labour is to be bought and sold like the materials of the earth'. This Keown links in turn to the Great War, driven as it was by 'the brutal persistence of the acquisitional impulse', which is well captured by 'the pronounced staccato rhythm' of the narrative. Finally, by teasing out a wealth of intertextual connections between Piñol's novels and other work of 'fiery exoticism and adventure' ('hot imperial literature', according to Joan Ramon Resina) such as that of Verne, Wells, Kipling or Defoe, as well as 'more sceptical and disconcerting' narratives like those of Conrad, Jack London, William Golding or Bioy Casares, Keown shows that Sánchez Piñol's innovative and popular work represents the beginning of a much-needed thematic expansion in contemporary Catalan literature.

The work of Avel·lí Artís-Gener/Tísner is addressed in two chapters. Rhiannon McGlade's topic is the complexity of humour and identity in three novels written during Tísner's Mexican exile: *556 Brigada Mixta* [556 Mixed Brigade] (1945), *Les dues funcions del circ* [The Two Functions of the Circus] (1966), and *Paraules d'Opòton el Vell* [The Words of Opòton the Elder] (1968). McGlade begins by noting that for humour and satire to occur there must be 'a shared system of historical, social, linguistic and/or aesthetic references'. That was the case not only for the Catalan Republican exiles in Mexico, for whom Tísner's irony was easy to understand, but also for those who endured Franco's repression in Catalonia. McGlade then shows how Superiority, Release-relief, and Incongruity theories of humour can be mapped onto the writer's fiction in inclusive and complementary ways. *556 Brigada Mixta* is an anti-epic and one of the first novels about the Spanish Civil War written from the Republican perspective, and these three theories of humour are key to understanding its understated approach to war, which seeks to counter the conflict's negative power, and its 'overt antimilitarism [...] reflected in the sustained leitmotiv of the lack of professionalism and incompetence in the higher echelons of the military [which] is typically manifest in those humorous episodes created through superior–inferior role reversal'. The essay relates this to Freud's 'belief that the aggression of a joke is bound to its rebellious nature whereby it facilitates the expression of criticism outside of accepted boundaries'. *Les dues funcions del circ*, written in Mexico but published in Barcelona after Tísner's return from exile, deals with two Catalan brothers who, on their way to exile, get stranded on the island of Martinique. Culture clashes and the longing for a Barcelona 'frozen in time' are central to the novel, which shows how geopolitical circumstances after the Second World War threaten to make the exile of the two brothers permanent. *Les dues funcions del circ*'s main elements are 'constructed along a series of binaries' which work to convey 'the duality of exilic identity'. Humour here is used to communicate 'a sense of otherness on the island and typically draw[s] upon the Superiority approach and its role in the construction of group identity'. McGlade then turns her attention to Tísner's best-known work, *Paraules d'Opòton el Vell*, an experimental novel with several narratological levels that challenges the 'Eurocentric discourse of "discovery"'. With an all-pervasive ironic tone which belies the seriousness of its subject matter, the book tackles issues of culture shock and alterity, and uses language itself as a tool in exposing the evils of colonialism. The novel's signature move is the fictional reversal of historical situations: before Columbus's arrival in the Americas, a group of Aztec explorers in search of the deity Quetzalcoatl is depicted arriving on Galician shores. McGlade's essay dwells on the cultural misunderstandings that result and how they are deployed to expose historical as well as contemporary injustices. It also shows that humour does not detract from the novel's political tension. If anything, the opposite is the case.

Avel·lí Artís-Gener's 1969 novel *Prohibida l'evasió* [Evasion Prohibited] is the subject of Sílvia Mas's essay. Tísner put the finishing touches to it in Barcelona having done the bulk of the work in Mexico, hence it bridges two periods of his life inevitably marked by the consequences of the Spanish Civil War for Catalan Republicans. When fleeing Catalonia and returning to it, Tísner had to leave a life behind, loved ones included, and these distressing experiences are related, explored and transformed in his literary fiction. The trauma manifests at a formal level in the novel's structure, 'which acts as a catalyst in exposing an absurd, claustrophobic and oppressive reality'. For Mas, placing *Prohibida l'evasió* in the wider context of Western literature of the first half of the twentieth century helps to explain its choral organization: the novel does not rely on a single narrator controlling the discourse and is 'composed of diverse plot-lines which are not readily synthesized in a single narrative thread'. Bearing in mind Patricia Waugh's definition of metafiction as writing that situates itself halfway between fiction and literary criticism, Mas also looks at the novel's metafictional elements. As a mode, metafiction suits Tísner's project of political critique through literature, and indeed this essay detects in *Prohibida l'evasió* a *mise-en-abyme* effect, since its readers in Franco's Spain were trapped in a 'distressing reality' just as the novel's characters are. Mas highlights how the presence of cinema is felt on different levels in this complex work: intradiegetically, as part of the characters' configuration, but also to evince the implication of the readers/spectators in constructing meaning while consuming the literary or cinematic product. Finally, Mas argues, although Brechtian alienation prevails in the novel and communication is mostly a failure, nevertheless it can be read more optimistically: Artís-Gener puts his hopes in a character, Viktor, who longs for freedom and has a sense of commitment that prevents him from evading his responsibility towards his own country and the world in general.

In *A Companion to Catalan Culture*, Dominic Keown writes:

> When we bear in mind that over the past three centuries there have been little more than four decades when that nation [Catalonia] and its signs of difference were not proscribed or prosecuted, its continued, dynamic presence nowadays is nothing short of astonishing. (2011: 13)

The present collection of essays amply attests to the accuracy of Keown's observation. As we write, Catalan politics is far more unstable even than when the conference took place. Some members of Catalonia's democratically elected government (the Generalitat), two civil activists, and the President of the Catalan Parliament, Carme Forcadell, have been sentenced, collectively, to more than one hundred years in prison — for sedition and, in some cases, for misuse of public funds, on the grounds that they organized the referendum on Catalan independence held on 1 October 2017 without the consent of the Spanish state. Other members of the Catalan Government are in exile, including the President of the Generalitat, Carles Puigdemont. The response to the sentence, which was made public on 21 October 2019, triggered massive demonstrations in Catalonia. Many protesters, most of them young, faced a brutal reaction from Spanish and, controversially, Catalan police forces. At the same time, the PSC (the Catalan branch of the PSOE — the Spanish Socialist Workers' Party, now in office) has questioned the Generalitat's pro-Catalan policies of linguistic immersion — policies implemented since Franco's death in 1975 by Catalan autonomous governments of different persuasions, and which the PSC had itself endorsed in the past (Ríos 2019). The future of the Catalan language, Catalan literature and Catalan culture in general is once again in the balance.

In 2005, Antoni Vilanova collected the articles on contemporary Catalan literature that he had published in the magazine *Destino* between 1950 and 1967, when resistance against Franco's repressive regime was gathering momentum. In these articles, Vilanova celebrates the rich Catalan literary tradition and points out that works by twentieth-century writers such as Carles Riba and Josep Pla did not appear out of nowhere. Rather, he says, they were 'fruto de un rico sustrato cultural que, a pesar de prohibiciones y censuras, permanece vivo entre nosotros después de la derrota' [the result of a rich cultural substrate which, despite prohibitions and censorship, remains alive among us after the defeat] (2005: 11). Unfortunately, his take on Catalan literature under the dictatorship applies just as well to the present moment, which is why it is necessary to keep reminding ourselves of how this rich literary history has played, and is still playing, a decisive role in keeping Catalan culture alive. Literary tradition would be a dead end, though, without the political determination of Catalans to defend their nation and 'its signs of difference'. In his contribution to *La modernitat cauta 1942–1963* [The Cautious Modernity 1942–1963] (2014: 306), Jordi Amat states that Francoism's self-construction was 'una realitat reaccionària, anti-il·lustrada i, per tant, antimoderna' [a reactionary, anti-Enlightenment, hence anti-modern, reality]. His words clearly resonate with today's political situation in Spain, where a modern and inclusive concept of democracy is being threatened by a political intransigence that has led to attitudes associated with the far right becoming mainstream. Yet against the odds Catalan culture in all its manifestations, whether popular or highbrow, lives on. We very much hope that this volume will be both a homage and a worthy contribution to its resilience.

Works Cited

AMAT, JORDI. 2014. 'La cautela com a estratègia de construcció', in *La modernitat cauta 1942–1963: resistència, resignació, restauració*, ed. by Antoni Marí and Albert Mercadé (Barcelona: Angle Editorial), pp. 305–21

CAMPS ARBÓS, JOSEP, and MARIA DASCA (eds). 2019. *La narrativa catalana al segle XXI, balanç crític* (Barcelona: Societat Catalana de Llengua i Literatura/IEC)

GRAÑA, ISABEL, and TERESA IRIBARREN (eds). 2008. *La literatura catalana en la cruïlla (1975–2008)* (Vilanova i la Geltrú: El Cep i la Nansa)

KEOWN, DOMINIC. 2011. 'Contemporary Catalan Culture', in *A Companion to Catalan Culture*, ed. by Dominic Keown (Woodbridge: Tamesis), pp. 13–40

MARRUGAT, JORDI. 2014. *Narrativa catalana de la postmodernitat. Històries, formes i motius* (Barcelona: Publicacions i Edicions de la Universitat de Barcelona)

RÍOS, PERE. 2019. 'Iceta defensa el canvi d'actitud del PSC sobre la immersió lingüística', *El País*, 23 November <https://cat.elpais.com/cat/2019/11/23/catalunya/1574509873_743361.html>

TERRY, ARTHUR. 2003. *A Companion to Catalan Literature* (Woodbridge: Tamesis)

VILANOVA, ANTONIO. 2005. *Auge y supervivencia de una cultura prohibida: literatura catalana de posguerra* (Barcelona: Destino)

Notes to the Introduction

1. See Graña and Iribarren (2008), Marrugat (2014), and Camps and Dasca (2019).
2. Some authors from different periods — Josep Carner, Mercè Rodoreda, Avel·lí Artís-Gener, Maria-Mercè Marçal, Albert Sánchez Piñol, and Marta Rojals — are studied in more than one essay.

CHAPTER 1

Autopsies of Everyday Life:
From Josep Carner to Marta Rojals
(and Joan Todó)

Enric Bou

Università Ca' Foscari Venezia

> For it is paradoxically the act of obliteration, the present absence of the former cafés which brings them so vividly to mind. Demolition and erasure bring with them a sudden appreciation of what is no longer there. (Graeme Gilloch 2004: 300)

In his essay *The Aesthetics of Disappearance*, Paul Virilio introduces the key concept of *picnolepsy*. Inspired by epilepsy — a neurological disorder marked by sudden recurrent episodes of sensory disturbance, loss of consciousness or convulsions — Virilio defines *picnolepsy* as the condition of brief lapses in time, momentary absences of consciousness or, as he puts it, fleeting instances of life escaping. *Picnolepsy* is produced by speed and is a characteristic of the pace at which we live our lives. As Virilio states, if epilepsy is 'little death', *picnolepsy* is 'tiny death'. Our awareness of living encompasses an infinite number of little deaths, little accidents, little breaks, little cuts in our life, made of sounds, visual effects, and that which is remembered. It corresponds to a montage of temporalities, which are closely related to the technologies of organizing time (Virilio 2008: 48).

The picnolept 'make[s] equivalents out of what [he] has seen and what he has not been able to see' (Virilio 1991: 10). Virilio presents the example of the awkward child, bothered by the adults who are in a position of authority over him:

> People want to persuade him of the existence of events that he has not seen, though they effectively happened in his presence; and as he can't be made to believe in them he's considered a half-wit and convicted of lies and dissimulation. Secretly bewildered and tormented by the demands of those near him, in order to find information he needs constantly to stretch the limits of his memory. When we place a bouquet under the eyes of the young picnoleptic and we ask him to draw it, he draws not only the bouquet but also the person who is supposed to have placed it in the vase, and even the field of flowers where it was possibly gathered. (1991: 10)

Referring to the kind of absence that occurs not only during particular states such as REM sleep but indeed in our general experience of space-time relations as a series of fragmented frames, the idea of *picnolepsy* lies behind Virilio's assertion that 'architecture is just a movie' (1991: 65), and as an experience can be likened to that of oblivion caused by disappearance. Even though he thinks of *picnolepsy* in terms of contemporary society, the concept can also be usefully applied to the problem of space disappearance and transformation. As Walter Benjamin wrote, 'articulating the past historically does not mean recognizing it "the way it really was". It means appropriating a memory as it flashes up at a moment of danger' (2003: 391). The present essay brings the idea of *picnolepsy* to bear on three explorations of the everyday, by Josep Carner, Marta Rojals and Joan Todó, paying special attention to matters of disappearance, and particularly to what we might call the invisible traditions recorded in literary texts of the early twentieth and twenty-first centuries.

★   ★   ★   ★   ★

The Jaussely Plan (1907) and the Reforma (1908, later the Via Laietana) were two important urban projects that transformed Barcelona in significant ways at the beginning of the twentieth century. Principally intended to create a direct link between the new neighbourhood of Eixample and the city's harbour, they led to the destruction of 2199 homes and many medieval palaces, and affected 10,000 people. Among the buildings demolished, particularly noteworthy were the palaces of the Marquis of Monistrol, the palace of the Marquis of Sentmenat (from which Jeroni Martorell saved a window which he used to restore the Casa dels Canonges), as well as the convents of Sant Sebastià and Sant Joan de Jerusalem, where Pau Claris's grave was located. Some buildings were saved and some were relocated to (or, I should say, reappeared in) the so-called Barri Gòtic [Gothic Quarter].[1] Josep Pijoan recounted the failed effort to build a huge catalogue that would record this important and now-disappeared part of Barcelona's past:

> No sé si fins volíem prendre l'índex antropomètric als aborígens barcelonins, ni si volíem conservar llur vocabulari de recargolats renecs, però sí recordo que comptàvem amb En Josep Carner, qui era aleshores *disponible* i ningú millor que ell per immortalitzar el perfum de les alcoves amb calaixeres, escaparates i relíquies i quadros de canemàs dels barcelonins del segle passat, amb llurs costums, mitologia, tradicions, tabús, creències d'ultratomba, fórmules màgiques, confraries, oracions, balls, etcètera.

> [I do not know if we even wanted to measure the anthropometric index to Barcelona's aborigines, or if we wanted to keep their expletive vocabulary, but I do remember that we were counting on Josep Carner, who was the best available to immortalize the perfume of the alcoves with drawers, and the display cabinets and relics and the canvas paintings of Barcelona citizens in the last century, with their customs, mythology, traditions, taboos, belief in afterlife, magic formulas, guilds, prayers, dances, etcetera.] (Pijoan 1927: 22)[2]

But Enric Prat de la Riba, the then-president of the Catalan Mancomunitat, decided to forget about that project, and the 'records etnogràfics de la gran ciutat s'han dispersat als quatre vents, sense possibles recuperacions' [ethnographic memories of the great city were scattered to the four winds, with no possible recovery] (Pijoan 1927: 23). On the other hand, Pijoan also recorded the reaction to this process of destructive renewal of Joan Maragall, who had no fond memories of the disappeared neighbourhood where he grew up, exasperated as he was by the stench of the sewers.

Clearly, reactions to this disappearance of an entire neighbourhood ranged widely, from the totally elegiac to, in Maragall's case, the plainly indifferent. In contrast to Maragall's cavalier attitude is that of Josep Carner, as portrayed by Pijoan, who undertook the ethnographic task of cataloguing the sensory details of the lost neighbourhood. This was indeed the kind of thing at which Carner excelled in poetry collections such as *Auques i ventalls* [Aucas and Fans] (1914), or in his many contributions to the Barcelona press that were compiled in volumes such as *Les planetes del verdum* [The Predictions of the Bird] (1918) or *Les bonhomies* [Positive Attitudes] (1925). Josep Pla believed that Carner was a 'considerable escriptor en prosa, cosa natural atesa la gran força expressiva de la seva poesia' [an excellent prose writer, understandably, given the great expressive power of his poetry] (Pla 1969: 278). Carles Riba claimed that one cannot read Carner's prose without thinking about his poetry (Riba 1967: 95). Estimates of Carner's achievement vary: Maurici Serrahima held the view that whatever worthwhile comments, jokes and observations might be incorporated in Carner's acute and often funny texts, the author was in the end successful in neither narrative nor essay, and that the topics he dealt with were always topics of general conversation (Serrahima 1968: 818). Alan Yates was unabashedly puzzled when he had to describe Carner's articles: 'La dificultat d'assignar-los una denominació exacta ("narracions curtes", "articles" — per qualificar-los d'alguna manera —) indica un dels trets peculiaríssims de la prosa carneriana' [The difficulty of assigning them an accurate label ('short stories', 'articles', to describe them somehow) indicates the peculiar characteristics of Josep Carner's prose] (Yates 1975: 123–24). Joan Fuster, on the other hand, thought that Carner's articles had considerable literary value: 'Transferits al llibre, ofereixen una unitat i una consistència que semblen premeditades i d'una peça' [Collated in book form, they exhibit a unity and consistency that seem premeditated and well thought-out] (Fuster 1964: 13). In the end, it was Fuster who unlocked the secret of Carner's prose, emphasizing precisely its ability to document a disappeared past. Fuster pointed out that Carner was writing from Italy, remembering a Catalan society of the 1920s that was fast fading away and populated by characters that were anachronisms in the modern world, and concluded:

> Avui, que tot això queda a penes diluït en l'enyorança dels ancians supervivents, nosaltres comencem a trobar-hi una nova curiositat, com en un àlbum de família. Ens hi sedueix la imatge d'una societat i d'una topografia que han canviat, o que fins i tot han desaparegut per sempre més, i que tanmateix conserven sobre el paper, embalsamades, una entranyable iridescència sentimental. I d'alguna manera *Les bonhomies* són també un document històric.
>
> [Today, when all this remains barely diluted in the nostalgia of the elderly survivors, we begin to find a new curiosity, as you might in a family album. We are seduced by the image of a society and a topography that have changed or

even disappeared forever more, and yet retain on paper, embalmed, a charming sentimental iridescence. And somehow *Les bonhomies* is also a historical document.] (Fuster 1964: 15)

In one article from *Les bonhomies*, 'Habitants de la nit' [People of the Night], Carner portrays with vivid imagination a series of human beings as they move through an urban landscape at night:

Un celibatari misàntrop, que surt a passejar el seu gos. — Un home estrany, de cara lluent, que us demana caritat en francès (¿qui ha demanat mai, de dia, caritat en francès?), aquell home necessita que sigui de nit i *que hi hagi una certa solitud.* — Un vidu que ha passat la cinquantena i s'arriba fins a Canaletes: havia tingut ideals i emocions, i avui no li resta sinó un culte meticulós de la higiene: és per higiene que dóna un miler de passes abans de ficar-se al llit, però com que l'ambient dels vidus és la paradoxa, surt a dar el seu passeig salutífer a l'hora que les porteres piquen les catifes de les escales. — Dos vellets suaus, marit i muller, que ixen cada nit una mica tard a sentir música: quan fa calor s'asseuen prop d'un teatre de sarsuela o d'opereta i quan fa fred van a un cafè on hi hagi pianista i es permeten el luxe de dues granadines. — El senyor que ha sopat a casa d'uns amics: porta una flor al trau i fuma un *Caruncho*; se sent encarcarat, entresuat i magnífic. — El marit que s'ha barallat amb la dona: heu-vos-el aquí amb el capell mal recolzat damunt la testa, les mans crispades: hom reconstitueix l'escena de la revolada amb què ha tancat la porta del pis per aquest senzill detall: *s'ha oblidat de posar-se la corbata.* Encara no se sap si va a un music-hall, a tirar-se a mar o a esperar el primer tren per la línia de Vilafranca.

[A celibate misanthrope, who goes out to walk his dog. — A strange man, with a shiny face, who is begging in French (who has ever begged during the day, in French?), it has to be at night and *there needs to be a certain solitude.* An over-the-hill widower walks to Canaletes: in the past he had ideals and emotions, and today he only has a meticulous worship of hygiene: it is because of hygiene that he walks a thousand steps before going to bed, but since widowers live in paradox, he goes out to perform his constitutional when the doorwomen clean the stairs' carpets. — A gentle old couple, husband and wife, who go out a little late every night to listen to music: when it's hot they sit near a zarzuela or operetta theatre and when it's cold they go to a café where there is a pianist and they allow themselves the luxury of drinking two grenadines. — The gentleman who has dined at some friends' house: he carries a flower on his jacket and smokes a *Caruncho*; he feels stiff, sweaty and magnificent. — The husband who has had an argument with his wife: here he is with an ill-fitting hat, his hands twitching: it is possible to reconstruct the scene of the slam with which he closed the door of the apartment because of one simple detail: *he has forgotten to put on his tie.* He still does not know if he is going to a music-hall, to jump into the sea or to wait for the first Vilafranca-line train.] (Carner 1981: 148)

What unites these characters is that all of them are out of place: they belong to a world that is disappearing. They include a misanthropic bachelor; a beggar who speaks in French; a widower obsessed with hygiene; an old couple who, after listening to a concert of popular music, indulge in a soft drink; a man with a flower on his jacket who smokes a cheap cigar; a husband without a tie who has just quarrelled with his wife and is hesitant in the middle of the street, not knowing what to do or where to go next. Carner portrays a human landscape of vices and attitudes that belong to the *genteta* [the contemptibles]. Gabriel Ferrater defended Carner against those who said that he was an 'estilitzador de manies de genteta' [an analyst of *genteta* idiosyncrasies] (Ferrater 1991: 7). But in *Les bonhomies* we encounter instances of the *genteta* that Carner liked to criticize in many of his poems as well. In yet another example, he puts together a catalogue of bad taste that is also a record of how Barcelona apartments were decorated at the time. In 'Les coses lletges' [Ugly things], he writes:

> Un nombre extraordinari de cases de la ciutat seran inundades, un altre cop, de les lletjors industrials: no li ve d'un pam a la dama que no ha conegut mai, en el seu vestit almenys, l'harmonia de la color, ni al seu marit, que, abandonant l'actuació civil a la seva dona, atorgant-li el monopoli, es dedica a la 'torre', que ha poblat de mil detalls 'rústecs'. Però els dolços infants que pugen en els grans caixons apel·lats 'pisos barcelonins', esdevenen una mica més tristos, amb el cor una mica més nuat. Quan s'és infant, i el col·legi, la presumpció naixent i altres malastres no ens han començat de viciar, la lletjor ens causa una tristesa que, naturalment, no podem referir a causes estètiques, però que ens emmetzina les hores. Un pastoret de color de rosa que aguanta una bombeta elèctrica, una tricromia amb una escena andalusa qualsevol, un gosset de guix per a clavar-hi l'escuradents, limiten cada dia, amb llur banalitat, com unes petites ídoles malèfiques, la imaginació, que és el do dels infants i de llurs padrines les fades. Creix llavors, a poc a poc, en els dolços infants, una cosa lletja i irresistible, com els 'desigs' de les dames en certs moments interessants de llur vida: una golafreria de coses que dringuen fals, que lluen fals, que encisen un dia la mirada grollera, i l'endemà degoten fàstic i desesperació. És el Mal Gust, una cosa que esgarrifa més que no el grinyol de l'esmolet.
>
> [An extraordinary number of houses in the city will be flooded, once again, by industrial ugliness: it does not matter a jot to the lady who, at least judging by the way she dresses, has never known which colour goes with which, nor to her husband, who, leaving things to his wife, devotes himself to decorating their 'villa' in a completely rustic fashion. But the sweet children that are brought up in those big boxes called 'Barcelona apartments' become somewhat sadder, and their hearts sink. When we are young and still unaffected by school, growing conceit and other disasters, ugliness causes a sadness that, of course, we cannot relate to aesthetic causes, but that poisons our days. A pink little shepherd who holds an electric bulb, a trichrome with an Andalusian scene, a plaster dog where one can leave used toothpicks, set limits every day, with their banality, like little evil idols, on the imagination, which is the gift of children and their fairy godmothers. And so, little by little, in those sweet children, an ugly and irresistible thing grows, like ladies' 'desires' at certain interesting moments in their lives: a gluttony for things that ring untrue and seem fake, that attract rude looks, and the next day drip with revulsion and despair. It's Bad Taste, something that makes your skin crawl more than a knifegrinder's screech.]
> (1981: 67–68)

Carner here itemizes the most horrifying objects one might find in any Catalan apartment, and abhors their effects during the early stages of life. He also establishes a catalogue of what Pijoan calls 'ethnographic memories of the big city' before they disappear without anyone having the chance to recuperate them, and the list is his method for doing so. Such a rhetorical device — enumeration — can be understood as an act of looking around to survey and record the wide variety of actions and people that populate the landscape of the everyday. Thinking about a Louvre exhibition, Umberto Eco makes some useful observations in this regard. As he points out, artists have resorted to a range of remarkable solutions in the attempt to represent the list, and he goes on to theorize them. As a good cataloguer, Eco relies on subdivisions. He considers the verbal (from Homer to Thomas Pynchon) and the visual (from a fifth-century Greek shield to Christian Boltanski installations), and concludes that the two major types of list are those that correspond to the 'poetics of everything included' and those expressing the 'poetics of the etcetera' (Eco 2009: 7). The first aims for comprehensiveness and closure, albeit temporary: the old phone book is at once a list of phone numbers and a comprehensive catalogue of the inhabitants of a city. The second exploits the human mind's capacity for association, as is the case in Carner's enumerations. Carner is also playing a well-known children's game: *Un, dos, tres, pica paret* [a variation of hide-and-seek] in which a player/observer facing the wall tries to catch the other players when they move, which corresponds to *picnolepsy* as defined by Virilio.

Sometimes Carner performs an autopsy of lost reality by enumerating what has disappeared. At the beginning of 'Un amic íntim' [A Close Friend], for example, he provides an elaborate theory of disappearances in our everyday landscape:

> L'home és fet així: gaudeix sense gratitud, i àdhuc sense parar-hi ment, la quieta carícia immòbil de les coses que el volten, però el canvi, tanmateix, l'adoloreix una mica. Cada dia travessem davant d'un arbre sense fer cabal de tota la seva successió de miracles, però el dia que hom l'abat, sentim, per un segon, una mena d'orfenesa. Tenim el costum de passar vora un cafè tot il·luminat, multiplicat pels miralls, atordit de converses; i fins el dia que el substitueix un Banc — paredat, com aquell qui diu, a encesa de llums — no ens adonem que el cafè ens feia un moment de companyia, amb el seu esclat heterogeni i vivent; i sentim, de cop i volta, una mica de solitud. Per a adonar-nos d'una gràcia necessitem en general adoptar un previ determini pedantesc: 'Avui esmerçaré una estona per dar un tomb inútil i sentimental'. Les coses, per a impressionar-nos si us plau per força, no tenen més remei que, amb llur desaparició, emportar-se'n una mica de la nostra vida. Tots nosaltres, amb alguna recança, amoixem reminiscències de coses que no veiérem sinó d'esma i que ja no hi són: conservem, talment, la flor emmusteïda que ens donà una noia de la qual no hem sabut ni sabrem mai la color dels ulls. Així, abans de morir, ja ens anem projectant gradualment en l'ombra.

> [People are like this: they enjoy without any gratitude, and even without thinking about it, the imperceptible caress of things around them, and yet any change causes them a little bit of pain. Every day we walk by a tree without realizing its string of miracles, but on the day it is cut, we feel for a second a kind of orphanhood. We are in the habit of walking past a café, with plenty of mirrors, filled with conversations; and until the day a Bank replaces it — fenced, one could say, in full daylight — we do not realize that the café, with

its heterogeneous and living activity, was good company; and we suddenly feel a little loneliness. To realize the elegance of something, we generally need to adopt a pedantic attitude: 'Today I will be doing some useless and sentimental walking'. Things, if they are to impress us, should take away a little of our life as they disappear. All of us, with some remorse, love reminiscences of things that we hardly saw but that are not there anymore: we keep, perhaps, a withered flower given to us by a girl, the colour of whose eyes we do not know and will never know. So, before dying, we are gradually entering the shadow.] (Carner 1981: 165)

Things that surround us cannot but take with them a little bit of our life when they disappear, and these sometimes insignificant, hardly noticed disappearances Carner emphatically links to death. Elsewhere in the text, he exhibits his exceptional ability to perceive and give a sense of invisible changes, for instance ending the article with an elegy for the decidedly quotidian object of the umbrella:

No us convido pas a les reminiscències literàries del paraigua: el paraigua de l'oncle rural de *vaudeville*, el paraigua panxa enlaire de l'estudiant i la modisteta, el paraigua nerviós i prim de la jove dama, el tendal solidíssim del capellà, el paraigua diminut de la *divette* amb el qual hom assenyala un espectador i amaga la fingida escena del bes, el paraigua oficial del senyor de copa alta que va a una cerimònia a l'aire lliure (dos estris a la vegada! — pensa el bon senyor — una desgràcia mai no ve sola!), el paraigua deformat i bruixenc de la castanyera, el paraigua tort del pagès, el paraigua perforat del fumador, el paraigua del poruc que obrint-lo i tancant-lo espanta els gossos, el paraigua del ric celibatari egoista i prudent, arborat per bé que no hi hagi sinó un cap de núvol a l'horitzó, contrapart elegant — seda, malaca i or — del baròmetre que hi ha en una repiseta, ben acuradament embeinat quan el somriure del cel és equívoc, mai no deixat a ningú, i només temerós d'haver de caure, després d'acompanyar cada vegada amb més freqüència el seu encirat senyor als enterraments, a les mans d'algun nebot inexpert.

[I do not invite you to the literary reminiscences about the umbrella: the vaudevillesque umbrella of a rural uncle, the upside-down umbrella of a student walking with a young dressmaker, the skinny and nervous umbrella of a young lady, the solid tent of a priest, the small umbrella of a *divette* with which she points to a spectator and fakes a kiss behind it, the business-like umbrella of a gentleman with his high hat on who attends an open air event (two objects at the same time! — he muses to himself — misery loves company!), the deformed and witchy umbrella of the chestnut-roasting lady, the peasant's twisted umbrella, the smoker's holed umbrella, the coward's umbrella that he opens and closes to scare dogs away, the rich bachelor's umbrella, selfish and pedantic, opened up even when there is no trace of an upcoming storm, stylish counterpoint — silk, Malacca cane and gold — to the barometer that sits at home on a little shelf, always at hand when a threatening sky sticks out, never lent to anybody, and in danger of becoming the property, after accompanying its uptight owner to increasingly frequent funerals, of an amateurish nephew.] (1981: 166)

The passage's keen sense of the relations between umbrellas and the particularities of their owners is remarkable. As Carner concludes, he turns towards the reader:

'No: us convido a considerar com el paraigua ha estat íntimament unit a l'evolució de la vostra personalitat' [No: I invite you to consider an umbrella as something closely linked to the development of your own personality] (1981: 166).

All these examples might make us think of the rapidity with which contemporary urban space evolves. Fast changes are characteristic of the urban environment and can instigate the unravelling of memory, affecting everyday life and changing imperceptibly how we relate to our surroundings: as Zoë Thompson puts it, 'the aesthetics of disappearance is intrinsically linked to the aesthetics of change as urban spaces evolve' (2015: 162). According to Thompson, Siegfried Kracauer stressed in his essay 'Street without Memory' (1932) that 'one's memories can be shocked into being, as familiar landmarks disappear, or are erased entirely by the destruction of the space in which they stood. For Kracauer, such erasure was the installation of an eternal now, a constant presentness' (Thompson 2015: 162). Thompson suggests that this is reminiscent of Baudrillard's fear that 'memory itself will be eradicated by the imposition of simulated versions of the past, synthetic histories engendered by a process of "museification" that produces an officially sanctioned form of cultural memory' (Thompson 2015: 162). As Baudrillard writes in a passage that resonates with Virilio's idea of *picnolepsy*: 'It is no longer buildings which burn or cities which are laid waste; it is the radio relays of our memories you can hear crackling' (cited in Thompson 2015: 162). Carner's itemizations of unravelling hidden spaces, his records of the physical and emotional network of which they are part, create a map of the city and of its inhabitants in the past, exploring space as a mute witness to changes in everyday life, and my contention is that *picnolepsy* offers an instructive key to this aspect of his work.

Transformation of urban space has long been a preoccupation for writers and artists alike. Christoph Asendorf claims that 'circulation finds its concrete expression in *démolitions*' (1993: 69). In Charles Baudelaire's poem 'Le Cygne' [The Swan], the poet witnesses the disappearance of a world, an entire Parisian neighbourhood swallowed up by Haussmann's reforms:

> [...]
> Le vieux Paris n'est plus (la forme d'une ville
> Change plus vite, hélas! que le cœur d'un mortel);
>
> Je ne vois qu'en esprit tout ce camp de baraques,
> Ces tas de chapiteaux ébauchés et de fûts,
> Les herbes, les gros blocs verdis par l'eau des flaques,
> Et, brillant aux carreaux, le bric-à-brac confus.
>
> [...]
>
> Paris change! mais rien dans ma mélancolie
> N'a bougé! Palais neufs, échafaudages, blocs,
> Vieux faubourgs, tout pour moi devient allégorie
> Et mes chers souvenirs sont plus lourds que des rocs.
>
> (Baudelaire 2014 : 226)

[[...]]
The old Paris is gone (the form a city takes
More quickly shifts, alas, than does the mortal heart).

I picture in my head the busy camp of huts,
And heaps of rough-hewn columns, capitals and shafts,
The grass, the giant blocks made green by puddle-stain,
Reflected in the glaze, the jumbled bric-à-brac.

[...]

Paris may change, but in my melancholy mood
Nothing has budged! New palaces, blocks, scaffoldings,
Old neighbourhoods, are allegorical for me,
And my dear memories are heavier than stone.]

(Baudelaire 1993: 174–75)

The poet voices how the past, the 'spirit' of the place, where now he finds new bridges and boulevards, lingers on in his mind.[3] The city of Modernity is used as a kind of clock or meter that measures variations accurately. Disappearances and transformations in the cityscape are read as indicators of the transience of life. The simile used to figure his memories of the city — stone — is also noteworthy.

Many of Gaziel's works elegize past times and missing spaces in a similar way. In his memoir *Tots els camins duen a Roma* [All Roads Lead to Rome] (1958), he provides a rich and eloquent chronicle of Barcelona at the turn of the twentieth century. He remembers that it was a city

molt comprimida, força allunyada encara de Montjuïc i, sobretot, de Collserola; s'alçava enmig de l'ample aiguamoll de la maresma, tota voltada d'un bosc de xemeneies. Aquest bosc fabril — del qual només queden ara restes, que aviat desapareixeran del tot — era llavors un espectacle imponent, la materialització mateixa de l'esperit de la centúria extraordinària que havia creat la màquina de vapor, la indústria moderna, la democràcia, el liberalisme i la grandesa de la capital de Catalunya. Contemplada de lluny estant i des d'una certa alçària, la ciutat, guarnida amb el seu cenyidor de xemeneies que anaven traient glopades de fum — blanques, negres, grises i groguenques — , semblava un pastís d'aniversari, fet de pinyó i ametlla, on havien clavat tantes candeles enceses com dies feiners té l'any.

[compact, still far from Montjuïc and above all from Collserola, it stood in the middle of the wide wetland of the marsh, surrounded by a forest of chimneys. This factory forest, of which nowadays very little remains and what does remain will soon disappear completely, was then an imposing spectacle, the very materialization of the century's extraordinary spirit that had created the steam engine, modern industry, democracy, Liberalism and the greatness of Catalonia's capital city. Looked at from afar and from a certain height, the city, decorated with its belt of chimneys that were belching smoke — whitewashed, black, grey and yellowish — looked like a birthday cake, made of pine nuts and almonds, into which had been stuck as many candles as there are working days in a year.] (1981: I, 30)

It was a city with no

> tramvies elèctrics, automòbils ni tampoc bicicletes, perquè encara no era inventat el pneumàtic. Només circulaven carruatges particulars, generalment luxosos, o cotxes públics, també anomenats 'pesseters', perquè des que arrencava el cavall fins que el passatger arribava a lloc, mentre pel camí no fes parada, el trajecte valia una *pesseta*; tartanes, molts carros, uns tramvies rudimentaris, també de tracció exclusivament animal, i uns ripperts de dues empreses en competència: *La Nueva Condal* i *La Catalana*. Tots els vehicles eren tirats per cavalls, eugues, mules o rucs.

> [electric trams, cars nor bicycles, because the tyre was not yet invented. Only private carriages were in circulation, usually luxurious, or public cars, also called *pesseters*, because from the moment the horse started walking to the passenger's arrival at his destination, provided it did not stop anywhere, the journey cost a *pesseta*; traps, many carts, rudimentary trams, also exclusively drawn by animals, and *ripperts* of two rival companies: *La Nueva Condal* and *La Catalana*. All the vehicles were drawn by horses, mares, mules or donkeys.]
> (1981: 1, 32)

The picture of Barcelona evoked in Gaziel's memoir is very much of a piece with the one that emerges from the newspaper articles he published in *La Vanguardia*. Assiduously avoiding the merely picturesque or superficial detail, there he manages to capture the poetry of living in the city even as he raises the questions and talks about the frustrations of the educated citizen.

In a memorable article entitled 'Pequeña elegía urbana' [Little Urban Elegy], Gaziel evokes the transformation of mechanical life in the city through an account of his forty-year personal relationship with the Sarrià train line. He writes as the tunnel under Balmes Street is to be inaugurated, with the result that the train will move underground and cease to travel along the surface of the city. The article ends thus:

> ¿Es un sueño? No; es algo parecido: cuarenta años de vida. [...] Al constatar sus extraordinarias mudanzas es forzoso sentir que, en nuestra brevedad, todo lo que fuimos en el seno de esa vida municipal gigantesca, se borra paulatinamente, y nuestra propia vida se va convirtiendo poco a poco en estampas del tiempo pasado.

> [Is it a dream? No. It is something similar: forty years of life. [...] When acknowledging its extraordinary changes we must feel that, in our short lives, everything that we witnessed within that giant municipal life is slowly being erased, and our life is gradually becoming a series of engravings from the past.]
> (1929)

As the subterranean world swallows a former surface train, Gaziel detects an important transformation in city life, and in his account of it there is an overlap between elegy for a time past, anxiety over the speed of change, and an awareness of transience: we are destined to be swallowed up and disappear. One cannot but recall Gilloch's reflection on disappearance: 'For it is paradoxically the act of obliteration, the present absence of the former cafés which brings them so vividly to mind. Demolition and erasure bring with them a sudden appreciation of what is no longer there' (2004: 300).[4] *Picnolepsy* is a way of labelling this phenomenon of the sudden and unnoticed disappearance of objects, parts of the city, attitudes and ways of living. Therefore, we could define it as the unremitting alternation between tiny moments of consciousness and diminutive 'deaths' of unconsciousness.

★   ★   ★   ★   ★

The 2008 financial crisis hit Southern European countries hard, leaving large groups of young graduates with little hope of finding a job. Consequently, a new and exceptional economic, cultural and social paradigm has arisen, which is not only multidimensional but also multidirectional. According to Manuel Castells et al.,

> the crisis of global capitalism that has unfolded since 2008 is not merely economic. It is structural and multidimensional. The events that took place in the immediate aftermath [of the financial crisis] show that we are entering a world with very different social and economic conditions from those that characterized the rise of global, informational capitalism in the preceding three decades. (Castells et al. 2012: 2)

Individuals and communities have articulated cultural and intellectual responses to such an unprecedented situation whose far-reaching effects transcend national borders. In Southern European countries including Spain, Portugal, Italy and Greece, the crisis has prompted a complete rethinking of democratic, social and cultural values, changes that literature is only now beginning to register and document.

Like Carner, many contemporary Catalan writers have engaged in chronicling disappearance and transformation in the everyday. However, they do so from a slightly different perspective. Some focus on the modern city. Others, hit hard by the financial crisis, return to the small rural communities where they grew up, viewing their hometowns from new urban perspectives and realizing how much (and how fast) the world around them has changed. I propose to analyse these upheavals and their depiction in two recent (auto)fictional texts. The characters/narrators in these texts, without jobs, and in some instances without a love life, go back to their hometown for sentimental reasons. In *Primavera, estiu, etcètera* [Spring, Summer, Etcetera] (2011), Marta Rojals has her protagonist Èlia return to a small town that resembles Rojals's own hometown, La Palma d'Ebre. In *L'horitzó primer* [First Horizon] (2013), Joan Todó revisits La Cènia.

Rojals's is a generational novel which centres on those in the mid-thirties demographic, paying special attention to their everyday lives in Ribera d'Ebre. One of the main issues is the dichotomy between city and village: the protagonist struggles constantly with the idea of returning to her hometown, and her struggles mingle with episodes and images from her childhood and adolescence (her first love and so on). Attention is also paid to the problems, disappointments and frustrations involved in migrating to Barcelona, where she now lives. Having left her hometown to study and work there, Èlia is puzzled by her new condition as a migrant. A friend tells her:

> — Ei, que per ser emigrant no cal anar a viure a l'altra punta del planeta, es pot ser emigrant de moltes coses, de realitats, de sentiments, de la llengua, també. Perquè cadascú té la pàtria que té, i se'n pot sentir allunyat encara que et trobis a deu quilòmetres, i la pots enyorar encara que siguis a tres hores de tren.
>
> [Hey, to become an emigrant it is not necessary to move to the other side of the planet. You can be an emigrant of many things, realities, feelings, language, too. Because everybody has a hometown, and you may feel far from it even though you are only ten kilometres away, and you may long for your hometown even if you can get there in three hours by train.] (Rojals 2011: 112–13)

To this Èlia answers that she has felt very lonely and foreign in Barcelona. She does not know anybody in the apartment building where she has been living for ten years, and finds it concerning that a new neighbour was surprised that she could speak Catalan: 'Va i em diu *Ay, "hablas catalán?, però ¿tú eres de aquí?"* T'ho pots creure, la tia?, d'on vol que sigui, de Singapur?' [And she tells me in Spanish, *'But do you speak Catalan? Are you a local?'* Can you believe it? Where does she want me to be from, Singapore!?] (Rojals 2011: 113). At the end of the novel, Èlia flies to Lisbon to visit her sister, who is expecting a baby. Through the plane's window she observes her hometown from a panoptic perspective that allows her to make unexpected connections:

> Recolzo el front a la finestreta de policarbonat i, en el moment precís, el Google Earth ja és un sotabosc de fulles de roure. Entre el trencaclosques de peces verdes i terroses, localitzo la serp negra de l'Ebre i li segueixo els capricis fins on gairebé es fa un nus: el Meandre. I ara he de mirar més amunt, i una mica cap a la dreta, i ja tinc ubicada la crosta verda del Montsant. [...] Però les coses que no es veuen, pel fet de no veure's, no tenen per què no existir. I *allí*, tot i que ara no ho veig, existeix un *patchwork* de teulades secretes, i sé que n'hi ha una amb una antena que sembla un penja-robes, i que dos pisos més avall hi té un telèfon inalàmbric que ningú no pensarà de carregar; sé que hi ha una altra teulada que, un pis més avall, hi té un sofà reclinable massa modern, i que al vespre hi jaurà un home que encendrà un Winston amb el cendrer al pit.
>
> [I lean my forehead against the polycarbonate window and, at the right time, Google Earth is already a vegetation of oak leaves. Among the earthy green puzzle pieces, I locate the black serpent of the Ebre river and I follow its whims until it almost becomes a knot: the Meander. And now I look a little to the right, and there I have located the green scab of Montsant mountain. [...] But things unseen do not cease to exist simply because they are not seen. And *there*, even though now I cannot see it, there is a patchwork of secret roofs, and I know that there is one with an antenna that looks like a clothes line, and two floors below there is a cordless phone that nobody will remember to charge; I know that there is another roof, a floor below, under which there is a recliner sofa that is too modern and in the evening a man will lie down on the sofa and light up a Winston cigarette with an ashtray on his chest.] (Rojals 2011: 362–63)

This very detailed description of what she sees, and what she does not see, from the plane's window is also a reconstruction of spaces she knows all too well, spaces that are the remnants of a world to which she no longer belongs. At the same time, without naming them, she surveys the novel's main characters and the repetitive actions they have performed in it, as if this passage were an abstract of the narrative as a whole. This unusual perspective, an intimate world seen from far above, gives the narrator a sense of security, but it also introduces a vanishing point, the point at which something that has been decreasing disappears altogether. She is daydreaming about what she sees, and remembering the details that her new perspective hides, when she is awoken by a stewardess who asks her '— ¿Café, señora?' [Coffee, Madam?]. She reacts forcefully: 'Señora? Señora tu!, no et fot?' [Madam?! Madam yourself, my foot!] (Rojals 2011: 363). The stewardess's use of 'señora' (rather than 'señorita' [Miss]) brings home for Èlia the passage of time, and from a panoptic perspective she now zooms in on a few houses she knows well, a move that encapsulates both the events in the novel and also a human geography only made visible by virtue of a piercing look at reality.

Joan Todó's *L'horitzó primer* likewise deals with the experience of being a foreigner at home. The narrator regards his situation as being of the kind that Victor Turner defined as liminal: a state of being 'neither here nor there; [...] betwixt and between the positions assigned and arrayed by law, custom, convention, and ceremony' (1969: 95). He perceives slight changes in his own behaviour and has many doubts about how to interact with his neighbors: 'Aquesta sensació de foranitat. Fa gairebé tres mesos que ets aquí, i tot ha canviat subtilment. Ja s'han adonat que has tornat per quedar-te. [...] Ja no saps, per exemple, quan saludar' [This feeling of being foreign. It has been almost three months since you arrived here, and everything has changed. They have already noticed that you're back to stay. [...] You do not know, for example, when you should say hello] (Todó 2013: 87). Also: 'No ha sabut endevinar quan és que la gent d'aquí va al bar, quan cal trucar-los, com funcionen les coses' [He has not been able to work out when people here go to the bar, when to call them, how things work] (Todó 2013: 88). He makes a long list of typical activities performed by families during the local festivities (Todó 2013: 57–59), but it does little good, and his isolation also reminds him of the passage of time (he is nearly forty). As a result of all this he comes to a pessimistic conclusion regarding the book he intended to write: 'Seria una novel·la sense protagonista únic, o potser l'únic protagonista seria el temps, o el mateix poble, la comunitat, una espiral de llenguatge, una novel·la sense argument que tu i jo no escriurem. ¿Qui la llegiria?' [It would be a novel without a main character, or perhaps the main character would be the time or the village, the community, a spiral of language, a plotless novel that neither I nor you will write. Who would read it?] (Todó 2013: 59). The quotidian pervades his memory:

> T'adones que, idèntics a si mateixos, aquests dies s'han perdut en un sospir. Aixecar-se, esmorzar, comprovar mails, llegir, passejar, comprovar mails, dinar, prendre notes per a una possible versió llarga del pregó de festes, comprovar mails: una rutina només trencada pels dies que has anat a ajudar el teu pare a carregar llenya a la finca, que després guardàveu al garatge, vora la caldera de la calefacció. La resta són hores que pareixen engolides per un forat negre, menys pesants que no marca el calendari, dies que semblen perduts. Ja és, però, el que vas aprendre aquells estius que anaves a treballar a la fàbrica: que les hores s'allarguen com un turment si estàs atent a elles, que es cremen com la

palla si en lloc d'estar comptant quantes peces falten per polir et concentres en la perfecció singular de cadascuna; al cap i a la fi, acabar la pila no volia dir res perquè, igual que la roca de Sísif, quan l'acabaves ja n'esperava una altra. Però després s'encongeixen en el record: en una situació de monotonia semblant Hans Castorp va descobrir que quan un dia és com tots, tots els dies són com un qualsevol, i el temps s'accelera. Les últimes setmanes mateix, les que has passat aquí navegant entre ofertes de feina, llegint, sense fer gaire res, atuït per la manca de sortides, aixecant projectes com estels que l'endemà deixaven d'interessar-te, ara semblen un sol minut angoixós; mentre que les Festes d'agost, quan vas fer el pregó, pareixen un any sencer.

[You realize that, identical to each other, these days have been wasted. Getting up, breakfast, checking mails, reading, walking, checking mails, lunch, taking notes for a possible long version of the speech at the *festes*, checking mails: a routine only interrupted by those days when you helped your father to load firewood at the farm, to store it in the garage, near the heating boiler. The rest are hours that seem swallowed up by a black hole, lighter than the calendar indicates, days that seem lost. It is, however, what you learned during those summers you worked at the factory: hours are excruciatingly long if you are aware of them, they go very quickly if, instead of counting how many parts are left to be cleaned, you concentrate on polishing each of them to perfection; in the end, finishing the stack did not mean anything because, like the rock of Sisyphus, as soon as one was finished another one was there. But afterwards they shrink in your memory: in a similarly monotonous situation, Hans Castorp discovered that when one day is the same as another, every day could be any other day, and time accelerates. Take these last weeks you have spent here considering job offers, reading, doing nothing much, devastated by the lack of opportunities, launching projects as if they were flying kites only to forget about them the next day, these weeks now seem like a single anguished minute; while the August festivities, when you made the speech, feel like a whole year.] (Todó 2013: 154–55)

Todó appears to be gesturing here towards *l'infra-ordinaire* [the infra-ordinary], a term coined by Georges Perec in 1973 to denote those unglamorous elements of reality on which he hoped to zero in: 'What happens everyday, the banal, the quotidian, the evident, the common, the ordinary, the infra-ordinary, the background noise, the habitual' (Perec 1999: 210). Perec reminds us that our eyes are conditioned to scan the horizon of our habitat only for the unusual, therefore we tend to neglect the anonymous *endotic* (another of his coinages, an antonym of *exotic*). And it was Walter Benjamin who described the process by which, without the aid of dreams or hashish, an individual perceives the most ordinary, overlooked objects of everyday reality — from obsolete train stations to out-of-place arcades — as uncanny, supernatural, and irrational, a process he called 'profane illumination' (1999: 209). These concepts, as well as that of *picnolepsy*, are useful to understand the texts examined here — by Carner, Gaziel, Rojals, and Todó — all of which detect major transformations in apparently insignificant changes in the everyday.

★   ★   ★   ★   ★

Milan Kundera invokes Herman Broch's reflection on the purpose of the novel: to discover what only a novel can discover is the *raison d'être* of the genre (Kundera 1986: 5). The sharpest writers have managed to condense narrative into a few topics. These topics are not mere plots (myth or elegy), but the inner filter that forces the writer to investigate large abstractions and to offer a reactive response, to express their ideas in a personal way that nevertheless reflects and speaks to the time in which they live. The texts examined here include names and places and temporal changes, and react to the absurdity of everyday life in a big impersonal city through elegy or by evoking mythical spaces and ways of life that have disappeared.

In a section of *The Arcades Project* that mocks the claustrophobic and chaotic mess of the bourgeois living room, Benjamin writes:

> Living in these plush compartments was nothing more than leaving traces made by habits. Even the rage expressed when the least little thing broke was perhaps merely the reaction of a person who felt that someone had obliterated 'the traces of his days on earth'. The traces that he had left in cushions and armchairs, that his relatives had left in photos, and that his possessions had left in lining and etuis and that sometimes made these rooms look as overcrowded as halls full of funerary urns. This is what has now been achieved by the new architects, with their glass and steel: they have created rooms in which it is hard to leave traces. (1999: 701–02)

Similarly, J. G. Ballard is fascinated by reality as a depository of quotidian objects with magic and poetic effects: 'I'm always struck by the enormous sort of magic and poetry one feels when looking at a junkyard filled with old washing machines, or wrecked cars, or old ships rotting in some disused harbor. An enormous mystery and magic surrounds these objects' (cited in Revell). What is the relevance of this for us as we conclude? Carner was an ethnographer of the near past and Rojals and Todó of the near present, but all three perform what I have called autopsies of the everyday and all three can be better understood by considering them in terms of *picnolepsy*. These writers look at reality from a very different perspective, as a special kind of autopsy. They assemble the materials of their mortuary investigation, treating reality almost as if it were a cadaver, or the contents of a special kind of forensic inquisition.

Works Cited

ASENDORF, CHRISTOPH. 1993. *Batteries of Life: On the History of Things and Their Perception in Modernity* (Berkeley: University of California Press)

BAUDELAIRE, CHARLES. 1993. *The Flowers of Evil*, trans. by James McGowan (Oxford: Oxford University Press)

——. 2014. *Les Fleurs du mal (édition posthume et Les épaves): nouvelle édition augmentée* (Paris: Arvensa Editions)

BENJAMIN, WALTER. 1969. 'The Image of Proust', in *Illuminations* (New York: Schocken Books), pp. 201–15

——. 1999. *Selected Writings, 1931–1934*, vol. II (Cambridge, MA: Harvard University Press)

——. 2003. *Selected Writings, 1938–1940*, vol. IV (Cambridge, MA: Harvard University Press)

CARNER, JOSEP. 1981 [1925]. *Les bonhomies i altres proses* (Barcelona: Edicions 62)

CASTELLS, MANUEL, JOÃO CARAÇA, and GUSTAVO CARDOSO (eds). 2012. *Aftermath: The Cultures of the Economic Crisis* (Oxford: Oxford University Press)

CAVALLIN, JEAN-CHRISTOPHE. 2006. 'Baudelaire et "l'homme d'Ovide"', *Cahiers de l'Association internationale des études françaises*, 58.1: 341–57

CÓCOLA GRANT, AGUSTÍN. 2011. *El Barrio Gótico de Barcelona: planificación del pasado e imagen de marca* (Barcelona: Ediciones Madroño)

ECO, UMBERTO. 2009. *The Infinity of Lists: An Illustrated Essay* (New York: Rizzoli)

FERRATER, GABRIEL. 1991. 'Pròleg', in Josep Carner, *Nabí* (Barcelona: Edicions 62), pp. 5–23

FUSTER, JOAN. 1964. 'Pròleg', in Josep Carner, *Les bonhomies* (Barcelona: Edicions 62), pp. 7–15

GAZIEL/AGUSTÍ CALVET. 1929. 'Pequeña elegía urbana', *La Vanguardia*, 26 April

——. 1981 [1958]. *Tots els camins duen a Roma: història d'un destí (1893–1914). Memòries*, 2 vols (Barcelona: Edicions 62)

GILLOCH, GRAEME. 2004. 'Impromptus of a Great City: Siegfried Kracauer's *Strassen in Berlin und anderswo*', in *Tracing Modernity: Manifestations of the Modern in Architecture and the City*, ed. by Mary Hvattum and Christian Hermansen (London: Routledge), pp. 291–306

KUNDERA, MILAN. 1986. *The Art of the Novel* (New York: Grove Press)

NAVAS, TERESA. 1995. 'La ciutat metropolitana (1897–1939)', in *Retrat de Barcelona*, vol. II (Barcelona: Centre de Cultura Contemporània; Publicacions de l'Ajuntament de Barcelona), pp. 25–55

PEREC, GEORGES. 1999 [1973]. *Species of Spaces and Other Pieces*, ed. and trans. by John Sturrock (London: Penguin Group)

PIJOAN, JOSEP. 1927. *El meu don Joan Maragall* (Barcelona: Llibreria Catalònia)

PLA, JOSEP. 1969. *Notes disperses* (Barcelona: Edicions Destino)

QUINTANA I TRIAS, LLUÍS. 2007. 'Joan Maragall, el Pla Jaussely i la Reforma de 1908 a la ciutat de Barcelona', *Zeitschrift für Katalanistik*, 20: 149–65

REVELL, GRAEME. 'Interview with J. G. Ballard' <http://www.researchpubs.com/products-page-2/excerpt-from-interview-with-j-g-ballard-by-graeme-revell/>

RIBA, CARLES. 1967. 'Josep Carner, *Les planetes del verdum*', in *Obres completes* (Barcelona: Edicions 62), p. 95

ROJALS, MARTA. 2011. *Primavera, estiu, etcètera* (Barcelona: La Magrana)

SERRAHIMA, MAURICI. 1968. 'La prosa de Josep Carner', in Josep Carner, *Obres completes* (Barcelona: Editorial Selecta), pp. 807–25

THOMPSON, ZOË. 2015. *Urban Constellations: Spaces of Cultural Regeneration in Post-Industrial Britain* (Aldershot: Ashgate Publishing Limited)

TODÓ, JOAN. 2013. *L'horitzó primer* (Barcelona: L'Avenç)

TURNER, VICTOR. 1969. *The Ritual Process: Structure and Anti-Structure* (Chicago, IL: Aldine Publishing)

VIRILIO, PAUL. 1991. *The Aesthetics of Disappearance*, trans. by Philip Beitchman (New York: Semiotext(e))

——, and SILVÈRE LOTRINGER. 2008. *Pure War*, trans. by Mark Polizzotti (Los Angeles and New York: Semiotext(e))

YATES, ALAN. 1975. *Una generació sense novel·la?* (Barcelona: Edicions 62)

Notes to Chapter 1

1. See Navas (1995), Quintana i Trias (2007) and Cócola Grant (2011).
2. Unless otherwise indicated, all translations are mine.
3. See Cavallin: 'En troisième lieu, les strophes du Cygne comme le premier chant des Métamorphoses s'écrivent sur un motif de construction. Tandis que le démiurge ovidien construit le cosmos à partir du vieux chaos de la matière, Napoléon III tire une ville impériale du chaos du vieux

Paris. Dans le Cygne, l'apparition de l'Andromaque de Virgile s'inscrit dans cette réflexion sur la construction ou l'architecture. Si Baudelaire pense brusquement à elle alors qu'il traverse "le nouveau Carrousel", c'est que les chantiers du nouveau Paris lui rappellent le chantier de la ville qu'Hélénus, mari de la princesse troyenne, est en train de construire quand Enée la rencontre sur un rivage désert de l'actuelle Albanie. L'allusion au "Simoïs menteur" illustre la méthode d'Hélénus. L'ancien esclave de Pyrrhus crée la ville de Buthrote à l'image de Troie détruite. Il construit "une petite Troie, une copie faite sur le modèle de la grande Pergame", "simulataque magnis | Pergama (1)". Il appelle respectivement les deux fleuves qui longent la ville le Xanthe et le Simoïs, en souvenir des fleuves de la cité phrygienne. Sa translation onomastique imprime sur le support neutre de ce rivage inconnu une ville archétypique. Sous le roitelet bâtisseur, à la fois cadet d'Hector et sa copie en miniature, se profile la silhouette de "Napoléon le petit", singe et médiocre neveu de Napoléon 1er, transformant le vieux Paris en une ville impériale, conçue comme la figure du rétablissement de l'Empire. À l'exemple d'Hélénus produisant ex nihilo un simulacre de Troie, Napoléon III efface le "bric-à-brac" du "vieux Paris" et y substitue une idée de ville. Le démiurge des Métamorphoses, l'Hélénus de l'Enéide et l'empereur urbaniste, tous trois architectes et bâtisseurs, forment une séquence analogique qui invite à lire le poème comme une méditation sur l'acte créateur et donc sur la poïesis' [Thirdly, the stanzas of The Swan as the first song of the Metamorphoses are written on a construction motif. While the Ovidian demiurge builds the cosmos out of the old chaos of matter, Napoleon III draws an imperial city out of the chaos of old Paris. In The Swan, the appearance of Virgil's Andromache is part of this reflection on construction or architecture. If Baudelaire suddenly thinks of her as he crosses 'le nouveau Carrousel', it is because the building sites of the new Paris remind him of the city that Helenus, husband of the Trojan princess, is building when Aeneas meets him on a desert shore of present-day Albania. The reference to the 'liar Simoy' illustrates Helenus's method. The former slave of Pyrrhus creates the city of Buthrote in the image of destroyed Troy. He builds 'a little Troy, a copy made on the model of the great Pergamos', 'simulataque magnis | Pergama (1)'. He calls respectively the two rivers that border the city Xanthe and Simois, in memory of the rivers of the Phrygian city. Its onomastic translation stamps on the neutral support of this unknown shore an archetypal city. Under the little king, both Hector's younger brother and his miniature copy, stands the figure of 'Napoleon the Little One', mediocre nephew of Napoleon I, transforming old Paris into an imperial city, conceived as a symbol for the restoration of Empire. Following the example of Helenus producing ex nihilo a simulacrum of Troy, Napoleon III erases the 'bric-a-brac' of 'old Paris' and substitutes it for an idea of a city. The demiurge of the Metamorphoses, Helenus of the Aeneid and the urbanist emperor, all three architects and builders, form an analogical sequence that invites us to read the poem as a meditation on the creative act and therefore on poiesis] (2006: 342–43).

4. As Benjamin said, '[t]he important thing for the remembering author is not what he experienced, but the weaving of his memory, the Penelope work of recollection. Or should one call it, rather, a Penelope work of forgetting? Is not the involuntary recollection, Proust's *mémoire involontaire*, much closer to forgetting than what is usually called memory? And is not this work of spontaneous recollection, in which remembrance is the woof and forgetting is the warp, a counterpart to Penelope's work rather than its likeness? For here the day unravels what the night has woven' (1969: 204).

CHAPTER 2

Walking through the World Republic of Letters: The Narrative Practice of Maria-Mercè Marçal

Helena Buffery

University College Cork

Al costat del llegat poètic marçalià, n'hi ha un de teòric i metodològic, indestriable del primer, en tant que es va desenvolupar encreuadament en els textos assagístics i en els poètics i narratius, al ritme de les reflexions i sensacions de la Maria-Mercè, que s'afuaven en la lectura, passaven per la verbalització i aterraven en l'escriptura. L'obra marçaliana és un microcosmos que no es pot mutilar amb el bisturí d'una pretesa lògica de puresa de gèneres o de literatures nacionals. T'arriba sencera i t'hi has d'aventurar sencera, has de gosar poder fer el teu camí.

[Alongside the poetic legacy of Marçal there is a theoretical and methodological legacy that is inseparable from it in so far as it developed interrelatedly in her essayistic, poetic and narrative texts, in time with the reflections and sensations of Maria-Mercè, which emerged from her readings, and passed through a stage of verbalization before landing in her writing. Marçal's *oeuvre* is a microcosm that cannot be mutilated with the surgical knife of generic purity or of national literatures. It arrives before you whole and you have to launch yourself into it whole, you have to dare to make your own path.] (Torras 2015: 9)

First published in 1994, Maria-Mercè Marçal's multiple award-winning *La passió segons Renée Vivien* [The Passion according to Renée Vivien] tells the story of an incomplete intermedial translation undertaken by the fictional documentary film-maker Sara T. (often identified as Marçal's fictional alter ego) of the lives and works and passion(s) of hybrid Anglo-French Parisian-based cross-dressing *fin-de-siècle* writer and female *flâneuse* Pauline Tarn, the body behind the pseudonym Renée Vivien. The novel is based on extensive literary, archival, archaeological, cartographical and genealogical research and reenactment, including translation into Catalan of English and French sources, most notably in the final chapter or 'monody', which is a collage made up entirely of Maria-Mercè Marçal's own renderings of fragments from her precursor's works (see Fons de Maria-Mercè Marçal, Box 11). The diverse, overlapping narrative layers in this palimpsest of a novel initially produce a sense of disorientation in the reader, who is left to reconstruct their own version of Vivien from the always provisional and partial visions, accounts and sketches provided.

Written in Catalan, *La passió segons Renée Vivien* has so far been translated into four different languages: Spanish, German, Italian and Slovenian, but notably not French (even though we know from Marçal's letters to Jean-Paul Goujon [Marçal 2014: 143–44] that the rights for a French translation were acquired before the author's death), or English.[1] As such, it proffers material aplenty to reflect on both the politics and problematics of translation to and from different languages and cultures, ranging from questions of where Marçal's decision to translate Pauline Tarn/Renée Vivien's process of interlinguistic and intersemiotic self-translation places her in debates over world literature, to how the different translators deal with the multiple, meticulously researched voices in the novel (all of whom seek to translate Pauline-Renée into their own personal frames). A particular problem faced by all who attempt to translate the novel is the challenge of reproducing the multi-valency of particular instances of wordplay in Catalan, most notably Marçal's rendering of *l'ébauche* [the sketch] as 'l'esbós', itself a palimpsestic translation of Vivien's fascination with *ébauches*, *ésquisses* and *croquis*: 'Le charme douloureux des ébauches m'attire' (Vivien)/'*L'encís tan dolorós dels esbossos m'atreu*' [The painful charm of sketches attracts me] (Marçal 1994: 334).References to *esbossos*, *esbós* and *l'esbós* become a central metafictional motif of the novel, simultaneously evoking the fragile provisionality of the lines required to capture and transmit such a mobile, protean subject, and the mythical haven of Lesbos, where Vivien and Natalie Barney are able to escape, if only fleetingly, from the complex performative geography of turn-of-the-century Paris and openly display and enjoy lesbian love. The play between 'L'esbós' and 'Lesbos' was even considered by Marçal in searching for a title for her novel, with version 2 prefaced by the hand-written *L'esbós o la passió segons Renée Vivien* [The Sketch or the Passion according to Renée Vivien] alongside *Lesbós de la memòria* [Lesbos of Memory] in pencil (Fons de Maria-Mercè Marçal, Box 11).

If my initial return to a text I first read at the very beginnings of my interest in Catalan Studies was fuelled by the desire to see it translated for an English-speaking audience, then the research that followed, including intense archival engagement with the materials Marçal used to elaborate her novel (Fons de Maria-Mercè Marçal), led to a wider exploration of the tactics she developed to negotiate literary space throughout the long period of its gestation (1984–94). Sensitive to the blurring of disciplinary boundaries characteristic of her practice, I have opted to approach her work from three overlapping perspectives: the spatial, focusing on the way in which she navigates and re-shapes different social, cultural and historical spaces; the translational, attending to the processes of interlinguistic, intersemiotic and intercultural translation enacted in and through her work; and the comparative, identifying the particular mode of worlding put into practice in her texts.

Inspired by Meri Torras's invocation that what we learn by working with Marçal is 'com relacionar-nos amb els textos' [how to relate to/enter into relation with texts] (Torras 2015: 8), including in this the layers of intertexts that infuse the pages of her works, I will begin by walking with the Catalan poet through a shorter narrative piece she first published midway through the lengthy process of composition of *La passió segons Renée Vivien*. The text extends a useful introduction to the way in which her self-consciously performative and embodied narrative practice overlaps and interacts with other readings, writings, memories, experiences and tactics, a web that is itself mirrored in the processual mode of composition displayed in the 1994 novel. Shifting my attention to critical prioritization of the motif and metaphor of the mirror as Marçal's preferred mode of projecting the relationship between self and other in her writings, I will explore how the play of mirrors deployed in and between the different narratives creates a *mise en abîme* in which there is a more performative process of multiplication and repetition through surrogation. This, in turn, motivates a return to the model of translation practice rehearsed and enacted in and through Marçal's novel, as a guide to negotiating the complex interpretive, ethical and erotic demands of standing in for and reenacting another's work, evoked in the embodied and situated sense of 'walking through' of my title. Taking my lead from Marçal's own narrative practice and performance of interlinguistic and intercultural relations, I go on to investigate what *La passió segons Renée Vivien* tells us about her self-positioning, as a Catalan woman writer, in relation to the World Republic of Letters, reflecting also on the challenges this presents for translation of the novel into English (given the primarily historical-thematic focus of the framing and marketing of literary translations into English at the current time).[2]

Turns and Returns

In 'Viratges, reminiscències' [Turns, Returns], Maria-Mercè Marçal's contribution to the 1989 volume *Barceldones* (reproduced in Julià 1998: 16–21, and in Marçal 2004: 25–34), the Catalan writer takes her readers on an intimate spatio-temporal journey through heterogeneous landscapes of the Catalan capital, simultaneously inserting herself in the twists and turns of its topography and transmitting a vision of a city shaped by bodily encounters in and between public and private spaces, in the shuttling between centre and margins. From her vantage point in the Putget area of Barcelona, she weaves back and forth, taking in her own origins and place in a genealogical line that marks out the city as a space of liberation for women, before reflecting on her connectedness to the everyday social, cultural and environmental ecology of her district. In waves, she reminisces on her political, educational, literary and sexual history, sharing intimate details of her experience of pregnancy, childbirth and motherhood, and of female love, friendship, care and companionship, via a network of shared sites and routes through the Born, Baix Llobregat, Eixample, Ciutadella, Barri Sant Just, Raval, Gràcia, Horta, platja de Sant Sebastià, Plaça de Catalunya, Turó de la Peira, amongst others.

The home from which she writes, as if in answer to her daughter's question 'on acaba, on comença Barcelona' [where ends, where begins Barcelona] (Marçal 1998

[1989] : 21), lies in a district that seems to her 'fet a mida per a un esperit híbrid, indecís, instal·lat de forma permanent en el solc entre dos mons, en el llindar entre dos paisatges, dues temptacions, dos codis' [made to measure for a hybrid, undecided spirit, installed permanently in the groove between two worlds, the threshold between two landscapes, two temptations, two codes] (17); a metaphorical 'port' in this maritime city presented as an inbetween space nestling between land and sea, as both a place of respite from her nomadic wanderings and a vantage point over the network of significant individual and group memory sites spread out across the city beneath her. Her journey is both a mental, intellectual and discursive one, through a 'xarxa dins de la qual em debato' [network within which I move and debate myself], and a physical, emotional and recursive one, which she re-traces 'amunt i avall, per dins, corrent darrere d'amors i d'altres coses...' [up and down, inside, chasing after lovers and other things...] (17). It is a network that can be traversed in various directions in order to achieve some form of autopoietic completion: 'Reprenc, trio de nou els camins que m'han dut fins aquí' [I take up, choose again the paths that have brought me here] (18). Nevertheless there is a remainder: 'Incrustada a la ciutat, espargida, difosa arreu, la vasta cambra fosca, opaca, quasi sempre invisible de l'amor entre dones' [Encrusted in the city, spaced out, spreading everywhere, the vast dark chamber, opaque, almost always invisible, of love between women] (20). Ultimately, hers is a tightrope walk, '[t]entinejant sobre l'estreta paret imperceptible que separa els espais acotats de la terra de ningú que queda en els marges...' [balancing on the narrow and imperceptible wall that separates the cultivated spaces from the no-man's-land that remains in the margins] (20), skirting the invisible, silenced, abject space of lesbian desire, on the margins of the symbolic and the normative. The desire lines she traces in her different moments and modes of walking in and through her city evoke the 'mobile infinity of tactics' of evasion, resistance and contestation celebrated by Michel de Certeau in *The Practice of the Everyday* (1984: 110). They offer an enticing key to the narrative practice of Marçal, her resistant reading/writing of the relationship between literature and world.

A Performative Play of Mirrors?

Written during the long period of elaboration of Marçal's only completed and published novel, 'Viratges, reminiscències' presents a tantalizing mirror to *La passió segons Renée Vivien* and to the 'joc de miralls' [play of mirrors] that is one of the latter's central metafictional motifs (see, for instance, Marçal 2004: 206), in the desire of its late twentieth-century protagonist, documentary film-maker, Sara T., to find her own passions reflected in the life and works of the *fin-de-siècle* lesbian poet. References to mirrors appear throughout the novel, particularly in relation to Sara T.'s at times anguished self-questioning about her motivations in seeking to retrace and reconstruct the poet's lived experience. Yet, this is often, as below, in the context of failure: because the image produced is blurred, deformed, fragmented or contradictory; because her object is characterized by constant metamorphosis and motility; because all that is reflected back to her is traces of her own likeness. In wondering how to re-orient her poet-other, she conjures images of movement, travel, performance, ephemerality and ruins, reminiscent of the fragile, provisional and palimpsestic topography we have seen traced in her earlier text:

> A partir d'un reflex que serpeja aigua endins, on m'és fàcil de destriar només els traços que em retornen la meva imatge, deformada, estiraganyada, contrafeta o agegantada com els miralls de fira, de quina manera redreçar-te a tu, més enllà d'aquest estrany joc d'encaixos, de peces movedisses, que intento de confegir a les biblioteques, als museus, pels carrers de París, a les llibreries, al Bois, a les guies turístiques, en els mapes de les illes gregues, en les reconstruccions escenogràfiques del cinema [...]. Peces canviants i indòcils, que ballen i s'encarcaren, fugen i s'apropen, desapareixen i es recreen, en contínua metamorfosi. Peces mòbils fetes amb fragments de peces fixes, trossos de papers esquinçats i restaurats, documents on les rates han fet el seu niu i que mostren en blanc els seus fulls més sencers, fotografies on sovint el rostre més decisiu apareix més borrós; testimonis escrits que sovint són actes de defensa, d'acusació i, sempre, d'autojustificació; cases que han estat enderrocades, carrers que han canviat de nom. I els mateixos escrits, màscares sobre màscares sobre màscares. I, així i tot, per les clivelles, des de dins, com una gran teranyina vella, la nafra, traspuant i envaint-ho tot amb el seu color de ponent i de vi.

> [From a reflection that twists deep in the water, where the only thing I can make out clearly is the traces that return to me my own image, deformed, stretched out of shape, distorted or magnified as in a fairground hall of mirrors, how can I return you to yourself, beyond this strange jigsaw puzzle of movable pieces, which I am trying to put together in the libraries, the museums, the streets of Paris, its bookshops, and the Bois, in tourist guides, in maps of the Greek islands, in the scenographic reconstructions of the cinema [...]. Mutable, indocile pieces, that dance and are petrified, that flee from me and come closer, disappear and are recreated, in continuous metamorphosis. Mobile pieces made of fragments of fixed pieces, and of torn paper restored, documents in which the rats have made their nest and whose most intact pages are blank, photographs where often the most significant face appears blurred; written testimonies that are often acts of defence, of accusation and always of self-justification; houses that have been demolished, streets that have changed names. And your own writings, masks upon masks upon masks. Even so, between the cracks, from deep inside, like a great red cobweb, there is the wound, seeping and invading everything with its colour of sunset and of wine.] (Marçal 1994: 78–79)

Here, though, the fragile network of lines that trace the almost always invisible spaces of 'la vasta cambra fosca [...] de l'amor entre dones' [the vast dark chamber [...] of love between women] of the 1989 piece are translated into the more abject imagery of an immense, ancient cobweb over an open, wine-coloured wound.

As Rosa Cabré (2004) reminds us, drawing on evidence in the afterword to the novel, Marçal's own encounter with the poetry of Renée Vivien leaves imprints on her poetic production from as early as *La germana, l'estrangera* [*Sister, Stranger*] (1981–84). Furthermore, in a later letter to the Vivien specialist, Jean-Paul Goujon, Marçal admits the importance of her discovery of the first modern poet to write openly of love between women, not only for her writing but also for her ability to function in society: 'Renée Vivien a joué là un rôle capital, car je l'ai placée entre moi et mon ombre [...] Voilà la histoire [*sic*] du roman! Au-delà ou en-deçà de la littérature, ce geste (ou cette métamorphose!) a supposé une vraie réussite dans le domaine de ma vie "réelle"' [Renée Vivien has played a key role in this, because I have placed her between me and my shadow [...] Here is the history of the novel! Above and beyond literature, this gesture (or this metamorphosis!) has been a real success story in the domain of my 'real' life] (cited in Cabré 2004: 174; full letter reproduced in Catalan in Marçal 2014: 84–89). Rather, then, than the narcissistic mirror lamented by Neus Real (1995: 115) in her early review of the structure of the novel, the encounter with Vivien signals a multi-directional mirroring that inspires the creation of a 'real-life' network of women writers, thinkers and artists, the network that inhabits, embodies and shapes Marçal's richly evocative Barcelona map. Like the later collective project with the Catalan branch of PEN, *Cartografies del desig* [Cartographies of Desire] (Marçal 1998), this forms part of a process of mapping a space of encounter for women past, present and future, as recognized by Caterina Riba (2015b: 471). Indeed, there is manuscript evidence in the Maria-Mercè Marçal archive in the Biblioteca de Catalunya that the writer had begun work on a novel about this very same network, mirroring the procedures and tactics followed in *La passió segons Renée Vivien*, but translated to the place she considered home: Barcelona (Fons de Maria-Mercè Marçal, Box 12/6).

Not only has the mirror constituted one of the prevalent tropes for reading Marçal's output, overarchingly characterized as a search for a feminine symbolic, through the recovery of literary (m)others (see, especially, Julià 2003), but even the shorter piece, 'Viratges, reminiscències', has been interpreted primarily from the perspective of identification, as in Rafael Mérida's essay (2012: 103), without always attending to the abject, invisible remainders beyond the frame of the mirror, or the complex, spatio-temporal multi-directionality of the cartographies it contains. Just as in the 1989 text we end with literary recognition in difference, through the way in which Marçal's own mapping and retracing of the meandering trajectories of home leads her to inhabit also the nostalgic landscape of Clementina Arderiu in exile, by remembering her poetic voice — '"Ara que ja de tanta casa torno"' ['Now that at last I return from so much home'] — and its history (1998 [1989]: 21), so it is important to attend to the simultaneous complexity, fragility and recursivity of the cartography traced in the 1994 novel, as we accompany Sara T. on her journey of creative reconstruction, marked by 'la por de repetir, cíclicament, [...] tots els passos de la passió segons Renée Vivien' [the fear of repeating, cyclically, [...] all the steps in the passion according to Renée Vivien] (Marçal 1994: 189).

For Pilar Godayol, Marçal's is a mirror that eschews beauty, associated with the realms of hegemonic discourse; instead, hers is 'una altra mena de mirall trencat en infinits bocins que reflecteix un ésser complex, híbrid i contaminat, abocat a viure entre Atenea i la Medusa, "movent-se entre la Llei del pare [...] i el femení inarticulat, caòtic"' [another type of mirror, broken into infinite pieces, that reflects a being that is complex, hybrid and contaminated, determined to live between Athena and the Medusa, 'moving between the Law of the Father [...] and the inarticulate, chaotic feminine'] (Godayol 2012: 221; see also Godayol 2008). If this broken, fragmented mirror recalls the palimpsestic writing of an earlier novel, Mercè Rodoreda's *Mirall trencat* [Broken Mirror] (1974), with its origins in the short play, *Un dia* [One Day], of 1959, then Rodoreda's repetitive and recursive reconstruction of a life after trauma in *La plaça del Diamant* [The Time of the Doves/In Diamond Square] is explicitly cited in notes by Marçal as a key intertext for her own narrative of ghostly presences (Fons de Maria-Mercè Marçal Box 8/4.3). Nor is Rodoreda's the only Catalan literary voice echoed in *La passió segons Renée Vivien*, as it includes excerpts from Carles Riba, Josep Maria de Sagarra, Rosa Leveroni and J. V. Foix, and there are references to Eugeni d'Ors, Joan Maragall and Josep Carner in the author's manuscript notes (Fons de Maria-Mercè Marçal, Box 8/5).

Furthermore, Marçal's working papers reveal the full extent of her navigation and immersion in the subject of her novel. Emerging from a moment of identification reflected also in the narrative of Sara T., her research leads her to read all of the Anglo-French lesbian writer's production, her literary influences, the writings of her contemporaries and their accounts of the Parisian *fin-de-siècle* scene; essays and analyses by critics and literary biographers; socio-historical accounts of nineteenth- and early twentieth-century French and British culture and society; newspapers and journal articles from and about the period; maps, travelogues and tour guides; as well as visiting and photographing all the key sites and sketching the relationships between the different spaces (Fons de Maria-Mercè Marçal, Boxes 6, 7, 8, 10). It is a novel that does not just seek to represent these multiple voices and perspectives, but to reenact them through the translations that Dolors Udina (2008: 211) repeatedly describes as being '*incrustades* en la novel·la' [encrusted in the novel], thus echoing the ambivalence of the metaphor's usage in 'Viratges, reminiscències', in its simultaneously artistic evocation of the setting of precious stones and the more abject depiction of encrusted remains.

Modelling the Reader/Writer as Translator

As Caterina Riba (2015a/b), Mercè Ibarz (2004) and Dolors Udina (2008) all note, Marçal's mode of translation is a radical one that consumes and incorporates her literary forebears. Riba (2015b: 479) connects such practice with the Anthropophagic movement of Brazilian Modernism, quoting Susan Bassnett on Haroldo de Campos: 'Translation is for him a physical process, it is a devouring of the source text, a transmutation process, an act of vampirization. Translation, as he says, "como transfusão. De sangue" [like a transfusion. Of blood]' (Bassnett 1998: 155). Marçal herself, in the various drafts for a 1991 talk on translation (Fons de Maria-Mercè Marçal, Box 13/1), reflects as follows on the reasons to translate to and from a minority language like Catalan, which she nevertheless celebrates for its great tradition of translations: 'crec que hi ha un altre impuls més primordial, que s'assembla a l'amor o a la passió que cerca apropiar-se en certa manera del text, menjar-se'l o ésser menjat, convertir el jo en el tu i el tu en el jo' [I think there is another more primordial impulse, similar to love or to the passion that seeks to

appropriate the text in some way, to eat it or to be eaten, to convert the I into you
and the you into I]. The regenerative power of translation to which she attests — 'a
través de la traducció es pot renovar' [through translation one can renew oneself] —
both through providing access to different poetic experiences, traditions and turns
of phrase, and through the opportunity to rework and expand the target language, is
now almost a commonplace, thanks to the 'cultural turn' in Translation Studies and
especially to descriptive and postcolonial approaches to translation. What stands out
is the metaphorical force of the embodied agency Marçal associates with translation,
as resembling a love story characterized by passion or desire. It is a formulation
that brings to mind Gayatri Chakravorty Spivak's slightly later advocation of erotic
openness to enable surrender to the particular rhetoric and silences of the source
text in her discussion of 'The Politics of Translation' (1993).

It is in part a return to Spivak's 1993 theory/praxis of the reader-as-translator that
has inspired my approach to Marçal's narrative practice. In her seminal essay, Spivak
calls for a mode of reading and/as translation that is more sensitive to the rhetoricity
of the text: 'The history of the language, the history of the author's moment, the
history of the language-in-and-as-translation, must figure in the weaving as well'
(1993: 186). Hence, what I want to focus on in the remainder of this chapter is the
way in which the processual model of translation rehearsed and enacted in and
through the novel can itself be translated to produce more sensitive awareness of
the situatedness of Marçal's narrative practice, beyond the now extensive readings
of her importance in reconstructing a space for reading and writing by women. I
will take as my guide the rather brilliant alternative to Baudelaire's albatross we
glimpse as an alter ego for the writer in the pages of the novel, in the invisible
wings of an ancient, mutilated Victory, which once again return us to the fragile
and provisional motility of 'l'esbós':

> Deies, Renée, i et planyies d'haver deixat mai aquest estadi alhora truncat i
> sense límits, on es troben les obres inacabades dels artistes i les que el temps ens
> ha llegat incompletes i fragmentàries: espai per al no-dit, per a l'irreal, per al
> somni, per al vertigen. Per a les ales invisibles d'una antiga Victòria mutilada.

> [You said this, Renée, and you regretted having ever left this simultaneously
> truncated and limitless state, in which the unfinished works of artists can be
> found and which time has left us incomplete and fragmentary: a space for the
> unsaid, for the unreal, for dreams, for vertigo. For the invisible wings of an
> ancient mutilated Victory.] (Marçal 1994: 76)

Instead of the idealized vision of the superiority of the Modernist writer able to
rise and soar above the decadent world below, we are presented with a truncated
version, firmly situated in the world:

> [Charles] Evocava Renée: de vegades li agradava anomenar-la així, amb aquell
> nom de so ambigu, sense sexe ni gènere, que ell mateix li havia ajudat a trobar;
> i en fer-ho, deixava endarrere la Pauline de terra que la terra havia reprès —
> aquella que lluny de ser la seva veritable personalitat era la seva involuntària,
> material personalitat — per destacar l'àngel: un àngel que, com l'albatros de
> Baudelaire, era tan maldestre quan abandonava la immensitat de l'espai.

[He invoked Renée: sometimes he liked to call her that, the ambiguous-sounding name without sex or gender which he himself had helped her find; in doing so, he left behind that Pauline of the earth which the earth had taken back — far from being her real personality it was her involuntary, material personality — to bring forth the angel: an angel like Baudelaire's albatross, so awkward when it abandoned the immensity of space.] (Marçal 1994: 88)

Walking in the World Republic of Letters

Having attended to different aspects of Marçal's narrative practice, in particular the eminently performative tactics unravelled in her writings to reshape the literary establishment from the margins, I will now turn my attention to the novel's place within recent debate around the existence, status, teaching and dissemination of something — a network of relations, perhaps? — called world literature. Drawing on Pascale Casanova's (2004) reconceptualization of the World Republic of Letters to underpin analysis of the diverse factors determining the production and dissemination of international literary capital, I wish to explore how the reader/writer as translator negotiates the operation and implications of multiple overlapping relations between centre and periphery in the novel. Casanova's work affords a useful guide because it sets out to counter the logic of Anglo-American dominance of the international literary marketplace, torn between the interests of a comparative literature taught through English and the market force of global English as lingua franca, with the need to see this capital always relationally. Indeed, this is something that can be illuminated by considering how to map the shifting flows of symbolic capital in relation to the triangle between Marçal, Vivien and world established by *La passió segons Renée Vivien*.

Following Casanova (2004: 23–34), for instance, we might want to highlight the function and operation of Paris as capital of the World Republic of Letters *par excellence* as central to Pauline Tarn's construction of her identity as a writer. Yet this is to ignore the *fin-de-siècle* poet's relative invisibility within and beyond her own lifetime, which we might attribute to diverse factors, such as literary fashions, her resistant affinity to the outmoded forms of Parnassian symbolism, and above all her identity-political positioning, as described within Marçal's novel itself as the first woman to openly extol lesbian desire since Sappho. It is also to ignore the particular situatedness of her choice to replace her mother tongue (English) with another, adopted language (French). Is this to be read as an instance of a process of aiding the minor in becoming major by making the major minor, as Kafka's replacement of his minorized tongues with German is portrayed by Casanova (2004: 200–04, via Deleuze and Guattari 1986), thus ultimately underpinning the dependency of minority languages and literatures on entering into relations with the major centres of cultural capital? Or is it simply part of a desire to break free of the normalizing, economic, rational focus of English culture by choosing French (as in Casanova's [2004: 125] rendering of William Faulkner's literary consecration)? Given that the positioning of figures like Algernon Charles Swinburne in Marçal's novel, and the influence of Pauline's encounters in the US, would pull against such a reading, perhaps an alternative would be to see Pauline Tarn's case as more similar to Samuel Beckett or James Joyce, where turning to another tongue can be perceived as a mode of resisting, evading and derailing the colonizing power of English (Casanova 2004: 315–20).[3]

In Tarn's case, of course, it is not the traces of political, economic and territorial domination through imperialism that are to be avoided by the self-translation to another language, but the more immediately felt objectification, fetishization and colonization of women's experience, identity and expression by and within patriarchy. Here, it is nevertheless important (if perhaps a little obvious) to dwell briefly on a particular feature of Renée Vivien's rebellion against patriarchal language that is generally passed over in other critical readings: this rebellion begins with rejection and emancipation from the mother tongue (not just the mother). I'll return to this feature in a moment, as it raises questions around the relationship between (un)translatability and world literature presented by the novel, but there are two key points I want to make first. It draws attention to the need to account for the situatedness of such choices, beyond reading for personal biographical details as can be the temptation when faced with a *roman-à-clef* dynamic. The pull of the autobiographical intertext strikes me as being a recurring tendency in extant readings of the novel, which almost always collapse Marçal, 'la narradora' (that is, the omniscient narrator), and Sara T. into each other, and justify this through the novel's own partial elucidation of Renée Vivien's only novel, *Une femme m'apparut* [*A Woman Appeared to Me*], first published in 1904, so exactly ninety years before Marçal's. By going beyond such readings, I respond to the need to situate the Tarn-Vivien choice within the operations of the relevant literary fields, and in this case within a context in which, as Elaine Showalter taught us all in her seminal work *Sexual Anarchy* (1991), one of the most salient features of the obsessive anxiety around representations of the new woman in *fin-de-siècle* English literature is the fact that it appears alongside the relative disappearance of the woman writer herself (if compared with the situation up until 1880). Furthermore, investigation of what lies behind this linguistic choice underlines the limitations of simply applying unreflexive appropriation of the metaphor of the mirror to readings of the representational economy of Marçal's novel itself. For, we might ask ourselves, what kind of mirror does Pauline Tarn's self-translation into French offer for Marçal in her search for a literary language with which to structure or, to borrow the more corporeal terms she uses, 'vertebrate' her production? Is it enough to read this in terms of the search for a feminine genealogy (later to be refashioned and confirmed in projects like *Cartografies del desig*), as a kind of enforced 'worlding' due to the relative lack of literary models and mothers in any language in the World Republic of Letters? Or is it worth looking again at the implications of the situatedness of Marçal's project to walk the World Republic of Letters in the wake of Renée Vivien beyond circumstantial reference to her fascination with the writer? There are numerous sections within the novel where consideration of the exclusion and marginalization of women in relation to a dominant patriarchal order, and the difficulties in occupying the margins, are compared also with the experience of minority languages and cultures assimilated by a dominant force. In other words, there are aspects of the novel that are more or less openly resistant to the implications of Pauline's choice of self-translation for a Catalan woman of lower-class social origin.

Re-orienting Maria-Mercè Marçal

This particular process of mirroring can be viewed most clearly, as Julià (2003) has recognized, in the situated reading of Charles Brun's federalism in the novel, through the account given of his history of commitment to Occitan culture, symbolized on the one hand by his investment in symbolic figures like Frédéric Mistral and Emma Calvé, but also, on the other hand, by his critique of the macrocephalic structure of French culture, with all symbolic power sited in Paris, as expressed below:

> Hi havia alguna cosa, més enllà o més ençà de la llengua que definia aquell país d'Oc, una mena d'essència que s'expandia des d'un paisatge, que vivia en la sang de les vinyes, en el bleix de la Mediterrània, en l'herència clàssica que s'enllaçava sense aparent contradicció amb el simbolisme fosc dels faidits de Montsegur o dels màrtirs de Besiers, en els trobadors lírics en occità i en la cançó èpica, en francès, dels Aliscans i del cavaller Vivien. Calia treballar per una plasmació política d'aquella realitat, que no era pas única dins i fora de l'hexàgon: Flandes, Bretanya, Còrsega, el Rosselló, que posseïen també llengües pròpies reduïdes a la categoria de patuès pel centralisme jacobí. Però també Normandia, la Borgonya, l'Alta Savoia... víctimes, igualment, d'aquella macrocefàlia que inflava París amb menysteniment de tota la resta.

> [There was something else, beyond the language that defined that land of Oc, a sort of essence emanating from the countryside, living in the blood of the vineyards, in the breath of the Mediterranean, in the classical inheritance that brought together with no apparent contradiction the dark symbolism of the *faidits* of Montsegur or the martyrs of Béziers, in the troubadour lyrics in Occitan and the epic song, in French, of the Aliscans and the Knight Vivien. Hard work was needed to create a political form out of that reality, which was not in itself unique to the hexagon: Flanders, Brittany, Corsica, the Roussillon, all of which had seen their own languages reduced to the category of patois by Jacobin centralism. Normandy too, Burgundy, High Savoy... all victims of that macrocephaly that inflated Paris at the expense of all the rest.] (Marçal 1994: 85–86)

His is a critical positioning that might fruitfully be compared with Joaquim Molas's notorious representation of Catalan culture as an enormous head with a very small body, via Josep-Anton Fernàndez's reading of *El malestar en la cultura catalana* (2008). Marçal was critical of this tendency, too, which was part of the reason she was proud to present herself as a poet from Ivars d'Urgell, even though, as we learn in 'Viratges, reminiscències', she was actually born in Barcelona. Above all, it is interesting that both of the male characters and narrators who are readers-as-translators of the life and work of Pauline Tarn/Renée Vivien — Charles Brun and Salomon Reinach — are themselves partly positioned on the periphery, which is what makes them capable of perceiving and relating to other margins.

Similarly, in the early sections reconstructed from Pauline Tarn's epistolary relationship with the middle-aged Amédée Moullé, Marçal slips in a reference to Francesc Ferrer i Guàrdia's execution as recounted in the same newspaper, *Le Figaro*, in which the ageing bourgeois gent learns that his own unattainable object of desire has died: 'Sí, allà hi havia una petita notícia indirectament relacionada amb els fets de Barcelona: el Consell del Sena havia elevat una protesta per l'execució d'aquell Ferrer i Guàrdia que havia fet córrer tanta tinta i aixecar tantes veus arreu d'Europa. Res més' [Yes, there was a report indirectly related to events in Barcelona: the Council of the Seine had protested against the execution of that Ferrer i Guàrdia fellow, who had provoked so much commentary and raised so many voices throughout Europe. Nothing else] (Marçal 1994: 41–42). This reference to a key figure in early twentieth-century urban working-class culture in Catalonia appears almost immediately after the introduction of the only Catalan character portrayed in the *fin-de-siècle* Parisian milieu, that of Amédée's beautiful new maidservant. The lack of two-way mirrors in the World Republic of Letters is surely indicated here in the fact that the widower renames her as Carmen, the symbol of northern European orientalizing readings of Spain, that are traceable in other French representations of Catalan culture in the nineteenth and early twentieth century:

> Era molt bonica, Carmen, li esqueia la tristesa, l'indici de la passió. Per això, quan l'havia admès al seu servei, l'havia anomenada així. Era el primer cop que posava nom a una cambrera: en vida de madame M. totes s'havien dit invariablement Françoise. I ell s'havia permès aquell petit caprici de lletraferit, ben convençut que això afalagaria la serventa. Però ella havia restat inexpressiva, en aparença indiferent: segur que mai no havia sentit parlar ni de Mérimée ni de Bizet, ni potser d'Emma Calvé.

> [Carmen was very pretty; there was a sadness in her that indicated passion. That is why he had decided to call her Carmen when he employed her. It was the first time he had assigned a name to a maid: while Madame M. was alive, she had invariably called them all Françoise. He had permitted himself that minor whim of a man of letters, convinced that it would flatter the servant. But she remained inexpressive, apparently indifferent: she had probably never heard of Mérimée or Bizet, or even of Emma Calvé.] (Marçal 1994: 40)

Just as names are never entirely accidental in this mousetrap of a novel, it is surely significant that the death of Pauline Tarn/Renée Vivien is linked to the execution and sacrifice of one of the key figures associated with working-class Catalan rebellion and the Setmana Tràgica of 1909. Furthermore, Charles Brun himself is gently lampooned for his own 'perverse' relationship with an idealized, distant and nostalgic representation of home and mother tongue, in the account of his unorthodox marriage in the novel, and this benefits from being compared with Tarn's 'feminization' of him as San Giovanni/Suzanne in her own *roman-à-clef*.

Translatability: triar/trair [to choose/to betray]

The other key element of the novel in which we see reflection of a double or triple minority is, of course, in the disquisitions of Sara T., especially if we consider the passage on the triangle in the chapter 'Papers privats de Sara T. (6)' (Marçal 1994: 147–49), which is the very passage used on the PEN Català website to showcase the four published translations of the novel (Visat, n.d.). Presented simultaneously as the symbol that frames the eyes of God in pious representations, the frame that limits our grammatical perception to three persons of the verb, and the obstacle that brings conflict to the immobile harmony of the two, the triangle is to be seen as an image of perpetual trial and perpetual betrayal ('perpètua tria' and 'perpetu trair'), on whose third corner we find the world. Not only does this provide an instance of impossible word play for the translator, reminiscent of the notorious Italian pun on 'traduttore, traditore', but the passage that follows articulates the individual's struggle with the world as a lesbian woman in relation to the demands of the norm and, above all, their embodiment in the subject, in terms reminiscent of the Catalan struggle — as stateless nation — for visibility:

> És, potser, aquesta estira-i-arronsa amb el món allò que ens defineix d'una manera més singular. No hi ha fugida, no hi ha un 'fora del món': per un instant, la passió, que t'allibera del clos de tu mateixa, dissol els límits i nega tota llei i tota culpa. Per la passió, oblidar-se, oblidar el món. O pactar-hi una treva: el privat i el social articulats per institucions — matrimonis o similars... Fer extensiu a l'àmbit dels sentiments allò que en un estat de dret fóra una constitució. He oscil·lat, durant aquests anys, entre aquestes dues sortides (?). He tingut la sensació de viure el pitjor de cadascuna sense cap dels seus avantatges respectius. Aquesta hibridesa, al capdavall, estableix la monotonia del perpetu sobresalt, de la manca de projectes — de projecte —, la instal·lació en el continu present que arriba a ser a la llarga tan rutinari com el dels pitjors matrimonis. La incertesa sobre el propi lloc, l'angoixa, la incomoditat del perpetu esforç, absorbent com la passió, mecànic com qualsevol habit... ¿Aquesta hibridesa és connatural — no pas en exclusiva, però — a aquells vincles que 'el món' ha declarat contra-natura? L'absència d'una 'constitució' reconeguda legalment i socialment, ¿estableix la lluita de poders en estat pur, l'articulació salvatge de tots i cadascun dels extrems? ¿O, a l'altra punta, només hi ha la possibilitat d'imitar — i la imitació esdevé sempre grotesca — allò que, amb la nostra peculiar evolució hem volgut, potser, evitar a tot preu?

> [It is perhaps this tug of war with the world which defines us in the most singular manner. There is no escape, there is no 'outside the world': for an instant, passion, which frees you from the prison of yourself, dissolves the limits, refuses all law and denies all blame. For passion's sake, forget oneself, forget the world. Or make a truce with it: with the private and the social as articulated by institutions such as marriage or other such... To extend to the ambit of the emotions that which under the rule of law is a constitution. I have oscillated over the last years between these two solutions (?). I have had the sensation of living the worst of each of them without any of their respective advantages. At the end of the day, this hybridity establishes the monotony of perpetual shock, of a lack of projects — of a project — , and the installation in a continuous present which ends up being just as routine as the worst of marriages. All that

uncertainty and anxiety about one's own place, the discomfort at having to make a continual effort, as absorbent as passion, as mechanical as any sort of habit... Is this hybridity connatural — not exclusively so, though — with those attachments which 'the world' has declared as being against nature? Is it the absence of a legally and socially recognized 'constitution' that establishes the power struggle in its pure state, as the savage articulation of each and every one of the extremes? Or at the other extreme, is there only the possibility of imitating — and imitation always becomes grotesque — that which, with our own particular evolution, we have sought to avoid at all costs?] (Marçal 1994: 148–49)

These connections are, of course, made possible by knowledge of Marçal's biography and political positionings, just as her choice to walk through the World Republic of Letters in pursuit of Renée Vivien is clearly governed by her own knowledge of French rather than English, and her shared passion for classical languages and cultures from her undergraduate days. Indeed, Renée Vivien's own attitude to the importance of openness to other languages in order to enter into relations with world literature is exemplified in the fact that she is presented as teaching herself Greek in order to read Sappho, just as she had done previously with Italian in order to read Dante, even though there are other more complex circumstantial factors that influenced these encounters. In other words, it is at least as important to recognize how this positioning takes place in relation to a wider literary field; one that in Marçal's case we can find summarized very clearly if we look at the essay on contemporary Catalan poetry she co-authored with Lluïsa Julià (2006). In this essay, the poet's own early affinities for symbolism and Parnassianism are set very overtly within the context of the network of writers connected to the Llibres del Mall from 1973 to 1988, and to a different course from that of the more central and dominant trends associated in their analysis with the rise of the 'poètica de l'experiència', with its roots in Robert Langbaum's *The Poetry of Experience* (1957) and, thus, relative translatability into English. Above all, it is made patent that this was both an aesthetic and a political choice, which distances her from accepting the economy of the cultural field that became dominant with the enshrinement of 'la cultura de la normalització' [the culture of normalization] in the 1980s and the push for Catalan culture to model itself on contemporary Anglo-American models. Marçal's own decision as a reader, writer and translator to engage in intimate translation and negotiation of the margins of the French literary field, and in particular through the work of a writer who turned against what she perceived as the excessive provincialism and commercialism of British culture ('Pregàries i rosbif' [Prayers and roast beef], Marçal 1994: 22) and the empty aspirations of her American mother, is one that must appear particularly relevant in such a context.[4] Indeed, it is one that, for me, calls into question the translatability of this novel into English, a language that in many ways it is written against. That is not to say that the novel cannot or should not be translated, but that it throws into relief the kind of questioning of the relationship between (un)translation and world literature posited by Emily Apter in her *Against World Literature* (2013): the need to pause before accepting the utopian myth of a transnational circulation of certain literary texts that are somehow more necessary or communicate more fully when translated than in their national source cultures. Is there not something about the transcreational narrative practice of Marçal in this novel — in its layering of frames, voices and fragments, in its negotiation of different cultural and geographical spaces, in its exploration of interartistic practice, shuttling constantly between archive and repertoire, bodies and ruins, language and the visual — that confronts us with precisely the kind of translation zone envisioned and celebrated by Apter (2006) in an earlier volume?

To conclude, I wish to reflect briefly on the simultaneous call and challenge to translation this novel presents, modelled in the cartography of desire that is the triangle between I/you/world in which the subject appears condemned to 'triar' and 'trair': '¿Com donar-te cos, encarnar-te, arrelar-te, fer que la meva sang recorri la teva ombra i, sense substituir-la, la converteixi en vida, en saba, en moviment?' [How to give you a body, to incarnate you, to root you, to make my blood run through your shadow and, without substituting it, convert it into life, into sap, into movement?] (Marçal 1994: 78). There is strong indication that one way to overcome this double bind is by taking the more nomadic, mobile, genealogical and performative route through this geography, suggested by the ruined image of Winged Victory as well as the layering of reenactments and performances throughout the novel (with different figures trying out different roles, wearing each others' clothes, cross-dressing, re-animating, even providing a skeleton for the skin of the dead). But it is found above all in the 'esbós', the motility of the sketch or desiring line, that gives an afterlife to that which is dead and immobile, and leaves a legacy for posterity.

Works Cited

APTER, EMILY. 2006. *The Translation Zone: A New Comparative Literature* (Princeton, NJ: Princeton University Press)

——. 2013. *Against World Literature: On the Politics of Untranslatability* (London and New York: Verso)

BASSNETT, SUSAN. 1998. *Comparative Literature: A Critical Introduction* (Oxford: Blackwell)

BUFFERY, HELENA. 2015. 'Traumatic Translations of *La plaça del Diamant*: On the Transmission and Translatability of Cultural Trauma', in *Funcions del passat en la cultura catalana: institucionalització, representacions i identitat*, ed. by Josep-Anton Fernàndez and Jaume Subirana (Lleida: Punctum), pp. 197–219

CABRÉ, ROSA. 2004. '*La passió segons Renée Vivien* i el miratge-miracle del mirall', *Lectora*, 10: 173–90

CASANOVA, PASCALE. 2004. *The World Republic of Letters*, trans. by M. B. DeBevoise (Cambridge, MA, and London: Harvard University Press)

CERTEAU, MICHEL DE. 1984. *The Practice of Everyday Life*, trans. by Steven Rendall (Berkeley: University of California Press)

DELEUZE, GILLES, and FÉLIX GUATTARI. 1986. *Kafka: Toward a Minor Literature*, trans. by Dana Polan (Minneapolis and London: University of Minnesota Press)

FERNÀNDEZ, JOSEP-ANTON. 2008. *El malestar en la cultura catalana* (Barcelona: Editorial Empúries)

FONS DE MARIA-MERCÈ MARÇAL. Biblioteca de Catalunya. Boxes 6–13

GODAYOL, PILAR. 2008. 'Entre Atenea i la Medusa: les mares literàries de Maria-Mercè Marçal', *Reduccions, revista de poesia*, 89/90: 190–206

——. 2012. 'Maria-Mercè Marçal en el mirall: sobre l'imaginari femení i el llenguatge poètic', *Reduccions, revista de poesia*, 100: 220–33

IBARZ, MERCÈ. 2004. 'Silencis, interrupcions, mites', in Maria-Mercè Marçal, *Sota el signe del drac: proses, 1985–1997*, ed. by Mercè Ibarz (Barcelona: Proa), pp. 7–18

JULIÀ, LLUÏSA. 1998. *Album Maria-Mercè Marçal* (Barcelona: Centre Català del PEN Club; Proa)

——. 2002. *Fons de Maria-Mercè Marçal: inventari* (Barcelona: Biblioteca de Catalunya)

——. 2003. 'Cap a l'ordre simbòlic femení: *La passió segons Renée Vivien* de Maria-Mercè Marçal', *Jornada d'estudi sobre l'obra de Maria-Mercè Marçal. Universitat de Barcelona*, 17 October. Available online at the Associació d'escriptors en llengua catalana website: <https://www.escriptors.cat/?q=publicacions_atextos_vivienr> [accessed July 2018]

——. 2007. *Tradició i orfenesa : per a una genealogia de l'escriptora catalana del segle XX* (Palma de Mallorca: Lleonard Muntaner)

MARÇAL, MARIA-MERCÈ. 1989. 'Viratges, reminiscències', in *Album Maria-Mercè Marçal*, ed. by Lluïsa Julià (Barcelona: Centre Català del PEN Club; Proa, 1998), pp. 16-21. Available online at the PEN Club català website: <https://www.pencatala.cat/wp-content/uploads/2016/06/marcal.pdf> [accessed July 2018]. Also in *Sota el signe del drac: proses, 1985–1997*, ed. by Mercè Ibarz (Barcelona: Proa), pp. 25–34

——. 1994. *La passió segons Renée Vivien* (Barcelona: Columna)

—— (ed.). 1998. *Cartografies del desig: quinze escriptores i el seu món* (Barcelona: Proa)

——. 2004. *Sota el signe del drac: proses, 1985–1997*, ed. by Mercè Ibarz (Barcelona: Proa)

——. 2014. *El senyal de la pèrdua: escrits inèdits dels últims anys* (Barcelona: Editorial Empúries)

——. 2020. *The Passion according to Renée Vivien*, trans. by Kathleen McNerney and Helena Buffery (London: Francis Boutle Publishers)

—— and LLUÏSA JULIÀ. 2006. 'Diferència i/o normalització: la poesia catalana dels darrers trenta anys', *Rels. Revista d'Idees i Cultures*, 8: 39–56

MÉRIDA, RAFAEL M. 2012. 'Viratges, visibilitats i reminiscències de Maria-Mercè Marçal', in *Accions i reinvencions: cultures lèsbiques a la Catalunya del tombant de segle XX–XXI*, ed. by Meri Torras (Barcelona: Editorial UOC), pp. 99–106. <cositextualitat.uab.cat/invisibles/wp-content/uploads/2011-11-RAFAEL-M.-MERIDA_accions-i-reivinvencions.pdf> [accessed July 2018]

REAL, NEUS. 1995. Review of Maria-Mercè Marçal, *La passió segons Renée Vivien*, *Els Marges*, 53: 112–15

RIBA, CATERINA. 2015a. *Cos endins: maternitat, desig i malaltia en l'obra de Maria-Mercè Marçal* (Girona: Curbet edicions)

——. 2015b. 'Maria-Mercè Marçal: tradició/traducció/creació', *Estudis Romànics*, 37: 471–81

SHOWALTER, ELAINE. 1991. *Sexual Anarchy: Gender and Culture at the Fin de Siècle* (New York: Viking)

SPIVAK, GAYATRI CHAKRAVORTY. 1993. 'The Politics of Translation', in *Outside in the Teaching Machine* (London and New York: Routledge), pp. 179–200. Reproduced in *The Translation Studies Reader*, ed. by Lawrence Venuti (London and New York: Routledge, 2000), pp. 397–416

TORRAS, MERI. 2015. '*Corpus* endins i enfora corpus', in Caterina Riba, *Cos endins: maternitat, desig i malaltia* (Girona: Curbet edicions), pp. 7–10

UDINA, DOLORS. 2008. 'L'altra mirada que perfà la pròpia: Maria-Mercè Marçal com a traductora', *Reduccions, revista de poesia*, 89/90: 207–17

VISAT. (n.d.). *La Revista Digital de Literatura i Traducció del PEN Català*. Traduccions de la literatura catalana/*La passió segons Renée Vivien* <http://www.visat.cat/traduccions-literatura-catalana/esp/fragments/85/0/cat/0//.html> [accessed July 2018]

Notes to Chapter 2

1. Since completing the initial version of this chapter, I have gone on to prepare a co-translation of the novel with Kathleen McNerney, to be published in 2020.
2. For further discussion of this issue, see Buffery (2015).
3. There is repeated evidence in Marçal's working papers for the novel of awareness of the colonization process in Ireland. See, for instance, the Fons Maria-Mercè Marçal, Box 6/1.4 where she underlines reference in photocopies from a 1974 PUF volume on *L'Ère victorienne* to Ireland's 'lutte agraire et bataille pour l'autonomie politique, conflits de mentalités avec les Anglais et attachement têtu à l'identité irlandaise' [agrarian struggle and battle for political autonomy, differences and conflicts with the English and stubborn attachment to Irish identity]. In Box 7/16 there is a cutting from the *New Statesman* that includes a review of *Nora: A Biography of Nora Joyce* in which Joyce's paean to his wife, 'wherever thou art shall be Erin to me', reminds us of Charles Brun's relationship to his maternal and matronly Occitan life partner in *La passió segons Renée Vivien*.
4. Once again, such a reading is supported by underlinings in the primarily French sources Marçal turns to for her understanding of Victorian English culture (see Fons de Maria-Mercè Marçal, Boxes 6–7). Furthermore, in the same notes for the elaboration of the overarching themes in the novel in which there is reference to the connection with *La plaça del Diamant*, we find listed amongst various ideas about mirroring, identification and desire, the sense of a conflict between 'França v Anglaterra' (Fons de Maria-Mercè Marçal, Box 8/4.3).

CHAPTER 3

Multilingualism in Contemporary Catalan Narrative

Jordi Cornellà-Detrell

University of Glasgow

Introduction: Literary Multilingualism in Context

This chapter focuses on the role of literary multilingualism — that is, the use of two or more languages within a single literary text — in contemporary Catalan literature. The appearance of more than one language within the space of the text is a discursive strategy which until recently has received limited attention. Claudio Guillén pointed out that 'asentada por una parte en el nacionalismo excluyente y centralizador, y por otra en el concepto romántico del alma o genio inconfundible de cada idioma, [Comparative Literature] no atendió con suficiente simpatía a los fenómenos de multilingüismo, tan importantes a lo largo de toda la historia literaria de Occidente' [Comparative Literature, emerging from centralizing and exclusionary nationalism and the Romantic concept of the soul or genius of language, did not regard in a positive light multilingual phenomena, very important in Western literary history] (1985: 327). Delabastita and Grutman, confirming Guillén's words, argue that in the 1980s this discursive strategy was still considered an anomaly, an odd curiosity which did not deserve serious study (2005: 11). Since then, however, the perspective on multilingualism has changed substantially, to the extent that not long ago Meylaerts postulated the existence of a 'multilingual turn' in cultural studies (2006: 2). This turn is no doubt a consequence of the fact that, as Steiner already observed in the 1970s, 'the conditions of language stability, of local, national self-consciousness on which literature flourished between the Renaissance and say, the 1950s are now under extreme stress' (1971: 17).

While the new century has seen an increase of interest in the phenomenon here analysed, the fields of Catalan and Hispanic Studies have remained largely oblivious to this area of inquiry. There exists a small body of research devoted to literary multilingualism (see Canonica and Rudin 1993; Villanueva and Cabo 1996), but studies usually lack a strong theoretical foundation or fail to relate the characteristics of the text to wider social and cultural forces. This chapter, which draws on current scholarship on textual multilingualism and sociolinguistics, explores the function and forms of this discursive strategy in contemporary Catalan writing. The texts to be analysed include Ramon Solsona's *No tornarem mai més* [We will Never Return] (1999); Joan-Daniel Bezsonoff's *Els taxistes del tsar* [The Tsar's Drivers] (2007) and *Les amnèsies de Déu* [God's Amnesias] (2005); and Marta Rojals's *L'altra* [The Other] (2014). The comparative analysis of a corpus of four works by three different writers aims to demonstrate that the perception of critics as well as the public regarding Catalan literary language has changed: despite a few instances of criticism directed at Solsona or Rojals for their transgressive linguistic usage, the overall reception of their work is very positive. Controversies over linguistic purism in Catalonia have been so frequent since the 1950s (see Solà 1977) that this greater tolerance towards lexical and grammatical interference seems to signal the emergence of a new attitude vis-à-vis literary language. This trend has already been detected by sociolinguists: Pujolar and González, for instance, observe that in the metropolitan area of Barcelona, 'accents and interference phenomena have become less salient to the community of speakers' (2013: 141; see also Woolard 2011).

The notions of Catalan and Spanish literature have been largely based on the Romantic paradigm alluded to by Guillén. On the one hand, this paradigm presupposes that languages and cultures are discrete units that exclude each other; on the other, it assumes that national identity is intrinsically linked to the national language, the only one that can faithfully translate the community's experience. These two premises have led to monolingualism being regarded as the unmarked, preferable situation in written and oral communication. As a result, code-mixing has been described as unnatural, both an indication of lack of competence and an attack on the integrity of the codes involved. This viewpoint, which renders invisible the contact zones where linguistic and cultural borders blur, can alienate or exclude those individuals at the crossroads who reject linguistic and cultural divides or do not want to choose between them. The transgressive force of multilingual texts lies precisely in the fact that they do not present tongues as separate entities which exist in isolation, but as an amalgam of correlations and interdependencies.

Writing is a highly self-conscious activity and, therefore, if writers resort to heteroglossic discourse it is with a view to creating a number of effects that could not be achieved by monolingual means (at least to the same extent). Catalan writers often include interlinguistic elements in their texts, mainly for ironic purposes or because an idea or concept can be more easily and adequately conveyed in one code than in the other. Bilingualism provides stylistic alternatives, occasionally allowing authors to combine the semantic strength of both tongues. For the purpose of this chapter, I will only focus on works where languages are blended to a significant degree and there is a high level of interaction between them. What cannot be determined, of course, is the percentage required of any given language in a text for such a text to be considered multilingual, because boundaries are not — and cannot be — clear-cut. As my analysis intends to demonstrate, multilingual texts, by subverting the monolingual norm, call attention to language as action and process, foregrounding its materiality and exposing its fabric for all to see.

Kramer, in an interesting yet misguided remark, accuses Catalan writers of blocking the development of multilingual literature on the grounds that they pursue the impossible dream of a linguistically and culturally uniform autonomous field: 'Nella letteratura vive il sogno di quello che la sociolinguistica catalana chiama con un termine rivelatore: *normalització* — il sogno di una normalità monolingue copiata sul modello del monolinguismo vissuto ogni giorno dei parlanti delle grandi lingue' [the literary field believes in a dream which Catalan sociolinguists have tellingly labelled as 'normalization': the dream of a monolingual society based on the daily monolingual realities of speakers of widely used languages] (2002: 326). Kramer claims, in short, that writers ignore linguistic reality for the sake of a monolingual fantasy. Two important objections to this argument can be made: first, while it is true that most Catalan novelists do not reflect social linguistic usage in their novels, this is not at all restricted to Catalan writers. Tom Stoppard's trilogy *The Coast of Utopia* (2002), for instance, is set in Russia, yet the characters speak perfect English. What Kramer does not take into account is that literature is by definition a highly elaborate and conventional construct. Chan cleverly observes that, paradoxical as it may seem, many original texts — such as *The Coast of Utopia* — are presented to readers as already 'translated' from another language, and therefore they read foreign and convey a sense of otherness even if the public understands every single word (2002: 57). The second objection is that, in reality, in Catalan literature multilingualism has historically been the norm and not the exception: in the nineteenth century, for instance, hundreds of heteroglossic plays were published and performed in Barcelona (see Rossich and Cornellà 2014).

As indicated by Grutman, well-established literary traditions such as those of England, France, Germany or Spain have been able to build up a self-sustaining literary field which functions with a great degree of autonomy (2006: 39). Literatures that have attempted to develop at a later stage, however, have found it more difficult to secure a niche for themselves in their area of influence, have struggled to create their own aesthetic models and, also, to consolidate the process of language standardization. This explains why they tend to be more open towards literary multilingualism, as the cases of Quebec, Catalonia and the Chicano literature in the United States prove. Québécois writers resort to anglicisms and dialectal features in order to stress the differences between their own literature and that of France (Grutman 2006: 30). Hispanic authors in the US have often employed Spanish lexical items to express a sense of bicultural belonging (Mendieta-Lombardo and Cintrón 1995; Rudin 1996). More recently, the immigration waves of the 1980s and 1990s have resulted in the emergence of a European migrant writing which uses multilingualism to varying degrees (for the case of Germany, see von Flotow 2000). This phenomenon appears to be growing in importance, but as Sebba points out, 'it is difficult to say for certain whether written multilingualism is on the increase, or whether it has simply been less prominent or less noticed by linguists in the past' (2013: 100). More comparative research is needed in order to answer this question. In any case, examples of multilingual texts abound in contemporary Catalan literature, and Kramer is not the only scholar who has failed to locate them. Rudin, for instance, has argued that in Chicano literature the interplay of languages is much more frequent than in that of Switzerland or Catalonia (1996:

15). Similarly, Heinemann posited the question of why textual multilingualism is uncommon in Catalonia, and her answer was that the uncertain and precarious state of the language explains the need to protect it from external influences (1996: 97).

In Kramer's, Rudin's and Heinemann's defence, it must be said that in the 1990s Catalan writers had significantly less scope for subverting established norms. During Franco's dictatorship, literature was the only prestigious domain where Catalan could be used, and the importance of the language in the legitimation of Catalan identity led to strict control over linguistic usage. The aversion to Spanish interferences or loanwords — the so-called *castellanismes* or *barbarismes* — needs to be interpreted as a symbolic fear that links language atrophy to social and cultural decline (see Aitchison 1991). The situation did not change much after the regime's demise, when Catalan could be used again in the public sphere, because interferences were perceived as a danger to the recovery of the language and the cohesion of the cultural field. Incidentally, the use of *catalanismos* [Catalan loanwords] in Spanish novels has provoked similar reactions. Upon publication, for instance, Juan Marsé's *Caligrafía de los sueños* [The Calligraphy of Dreams] (2011) merited the following remark: 'hay muy pocas máculas en el texto: algunos catalanismos, como "parar [la] oreja" [...] o "ginesta" [...] por "retama"' [the text doesn't contain many mistakes, just some Catalan loanwords, such as 'eavesdrop' ... and 'brum' instead of 'broom'] (Senabre 2011). Marsé and Manuel Vázquez Montalbán have made use of the occasional borrowing, but for the most part their Spanish is perfectly standard. Vázquez Montalbán himself poked fun at such comments in *El premio* [The Prize]: 'habría que descatalanizar la literatura española. ¡Qué horror! ¡Ese castellano periférico de los Marsé, los Mendoza, los Azúa y los Goytisolo! Apestan a pan con tomate y al María Moliner' [we should rid Spanish literature of Catalan words. How disgusting! The peripheral Spanish used by Marsé, Mendoza, Azúa, Goytisolo and the likes! They stink of bread with tomato and María Moliner's dictionary] (1996: 27). Vázquez Montalbán, appears to proudly suggest that nobody writes in Spanish as Catalans do.

Save for a few exceptions, Catalan novels assume that Catalonia is either Castilian or Catalan speaking, depending on the language in which the text has been written. Heinemann and Kramer direct their attention to authors who express themselves in Catalan, somehow overlooking that those who write in Spanish adopt the same strategy. As Simon puts it, '[t]his language-neutralization [...] indicates that the language of the Barcelona [or Catalan] novel will always be in some ways out of kilter, misaligned, with the sociolinguistic reality of the city. Choosing to write in one language or the other dictates which social or linguistic references will be excluded' (2012: 93). The border between these two languages is still very clear and, as a result, writers on both sides of the divide tend to avoid interferences from the other tongue. This is one of the rules governing both literary fields, which are largely autonomous from one another. Having said that, there is no denying that Catalan and Spanish are closely related languages that have been in contact for a long time and this has altered them both — even if influences have not been symmetrical: as Galindo reveals, Catalan is under significant more pressure (2003:

19). Galindo also notes, and this only confirms the extent to which the two literary fields have strived to preserve their independence, that little research has been done on the variety of written and spoken Spanish used in Catalonia.

Ramon Solsona, Joan-Daniel Bezsonoff and Marta Rojals are the Catalan writers who employ code-mixing in more provocative and imaginative ways. In their texts, this discursive strategy is not limited to brief dialogues or a few scattered borrowings: the blending of codes is a key stylistic feature at the service of the plot. Solsona is from Barcelona; Rojals was born in Palma d'Ebre, a very small town in the province of Tarragona, but studied in Barcelona, and Bezsonoff is a French national born in Perpignan who has published most of his work in Barcelona. Bezsonoff's case is particularly relevant as it signals that it is paramount to go beyond the dichotomy Catalan–Spanish, since his novels deploy other languages, including French, English, Italian, German, Rumanian, Afrikaans, Russian and Vietnamese. This shows that the study of literary multilingualism should transcend mere sociological or sociolinguistic explanations. Scholars have given priority to the mimetic function of multilingualism (see, for instance, Lüdi 2001), but even when this phenomenon is grounded in social reality its functions tend to far exceed mimetic uses (see Grutman 2002). While it is tempting to present Catalan literary multilingualism as highly conditioned by Catalonia's sociolinguistic situation, literature 'does not have to reflect the community's bilinguality nor even be semantically or syntactically acceptable in the ordinary sense' (Keller 1984: 184). In reality, not all situations of social multilingualism have stimulated literary heteroglossia — and, by the same token, neither are monolingual societies safe from this discursive strategy.

Ramon Solsona's *No tornarem mai més* (1999): Mimesis and Power Struggles between Languages

Since his first novel, *Figures de calidoscopi* [Kaleidoscope Patterns] (1989), Ramon Solsona's work has been characterized by urban realism, irony and formal complexity, both in terms of narrative structure and style. In the context of the Catalan literary field, Solsona's linguistic ideology is unique: on the one hand, he contends that writers have the right to use non-standard forms according to the needs of their fictional world (Solsona 2015: 166–68); on the other, he rejects the pessimism towards the future of Catalan that has dominated public opinion for decades.[1] Solsona has tellingly declared that '[c]om que la llengua catalana està tan associada a patiments, frustracions i pessimismes, m'agrada transmetre una certa alegria del llenguatge' [since Catalan language is often linked to suffering, frustration and pessimism, I try to convey a sense of linguistic joy] (Domínguez 2004: 3). In the face of recurrent controversies about language purity and the idea that Catalan is on the brink of extinction, Solsona has chosen to adopt a more relaxed and positive attitude, stressing that defeatism is misguided and counterproductive, since '[p]erdem paraules però també en guanyem. El llenguatge és una festa' [we lose words, but we also gain them. Language is a constant surprise] (Bibolas 2007: 8). In order to understand the writer's stance, it is important to take into account his belief that 'les llengües són promísqües per naturalesa' [languages are promiscuous by nature] (2015: 161), and also that '[l]a barreja de llengües sempre ha estat una font de diversió' [code-mixing has always been a source of humour] (2015: 160). Solsona's viewpoint has led him to exploit bilingualism in a free and transgressive manner. *No tornarem mai més* begins with the following dialogue:

> — Si este fusil está limpio, mis cojones son perlas.
> — Pues son perlas, mi comandante.
> La companyia, encarcarada en un firmes paralític, va suspendre la respiració amb alarma.

> ['If this gun is clean, my balls shine like pearls.'
> 'Then they are pearls, Sir.'
> The members of the squad, standing at attention, held their breath in fear.]
> (1999: 11)

As *No tornarem mai més* focuses on a group of conscripts in the Spanish army towards the end of Franco's regime, the use of Spanish in dialogues might be interpreted as a simple case of mimetic code-mixing: officers always express themselves in Spanish, whereas rank-and-file soldiers adopt one communicative code or the other depending on the addressee. Such a straightforward explanation, however, is not entirely satisfactory as it overlooks the shock value of the above passage: as far as I know, this is the only novel written in Catalan that starts in Spanish. What would appear as a logical reflection of linguistic use, involved a rather controversial choice on the writer's part, whose aim was to establish the distinctive style and tone of the novel from the outset. The intended effect is heightened by the use of profanity, which further emphasizes Solsona's provocative literary strategies.

Literary norms permit the occasional use of a supplementary tongue, but in a limited and conventionalized way: only short exchanges between characters and scattered borrowings are allowed. Sternberg (1981) argues that writers can adopt three different approaches to what he calls 'heterolingual mimesis': first, they may avoid multilingualism altogether by not even mentioning the existence of another tongue different to that of the text; second, they may try to mimic real language usage; third, they may favour a number of intermediate strategies, such as deploying a few foreign words, simplifying syntax, including some grammatical inaccuracies or, in the most superficial case, stating that characters are speaking in one tongue but making them speak another. When the third approach is adopted, Lennon (2010) claims that three main strategies are used to prevent the guest code from contaminating the hegemonic language of the text: first, the supplementary tongue is often limited to a few isolated token words or well-known formulas which are easily recognizable, mainly in dialogues; second, these token words are generally italicized in order to highlight their foreignness within the text; third, they are often translated or paraphrased in the very same text. As Blake observes, in spite of conveying a sense of alterity, these strategies are problematic because the guest language(s) are clearly given an inferior status and therefore occupy a subaltern position (1999: 327). Used in this way, multilingualism not only does not call into question the Romantic axiom but reinforces it, since it shows that exogenous forms can be easily domesticated and assimilated by the hegemonic system, which is strong enough to allow a degree of deviance from the norm. What emerges from Sternberg's and Lennon's analyses of the literary conventions governing multilingual discourse is that writers often 'translate' the different codes that should appear in the text so they are perfectly understandable to the reader but still convey a sense of otherness. It must be stressed, however, that as a result of the proximity of Catalan and Spanish, and the bilingualism of potential readers, Catalan multilingual writing tends to be significantly more complex than suggested by Sternberg and Lennon: *No tornarem mai més*, for instance, contains long stretches in Spanish which are neither translated nor distinguished by means of italics.

Apart from frequent dialogues and military songs and poems in Spanish, in *No tornarem mai més* the narrator's voice often incorporates this code in the form of free indirect discourse modelling the speech of other characters: 'El tinent amenaçava sempre amb la mateixa fórmula: Ojo al parche y que nadie se llame a engaño. ¿Está claro? Però, a l'hora de la veritat, es feia respectar xorrejant i imposant petits puros perquè sí' [The Lieutenant always used the same threat: *Stay alert and never drop your guard. Do you understand me?* Truth is, he asserted his authority by shouting at us and imposing mild punishments for the sake of it] (1999: 16). Linguists have observed that bilingual individuals often repeat the speech of other people in the language that it was uttered in order to clearly indicate who is speaking, lend particular emphasis to a part of a sentence, enhance the vividness of what is being told and establish a clear contrast between what comes before and after the utterance (Gardner-Chloros et al. 2000: 1323). Solsona uses this mechanism throughout the novel because the narrator's bilingual repertoire reinforces the distance between the language sanctioned by the state and his own. Multilingualism allows him to achieve this objective in a subtle way; in fact, there are only two instances in which the narrator explicitly addresses language discrimination: first, he points out that in the barracks books 'eren suspectes per definició, especialment els de poesia i els escrits en català o en qualsevol altra llengua que no fos la castellana' [were treated with suspicion by default, especially collections of poetry and those written in Catalan or any language other than Spanish] (1999: 95); second, Captain Labuén humiliates a Majorcan recruit because he bears non-Castilian surnames: ' — Vaya, vaya. mallorquín y con un apellido que no entienden ni las culebras. Para eso mejor llamarse Mierda' ['Look who is talking! From Majorca and with a surname that not even snakes can understand. You should rather be called Shit'] (1999: 33). In both examples Spanish is clearly associated with the repressive, Castilian-centric policies of Franco's dictatorship, yet it would be erroneous to conclude that in the novel Catalan is simply set off against Spanish: when the conscripts talk to each other the resulting dialogue is often mixed, this depending on the origin of who is speaking. In addition, the plot revolves mainly around the clash between Major González, a relatively sensitive and open-minded officer who embodies the spirit of the Transition, and Captain Labuén, a bigoted, embittered and sadistic Falangist who ruins the life of those around him. The narrator frequently reports their thoughts in Spanish, but the former is presented in a much more positive light than the latter. In any case, what cannot be denied is that the source of power largely lies in the code promoted by the state; heteroglossia, therefore, allows Solsona to thematize power struggles between languages. Nevertheless, although his antimilitaristic and anti-Franco stance is obvious, the form it takes could be deemed contradictory: while advocating the Generalitat's linguistic and cultural policies and maintaining that Catalan literature is exclusively written in Catalan, Solsona is not opposed to the use of Spanish, which has become part of the stylistic fabric of his novels. This indicates that linguistic ideologies in Catalonia are more complex and multiform than often acknowledged.

Joan-Daniel Bezsonoff: Post-Babel Anxiety and Metalinguistic Reflection

To date, Joan-Daniel Bezsonoff has published nine novels and four autobiographical narratives. The former focus on several twentieth-century military conflicts (World War I, World War II, the Indochina and Algerian wars) and their protagonists are members of the French armed forces or intelligence services on overseas operations; the latter focus on the writer's family and cultural background: his Russian heritage (*Els taxistes del tsar*, 2007), his French education (*Una educació francesa* [A French Education], 2009); *Les meves universitats* [My Universities], 2012) and his allegiance to Catalan culture (*Un país de butxaca* [A Pocket-Sized Country], 2010). Despite their thematic differences, all of Bezsonoff's texts make extensive use of multilingualism, place metalinguistic reflection at their core and describe in great detail the sociolinguistic reality surrounding narrators and characters. Heteroglossia seems to be the main thrust behind the author's highly personal literary universe, which is surprisingly coherent: his first published novel, *Les rambles de Saigon* [Saigon Avenues] (1996), already included several tongues and frequent linguistic remarks. The emphasis on these topics is no doubt linked to the fact that Bezsonoff has witnessed first-hand the disruption of the sociolinguistic structure in the South of France, where Occitan and Catalan, widely spoken not so long ago, have almost disappeared.

Els taxistes del tsar reconstructs the life of the Russian officer Mitrofan, the writer's grandfather, who went into exile after the October revolution and became a taxi driver in Paris. Mitrofan did not speak Russian to his children, and the narrator explains his attempts to come to grips with this language as an adult and the identity problems caused by having a Russian surname, being a French national and his choice to write in Catalan. The narrator, haunted by a sense of being 'other' from an early age, sets out to explore '[q]ui és aquest home nascut a Perpinyà, d'origen rus, que escriu novel·les en català?' [who is this man born in Perpignan, of Russian origin, who writes novels in Catalan?] (2007: 94). The whole of Bezsonoff's *oeuvre* may be read as an attempt to answer this complex question. In *Els taxistes del tsar*, the narrator challenges readers with passages like this:

> Eufòric, estava bevent una copa de xampany al darrer pis del Palau de Congressos de Perpinyà quan se'm va atansar un senyor.

— Поздравляю вас с успехом.
— Извините, я не говорю по-русски.[2]
    I es va presentar en francès. Era un antic diplomàtic francès, d'origen rus.

[Exhilarated, I was drinking champagne on the top floor of Perpignan's Exhibition Centre when a man approached me.
    'Поздравляю вас с успехом.'
    'Извините, я не говорю по-русски.'
    And he introduced himself in French. He was a French diplomat of Russian origin.] (2007: 58)

Bezsonoff employs some of the strategies criticized by Lennon (such as offering a translation in inverted commas or in footnote) to ensure that Russian can be understood by readers. Nevertheless, this cannot be seen as trivializing multilingualism, since adding a few italicized words from a relatively similar tongue is significantly different from including a string of non-Latin characters which the vast majority of readers will not be able to decipher. Even if sometimes a rendition is offered, the incomprehensibility of the Cyrillic alphabet brusquely disrupts the flow of discourse. To press the point, on occasion Bezsonoff opts for further alienating the audience with sentences such as 'M'havia confiat que li agradaven particularment les sonoritats de la paraula пожалуйста' [He confided to me that he particularly liked the sound of the word пожалуйста] (2007: 21), which invites readers to reflect on the sound of a word which they are very unlikely to be able to pronounce. The narrator, therefore, is making readers aware of their linguistic limitations, but this is not just a prank at the expense of their ignorance: on several occasions the narrator himself bitterly acknowledges that he will never have the skill or the time to master Basque, Chinese, Vietnamese... Distressed by his own shortcomings, he conveys his post-Babelian anguish by means of a number of lexical items and sentences that the public will not understand.

    Multilingualism in Bezsonoff's work serves a variety of purposes: a) it sets a cultural and historical background for the story to unfold; b) helps to establish the personality traits of characters; c) challenges literary conventions; d) reflects and refracts the identity crisis of the 'other' (the displaced, the migrant...); e) criticizes the utilitarian drive towards linguistic homogenization and, also f) questions the disengagement of the concepts of language, culture and territory. In relation to the first point, the frequent songs and poems in other languages which punctuate his novels allow the narrator to delineate the cultural background and mind-set of the characters. In *Les amnèsies de Déu*, which explores the ways in which World War II impacts on a French bourgeois family, Bezsonoff reproduces in their original language two poems by Baudelaire; some lines of dialogue by Corneille; a poem by Goethe; six chansons by Tino Rossi, Luis Mariano, Fernandel, Ray Ventura and Léo Marjane; three anonymous French popular songs; an aria by Puccini; and two songs by Frank Sinatra and Vera Lynn.

    Although written for the most part in Catalan, Bezsonoff's novels contain a plethora of references to French culture which are not always easy to grasp on the other side of the Pyrenees. The Catalan reading public, then, is thrown into a cultural, social and historical world which is unapologetically French, and this has puzzled some critics, who claim that the author does not provide enough context (Montferrer 2006: 14; Pons 2011: 1). The disjunction between the cultural framework underpinning the narrative and the language(s) in which it has been written, however, is precisely one of the most innovative aspects of Bezsonoff's texts. Authors frequently write about cultures other than their own, but this does not normally estrange the audience, as every effort is made to ensure that the events described resonate with the reader's own experiences. As Chan points out, many original works are already 'translated', in the sense that writers force us to imagine — or simply disregard — that the language we are reading should be another one (2002: 54–57). Bezsonoff, however, refuses to 'translate' in two different ways: on the one hand, all his works contain other tongues; on the other, he makes no attempt at bridging cultural gaps. As a result, the implied reader of his texts is an individual totally immersed in French culture and society but who reads in Catalan. Not surprisingly, Bezsonoff himself has claimed to write French literature in Catalan (Bombí-Vilaseca 2008: 27).

Multilingualism and linguistic remarks are constantly used for characterization purposes. In *Les rambles de Saigon*, we are introduced to Catalan-speaking French officer Daniel Valls, who 'parla totes les llengües del planeta: l'annamita, el català, el castellà i a vegades el francès...' [speaks all the languages in the world: Vietnamese, Catalan, Spanish and, sometimes, French...] (1996: 31). In *Les amnèsies de Déu*, one of the protagonists is a priest who quotes — in Latin — Lucretius, Seneca and half a dozen lengthy passages from the Bible. Bezsonoff carefully delineates the linguistic biographies of his characters: each and every single one of them is described by their accent and the languages they speak, information which becomes a source of dramatic tension and ambiguity. Daniel Valls, for instance, is a misogynistic, conservative officer who, during the Indochina war, perpetrates brutal acts of violence in the name of France. As argued by Cortadellas (2014: 12), Bezsonoff's characters are not particularly likeable, mainly because their actions and ideas are often at odds with contemporary values. Multilingualism, though, helps the writer to present their gentle side: they may be shady figures and uphold reactionary views, but they are also cultured individuals who cite Baudelaire, Corneille or Goethe, and keen linguists who, as Pagès puts it, 'estimen el llenguatge encara que siguin sicaris' [love language even if they are criminals] (2008: 28).

Bezsonoff refuses to fully translate cultural alterity and, in relation to literary conventions, uses mimetic realism in unsystematic and contradictory ways. In *Les amnèsies de Déu*, a character called Leccia states that '[m]ai no m'han agradat els alemanys! *Je n'ai jamais pu blairer les Boches* en versió original' [I've never liked Germans! *Je n'ai jamais pu blairer les Boches* in the original version] (2015: 49). Leccia uses Catalan in the first part of the sentence, and therefore in principle there is no need to translate the already 'rendered' utterance back into its original language. Adding to the confusion, it is not clear whether the phrase 'en versió original' belongs to Leccia or to an omniscient narrator who is controlling what the character says and in which language. The narrator, by stressing the incongruity of using a language different to that of the original enunciation, relies on multilingualism to break the fourth wall and, in the process, inverts the normal hierarchy of languages:

instead of offering a sentence in the guest code and then unobtrusively translating or paraphrasing it, which is what literary conventions dictate, he adopts the opposite strategy. Bezsonoff, therefore, mocks and undermines his own discursive strategies by means of unexpected remarks that foreground language as a subject. Contradictions of this sort abound in his novels: in *Les amnèsies de Déu* the priest may quote long fragments of Lucretius, Seneca and the Bible in Latin, but he also quotes Petronius directly in Catalan or provides the original passage in footnote (2005: 99). More often than not, however, languages appear unmediated. In the following two sentences in Rumanian and German, readers are left to their own devices, forced to infer their meaning from the context:

> L'oficial romanès va insultar en Leccia:
> — Îţi baţi joc de mine, dobitoc? Ce surpriz plăcută! Eşti bolnav? Hai sictir! Pizda mătii!

> [The Rumanian officer insulted Leccia:
> 'Îţi baţi joc de mine, dobitoc? Ce surpriz plăcută! Eşti bolnav? Hai sictir! Pizda mătii!] (2005: 110)

> Estava orinant dret contra un arbre quan un policia el va renyar.
> — *Na sowas! Ein Fräulein wie Sie, und Sie pissen im Stehen, wie ein Mann!...* Ausweis, bitte...

> [He was urinating against a tree when a policeman told him off.
> 'Na sowas! Ein Fräulein wie Sie, und Sie pissen im Stehen, wie ein Mann!... Ausweis, bitte...] (2005: 117)

French, the most common guest tongue in Bezsonoff's novels, is not much of a problem for educated Catalan readers, although its use is inconsistent, to say the least. Dialogues that 'should' take place in French are sometimes reported in Catalan, and yet on numerous occasions the language inexplicably changes mid-way through. *Les rambles de Saigon* goes as far as to include dialogues in Vietnamese but, when it comes to citing Flaubert, the narrator translates the passage into Catalan. The degree of randomness to which languages are subject underlines the linguistic nature of the text and brings to light the conventionality of literary norms.

Bezsonoff's style has been praised as well as criticized for being sparse, for his tendency to summarize and condense. However, while it is true that his novels include little description in the traditional sense, they portray a varied and rich multidimensional sociolinguistic space which is rarely found in literary discourse. They also open up to the inflections of other tongues and show how languages are inevitably caught up in a complex, wider set of relations and assumptions that operate in already existing cultural and linguistic networks. In Bezsonoff's texts, situated at the junction between fiction and sociolinguistics, the carnival of languages undermines and dislocates the narrative at every turn, bringing unexpected tongues together at the risk of mystifying potential readers.

Interestingly, the reviews devoted to Bezsonoff's work have rarely dealt with their multilingual fabric (the exception being Murgades 2006). Given that his novels tend to contain at least half a dozen tongues, this may appear surprising, but it is not: critics who would find the interaction between Spanish and Catalan problematic are less concerned when the equation includes more remote variables such as Rumanian, Vietnamese, Italian, Occitan, German, Russian or English. As for Spanish, its presence is minimal; in *Les amnèsies de Déu*, it is reduced to a single sentence sandwiched between Italian and Catalan:

> En Leccia, segur de la seua falsa documentació, va protestar.
> — *Sono italiano, sono italiano! Chè cosa fanno? Sono un intimo amico personale del console d'Italia a Barcellona.*
> — *¡Muy bien señor! Ya lo comprobaremos...*
> En Leccia es retrobà internat a la presó de Figueres.
>
> [Leccia, confident with his fake documents, protested.
> 'Sono italiano, sono italiano! Chè cosa fanno? Sono un intimo amico personale del console d'Italia a Barcellona.
> '¡Muy bien señor! Ya lo comprobaremos...'
> Leccia found himself again locked in Figueres prison.] (2015: 159)

Overall, Bezsonoff's emphasis on multilingual discourse defamiliarizes language; points to the representational inadequacies (or arbitrariness) of literary conventions; underscores the importance of language in the construction of reality; questions the hegemony of national languages; and examines the links between the concepts of culture, identity, territory and language.

Marta Rojals's *L'altra* (2014): Concerns over Language Purity against the Backdrop of Barcelona's Soundscape

Marta Rojals's first two novels — *Primavera, estiu, etcètera* [Spring, Summer, Etcetera] (2011); *L'altra* (2014) — have received unanimous acclaim, and only a couple of critics have mildly questioned the author's 'llibertats lingüístiques' [peculiar linguistic uses] (Pagès 2014: 56; Puigdevall 2014: 6). Solsona, who no doubt saw echoes of his own work in Rojals's opera prima, which contains abundant dialectal features and borrowings, was quick to praise her literary style in the press (2011: 25). Rojals has often criticized the deterioration of Catalan but, not unlike Solsona, she has no qualms when it comes to including Spanish in her novels. She has complained that '[s]embla que parlar bé el català ha quedat estigmatitzat, deu ser l'únic país del món on l'excel·lència es ridiculitza' [it appears that speaking proper Catalan is frowned upon, it is the only country in the world where linguistic excellence is subject to derision], yet at the same time she defends the right to use non-standard language in the name of verisimilitude: 'com que la parla mitjana de Barcelona és d'un nivell molt baix, els personatges segueixen aquest patró en diferents graus' [since average linguistic skills in Barcelona are very low, characters follow this trend to varying degrees] (Llobet 2015).

The setting of *L'altra* is Barcelona, and the narrator, Anna, is a woman in her late thirties who experiences problems with her boyfriend and has been severely hit by the economic crisis. The long list of borrowings present in the narrative (*curro, adelanto, arrebato, algo, vaya, parque, pillar, quarentons, manitas, hasta, empastes, papeleo*, among many others) are mostly uttered by Cati, a character who draws indiscriminately from the lexicon and grammar of either language. *L'altra*, however, displays a complex polyphony of voices which goes well beyond the mere hybridization of Catalan and Spanish. While walking down the streets of the city, the narrator finds herself surrounded by tongues that cannot be identified with any specific standard: 'Per les oïdes li passen accents argentins, xilens, del nord — *si vos tenés un proshecto... Po' no queda otra, po'... M'està cardant dels nervis...*' [She hears Argentinian, Chilean, Northern accents: — If you have a project... We haven't any left, any... It's affecting my nerves...] (Rojals 2014: 141). The fact that the Argentinian and Chilean accents she hears overlap with a northern accent (from the North of Catalonia, of course) is indicative of the author's intention to evoke the complex soundscape of the city. Solsona, who belongs to an earlier generation, fundamentally depicts a bilingual metropolis; this is no longer possible in Rojals's crisis-ridden Barcelona, which during the boom times attracted 280,000 immigrants (17.4% of the city's current population).

The different interpretations that Cati has merited attest to the difficulty of clearly pinpointing the purpose of literary multilingualism and the contrasting reactions that it elicits. Rojals has explained that linguistic usage in *L'altra* is a consequence of the realistic nature of the text. Alós (2014), however, considers that Spanish borrowings have a comic function, and Nopca (2014), who seems to be trying to ease the potential anxiety caused by Spanish interferences, suggests that their function is to criticize the decay of Catalan. As argued by Solsona, '[a]pel·lar a la correcció o incorrecció d'una paraula o expressar dubtes en veu alta és una manera de tranquil·litzar la mala consciència crònica dels catalanoparlants' [discussing the proper use of words or openly expressing linguistic doubts helps to alleviate the ever-present bad conscience of Catalan speakers] (2015: 168). While Rojals does not object to Nopca's interpretation, she cautiously states: 'M'agrada que hi hagis vist un punt de crítica. Amb tot, la voluntat primera era que les converses fossin versemblants, i si els fets passen a Barcelona no podia fer veure que el castellà no hi és present, que no contamina en major o menor grau la manera de parlar del carrer' [I like the fact that you interpret it as criticizing linguistic errors. However, the main goal was to create realistic dialogues, and since the narrative takes place in Barcelona I could not pretend that Spanish wasn't there or forget that, to a lesser or greater extent, Spanish contaminates popular speech] (Nopca 2014). The problem, of course, is that denouncing the decline of Catalan through one of the most hybrid literary languages to appear in print is a controversial option at best. Rojals, well aware of the anxieties caused by linguistic interference, appears to have taken an ambiguous stance in order not to alienate the audience: on the one hand, she has extensively borrowed from Spanish; on the other, she has tried to compensate for this by inserting negative comments on Cati's hybrid diction. Readers uncomfortable with her speech habits can always cling on to this passage, in which the narrator censures her friend:

> — Per una vegada que començo a sortir amb algú una mica en *sèrio* i que *desatasco* les *canyeries*... Però *bueno*, ja li he dit que per fer la *siestecita* m'escaparé, *vaya* si m'escaparé.
> Aquestes insinuacions incomoden l'Anna, i no només pels barbarismes.

['For once that I seriously date somebody and start unblocking the pipes...
But, well, I've already told him that I'll leave work for a quickie, you can count
on it...'

These remarks make Ana uncomfortable, and not only because of the
Spanish borrowings.] (124)

Despite Anna's reproach, *L'altra* does not seem to be particularly concerned with
linguistic accuracy (or the lack thereof); rather, what this novel attempts to do is to
offer an artistic representation of the variety of accents that can be heard in the streets
of Barcelona. This is why, as well as *castellanismes*, it includes a number of anglicisms,
non-standard Catalan forms (*sapigut, enradera...*), sentences in pseudo French: 'Ah,
mon amour, et prova, l'*air* de la *Barcelonette?*' [Oh, my love, does the air in Barceloneta
reinvigorate you?] (118); and pseudo Andalusian: '*vozotra mizma, pero no eztá el tiempo
mu fino*' [It's up to you, but the weather is not very good] (108). Spanish is also used
to mock certain linguistic ideologies associated with Franco's regime, such as the
concept of imperialism: 'Tu creus que l'hauria d'escriure directament *en la lèngua
del impèrio* o te la deixen *tradusirt?*' [Do you think I should have written it directly
in the Imperial language or they let you translate it?] (130). The fact that criticism is
exerted in a phonetically hybrid idiom (*lèngua, impèrio* and *tradusirt*) further adds to
the ambiguity of *L'altra* which, to complicate matters further, also uses Spanish to
make fun of the accent of Catalan speakers: '*Ustet póngale* força *lío que no lo entienda
ni dios*' [let's mess things up so nobody understands a word] (15). This ambiguity
extends to typographical conventions: while Spanish borrowings are italicized, the
ungrammatical use of the neuter article 'lo' by the narrator is not, and therefore this
non-standard form is presented as acceptable.

Overall, *L'altra* displays a variety of linguistic uses and ideologies which intersect
and clash with each other: Spanish can be the language of Latin American
immigrants, that of the Castilianized urban area, or the language imposed by
Franco's regime; Catalan, on the other hand, is seen as an exotic tongue when
spoken with an accent from outside Barcelona or as a language receding into its
own territory. In addition, both tongues often appear mixed, giving rise to a hybrid
code, a sort of pidgin that is becoming increasingly frequent in the metropolitan
region. Their crossbreeding can be taken as an ironic criticism of linguistic
impurity, as a statement on the marginal situation of Catalan in certain areas of
Barcelona, it can be justified in the name of realism or, even, seen as a way to
attract a new kind of public that lacks an assured command of this tongue and is
unconcerned about linguistic accuracy. The title of the novel, *L'altra*, refers to the
narrator, affected by an economic and personal crisis that shatters the foundations
of her life. Anna's sense of otherness is reflected in the complex, mixed idiom that
translates the lack of certitude and stability in her life and, by extension, the city
where she lives, which is undergoing dramatic social and economic changes. That
this should be described in a language other to itself is all the more fitting.

Conclusion: The Uses of Textual Multilingualism and the Literary Field at the Turn of the Twenty-First Century

Solsona's, Bezsonoff's and Rojals's works explore how languages interact with each other, the sociocognitive experiences of speakers and their interpersonal and social linguistic behaviour. Their highly elaborate textual constructs present languages as artefacts that are controlled and manipulated according to the sociocultural needs of their users and, by doing so, they highlight the unavoidable political dimension of linguistic phenomena. If in Rojals's and Solsona's work multilingualism can be misguidedly seen as conventionally realistic by readers and critics, the sudden irruption of Russian or Vietnamese in Bezsonoff's texts points to the evidence that the linguistic and cultural networks in which individuals participate are more complex than often acknowledged. Beyond simple mimesis, literary heteroglossia exposes the fallacy of monolingual ideologies: instead of presenting languages as independent, homogeneous and static constructs evolving on their own, they are presented as dynamic, intersecting systems constantly permeating each other and redefining their boundaries.

The reviews devoted to Solsona's, Rojal's and Bezsonoff's novels, for the most part very positive, appear to indicate that the controversies over linguistic purism that affected the literary field in the 1980s and 1990s are no longer at the centre of intellectual debate. Overall, the greater acceptance of less rigid conventions certifies the versatility and flexibility of the Catalan literary language. This does not mean that the field has ceased to be governed by linguistic rules: Rojals, Solsona and Bezsonoff may have resorted to multilingualism, but the vast majority of writers continue to use the standard variety.

In the novels here analysed, multilingualism serves a clear narrative purpose, but this discursive strategy comes with a caveat: no literary field is likely to tolerate a general and indiscriminate use of another language without putting at risk its own prestige and autonomy. If the blending of Catalan and Spanish were to intensify to such an extent that it became an inherent characteristic of the field, Catalan would most likely cease to be perceived as an independent code and the field itself would eventually collapse: it would be a mere dialectal extension of Spanish literature. Furthermore, the generalization of this strategy would result in negative attitudes towards Catalan and a new complex of linguistic inferiority. This is a remote yet not entirely impossible scenario, as an article by the editorial team of *Els Marges* entitled 'Una literatura en crisi, un país sense cultura?' [A Literature in Crisis, a Country without Culture?] suggests:

> No tindrem més lectors si fem novel·les més bones, perquè, des dels paràmetres actuals, ja les fem. No tindrem més lectors si aprofundim en el bilingüisme literari — cada cop més hi ha obres que es complauen a posar-hi personatges que parlen en castellà — ni en l'hibridisme lingüístic — una tendència que no es pot portar més lluny sense que perilli tot.

> [Readership will not increase with better novels, because from a contemporary perspective Catalan literature is good enough. Literary multilingualism is not an option — there is a growing tendency to include Spanish-speaking

characters in novels — , and neither is linguistic hybridization, a trend that cannot be further developed as it would put everything at risk.] (*Els Marges* 2014: 12)

The possibility of a gradual merging of Spanish and Catalan in literature cannot be entirely ruled out, but there exist at least four main arguments against it. The first point is that, in Bezsonoff's texts, French, Occitan and even Russian or Vietnamese are much more common than Spanish, hence multilingualism should not be automatically linked to the use of a specific language. Secondly, examples of works that include abundant Spanish are still few and far between and, in them, the guest tongue does not permeate the whole narrative. Rather, it is often part of an ironic strategy which seeks to establish a rapport with the reader, who is perfectly able to distinguish between languages and between standard and non-standard varieties. Thirdly, the editorial team of *Els Marges* fail to mention that linguistic hybridism is already widespread in radio and television broadcasts, which are significantly more influential than literature. In the fourth place, literary multilingualism has a very long tradition in Catalan literature (see Rossich and Cornellà 2014), but this discursive strategy has not prevented its historical continuity. At this stage, therefore, to say that this phenomenon is threatening the independence of the literary field is, perhaps, an overstatement. Nevertheless, it is a reasonable concern. According to the publisher, *L'altra* sold 30,000 copies in one month: what would happen if literary multilingualism became more widespread, in the belief that it boosts sales?

The novels analysed in this chapter place the reflection on, or ironic distortion of, sociolinguistic reality at its very centre, self-referentially playing with the linguistic perceptions of readers. In them, language is not a mere vehicle that is supposed to disappear in the act of referring, since heteroglossia is constantly foregrounded as the creative impetus behind the text and one of its thematic cores. However, it is worth distinguishing those works which, while introducing a supplementary code, make use of standard varieties from those which blend the lexis and syntax of both tongues. Bezsonoff, for instance, draws a very clear line between the different codes he uses; it is obvious what belongs to each. The naturalization of textual code-switching does not seem to be possible in his work: tongues clash or coexist, but they do not merge to a significant degree. *No tornarem mai més* and *L'altra*, on the other hand, reflect the language contacts of daily life in Catalonia — even though, as already mentioned, in the Catalan novel the language of lived experience is generally effaced by means of translation. Solsona includes Spanish in both dialogues and the narrator's voice — as free indirect speech. Rojals mainly limits hybridisms to dialogues and, in addition, she adopts compensatory strategies in order to avoid normalizing code-mixing: while she does not refrain from using Spanish borrowings, this is counterbalanced by the use of italics and the inclusion of positive linguistic remarks and characters, such as the narrator, 'que provi[n] de fer sexi el català correcte als lectors, que els influeixi[n] lingüísticament' [that try to make standard Catalan appealing to readers, that influence readers from a linguistic point of view] (in Llobet 2015). What is obvious is that Solsona and Rojals no longer pine for the recovery of a pre-existing uncontaminated language nor do they nostalgically mourn its disappearance; rather, they discover in the present situation a continuum of interlocked cultural and linguistic possibilities that are reflected in and refracted by their characters. The main difference is that Rojals, by linking economic and personal crisis to the precarious position of Catalan in Barcelona, appears to be implicitly questioning whether this language alone can be used to represent the city. In any case, Solsona and Bezsonoff have been exploiting multilingualism since the beginning of their careers, and therefore this is an integral element of their style. Rojals has only written three novels, and the success of *L'altra* may have encouraged her to go down a similar route in *El cel no és per a tothom* [The Sky Is Not for Every One] (2018). However, it is still unclear whether Rojals' popularity will inspire other writers to follow her example, which is what the editorial team of *Els Marges* seem to fear.

To conclude, multilingual texts highlight the problematic ways in which the notions of culture and literature are linked to that of language by 'oppos[ing] monolingual complacency and disrupt[ing] the myth of the singularity, separateness of cultures' (Choudhuri 1997: 25). This chapter has shown that contemporary Catalan writers are increasingly allowed to explore previously uncharted linguistic territory. Echoing Moth's words in Shakespeare's *Love's Labour's Lost* (Act V, Scene 1), by bringing to light peripheral linguistic phenomena which literary norms and the ideology of the standard have forced to ignore, Solsona, Bezsonoff and Rojals 'have been at a great feast of languages, and stolen the scraps'. In their quest for transgressing the barriers of expressiveness set by existing norms, they often make ironic, self-reflexive and self-critical linguistic remarks and mock some of their own stylistic choices. In their novels, languages appear in flux, freeing the text from conventional constraints, enhancing the metalinguistic and metafictional possibilities of the narrative, and highlighting the ethical and political dimension of communication. Overall, their use of multilingualism to reflect on cultural, political and social issues ensures that this strategy is not just the means, but also the message.

Works Cited

AITCHISON, JEAN. 1991. *Language Change: Progress or Decay?* (Cambridge: Cambridge University Press)

ALÓS, ERNEST. 2014. 'El fenomen Rojals', *El Periódico*, 8 February

BAULENAS, LLUÍS ANTON. 2004. *El català no morirà mai* (Barcelona: Edicions 62)

BEZSONOFF, JOAN-DANIEL. 1996. *Les rambles de Saigon* (Perpinyà: Trabucaire)

——. 2007. *Els taxistes del tsar* (Barcelona: Empúries)

——. 2015 [2005]. *Les amnèsies de Déu* (Barcelona: Labutxaca)

BIBOLAS, NOEMÍ. 2007. 'Quan escrivim anem amb el fre de mà posat', *Avui, Cultura*, 1 March, pp. 8–9

BLAKE, N. F. 1999. 'Afterword', in *English Literature and the Other Languages*, ed. by Ton Hoenselaars and Marius Buning (Amsterdam: Rodopi), pp. 232–341

BOMBÍ-VILASECA, FRANCESC. 2008. 'La peça Joan-Daniel Bezsonoff al trencaclosques identitari català', *Caràcters: Revista de Llibres*, 45: 27

CANONICA, ELVEZIO, and ERNST RUDIN (eds). 1993. *Literatura y bilingüismo: homenaje a Pere Ramírez* (Kassel: Reichenberger)

CHAN, TAK-HUNG. 2002. 'Translating Bilinguality: Theorizing Translation in the Post-Babelian Era', *The Translator*, 8.1: 49–72

CHOUDHURI, INDRA NATH. 1997. 'Plurality of Languages and Literature in Translation: The Post-colonial Context', in *Translation and Multilingualism: Post-Colonial Contexts*, ed. by S. Ramakrishna (Delhi: Pencraft International), pp. 25–33

CORTADELLAS, XAVIER. 2014. 'Els herois batuts', *Avui, Cultura*, 17 October, p. 12

DELABASTITA, DIRK, and RAINIER GRUTMAN. 2005. 'Fictional Representations of Multilingualism and Translation', *Linguistica Antverpiensia*, 4: 11–34

DOMÍNGUEZ, LOURDES. 2004. 'Ramon Solsona: "la realitat és un estímul constant de la imaginació"', *Avui, Cultura*, 26 February, pp. 1–3

GABANCHO, PATRICIA. 2007. *El preu de ser catalans: una cultura mil·lenària en vies d'extinció* (Barcelona: Meteora)

GALINDO SOLÉ, MIREIA. 2003. 'Language Contact Phenomena in Catalonia: The Influence of Catalan in Spoken Castilian', in *Selected Proceedings of the First Workshop on Spanish Sociolinguistics*, ed. by Lofti Sayahi (Somerville, MA: Cascadilla Proceedings Project), pp. 18–29 <http://www.lingref.com/cpp/wss/1/paper1004.pdf>

GARDNER-CHLOROS, PENELOPE, REEVA CHARLES, and JENNY CHESHIRE. 2000. 'Parallel Patterns? A Comparison of Monolingual Speech and Bilingual Codeswitching Discourse', *Journal of Pragmatics*, 32: 1305–41

GRUTMAN, RAINIER. 2002. 'Les Motivations de l'hétérolinguisme: réalisme, composition, esthétique', in *Eteroglossia e plurilinguismo letterario*, vol.II, ed. by Furio Brugnolo and Vincenzo Orioles (Rome: Centro internazionale sul plurilinguismo dell'Università degli Studi di Udine), pp. 337–41

——. 2006. 'Refraction and Recognition: Literary Multilingualism in Translation', *Target*, 18.1: 17–47

GUILLÉN, CLAUDIO. 1985. *Entre lo uno y lo diverso: introducción a la literatura comparada* (Barcelona: Crítica)

HEINEMANN, UTE. 1996. *Novel·la entre dues llengües: el dilema català o castellà* (Kassel: Reichenberger)

KELLER, GARY D. 1984. 'How Chicano Authors Use Bilingual Techniques for Literary Effect', in *Chicano Studies: A Multidisciplinary Approach*, ed. by Eugene E. García, Francisco A. Lomelí, and Isidro D. Ortiz (New York: Teachers College), pp. 171–92

KRAMER, JOHANNES. 2002. 'Testi mistilingui per una società bilingue: Plauto, Raimbaut, Osvaldo, Lutero, Goldoni, Reuter e Candinas', in *Eteroglossia e plurilinguismo letterario*, vol. II, ed. by Furio Brugnolo and Vincenzo Orioles (Rome: Centro internazionale sul plurilinguismo dell'Università degli Studi di Udine), pp. 309–28

LARREULA, ENRIC. 2002. *Dolor de lengua* (Valencia: Edicions 3i4)

LENNON, BRIAN. 2010. *In Babel's Shadow: Multilingual Literatures, Monolingual States* (Minneapolis: University of Minnesota Press)

LLOBET, ALEXIS. 2015. 'Entrevista a Marta Rojals', *Visat*, 19 <http://www.visat.cat/articles/eng/107/entrevista-a-marta-rojals.html>

LÜDI, GEORGES. 2001. 'Le "mélange de langes" comme moyen stylistique et/ou comme marqueur d'appartenance dans le discours littéraire', in *Écrire aux confins des langues. Actes du colloque de Mulhouse 30, 31 janvier et 1er février 1997*, ed. by J. Bem and A. Hudlett (Mulhouse: Centre de Recherche sur l'Europe Littéraire), pp. 13–31

Els Marges. 2004. 'Una literatura en crisi, un país sense cultura?', *Els Marges*, 103: 7–24

MENDIETA-LOMBARDO, EVA, and ZAIDA A. CINTRON. 1995. 'Marked and Unmarked Choices of Code Switching in Bilingual Poetry', *Hispania*, 78.3: 565–71

MEYLAERTS, REINE. 2006. 'Heterolingualism in/and Translation', *Target*, 18.1: 1–15

MONTFERRER, ÒSCAR. 2006. 'Natura viva amb circumstàncies', *Avui, Cultura*, 1 February, p. 14

Murgades, Josep. 2006. 'Joan Daniel Bezsonoff, *Les amnèsies de Déu*', *Els Marges*, 79: 124–25

Nopca, Jordi. 2014. 'Marta Rojals: "Ara ens comuniquem més i pitjor"', *Ara Llegim*, 18 January, pp. 40–41

Pagès Jordà, Vicenç. 2008. 'Un estil característic', *Caràcters: Revista de Llibres*, 45: 28

———. 2014. 'Més enllà del costumisme', *El Periódico de Catalunya*, 15 January, p. 56

Pons, Pere Antoni. 2011. '*La melancolia dels oficials*: això és la guerra (d'Algèria)', *dBalears. L'Espira*, 523, [1]

Puigdevall, Ponç. 2014. 'El mèrit de l'oportunitat', *El País, Quadern*, 16 January, p. 6

Pujolar, Joan, and Isaac González. 2013. 'Linguistic "mudes" and the De-ethnicization of Language Choice in Catalonia', *International Journal of Bilingual Education and Bilingualism*, 16.2: 138–52

Rojals, Marta. 2011. *Primavera, estiu, etcètera* (Barcelona: La Magrana)

———. 2014. *L'altra* (Barcelona: La Magrana)

———. 2018. *El cel no és per a tothom* (Barcelona: Anagrama)

Rossich, Albert, and Jordi Cornellà-Detrell. 2014. *El multilingüisme en la literatura catalana* (Bellcaire: Edicions Vitel·la)

Rudin, Ernst. 1996. *Tender Accent of Sound* (Tempe, AZ: Bilingual Press/Editorial Bilingüe)

Sebba, Mark. 2013. 'Multilingualism in Written Discourse: An Approach to the Analysis of Multilingual Texts', *International Journal of Bilingualism*, 17.1: 97–118

Senabre, Ricardo. 2011. 'Caligrafía de los sueños', *El Cultural. El Mundo*, 25 February <http://www.elcultural.es/version_papel/LETRAS/28741/Caligrafia_de_los_suenos> [accessed 18 November 2011]

Simon, Sherry. 2012. *Cities in Translation: Intersections of Language and Memory* (London: Routledge)

Solà, Joan. 1977. *Del català incorrecte al català correcte: història dels criteris de correcció lingüística* (Barcelona: Edicions 62)

Solsona, Ramon. 1989. *Figures de calidoscopi* (Barcelona: Quaderns Crema)

———. 1999. *No tornarem mai més* (Barcelona: Quaderns Crema)

———. 2011. 'L'Eliete es fa estimar', *Avui*, 20 March, p. 25

———. 2015. 'El malentès del català popular', in *Canvi d'agulles*, ed. by Enric Gomà (Barcelona: RBA), pp. 152–68

Steiner, George. 1971. *Extraterritorial: Papers on Literature and the Language Revolution* (New York: Atheneum)

Sternberg, Meir. 1981. 'Polylingualism as Reality and Translation as Mimesis', *Poetics Today*, 2.4: 221–39

Stoppard, Tom. 2008 [2002]. *The Coast of Utopia: Voyage, Shipwreck, Salvage* (London: Faber & Faber)

Vázquez Montalbán, Manuel. 1996. *El premio* (Barcelona: Planeta)

Villanueva, Darío, and Fernando Cabo Aseguinolaza (eds). 1996. *Paisaje, juego y multilingüismo. X Simposio de la Sociedad Española de Literatura General y Comparada (Santiago de Compostela, 18–21 de octubre de 1994)* (Santiago de Compostela: Universidade de Santiago de Compostela)

Von Flotow, Louise. 2000. '*Life is a Caravanserai*: Translating Translated Marginality, a Turkish-German *Zwittertext* in English', *Meta: Translators' Journal*, 45.1: 65–72

Woolard, Kathryn. 2011. 'Is There Linguistic Life after High School? Longitudinal Changes in the Bilingual Repertoire in Metropolitan Barcelona', *Language in Society*, 40.5: 617–48

Notes to Chapter 3

1. The bleak prospects facing Catalan have been discussed in a considerable number of books, among them Larreula (2002), Baulenas (2004) and Gabancho (2007).
2. '— Us feliciti pel vostre èxit. | — Perdoneu, no parli rus.' [Bezsonoff's translation] ['I congratulate you on your success.' | 'Sorry, I don't speak Russian.']

CHAPTER 4

Reimagining the
Catalan National Family in the
Twenty-First-Century Historical Novel

Kathryn Crameri

University of Glasgow

The twenty-first century has so far seen a significant increase in the publication and consumption of historical novels set at key moments in Catalonia's past. Ranging in time from Catalonia's medieval expansion as part of the Crown of Aragon, through to conflict with the Crown of Castile in the 1640s, the War of Spanish Succession in the early eighteenth century, the nineteenth-century Peninsular War, the Carlist wars and beyond, these fictional explorations have reflected an interest in history that has been stimulated by recent debates on Catalonia's potential independence (Crameri 2014: 73–99). There has also been a proliferation of historically themed conferences, exhibitions, documentaries, board games, musicals and poetry, alongside popular movements designed to restore the repressed voices of Catalonia's past to their rightful place in Spain's history.[1] The celebration of the 300th anniversary of the Siege of Barcelona (1714), in which the city was defeated by Philip V's Bourbon army, has been particularly important as a catalyst both for pro-independence sentiment and historically based cultural production. This chapter analyses several historical novels in order to examine some of what they can tell us about contemporary conceptions of the Catalan national past within this new political context.

Modern Catalan narrative has always featured the historical novel among its genres, even though the extent of this presence has tended to fluctuate over time. The very first novel of the modern era written in Catalan (after the centuries-long *Decadència*) was the historical novel *L'orfaneta de Menargues o Catalunya agonitzant* [The Orphan Girl from Menargues, or The Death Throes of Catalonia] by Antoni de Bofarull (1993 [1862]). First published in 1862, it was set at the beginning of the fifteenth century, at the time of the *Compromís de Casp* that put a Castilian-born King on the Aragonese throne, and had a clearly socio-political inspiration based on the view that this historical moment was the origin of many 'injustícies' [injustices] subsequently suffered by the Catalans (Serrahima and Boada 1996: 46). Further publications in the 1870s consolidated the historical novel both as a part of the revived Catalan literary polysystem and as an 'arma de combat' [tool in the arsenal] for the cultural values of the *Renaixença* (Serrahima and Boada 1996: 63, 118). If this was a propitious moment for the historical novel, then so — according to Àlex Broch (1991: 85, 87) — was the transition to democracy after the dictatorship of Francisco Franco, which produced many prize-winning examples of the genre. It is therefore not surprising that there would be another boom in historical novels in the early twenty-first century, during a period in which there occurred a fundamental shift in the goals and rhetoric of Catalan nationalism. As Broch says (1991: 106–07), historical novels flourish only when there is demand from readers, who share the same 'estat d'època' [state of the era] — and therefore the same thirst for knowledge and understanding — as the authors.

However, this apparent linkage between recent political changes and a surge in interest in Catalonia's history requires some examination, since one of the most significant features of the current pro-independence movement is its attempt to be as inclusive as possible. Ethnic ties to Catalonia have ceased to be a pre-requisite for either supporting independence or joining in the many activities organized by political and civil groups. As Gabriel Rufián put it in a speech during the mass demonstration on 11 September 2015, 'este proceso trasciende cualquier origen, cualquier bandera, cualquier apellido, cualquier barrio' [this process transcends any origin, any flag, any surname, any location] (Font 2015). On the other hand, the *Onze de setembre* itself is a commemoration of an event in Catalonia's history — the last day of the siege of Barcelona in 1714 — that is intimately associated with a very particular ethnic community. There is a clear tension here between the need to broaden the independence movement and the symbolic value of a distinctive ethnic past.

The Catalan independence movement is not alone in confronting this conundrum. According to Steven J. Mock, 'the word that best describes a nation's attitude and relationship to its ethnic heritage is *ambivalence*':

> in order to give ethnicity relevance in the modern world, the signifiers that determine ethnic communities must shift in the process of nation formation to account for modern institutions and instrumentalities. There is, therefore, a complex dialectic between preservation and invention in that process. The nation must be both preserved and invented insofar as, broadly speaking, it is the former that satisfies the cultural-psychological and the latter that addresses the sociopolitical. (Mock 2012: 44)

It is true that this push and pull of preservation and invention might go so far as to require what Mock calls 'a radical inauthenticity' (Mock 2012: 44) — such as welcoming people with no ethnic ties to Catalonia into the independence movement. However, cultural-psychological motives still seem to demand that there be some place for the ethnic past in the nation's present.

Indeed, Oriol Junqueras, leader of the pro-independence *Esquerra Republicana de Catalunya*, sees the continuing importance of the ethnic past as one of the main reasons why some Catalans wish to be independent, 'perquè existeix un seguit de vincles emocionals, vincles històrics, culturals, de referències que fa que alguna gent vulgui fer alguna cosa' [because there is a set of emotional ties, historical and cultural ties, references, that make certain people want to do a certain thing].[2] History cannot simply be jettisoned in order to foster an inclusive mass movement to achieve the political goal of independence, because without history the goal itself makes no sense. Nevertheless, it is clear from Junqueras' comments that, when looking at Catalonia's past, ethnicity is best defined from the perspective of social anthropology, in which the term 'simply refers to aspects of relationships between groups which consider themselves, and are regarded by others, as being culturally distinctive' (Hylland Eriksen 2010: 5). The past to which Junqueras refers is ethnic in the sense that it is identified as 'belonging to' the present-day group of people who label themselves Catalans, and who — in that way — define some kind of boundary that conditions their relationships with other groups. Ethnicity is still relevant, then, as a category of practice within the Catalan independence movement; that is, it continues to be part of the mechanism by which the community is imagined.

However, Lauenstein, Murer, Boos and Reicher (2015) question the usefulness of the very idea of the imagined *community*, and claim that the concept of the imagined *family* more accurately represents the way we generally conceive of the nation. They argue that the notion of the imagined community puts too much stress on the equality of members of that community, hiding the fact that any society will necessarily be structured hierarchically. Being a member of a nation comes with certain roles and responsibilities that are determined by our position within the community. The family as a metaphor captures this reality because children are supposed to defer to parents, and both in turn to grandparents. Not only this, but mothers traditionally defer to fathers and sisters to brothers, which means that the metaphor captures society's ingrained gender inequalities as well as the authority of elders. Furthermore, family has a clear association with a place — 'home and hearth' — which represents safety and emotional wellbeing (Lauenstein et al. 2015: 312), just as the nation is supposed to, even for those who are temporarily or permanently absent from it. Our ancestry also provides a sense of continuity through the ages and an assurance that this will persist into the future. In other words, the nation as an imagined family is first and foremost an ethnic community.

In contrast, Thomas Hylland Eriksen (2004) argues that it is possible to create a sentimental attachment to a national identity without invoking ethnic factors at all, since in some cases aspects such as place and kinship can be used to forge 'alternative kinds of imagined communities, based not on fictional bloodlines and shared history but on shared futures and multiple pasts' (61). However, if the imagined family is indeed a better metaphor for the nation than the imagined community, as Lauenstein et al. contend, then Hylland Eriksen is presumably misguided in thinking that a national identity can ever function properly without a shared past, even if there are contemporary forms of kinship that provide some sense of community. We seem to have returned full circle to the problem of 'ambivalence' towards an ethnic past that is both indispensable and highly problematic.

How might the contemporary historical novel help us untangle this conundrum?

Speaking about the transition to democracy in Spain, Broch (1991: 106) contends that the popularity of the Catalan historical novel at that time was related to 'aquesta situació política que ens fa creure que la història torna a enllaçar amb el passat i que el nostre projecte tira endavant' [this political situation that makes us believe that our history is once more linked to the past and our project is moving forward]. This linking of past and present is clearly occurring again with the shift of mainstream Catalanism towards independence. Even though Catalan novelists are now more profoundly influenced by a Western 'postmodern climate which is, almost by definition, cosmopolitan, supra-national and sceptical towards such closed entities as the nation', like the British historical novelists studied by Mariadele Boccardi, 'the retrospective dwelling on the past that is required of them [...] and that past's uncertain transmission and ideologically bound representation inevitably leads these authors to a reflection of the particular national experience that shapes the present's relationship to the past' (Boccardi 2009: 16). This reflection will be even more apparent in the case of novelists with pro-independence sentiments, some of whom have set out to give specific messages about the present through their writing (as can be seen from various dedications, epigraphs, prefaces, afterwords and press interviews).

The aim of this chapter is therefore to examine this push and pull between past and present in a sample of historical novels published in the twenty-first century. Given the need for focus in a relatively brief chapter, and the significance of the *Onze de setembre* commemorations within the current independence movement, the sample will only include novels set during the War of Spanish Succession that culminated in the fall of Barcelona in 1714. Furthermore, in the light of the interesting recent contentions of Lauenstein et al. regarding the usefulness of the concept of the imagined family as a metaphor for the nation, the discussion will concentrate on elements of these novels that appear to be designed to construct a particular image of the Catalan national family in both the past and present. The analysis centres around apparently opposing views of the family, on the one hand as a fixed biological construct and on the other as a porous container that allows for voluntary membership. I will argue that despite the predominance of depictions of the Catalan national family as inclusive and not in any way reliant on blood ties, one element remains constant: the assumption that members will be willing to sacrifice themselves for the good of their real and imagined family.

Most of the novels under discussion fall easily into the category of Catalan narrative, in that they were originally written in Catalan. This is the case with Alfred Bosch's *1714* trilogy (2008), published at the start of this century, Víctor Jurado Riba's *No s'hi enterra cap traïdor* [No Traitor is to Be Buried Here] (2014), and *Lliures o morts* [Either Free or Dead] by Jaume Clotet and David de Montserrat (2012).[3] However, the most famous historical novel of the last few years by a Catalan, *Victus* by Albert Sánchez Piñol (2012), was originally published in Spanish, despite its author having previously written a number of (sometimes prize-winning) novels in Catalan. Sánchez Piñol's decision to write in Spanish, apparently because the writing process was not 'flowing' in Catalan, is just one of many examples of the fluid boundaries between literature in Catalan and literature by Catalans in other languages (J. V. 2012).[4] The fact that it is written in Spanish throws into relief some of the very questions surrounding the characteristics of the Catalan national family that these novels seek to address.

National Families

Lauenstein et al. say that the model used to shape the national consciousness has always been the 'abstract ideal of the nuclear family' (2015: 312), often in a very clichéd form (325). However, by the twenty-first century the concept of the nuclear family appeared to be in crisis, because of challenges to the patriarchal structure of society and the increasing need for mobility and flexibility in the contemporary workforce to meet the demands of global capitalism (Carrington 2001: 186–87). This might therefore call into question the family's use as a metaphor for the nation. There are aspects of these changing family relationships that can certainly be described as significant — such as a growing acceptance of same-sex and interethnic relationships and blended families — but this does not imply that the normative power of the nuclear ideal has simply disappeared. As Victoria Carrington says (2002: 142–43), it 'will continue to have a significant potency', since its residual effects will be felt in generations to come. This means that the metaphor can still be drawn upon in a way that 'reifies social relations as biologically determined' (Lauenstein et al. 2015: 312). Nevertheless, some of the visions of the family offered by our 'novels of 1714' seem to be firmly based on more contemporary ideas of voluntary belonging and the family-of-choice (Carrington 2002: 140).

Perhaps the most extreme version of this kind of family would be the eclectic pseudo-family of Martí Zuviría, protagonist of Sánchez Piñol's *Victus*. Martí's amorous adventures as he weaves his picaresque way between the Bourbon and pro-Austrian camps include a passionate affair with the Duke of Berwick. He acquires his eventual partner Amelis first by taking her hostage as he flees from an attack by *miquelets*,[5] and then rescuing her from assault after a chance meeting while she is working as a prostitute in Barcelona. Their adopted 'children', Nan and Anfán, are a dwarf and a boy Martí first encounters as they perform sexual favours for Bourbon soldiers in the trenches in order to rob them. Also living with Martí is his boyhood servant, Peret. Martí describes him as 'aquel despojo humano' [that piece of human garbage], but at the same time 'el único sucedáneo de madre que conocí. Me resultaba imposible no sentir afecto por quien me peinaba, abotonaba y acariciaba mucho más que mi padre' [the only mother substitute I ever knew. It was impossible not to feel affection for someone who combed my hair, dressed me and caressed me much more than my father did] (Sánchez Piñol 2012: locs 3478, 756). Amelis and Martí's cramped 'semisótano' [semi-basement flat] becomes home to these five people he comes to regard as his family, and the five of them even share the only bed (locs 5925, 7759, 3752). Small homely connections come to represent the meaning of family for Martí, to the point where '[l]o que en verdad me unía a ellos no eran los actos sublimes, sino la acumulación de banalidades. No hay nada más significante que la suma de un millón de insignificancias' [what really bound me to them were not sublime acts, but an accumulation of banalities. There is nothing more significant than the sum of a million insignificancies] (loc. 10250). However, in the final battle he loses first Amelis, then Nan, then Anfán, who calls out '[p]are, pare, pare' [father, father, father] as he dies. Martí (as first-person narrator) then says: 'El fin del mundo era eso: cuando tu hijo te trata de "padre" por vez primera, y esa vez es el instante antes de que se muera' [That was the end of the world: when your son calls you 'father' for the first time, and that time is the moment before he dies] (loc. 10407).

Sánchez Piñol's vision of the family as built on everyday proximity rather than ancestry or deep emotions echoes Thomas Hylland Eriksen's observations (2004: 56) that all communities form around 'taken-for-granteds', and the 'sense of kinship felt by well-integrated members of any nation grows out of shared experiences'. Indeed, Sánchez Piñol returns to the theme in the sequel to *Victus*, *Vae Victus*, in which Martí, having fled Catalonia, becomes first involuntarily and then willingly part of a new family of Native Americans. Held as a sex slave for the chief's stepsister Mausi, Martí is also given the task of watching over a child known as Abuelo who does all he can to make Martí's life a misery. Nevertheless, Martí comes to love them both for the same reason he loved Nan and Anfán: 'las menudencias' [the little things] (Sánchez Piñol 2015: loc. 1626). Biological parenthood as a necessity for parental love is dismissed: 'No amamos a un hijo porque somos padres; somos padres porque amamos a un hijo' [We don't love a child because we are parents; we are parents because we love a child] (loc. 1633). In other words — those of David Morgan (2011: 177) — 'family is something people "do" and in doing create and recreate the idea of family'.

Although not as outlandish, the family structure in Víctor Jurado's *No s'hi enterra cap traïdor* mirrors some of the main features of the Zuviría family in *Victus*. The protagonist is Pere, a shoemaker who lives with his two sons, Joan and Ignasi, and Roser, an orphan adopted as a baby who acts as their maid. His wife Joana has been killed in the Bourbon attacks on the city in 1706, and he later brings into the household, as his partner, Margarida, herself widowed during the 1706 attacks, when her house was destroyed during the final siege. Along with Margarida, he ends up sheltering Francesc (a friend who was blinded during earlier fighting) and the apprentices from his shoemaking business. It also transpires that his son Joan has made Roser pregnant and then wants nothing more to do with her. The baby girl is born just as Pere is killed trying to defend the flag of Santa Eulàlia after Rafael Casanova — the head of Catalonia's civilian defence force, who had taken the flag out onto the battlements to rally the troops — is wounded. Although Roser has no way of knowing this, she decides to call the baby Eulàlia. The episode is based on one of the key moments in the dominant narrative of the historical events of 1714, and the naming therefore transforms the child into a symbol that the Catalan nation — and its fight — will continue. It is Pere's younger son Ignasi who will take care of Roser and the baby after the battle is over.

Like Martí, Pere takes in and defends those who need him, those who are weaker than himself, welcoming them into the family. However, there are other elements here. His relationship with Joan is not good and they often disagree either for personal reasons or because of their different views of the conflict. Joan is more concerned about fighting for an abstract idea of the nation, Pere more embittered by the various conflicts he has already lived through and certain that the only thing worth fighting for is other people. This is one of their heated conversations on this topic:

> [Joan] — De vegades cal lluitar per alguna cosa més gran que les nostres vides. Combatrem per una forma de ser i de viure, allò que ens fa catalans!
> [Pere] — Sembles un filòsof... Baixa a la terra, nano, i deixa de viure al teu món de fades! Les lleis ens distingeixen, però són només papers! El que importa són les persones i les seves vides, no allò que les ha de fer comportar-se d'una manera o d'una altra!
> [Joan] — Però aquestes lleis ens identifiquen com a poble!

> [[Joan] — Sometimes we have to fight for something bigger than our own lives. We will fight for our way of being and living, for what makes us Catalans!
> [Pere] — You sound like a philosopher... Come back down to earth, child, and stop living in fairyland. Our laws make us different, but they are only bits of paper! What matters are people and their lives, not what forces them to act in one way or another.
> [Joan] — But those laws mark us out as a people!] (Jurado Riba 2014: loc. 593)

Joan's apparent idealism does not stretch to welcoming others into the family home, and he complains bitterly when his father invites Margarida and Francesc to stay with them. His treatment of Roser is also less than gallant, and he and Pere actually come to blows over this, although Pere naturally mourns his son when he is killed towards the end of the siege. The message in the portrayal of their relationship is clear: a family member who does not put family loyalty first is little better than a *botifler*,[6] for what is a nation but a collection of people? As a minor character, Captain Bòria, puts it, 'mentre un català defensi la seva llar i la seva família, i no un rei, tots seguirem vius entre les moreres' [while there is still one Catalan who defends his home and his family, and not a king, we will all remain alive among the mulberry trees] (loc. 3395).

Biological Continuity and the Role of the Mother

Lauenstein et al. state (2015: 312) that, in the context of the nation as an imagined family, 'family ties are predominantly understood as biological ties of blood relatedness; therefore, drawing on the family as a metaphor reifies social relations as biologically determined'. However, it will be apparent from the preceding discussion that there is often little or no emphasis on blood relatedness in the families depicted in these historical novels: Martí's family in *Victus*, for example, shares no blood ties at all. In the case of *No s'hi enterra* the situation is more ambiguous: Ignasi as surrogate father to Eulàlia, and Roser who herself was adopted, do not represent a standard biological family. Nevertheless, Pere's blood line survives through Joan's paternity of Eulàlia. The effective continuity from Pere to Eulàlia is therefore the same, and it is Eulàlia that stands as the symbol of hope at the end of the novel.

Paternity as a form of continuity of the nation also forms part of the final message in *Lliures o morts* by Jaume Clotet and David de Montserrat. The novel is a fictionalized account of the life of Ermengol Amill, one of the heroes of the siege of Barcelona who survives to make a life at the service of the Holy Roman Emperor. Having lost his first son Ponç in a cruel act of revenge by his arch enemy Le Guerchois, he abandons Catalonia after the war with another son, whom he must leave in safety in Vienna while fighting for the Emperor. In 1732, while governor of Crotone in the Kingdom of Naples, he dictates his life story to a young Catalan lieutenant, only to find out when the story is finished that he has been dictating to his own son. The final words of the novel are the following:

> Pare i fill es van abraçar llargament i van compartir l'última copa de zibibbo. Poc després, el tinent Llorenç Amill, oficial de cavalleria imperial, sortia al galop del castell de Crotone en direcció al nord, Itàlia amunt. El vell governador l'observava des de la torre més alta del castell, on havia fet hissar aquella vella bandera negra que havia onejat a Santa Maria del Mar fins al mateix dia de la caiguda de la ciutat. L'havia amagat tots aquells anys i ara tornava a espetegar furiosa contra el vent. En aquell moment va comprendre que, quan havia abandonat Catalunya, quasi vint anys enrere, no ho havia perdut tot. Tenia un fill i una bandera. 'Potser no som lliures, però de ben segur que tampoc no som morts', va pensar.

> [Father and son shared a long embrace and the last glass of zibibbo. Shortly afterwards, Lieutenant Llorenç Amill, an Imperial cavalry officer, galloped northwards away from the castle of Crotone, up through Italy. The old Governor watched him from the castle's highest tower, on which he had given orders to fly the old black flag that had fluttered over Santa Maria del Mar right up to the day the city fell. He had hidden it all those years, but now it once again flapped furiously against the wind. At that moment, he understood that when he had left Catalonia, almost twenty years earlier, he had not actually lost everything. He had a son and a flag. 'Maybe we're not free, but we're certainly not dead either', he thought.] (Clotet and de Montserrat 2012: loc. 6182)

Given that he had in any case been in touch with his son regularly by letter, the significance of this final realization must be that it comes just as Ermengol has finished reviewing his lifelong dedication to his nation. The symbolism of the black flag — proclaiming that there will be no surrender — and the fact that he has a healthy son capable of continuing the fight give meaning to his own sacrifices, and those of others yet to come. Since the novel's dedication reads '[a] tots aquells que sempre han lluitat i lluiten en defensa de la llibertat dels catalans' [To all those who have always fought and still fight to defend the liberty of the Catalans] (loc. 27), this message of hope must also be interpreted as a call to action addressed to current members of the Catalan national family.

Missing from this account, of course, is Llorenç's mother, Marianna. Lauenstein el al. assert that '[a] strong nation rests in a strong family, including a strong and dedicated national wife and mother. Women not adhering to the ideal of a caring mother are letting down more than their own family; they neglect the biological and cultural continuity of the nation as a whole' (2015: 313). Marianna, however, gives her baby to Ermengol in order to stay in Catalonia to raise her niece and look after her family's house and lands. It appears, then, that she has abandoned her child — hardly the act of a caring mother. However, this is Marianna de Copons, the spy who elicited Bourbon secrets during the war and saved Ermengol himself from a trap set for his regiment in Mataró by diverting them to Canet. She is hardly a 'passive, emotional counterpart to the protecting and providing roles' of men, as Lauenstein et al. propose is typical in concepts of the national family (2015: 313). Her legacy is twofold, both the son she leaves with Ermengol and her care for her own family's heritage and wellbeing, and this means that once again there is a tension here between a rejection of biological determinism and the role of children as symbols of continuity and hope.

Another Marianna — this time the wife of John Sinclair in Alfred Bosch's trilogy *1714* — provides our last example of this tension. The daughter of an Afro-Cuban slave and Catalan heiress Marta de Vilana, Marianna is an enigmatic character who clandestinely assists John Sinclair in the first part of the trilogy, is feted as a reincarnation of the Black Virgin of Montserrat in the second, and bears John a son in the third while suffering from increasing mental instability. Finally, she disappears, leaving John to play his part in the defence of Barcelona at the end of the siege and then take their son to safety in Menorca. Not only is their son, Fidel, the grandson of a West African and the offspring of an Englishman, we are told that he looks nothing like his father. When Fidel asks John whether he is Menorcan (despite his skin colour and not having been born there), his father (as the narrator) says: 'Podrà ser d'on vulgui. [...] Ja pot triar la soca que més li plagui, si és robusta i arrelada, si és forta i autèntica. El que m'interessa no és d'on ve, sinó cap on va. Perquè ell és tot el meu país, i és damunt d'ell, damunt d'aquest país diminut, que s'edificarà un món nou — l'únic que podré adorar' [He will be from wherever he wants to be. [...] He can choose whichever root he likes best, as long as it is robust and well established, strong and authentic. I don't care where he comes from, but where he's going. Because he is my whole country, and upon him, upon this tiny country, a new world will be built — the only one I will be able to worship] (Bosch 2008: 728). Nevertheless, it is clear that he also represents some kind of continuity from the past. His birth allows John to understand for the first time his own mother's sacrifices in raising him (657), and gives meaning to John's life despite the defeat of the Barcelona he had fought for, and the loss of Marianna. As he says to his son in the very last line of the novel, 'John Sinclair no ha viscut debades' [John Sinclair has not lived in vain] (730). All this leaves a sense that it is not just what Fidel will become that matters, but where he came from too.

The Necessity of Sacrifice

Like Martí of *Victus* and Pere of *No s'hi enterra*, John Sinclair is sceptical about grand sentiments and bases his loyalties on personal relationships with those around him. Similarly, he is accepted by others into the fight for Barcelona on the simple premise that '*Hic domus, haec patria est*': 'Aquí hi teniu la casa, aquí hi teniu la pàtria' [Here is our home, here our country] (677). However, the second part of this statement makes no sense to him. 'El que jo veia era com nobles i plebeus, pagesos o ciutadans, rics i pobres, homes i dones, naturals i forasters, tots plegats sense distinció ja no érem més que un grapat de vides perdudes. La fatalitat ens agermanava' [It seemed to me that nobles and plebeians, peasants or city-dwellers, rich and poor, men and women, native-born or incomers, all of us without distinction, were now no more than a collection of lost souls. It was fate that brought us together] (677–78). Like Pere and Martí, he is willing to sacrifice his own life, not for a 'cause' but for the people around him (476).

The subject of sacrifice has already entered into the discussion here in various ways. Joan and Pere of *No s'hi enterra* disagree over what exactly they will sacrifice themselves for, but are equally prepared to do so. Ermengol sacrifices his physical connection with his country in order to ensure its continuity in the form of the son he carries safely to Vienna and who will eventually return to Catalonia (Clotet and de Montserrat 2012: loc. 6170). Family, nation and sacrifice go hand in hand — even if a mother has to risk giving up her young son, as we see in Andreu Martín's novel for teenagers *Cicatrius de 1714* (2013). On discovering that her son Bernat has slipped out of his bed in Badalona to find a way of warning troops in Barcelona that they are about to be attacked by sea, Amèlia is both horrified and proud of her son's daring, giving up the chance to raise the alarm and find him in favour of allowing him the time he needs to get away. 'La mare patidora havia estat desplaçada per la mare orgullosa i defensora del fill heroic' [The suffering mother had given way to the proud mother defending her heroic son] (135). Her love for her son is not contradicted by this act, but rather affirmed by it. In *1714*, Bosch paints a similar picture of wives and mothers urging their loved ones back into the heat of battle, defining in this way their own brand of feminine heroic sacrifice and a love of country that transcends personal loss (Bosch 2008: 644).

This connection between love and sacrifice is a common theme in all the novels we have examined so far. Love of family — that is, of those with whom one chooses to spend one's life — paradoxically implies the willingness to leave or lose them in order to preserve the context in which one has come to know them. If love derives from everyday closeness, as these authors suggest, then love is itself threatened when what constitutes 'the everyday' is under attack. John Sinclair links love and sacrifice explicitly in his imaginary conversation with his son on the last page of *1714*, telling him '[q]ue l'amor no em va commoure, fins que ella [Marianna] me'l va ofrenar. Que el sacrifici m'era estrany, fins que ella el va consumar' [love never moved me until she [Marianna] gave hers to me. Sacrifice was alien to me, until she consummated it] (730). Similarly, a minor character in *No s'hi enterra* attributes a (short-lived) Catalan victory to the fact that the Catalans had fought for those they love whereas Berwick's troops were just following orders (Jurado Riba 2014: loc. 3096). However, it is the story of Martí Zuviría which revolves most directly around the connection between love and sacrifice.

At the very beginning of *Victus*, Martí asks this question: 'Si el hombre es el único ser que posee una mente geométrica y racional, ¿por qué los indefensos combaten al poderoso y bien armado? ¿Por qué los pocos se oponen a los muchos y los pequeños resisten a los grandes? Yo lo sé. Por una palabra' [If man is the only being that possesses a geometrical, rational mind, why do defenceless people take on those who are powerful and well-armed? Why do the few oppose the many and the lowly resist the great? I know. Because of a word] (Sánchez Piñol 2012: loc. 58). He goes on to explain that 'la Palabra' was the answer to a question posed by his mentor, the master engineer Vauban, on his deathbed: to sum up in one word 'la defensa óptima de una plaza asediada' [the optimal defence of a besieged city] (loc. 1869). A correct answer would have validated the award of a fifth 'point' (tattooed on his arm) signifying his status as an engineer, but Martí is unable to answer and Vauban dies shortly afterward. His search for 'la Palabra' becomes a constant theme in his life, but it is not until Barcelona itself is besieged and facing its final defeat that Martí's understanding of the question shifts from the technicalities of physical defences to the realization that the answer actually lies in the people around him: 'La Palabra era eso. Esos críos, esas mujeres, esos hombres de cien orígenes distintos. Aglutinados tras el caballo de don Antonio' [This was The Word. These youngsters, these women, these men from a hundred different origins. Massed together behind Don Antonio's horse] (loc. 10597). 'La Palabra' itself is never stated, because any to be found in the dictionary, he says, would only be a pale reflection of the reality. Nevertheless, the reader might infer that the basis of 'la Palabra' is love, apparently combined with a broad range of other concepts such as family, community, pride, loyalty, sacrifice and even desperation.

The 'defensa perfecta' [perfect defence] (loc. 1876) then, does not actually result in victory in battle, but in a very different kind of 'victory': a collective transcendence of the moment of defeat. '[C]uanto más oscuro sea nuestro crepúsculo más dichoso será el amanecer de los que están por venir' [the darker our dusk, the happier the dawn of those who are still to come] (loc. 10653). As Steven Mock says (2012: 277), 'the fact that the nation continues to live on in spite of the defeat to commemorate the heroic act serves as concrete proof that those who altruistically choose suffering or death on behalf of the nation do not do so in vain'.

It is in this 'altruism' that some of the ambiguity of the idea of the imagined family emerges. These authors portray families — and therefore the nation — as relationships of choice more than blood. However, there is an unstated implication that making the choice to belong also implies a willingness to sacrifice oneself should this be necessary. Martí understands this only when a combination of Villarroel, a flashback to the dying Vauban and his own inner voice together whisper '[d]ese' [give yourself] at the moment before defeat (Sánchez Piñol 2012: loc. 10620). Similarly, the cynical Pere of No s'hi enterra spends much of the novel looking for 'alguna cosa per la qual valgui la pena lluitar' [something worth fighting for], truly finding it only in his last moments as he sacrifices himself to save the flag of Santa Eulàlia from capture (Jurado Riba 2014: locs 2211, 3685). If previously he had fought from a sense of obligation, now he gives himself willingly for a symbol of the people whose continued existence is represented first by this flag and then by his granddaughter. As Ermengol Amill puts it in Lliures o morts, in such cases 'no seria un sacrifici estèril, perquè la llavor del seu exemple acabaria germinant' [it would not be a sterile sacrifice, because the seed sown by this example would eventually sprout] (Clotet and de Montserrat 2012: loc. 5161).

Conclusion

It is clear that these contemporary authors are using the family as a metaphor for the nation, although in some of the novels this metaphor plays a more central role than in others. But this is not the ethnic model of the imagined family suggested by Lauenstein et al. (2015: 312), one that 'reifies social relations as biologically determined'. Relations in the contemporary Catalan historical novel are often anything but biologically determined, and in the case of *Victus* could hardly be said to be 'determined' in any way at all. Instead, these novelists are trying to imagine what Anderson calls 'a deep horizontal comradeship' by using the metaphor of the family as we might understand such relationships in the twenty-first century (Anderson 1991: 7). This new sense of family and community is 'linked with space rather than time; sharing the same space rather than entertaining notions of shared origins' (Hylland Eriksen 2004: 54). However, in applying this twenty-first century concept of the family to the fictionalized 'imagined family' of the Catalan nation in 1714, the authors we have examined are employing a shamelessly anachronistic perspective on both family and nation. Furthermore, the equality this implies — in contrast to the nuclear family's rigid hierarchies (Lauenstein et al. 2015: 312) — has a sting in its tail, since it means that ordinary Catalans have to be just as willing to sacrifice themselves as politicians and military leaders. In fact, this becomes something of a circular argument, given that it is the protagonists' realization of the equality and plurality of the community that is fighting alongside them that makes them willing to fight to the end themselves.

Lauenstein et al. are of course right to focus on the nuclear family and biological relations in the national anthems they use as their source material, so nothing said here calls into question their findings. Nevertheless, we also need to account for changes in conceptions of the imagined family as explored in more contemporary cultural products associated with political nationalism. Bearing in mind the (r)evolution that has taken place in both family life and the nation-state as they have been remoulded by the practices of twentieth-century global capitalism, Victoria Carrington argues (2001: 191) that '[w]hereas in traditional theorizations of family the connection between nation state and family (understood in relation to a narrow band of "normal" roles and practices) was taken for granted, this can no longer be the case'. The converse is also true: contemporary expressions of the nation-state cannot unproblematically rely on metaphors derived from a normative concept of the nuclear family. Instead, both the nation-state and the family are now 'dynamic, performative and open rather than closed and static' (195).[7] Indeed, there is perhaps another subtext related to this that can be discerned in our corpus of historical novels: the suggestion that the contemporary Catalan nation has accepted this new, inclusive reality, whereas the backward and monolithic Spanish state has not.

Like Hylland Eriksen's concept of a putative non-ethnic nation conditioned by 'space rather than time', Carrington's description of the twenty-first century family 'places emphasis on the activities and shared symbolic systems of people' rather than foundational structures, resulting in 'sociospace families' (193). However, despite this apparent emphasis on the here-and-now, the space shared by both the imagined and real family has already been moulded into a particular shape by the actions of those that came before them, as Oriol Junqueras clearly signalled when he listed the complex synchronic and diachronic ties that bind the Catalan nation together.[8] Even though these past actions can no longer dictate the membership of the present-day nation, they still retain the power to influence the actions of those that choose to belong to it. This means that the capacity for symbolic violence that Pierre Bourdieu associated with the nuclear family is still at play in the imagined national family (Carrington 2002: 49). In fact, this is perfectly clear from the messages to contemporary Catalans that these novels elicit from their exploration of the past. The nature of the ties that create the Catalan national family may have shifted, but they are still assumed to bind.

Works Cited

ANDERSON, BENEDICT. 1991. *Imagined Communities: Reflections on the Origin and Spread of Nationalism*, 2nd edn (London: Verso)

BOCCARDI, MARIADELE. 2009. *The Contemporary British Historical Novel: Representation, Nation, Empire* (Basingstoke: Palgrave Macmillan)

BOFARULL, ANTONI DE. 1993 [1862]. *L'orfaneta de Menargues o Catalunya agonitzant* (Barcelona: Laertes)

BOSCH, ALFRED. 2008. *1714* (Barcelona: Labutxaca)

BROCH, ÀLEX. 1991. *Literatura catalana dels anys vuitanta* (Barcelona: Edicions 62)

CARRINGTON, VICTORIA. 2001. 'Globalization, Family and Nation State: Reframing "Family" in New Times', *Discourse: Studies in the Cultural Politics of Education*, 22: 185–96

———. 2002. *New Times: New Families* (Dordrecht, Boston and London: Kluwer Academic Publishers)

CLOTET, JAUME, and DAVID DE MONTSERRAT. 2012. *Lliures o morts* (Barcelona: Columna)

CRAMERI, KATHRYN. 2014. *'Goodbye, Spain?' The Question of Independence for Catalonia* (Brighton: Sussex Academic Press/Cañada Blanch)

FONT, MARC. 2015. 'Acabaremos esta revolución en las urnas, donde terminan las revoluciones democráticas', *Público*, <http://www.publico.es/politica/acabaremos-revolucion-urnas-terminan-revoluciones.html> [accessed 26 February 2016]

HYLLAND ERIKSEN, THOMAS. 2004. 'Place, Kinship and the Case for Non-Ethnic Nations', *Nations and Nationalism*, 10: 49–62

———. 2010. *Ethnicity and Nationalism*, 3rd edn (London: Pluto Press)

JURADO RIBA, VÍCTOR. 2014. *No s'hi enterra cap traïdor* (Barcelona: Columna)

J. V. 2012. 'Sánchez Piñol remou el 1714', *El Punt Avui*, 11 July

KING, STEWART. 2005. *Escribir la catalanidad: lengua e identidades culturales en la narrativa contemporánea de Cataluña* (Suffolk and New York: Tamesis)

LAUENSTEIN, OLIVER, JEFFREY S. MURER, MARGARET BOOS, and STEPHEN REICHER. 2015. '"Oh Motherland I Pledge to Thee..": A Study into Nationalism, Gender and the Representation of an Imagined Family within National Anthems', *Nations and Nationalism*, 21: 309–29

MARTÍN, ANDREU. 2013. *Cicatrius de 1714* (Alzina: Bromera)

MOCK, STEVEN J. 2012. *Symbols of Defeat in the Construction of National Identity* (Cambridge: Cambridge University Press)

MORGAN, DAVID H. J. 2011. *Rethinking Family Practices* (Basingstoke: Palgrave Macmillan)

ROSSICH, ALBERT, and JORDI CORNELLÀ. 2014. *El plurilingüisme en la literatura catalana* (Bellcaire: Edicions Vitel·la)

SÁNCHEZ PIÑOL, ALBERT. 2012. *Victus* (Barcelona: La Campana)
——. 2015. *Vae Victus* (Barcelona: La Campana)
SERRAHIMA, MAURICI, and MARIA TERESA BOADA. 1996. *La novel·la històrica en la literatura catalana* (Barcelona: Publicacions de l'Abadia de Montserrat)

Notes to Chapter 4

1. See the webpage of the Institut Nova Història, <http://www.inh.cat/institut>.
2. Radio debate with Francisco Marhuenda, *Versió Estiu*, RAC1, 1 August 2012.
3. Where the Kindle edition of a book was used and no page numbers are provided, Kindle locations have been given in references.
4. See also King (2005) and Rossich and Cornellà (2014).
5. *Miquelets* were irregular troops drawn from local populations at specific times of need.
6. *Botifler* was a pejorative term used to describe Catalans who had opted to support the Bourbon cause.
7. N. B. Carrington was originally talking only about new forms of family.
8. See above.

CHAPTER 5

Oedipus and the Spanish Crown:
The Abject Imaginings of
Guillem Viladot

P. Louise Johnson

University of Sheffield

In 1995 Estanislau Torres published the unexpurgated text of an interview with the prolific and multifaceted Catalan writer, poet, and sculptor Guillem Viladot (1922–1999) which had first appeared two decades earlier, censored, in *Els escriptors catalans parlen* [Catalan Writers Speak] (1973). Viladot speaks candidly about his decision to consolidate his creative activity in Catalan, as a poet rather than literary critic, following the censorship of an article on Rafael Alberti he had written for *Labor* (Lleida, 1953–59), in 1956:[1]

> El meu lliurament a la llengua va ser furiós. Calia recuperar molt de temps perdut. Jo no havia seguit cap estudi en català, anteriorment... Era un retard que m'havia de marcar pel radicalisme que comportava. Un fet general en la meva generació, em sembla... No, ara en castellà no hi escric. No hi escric res, en absolut, i això que m'han ofert columnes temptadores... De tota manera no en faig una arma d'actitud irreductible perquè no sé si un dia el país, per manca de publicacions pròpies, ho podria necessitar. Perquè hi pot haver moments que el país ho necessiti tot, tot, absolutament tot: fins i tot que la seva cultura es difongui en castellà, que és una contradicció que no es produiria per primera vegada... Cal ser polític.

> [I threw myself passionately into the language. I had to make up for lost time. I hadn't studied in Catalan at all before... It was a delay that fed my radicalism, something quite common to my generation, I think... No, I don't write in Castilian now. Not at all, and I've been offered some attractive columns, believe me. But this isn't some unshiftable weaponized principle, because I don't know whether one day, through an absence of publications of our own, the country will need Castilian. There might be times when the country needs everything, everything, absolutely everything: even making its culture known through Castilian, which is a contradiction that's already happened... We have to be pragmatic.] (Viladot in Torres 1995: 49; original ellipses)

Viladot, like his father and grandfather before him, was a pharmacist. He studied in Barcelona, graduating in 1949, before marrying and returning to the family business in Agramunt (Lleida). Isidor Cònsul attributes the literary and cultural stagnation of the post-war and dictatorship in Lleida to the Instituto de Estudios Ilerdenses, created in 1942, accusing it of being largely and directly responsible for 'la mediocritat, el provincianisme, la irregularitat i la fossilització culturals' [mediocrity, provincialism, cultural irregularity and fossilization] (1991a: 24). The weight of this conservatism and inertia seems almost downplayed decades later as Viladot describes the shift to a militant linguistic position in defence of Catalan language and culture (Torres 1995: 49), and even to 'l'assumpció del nacionalisme' [the assimilation of nationalism] (Salvo Torres 2012: 94), but it is qualified, as we can see, by pragmatism, although this would never be substantially tested. At the same time, this pragmatism occasionally extended to his relationship with the Catalan literary establishment, provoking criticism from those who saw Viladot as a beacon of non-conformity. When, for example, *Poesia completa* [Collected Poetry] was published by Columna in 1991 with a prologue by Joaquim Molas — the very personification of the establishment — David Castillo wrote despairingly: 'La síndrome d'Estocolm sembla haver afectat un dels últims escriptors desinhibits i lliures' [Stockholm syndrome seems to have affected one of our last disinhibited and truly free writers] (1992: 46).

A lesser-known factor in Viladot's direction of linguistic and aesthetic travel in the years prior to the *Labor* incident is his correspondence and collaboration with Majorcan-language poet Bernat Vidal i Tomàs from about 1952, which included Viladot's public support for the then little-known novelist and poet Blai Bonet (see Salvo Torres 2012; Bonet's treatment of homosexual themes was highly controversial at the time). Viladot did, however, write creatively again in Castilian:[2] the 1991 novel *Joana*, for example, the sometimes tortuous interior monologue of Juana of Castile, was derived from a first-person Castilian version composed in 1987.[3] Viladot has suggested that he wrote in Castilian because that was the language of his sources, but concluded that somehow 'no funcionava' [it didn't work] (Bonada 1991: 66). One of his principal sources was psychiatrist Juan Antonio Vallejo-Nágera's *Locos egregios* [The Illustrious Insane] (1977) and *Joana* adheres closely to this overview, with notable and diverging embellishments. Viladot initially experienced difficulties locating a publisher for the novel in Catalan; in his words, '[v]a ser presentada a una de les grans editores catalanes i van dir, home, sí, està bé, però si fos una reina catalana, millor que millor. Tot plegat, que no hi va ser admesa' [it was presented to one of the big Catalan publishing houses, and they said 'yes, it's good, but it'd be much better if it were about a Catalan queen'. So that was that, they turned it down] (Bonada 1994: 75).[4] A Spanish version with the amplified title *Juana la loca* [Joanna the Mad] — a later Salvat edition added 'una mujer marcada' [a marked woman] — was eventually published in 1994. The companion volume, *Carles*, also from 1994, appeared in Castilian the following year as *Carlos, hijo y víctima de Felipe II* [Charles, Son and Victim of Philip II]. This version is undoubtedly Viladot's own (see Gutiérrez 1994), but the question of which was composed first is more fraught, and is not wholly illuminated by an anecdote concerning the author's relative lack of familiarity with the range of colloquial terms for 'penis' in Catalan, and his desire for linguistic authenticity: he credits Joan J. Vinyoles Vidal and Ramon Piqué's *Diccionari eròtic i sexual* [Dictionary of Sex and Erotica] (1989) with enriching his lexical knowledge in this area, necessitating in turn a revision of 'gran part del lèxic de *Vèrtex/zero*' [a large part of the lexis of *Vèrtex/zero*], a working title for *Carles* (Viladot 1990a: 45).[5] All versions in Catalan and Spanish have run to several editions, and critical reception, while for the most part limited to contemporaneous press notices, was overwhelmingly positive: Avel·lí Artís' review (1994) is an interesting exception, and we return to this below.[6]

Joana and *Carles* are two of Viladot's best-known works,[7] and their relative success seems to have mitigated any suspicion aroused by his focus on the history of the Kingdom of Castile, rather than on a Catalan noble. Our contention, however, is that these 'historical' novels need to be read from the perspective of resistance to male-gendered authoritarianism and oppressive structures of power in a psychoanalytic sense, rather than in the more simplistic and limited frame of a critique directed at Castile (and Spain) from Catalonia. At the same time, crucially, these two major novels cannot avoid being read as engagements with the extraordinarily persistent Black Legend of Spanish Catholic fanaticism and degeneracy,[8] for which the death of Don Carlos was a particularly potent catalyst. It is tempting to see the (re)publication of these works in both languages as a gesture of defiance from the geographical margins when confronted by a Barcelona-centric Catalan literary establishment (oft-cited, but see e.g. Johnson 2012). Josep Vallverdú has rightly emphasized Viladot's creative engagement with his 'fantasmes' [ghosts/ phantasms] (2004), articulated through an attitude of resistance or revolt in the face of Francoist hypocrisy and falseness, a complicit Church, and later, as he explores psychoanalysis in greater detail, through the Oedipal Father. Viladot's publicly stated dislike of the term 'historical' to refer to these novels,[9] while he nevertheless claims to respect their historical contexts, answers to a need to exalt what is resolutely human in the abandonment each protagonist suffers, at the hands of their literal and figurative fathers.

Under Francoism — and of course in earlier centuries — the body had been, in Viladot's words, 'la bandera negra de la societat' [society's flag of resistance], which 'una Església triomfant i patrocinadora d'un animisme ultrancer [...] atiava a ser dominada, assetjada'; '[per ser] responsable del pecat, de totes les misèries humanes' [a triumphant Church, championing an extreme form of animism [...] urged should be dominated and overcome; [because it is] responsible for sin, for all human miseries] (1981: 67). The Church's subordination of the body to the soul, depicted in the novelistic account of Joana and Carles' subjugation variously through imprisonment, rape, medical neglect, or gangrene and putrefaction, is recovered and raised up as an alternative standard of defiance, and in its diminishment and disintegration, the flesh takes on a more positive valence, or at least the threat of non-containment. Both novels, *Carles* in particular, move beyond the Oedipal. As Elizabeth Grosz writes,

> body fluids flow, they seep, they infiltrate; their control is a matter of vigilance, never guaranteed. In this sense, they betray a certain irreducible materiality; they

assert the priority of the body over subjectivity [...] They force megalomaniacal
aspirations to earth, refusing consciousness its supremacy. (1994: 194)

In *Joana* and in *Carles*, the body is both literal — as are its torments — and metaphorical, a *corpus mysticum* aligned with a sense of nationhood, or state, which
is discomposed by the very existence of the uncrowned queen (Juana) and the
errant, malformed prince (Don Carlos).[10] In their own materiality, and as the
waste products of a body politic which engenders them only then to seek their
containment and invisibility in lieu of expulsion, Joana and Carles become aligned
with defilement, which, as Julia Kristeva argues, is 'a variant of abjection' (1982: 68).
Salvo Torres had identified 'un realisme sovint escatològic' [an often scatological
realism] in Viladot's poetics as early as the 1950s (2012: 93), and it is clear that as
the writer's formal interest in psychoanalytic culture developed from the 1970s,
the scatological and excremental was reframed, and cast symbolically, as well as for
its realist immediacy. We must too, it seems, read Viladot as a thorn in the side of
cultural and political hegemony, as a cry for communication in the face of isolation
and reclusion at the periphery.

Viladot met Lleida psychologist Marta Trepat Secanell after the publication of
Ricard (1977), and the enduring friendship that developed was central in allowing
the author to explore his creative interest in different forms of psychoanalysis which
prior to *Ricard* he considered to have been merely, but strongly, intuitive:[11] he writes
of the novel that 'ja és una novel·la d'estructura lacaniana, perquè hi ha la dramàtica
psicoanalítica dels miralls, però és encara un procés psicoanalític intuïtiu. A *L'amo*
[The Master], en canvi, ja tenim una novel·la volgudament psicoanalítica' [the novel
already reveals Lacanian structuring, because the psychoanalytic drama of mirrors is
present, but the psychoanalytic process is still intuitive. In *L'amo*, by contrast, we have
a consciously psychoanalytic novel] (in Rendé 1982: 21).[12] Margalida Pons (amongst
others)[13] has also remarked on this point of transition, and of *Discurs horitzontal:
anàlisi sexual d'una dona* [Horizontal Discourse: Sexual Analysis of a Woman] (1982),
a work notable for its unorthodox textual layout, like *Ricard*, she comments: 'La
representació del procés psicoanalític no té, en aquest cas, vincles directes amb el
textualisme, sinó més aviat amb una assumpció personal de l'obra de Freud i Lacan
com a via d'exploració del jo' [The representation of the psychoanalytic process
doesn't in this case have direct links with textualism, but rather with the personal
assimilation of Freud and Lacan's work as a means of exploring the self] (Pons 2007:
45). There is no significant, or even minor, study of how Viladot's engagement
with psychoanalysis evolves across his diverse creative production (and this would
be an enormous task), but as Pons and of course Viladot himself have clarified, it
responds to a personal imperative rather than to fashion, the subject of extensive
reading, conversations and lectures: the naming and refinement of an approach
operative before 1977. The psychoanalytic models Viladot adopts and subsequently
confronts tend to be male-oriented and often Freudian, although Lacanian dramas
of mirroring are also prominent, as the author himself indicates (above, but see
especially *Ruth*, 2000).[14]

When *Carles* was published in 1994, Lluís Bonada asked the author: 'Aneu,
potser, a la recerca de personatges tarats de la monarquia castellana?' [So are you

specifically interested in 'damaged' figures from the Castilian monarchy?]. Viladot swerves the reference to Castile and responds: 'No són tarats en el sentit de mancats. Són intel·ligents però creen neures, tírries i fòbies. Joana no era pas boja. Va ser un instrument' [They're not damaged in the sense of lacking. They're intelligent but they arouse strong reactions, frenzies, phobias. Joana wasn't mad. She was an instrument]. Of *Carles* specifically, he explains: 'és un intent per demostrar fins on pot arribar el poder per anul·lar la personalitat' [it's an attempt to show how far power will go to obliterate the personality] (Bonada 1994: 75). Thus the problem for Viladot is power, however constituted, and if he rejects the designation 'historical' for these works, it is because, by his own rationale, he extracts his characters from history in order to distil from them what may be contemporary and universal, as Isidor Cònsul observes. Viladot remarks teasingly on giving up the idea of working painstakingly through the General Archive of Simancas — the principal archive of the Spanish Monarchy and project of Felipe II — travelling instead through Castile and León to Tordesillas, where Juana, daughter of Fernando of Aragon and Isabel of Castile, was confined from 1509 until her death in 1555 (Bonada 1991: 66). In reality, and as Magda Gutiérrez (1994: 37) clarifies in an interview with Viladot, the extensive reading the author carried out for *Joana* also served him for *Carles*. Viladot's assertion that the two works 'només tenen en comú la documentació aportada per múltiples lectures sobre Carles I i Felip II' [only have in common the documentation compiled from multiple readings on Carles I and Felip II] is questionable, however, and the novels need to be seen as part of a similar excremental trajectory.

Joana

The literary, artistic, visual and cinematic tradition surrounding the figure of Juana is extensive, and so too is the accompanying scholarly apparatus. María A. Gómez, Santiago Juan-Navarro and Phyllis Zatlin (2008: 252–54) list almost sixty creative reinterpretations of Juana's life between 1825 and 2008,[15] including Viladot's novel, the majority of which address the supposed necrophilic attraction to her husband Philip's corpse, and the persistent attribution of 'madness', the fact of which is disputed by fewer than those who merely debate the causes and underlying pathology. Bethany Aram points out that 'the proprietary queen who never ruled Castile or Aragon offers insights into the role of legend in Spanish history. Juana's image — as projected by others and by the queen herself — responded to concrete, shifting political ends' (2008: 33). In this sense, Juana, like her great-grandson Don Carlos a century later, provided material for the English and Dutch Black Legend (see David R. George 2008);[16] while as the 'last true Spanish monarch, a hinge at a key historical junction, albeit a problematic one', she played counterpoint to Isabel II in Romantic depictions of Spanish history, 'a visual landscape of female passivity and helplessness more in accordance with the values of the Restoration of a Spanish monarchy still firmly rooted in traditional patterns' (Soliño 2008: 177, 193). Scholarship on Juana as a cultural phenomenon is extensive, and we can only indicate trends here. In the twentieth-century context, for example, Jo Labanyi alerts us to the potential for public unease at the time of the social, political and military crisis of 1917, when the role of Santa Juana de Castilla in Galdós' play of the same name was taken by Catalan actress Margarida Xirgu.[17] Phyllis Zatlin sees the Francoist regime's 'efforts to view Juana of Castile as willingly taking refuge from a sinful world [...] as integration propaganda because they lead the spectator to set aside any concerns he or she may have had about the queen's imprisonment' (2008: 170). Santiago Juan-Navarro talks in similar terms about the regime's appropriation of the nationalistic legend for propagandistic purposes through the medium of the CIFESA film studio, and in particular Juan de Orduña's *Locura de amor*, from 1948 (2008: 210–27). As María Donapetry observes, the film intended to present the Spanish viewing public with 'una España coherente, atosigada por los malvados extranjeros que envidian siempre la nobleza natural del pueblo español' [a coherent Spain, poisoned by evil foreigners who have always envied the natural nobility of the Spanish people] (2005: 148).

Thus, the susceptibility of Juana to politicization by writers, regimes and recipients (readers, spectators) is well established, and it is difficult to resist this seduction in the case of Viladot's work, not least in light of his own linguistic and cultural trajectory. However, rather than attempt to situate *Joana* and *Carles* any more precisely in their respective cultural traditions, this essay works instead within the context of Viladot's aesthetics, characterized by an Oedipal discourse 'amb un Edip mal resolt' [with a badly resolved Oedipus] (Capdevila 1991: 29), an evolving interest in psychoanalysis in both cultural theory and clinical practice, and a self-reflective imperative. For example, in his 1991 poetic manifesto, the 'Guia gnòstica o de la perversió...' [Gnostic Guide, or Guide to Perversion...], Viladot defines '[n]ovel·la' as the 'escenificació en dues-centes pàgines d'un deliri per arribar al coneixement de la pròpia follia' [performance in two hundred pages of a delirious effort to attain knowledge of one's own madness] (58). 'Follia' here seems to be synonymous with 'fantasma' in Viladot's imaginary, the 'killing' of which is the condition for, and of, artistic creation. In other words, the novel is partly the achievement of capture, interrogation and subjection of unconscious phantasies, themselves the unresolved remainders of desire.

Joana, I want to suggest, is revealing for the aforementioned historical 'embellishments', and as a testing ground for the more successfully realized *Carles*. *Joana*'s originality, and the dimension most often lauded by critics, lies in the cross-gendered first-person narration which crucially supplies a privileged vantage point on and from a figure whom history has variously silenced, traduced and reinvented. At the same time, the absence of a contrapuntal voice — present in *Carles* — can seem restrictive. While Joana as a character shows borderline-anachronistic awareness of her mental instability, from a twenty-first century perspective much of her untoward behaviour comes across as eccentric, erratic or merely justifiably angry in response both to the philandering of her beloved husband, Philip the Handsome, and to her impotence before the Machiavellian dealings of first her husband, then her father (Fernando of Aragon), later Cardinal Cisneros, and finally her son, Carlos I of Spain (Carlos V, Holy Roman Emperor): Joana is in all aspects of her life subordinated to, when not consubstantial with, 'reason of state' (the doctrine thus named is anachronistic in the novel).[18] What Vallejo-Nágera describes as the 'relación pasional de reconciliaciones y rupturas alternantes' [a passionate relationship of alternating break-ups and reconciliations] (1977: 70) with her husband is replicated in the novel, and lends an almost metronomic rhythm to the first part of her history, while after his death, the necrophilic legend of Juana's attachment to the corpse of Philip is balanced to a degree in Viladot's account by the compensatory sexual encounters she enjoys with her new stepmother, Germaine de Foix (*Joana*: 132–35). These occasion a fleeting moment of regret that she had not taken advantage of more such opportunities with both women and men in Flanders (*Joana*: 135).[19] The second embellishment seems to be prompted by Vallejo-Nágera on Juana's first 'jailer' in Tordesillas, Luis Ferrer, who justifies '"haber usado de violencia" con la Reina ocasionalmente, "para preservarle la vida, pues se negaba a tomar alimento". En estas huelgas de hambre se llegó a "darle cuerda", cuyo significado no se especifica, pero tiene siniestra resonancia' ['having used violence' with the Queen occasionally, 'to save her life, because she refused to eat'. In these hunger strikes he would encourage her, the meaning of which isn't clear, but it has sinister resonance] (1977: 83). In Viladot's novel, Joana rejects Ferrer's sexual advances and is subject to seven years of beatings as a consequence, but the treatment she receives later at the hands of Don Bernardo Sandoval y Rojas, Marquis of Denia, charged with the queen's 'security', is even more brutal: Joana almost emasculates Denia during fellatio in an apparently faked seduction, which in turn occasions her public whipping and punishment rape, and a different kind of physical relationship which centuries later might be seen as co-dependent and sadomasochistic, or, recalling Castillo (1992: 46), indicative of Stockholm syndrome:

> Després de tantes calamitats, quan el temps ha deixat de barallar-se amb mi en forma de malsons, penso que el marquès de Dènia i jo érem, d'una forma o altra, amants, i que aquella violència, aquella mena d'animalitat, aquell domini irracional de l'un sobre l'altre, s'havia transformat en un acte d'amor que anava més enllà de nosaltres mateixos i de les nostres voluntats.

> [After so many disasters, when time had ceased its quarrel with me in the form of nightmares, I think the Marquis of Denia and I were, one way or another, lovers, and that the violence, the animality, the irrational dominion of one over the other, had become an act of love which went beyond us and our conscious wills.] (174)

This nadir is referred to by Joana as the 'desnonament d'amor' [eviction of love] (175). 'Desnonament' is a term Viladot uses frequently to refer to alienation, abjection and other processes of dehumanization, and its corollary is Joana's place in the body politic, where she becomes not merely marginal, but waste: 'A cops, quan m'arriba el ventet del riu, i la seva atmosfera puja a aquest castell, penso que allò que es mou és l'ànima del pare que em bressola, que m'amanyaga, que m'enlaira cap a un tron d'amor, i que, *en ser dalt de tot, renega de mi i m'excreta*' [Sometimes, when the river breeze reaches me, when its air rises to this castle, I imagine that what moves is the soul of my father who cradles me, nuzzles me, lifts me up to a throne of love, and when we are above everything, rejects me and shits me out] (105; emphasis added). Joana is literally the waste product of the body politic, a fate which will be inherited and magnified through Hapsburg in-breeding, by her great-grandson Don Carlos. Inverting the geopolitical reality in order to highlight her own subordination and sidelining from power, Joana depicts Castile as a colony of Flanders, subject to her son's will (159), and Viladot thus underlines her sense of abandonment by male authority through a very modern criticism of the male-gendered Divine. The Queen laments bitterly, 'Déu, ¿per què de tant en tant no t'encarnes en el cos d'una dona?' [Why cannot God, from time to time, become Woman?], and bemoans the fate of her devout *King*dom, which is also her own fate: 'Gràcies, Senyor. La nostra catoliquíssima Castella no t'ha mogut la misericòrdia. *Merda!'* [Thank you, Lord. You have shown our so very catholic Castile no mercy. Shit!] (160; emphasis added).[20] This exclamation exemplifies the inherent tension and unresolvability of Joana's situation both symbolically and in more immediate terms, caught as she is between her father's and later son's desire for her expulsion from the body politic, and the necessity of her reclusion (containment). Referring to Mary Douglas's essay 'Pollution' (1968; erroneously given as 1960), Pops writes that where shit is concerned, '[t]he crucial issue [...] is the reduction of dissonance in the preservation of boundary' (in 1982: 50). Joana is at the bodily and political boundary, but if she escapes containment and exceeds that boundary (if the body is purged) she will constitute a different order of threat: '[S]hit, the first extension of the self, is also the first instancing of the other' (Pops 1982: 50). As Marta Segarra reminds us, a conventional binarism affecting representations of the feminine and masculine renders the former '*agujereado y penetrable*' [full of holes and penetrable], and the latter '*entero* (o intacto, que es el sentido etimológico de "entero") e *impermeable*' [whole/entire (or intact, which is the etymological sense of 'entire') and impermeable] (2014: 91; original emphasis). Thus the 'excretion' of Joana calls up the anus and permeability of the father's body and the body politic, while abjection from the body opens up the possibility of penetration from without. Moreover, as Kristeva so acutely observes, '[e]xcrement and its equivalents (decay, infection, disease, corpse, etc.) stand for the danger to identity that comes from without: the ego threatened by the non-ego, society threatened by its outside, life by death' (1982: 71).

Viladot's reimagining of the (hi)story of Don Carlos takes the excremental a step further, to its logical extension: to coprophilia and cannibalism, since from its position of liminality, figurative shit (Carles) has no recourse but to consume itself, which Carles does indeed do. Seen another way, what we witness, following Deleuze and Guattari (in Segarra 2014: 97), is 'el "devenir agujero", un proceso que se asimila a la "desterritorialización" del cuerpo, la pérdida de sus referencias, marcas y fronteras, que le dan un sentido y una identidad' [the 'becoming hole', a process which assimilates to the 'deterritorialization' of the body, the loss of its references, frames and frontiers, which give it meaning and identity]. For Segarra, 'el colmo de la abyección es el cadáver que se descompone, porque todavía es y a la vez ya no es un cuerpo, pues pierde su carácter compacto [and therefore 'masculine'] al disolverse en la materia orgánica adyacente' [the pinnacle of abjection is the decomposing body, because it is still, and at the same time, no longer, a body, since it loses its compact [and therefore 'masculine'] character as it dissolves in the adjacent organic matter] (2014: 89). In Carles' case, he becomes increasingly 'perforated', feminine, and eventually something akin to a living corpse, breaking down into its constitutive liquids (re*juiced* to his fluids, we might say). But the textual revelling in this liquid horror, accompanied by an oral/anal eroticism which stands up in spite of Carles' impoverished manliness (understood in conventional terms), suggests a greater level of defiance to power than the relation of Joana's history can muster, as we will now see.

Carles

Carles, Viladot's fictionalization of the life of Don Carlos of Austria (1545–1568), son and heir of Philip II, is narrated in the first person by Sòcrates Laína de Torrebermeja i Negrete de Casaldàguila, a fictitious character of aristocratic descent who mediates the space between Carles and his household in the hybrid role of confidante, archetypal court dwarf, 'groom of the stool' and general factotum. Previously, and following the imprisonment of Sòcrates' father by the Inquisition as an Erasmian,[21] his mother had turned to prostitution to secure a living and Sòcrates himself entered service, eventually finding himself in the intimate employ of Prince (and later King) Felipe II of Spain. These scene-setting events are recounted without pathos, and the mode is Rabelaisian and celebratory, finding ideal subjects in the already caricatured figure of Sòcrates, whose misshapen physique, keen intellect and wit are extolled in the first of twenty-six 'plecs' (sections or chapters),[22] and in the ultimately less fortunate person of Carles/Don Carlos, who has been characterized by historians and propagandists as 'contrahecho, rebelde y sádico' [misshapen, rebellious and sadistic] (Aldea Vaquero 2003: 72). As F. Xavier Dilla observes, 'el bufó ens planta davant la figura mancada sexualment, familiarment i políticament del jove hereu i n'actua sovint com a substitut o doble, gairebé com una narcisística imatge familiar' [the buffoon positions us before the figure of the young heir who is lacking in sexual, family and political terms, and often acts as his substitute or double, almost as a familiar, narcissistic image] (1994: 72).

The subtitle of the Spanish version, 'hijo y víctima de Felipe II' [son and victim of Felipe II], foregrounds both Carlos' blaming of his father for his physical and psychological shortcomings, and the co-option by foreign reporters for political purposes of Carlos' disputed death, feeding the Black Legend.[23] The Spanish version also reproduces a schematic genealogy for Carlos not present in the original, contains a different epigraph and names the narrator 'Pedrillo', as well as incorporating numerous textual changes that remain to be examined.[24] What brief critical mention exists tends to focus on the sexual, autoerotic activities of the two protagonists, and their abject matters. Oriol Vergés, for example, refers to 'passages that horrify as much as by the harshness of the scenes they recreate as by the crudeness of their language', and considers that Viladot 'does not flinch from a description of raw details of a coprophilia scene between the jester and the prince that verges on pornography' (1995: 83). Artís takes issue, simplistically, with the novel's structuring around the castration complex ('Com es pot continuar parlant de castració quan, de fet, ha desaparegut la institució repressiva?' [How can one continue talking of castration when, in reality, the repressive institution has disappeared?]) and sees the tragedy of the protagonist rather in the 'absence' (surely inaccessibility?) of the father. He comments that '[s]i la censura encara existís, el llapis vermell hauria fet estralls en aquest text' on account of its being, in his view, 'gairebé injuri[ó]s', a fact which 'en una primera lectura, el desvirtua' [if we were still subject to censorship, this text would have been decimated by red pencil, on account of its being almost injurious, a fact which debases it on a first reading] (1994: 51). The tone of affront continues in Gerardo Moreno Espinosa's splenetic survey of historical and biographical sources on Don Carlos whose authors he refuses to name.[25] He chides one writer for ascribing homosexual proclivities to the Prince and suggests that he might have been 'inspired' by Viladot's novel, which he later refers to as 'esperpéntic[a]' [grotesque] (loc. 483):

> Este escritor, para rematar la fragilidad del infante [...], no se recata en censurar, proyectándose hacia una época más avanzada, 'que se acentuaban los síntomas de su demencia, manifiesta en extravíos sexuales y en sadismo'. Desconozco en qué fuentes ha bebido el redactor de estas líneas para sustentar, con estilo tan incisivo, que el príncipe podía ser homosexual o un sádico, salvo que tuviese facultades supranormales y hubiese intuido el contenido del *volumen de ficción elaborado por Guillem Viladot (1995) y en cuyas páginas se vierten, entre patéticas y deslenguadas procacidades, un sinfín de escabrosas escenas entre el bufón Pedrillo (Pedro Laína de Torrebermeja y Negrete de Casaldáguila) y su amo.*

> [This writer has no qualms about magnifying the fragility of the Infante [...], in critical comments reminiscent of a more modern era, saying that 'the symptoms of his demented state, evident in his sexual excesses and sadism, were pronounced'. I am unaware of the sources the writer of these lines has consulted to allow him to maintain so incisively that the prince might be homosexual or a sadist, unless he has supernatural faculties or has intuited the content of a *volume of fiction by Guillem Viladot (1995), in the pages of which we find, amongst pathetic and foul-mouthed obscenities, endless salacious scenes between the fool Pedro and his master.*]
> (Moreno Espinosa, loc. 236–41; emphasis added)

Moreno Espinosa cites 'Federico Baodero' (Federigo Badoaro, Venetian ambassador), to establish that Carlos at twelve years old (1557) was 'muy inclinado hacia las mujeres, a despecho de sus años' [very fond of women, in spite of his years] (loc. 698), but admits that the Venetian would have relied on second-hand accounts. Carlos's childhood attachment to his aunt, Juana (daughter of Charles V), and the affection in which he reportedly held Isabel de Valois, is well-known: Isabel was to have been married to Carlos, but instead became his father's third wife.[26] In Viladot's retelling, Carles holds Isabel in the highest regard and blames his father for prematurely deflowering her, as well, of course, for stealing her from him. Moreno Espinosa's low opinion of the novel notwithstanding, only a superficial and selective reading could insist on the 'homosexuality' of the Prince. Other historical commentators and propagandists made much of Carlos' reputed misogyny, as evidenced presumably by his reported aggressive behaviour towards women, and in this sense, the *Mémoires de Messire Pierre de Bordeille, seigneur de Brantôme* [Memoirs of Monsieur Pierre de Bordeille, Lord of Brantôme] (1666) are a case in point (see García Cárcel 2001: 17).

As in *Joana*, Viladot is broadly faithful to key historical and/or anecdotal events familiar to us from the vast literature available on the subject. To a greater extent than *Joana*, however, *Carles* invites consideration of glorious, corporeal excess in the frame of Kristeva's *Powers of Horror*, centred on the Prince. His complex and shifting relationship with the fictional Sòcrates makes possible a kind of split-Oedipal structuring that implicates both protagonists in parricidal desire and mother–son incest, a motif further developed from *Joana*. This endogamic patterning is reinforced by what I see as Viladot's *overflowing* depiction and, in particular, his focus on the ambiguous or *exiguous* genitalia of the heir to the Spanish throne, which brings into the frame, and partially conflates, the figures of both Don Carlos of Austria, son of Felipe II (our present focus), and Carlos II (1661–1700), last of the Hapsburgs, whose death without an heir in 1700 unleashed the War of the Spanish Succession. In January 2015, *ABC* newspaper cited a coefficient of consanguinity for Carlos of Austria of 0.211% ('casi el mismo que resulta de una unión entre hermanos' [almost the same as from a union between brother and sister]), below only Carlos II at 0.254% (Cervera 2015). Researchers in Álava and Lleida have concluded that Carlos II suffered 'un estado intersexual con genitales ambiguos [...] fruto de una reiterada política matrimonial endogámica' [an intersex state with ambiguous genitalia [...] the result of a long-standing policy of endogamy] (García-Escudero López et al. 2009: 179), and this characteristic already presents in the fictional depiction of his ancestor, as Sòcrates explains in *Carles*, with a certain levity:

> En trobar-se la criatura fora del tot, el metge de cambra li examinà el genitori, com si la resta del cos no valgués la pena, per saber com s'havia format l'infant. Davant la penjarolla que se li veia entre les cames, a la part baixa del ventre, i pel seu aspecte tan minso, el galè restà dubitatiu. Una llarga estona es rascà la calba, que tenia groga de tant pensar a les fosques; al final, en deduir que allò, encara que minúscul, només podia ser un carall, engegà a córrer per dur la notícia a Don Felip.

> [When the baby emerged fully, the doctor examined its genitals, as though the rest of its body was unimportant, to see how well-formed it was. Before the insignificant dangle of flesh visible between his legs at the lower part of his abdomen, the physician hesitated. For a long time he scratched his bald patch, yellow from so much thinking in the dark; finally, deducing that even though minuscule, it could only be a willy, he hurried away to convey the news to Don Felip.] (*Carles*: 27)

According to Moreno Espinosa, Adam von Dietrichstein, Austrian ambassador to the Court of Felipe II, alludes to widespread suspicions that Carlos, at the age of almost nineteen, 'no ha copulado con mujeres y que, cuando se comenta la cuestión delante de él, se muestra firme en su convencimiento de mantenerse casto y entregado a quien vaya a ser su esposa, por encima de que se burlen de su integridad y le atribuyan condición de eunuco' [he has not copulated with women and that, when the matter is raised with him, he is firmly committed to chastity, sworn to whoever becomes his wife, no matter that his physical integrity is mocked and he is believed to be a eunuch] (loc. 1077; see also locs 1798, 1803). Whether veiling impotency or exalting chastity, the conjecture surrounding Carlos's ability to bear issue anticipates the genealogical redundancy of Carlos II. More importantly, it looks backwards in the blame attached by the Prince to his father, the King (see below), for his incompleteness.

Carles's attitude of revolt, his anguished, angry and near-demented outbursts, lack any kind of counterpoint in guilt. Their articulation and performance are often scatological. Viladot presents an interpretation of Carles as profoundly and ontologically at odds with the Inquisition, both as a betrayal of Christianity, and as an extension of his father's brutal authority. Returning from an *auto de fe*, Carles tears out the pages of his Bible, tramples on it and, mimicking the defilement that he has just witnessed, first pisses and then shits on it: 'La veritat del Nostre Senyor Jesucrist ha estat vençuda, humiliada, escarnida, derrotada. El rei, el meu pare, s'ha cagat damunt seu davant els nassos de tothom. Treu-me les calces! Ara vull ser jo qui es cagui damunt el llibre sant' [The truth of Our Lord Jesus Christ has been vanquished, humiliated, derided, defeated. The King, my father, has shat on it in full sight. Remove my underwear! Now I want to be the one who shits on the holy book] (*Carles*: 48).[27] This shift from rhetorical to literal defecation and material excrement, ends in shit as salvation: 'La merda, Sòcrates, és la veritat. El foc la dissimula tot cremant-la. Aquesta és la diferència. Però ai d'aquells que prefereixen la crucifixió del foc a la salvació de la merda!' [Shit, Sòcrates, is truth. Fire conceals shit even while burning it. That's the difference. But pity those who prefer the crucifixion of fire to the salvation of shit!] (*Carles*: 48). Shit is then a positive force, life-affirming (while there is still life) and liberating; it is elemental and omnipresent, a political counter to the consuming flames of tyranny: Carles asks '[é]s que els poderosos no saben què fer amb el foc que els consumeix?' [don't the powerful know what to do with the fire that consumes them?] (48). We are reminded of Gilbert & George's virtually contemporaneous representation in *Shitty* 'of an 11-foot-tall crucifix constructed of excrement [which] takes the usual art-world expression of abjection and abnegation to a new level of strangeness' (Duncan 2008: 176). In *Carles*, the temporary co-opting of abject matter seems to be a coping strategy, as though embracing the abject, bringing it back into the system, is a further gesture of defiance. The Prince's rants become progressively incoherent in a movement that looks forward to the structuring of Viladot's epistolary novel *Ruth* (2000). These episodes of excitement, metaphorical ejaculation and deflation to a state of calm or sleep stand in place of literal sexual potency in the text, whose very pacing seems to replicate the climax and anti-climax of arousal and orgasm.

Carles can be read productively alongside Gilbert & George's 1994 *Naked Shit Pictures*, and also *The Fundamental Pictures* of 1996, in their exposition of naked mortality.[28] As Duncan notes, '[i]n the body-fluid and shit works, they [G&G] bring us face-to-face with the universal realities of flesh, unacknowledged in everyday culture and society' (2008: 177). This, at the very least, we can say of Viladot's *Carles* too. Natalie Daniel-Risacher has called the duo of Gilbert & George 'an amorous dialectic': a fusion (or synthesis, presumably) rather than complementarity. Referring to the fantasy element of certain works, she comments:

> Through their capacity to laugh at themselves and by placing themselves in deliberately absurd or ludicrous situations, the artists break obvious conformism. The repetition of gestures or the reduplication of the presence are comic forces which have always been abundantly used in the theatre, literature or the circus (Don Quixote and Sancho Panza, Bouvard and Pécuchet [...]). (1998: 24)[29]

Cüneyt Çakirlar similarly observes that in Gilbert & George '[t]he funny is confused with the serious', their 'pastiche of gender, their performance of a self-embarrassing, self-shaming masculinity, operat[ing] in similar multifaceted layers of ambiguity and aporia, parody and seriousness' (2011: 92). The confrontational aspect of *Carles*, its scatological and remarkably matter-of-fact revelry in eroticism, cannibalism (Carles wants to know what his flesh tastes like, and Sòcrates dutifully bites and eats a piece of his ear [99]), and bestiality (Sòcrates has to supply a goat to satisfy a client who is kept waiting by his mother), seems to have acted as a brake on criticism (Artís suggests humourlessly that Viladot is disrespectful of Don Carlos and castigates the author for his 'impertinències i grolleries sense límit' [limitless impertinences and vulgarity] [1994: 51]). We need in fact to ask what the role of this taboo dimension is in the dynamic of the Carles and Sòcrates duo, and what the interposition of Sòcrates achieves in the fictionalizing of one of the Spanish monarchy's most contested episodes, namely, the imprisonment and subsequent death of Carlos in 1568. Janet Ravenscroft is helpful in this latter regard, as she explains that '[o]ne of the dwarf's most important roles was to affirm a lesser degree of aberration from the idealized body in their masters by their own physical imperfections' (2006: 32).

The uncomfortable but humanizing absurdity of Sòcrates' narration is structured around moments of bathos that interrupt the young Prince's struggle with the seemingly irresolvable exile from his father, and therefore also from a role model or measure of his own manhood, which translates into a logic of hatred: if my father does not love me, he must hate me, and therefore I must hate my father (*Carles*: 42). But I lack a penis (I am castrated) and cannot rise against him (70): 'Arribarà un dia que destronaré el meu pare. Sòcrates, qui és el meu pare? On és? Com és? [...] Quan arribi l'hora de destronar-lo, a qui enderrocaré? A un fantasma?' [The day will come when I dethrone my father. Sòcrates, who is my father? Where is he? What is he like? [...] When the time comes to dethrone him, who will I dethrone? A ghost?] (42). Carles' aporetic despair only later gives way to a conspiratorial fantasy in which he will seek alliance with the rebellious nobles of Flanders to usurp his father's throne in this part of the empire; the more immediate relief plays out in intimate, physical contact with Sòcrates whereby the Prince's abject masculinity is supplemented by the well-endowed but otherwise similarly misshapen servant, who stands variously as slave, shit, guardian, dog and even putative father, in relation to his master. As the following fragments illustrate, and in line with the split structuring wherein one character compensates for the other's defects, the functions are often interchangeable:

> Tu ets encara més lleig que jo, de fet, ets una merda; a cops no sé si matar-te o prendre't per pare. Serà millor que siguis el meu guardià, si bé un home tan petit com tu i sense armes, què pot guardar? Jo sóc una altra merda i, per tant, no necessites gran cosa per ser-ne guardià i respectar-la.

> [You're even uglier than I am, you're a shit; sometimes I don't know whether to kill you or adopt you as my father. Better you were my guardian, but what can you guard, being so small and unarmed? I'm just more shit, so you don't need much to be its guardian and respect it.] (*Carles*: 37)

> Tu em diràs 'senyor' perquè jo sóc el teu amo i tu el meu gos, la meva merda, i jo la merda del meu Sòcrates.

> [You will call me 'lord' because I am your master and you are my dog, my shit, and I am the shit of my Socrates.] (*Carles*: 37)

> 'Es que la teva és més grossa?' [...] Si jo no em puc envanir de les meves penjarolles, almenys podré presumir de les teves...' [...] I dit això, s'ajupí i me les petonejà.

> [And so is yours bigger? [...] If I can't boast about my own crown jewels, at least I can show off yours... [...] And saying that, he crouched down and kissed them.] (*Carles*: 38)

> Merda hauria menjat del meu don Carles de l'ànima si en fer-ho hagués aconseguit salut per a ell.

> [I would have eaten my dear don Carles' shit if in doing so I could have made him well.] (*Carles*: 69)

> [V]aig apropar-me al príncep i vaig començar a xumar-li la xulina que, sigui dit de passada, fetia a merda i pixats podrits, però com que sabia que era el més bo que li donava en aquesta vida, m'hi vaig aplicar amb llavis suaus i llengua humida. Mentrestant, amb una mà jo em manipulava la meva perquè, arribada l'hora del gaudi, el meu amo la pogués engrapar i fruir de l'abundor espessa que en sortia, amb la il·lusió que aquell gènere tan ric era seu i, amb la calidesa i textura, pogués somiar que engendrava princeses i corones.

> [I went up to the prince and started sucking his member which, incidentally, stank of shit and putrid piss, but because I knew it was what gave him most pleasure in this life, I applied myself with soft lips and moist tongue. Meanwhile, with one hand I stroked my own, so that when it came to the moment of truth, my master could grasp it and enjoy the thick abundance that issued forth, under the illusion that this rich seed were his and, with its warmth and consistency, could dream that he was begetting princesses and monarchs.] (*Carles*: 132)

Shit slips effortlessly between the metaphorical and material, performing a kind of ubiquitous stickiness in the text, as inerasable as the Black Legend itself. Carles' status with regard to the figurative, as well as literal royal body, is unavoidably excremental, and the relation of excess materializes his abjection. He writes in a treasonous letter to the King that '[j]o no sóc jo. Els meus dits no són els meus dits. Els meus peus no són els meus peus' [I am not me. My fingers are not my fingers.

My feet are not my feet] (*Carles*: 146). The Lorquian resonances here reinforce a further expression of 'desnonament' and abjection. The humour and revelry that characterize Sòcrates' account of his service prior to the head injury suffered by the Prince as he is said to have hurried to a tryst with the daughter of the gate-keeper,[30] loses its force as the young Prince fights for his survival, eventually undergoing trepanation. The richly orificed Carlos is further 'perforated' by celebrated Flemish physician Andreas Vesalius, who drains abscesses from beneath his eyelids, restoring his sight and, in Viladot's re-telling, saving the Prince's life.[31] In the novel as a whole, these 'sucs de molta fetor i de colors insans' [fetid and unhealthily coloured juices] (93) mingle with the myriad fluids and semi-fluids into which the narrative presence of the royal body begins to dissolve, its contours becoming obscured: the 'desterritorialización del cuerpo' [deterritorialization of the body] that Segarra discusses. Absent from this scheme is, of course, the Prince's own seminal fluid, until in a final death agony he ejaculates weakly, calling out for his father.

Despite his parricidal desires (in Viladot's novel), Carles does not kill his father, and instead historians dispute whether Felipe II's actions to control his son's treacherous tendencies might have had a role in his death. The incest motif, however, is more marked: on the one hand is Carles' devotion to Elizabeth of Valois, his stepmother, a relationship dramatized by Friedrich Schiller amongst others (*Don Karlos, Infant von Spanien*, written between 1783 and 1787), and which the loyal Sòcrates insists is a 'pure friendship' (133–34). On the other hand, Sòcrates' one-off incestuous encounter with his own mother ('fotre's la pròpia mare és la cosa més bona d'aquest món' [fucking one's own mother is the best thing in the world] [147–48]) has a proxy function for Carles, who asks: 'deixa'm que te la xumi. Vull saber quin gust té la teva mare...' [let me suck you. I want to know what your mother tastes like] (148). Finally, Carles' scream of '[p]areeeeee!' [father], accompanied by his first and only orgasm, enacts a symbolic father–son incest in which not only does the King take everything 'com un lladre que aprofita qualsevol hora per saquejar les criptes genitals' [like a thief who at any hour might pillage the genital crypts] (172), but steals even his dying breath. When Sòcrates is released from service, he goes looking for a renowned prostitute who greets him by his name and full lineage; the reader assumes her to be his mother, and here the novel ends.

Viladot's playful manipulation of the heteronormative Oedipal frame in the supplemental complementarity of the Carles–Sòcrates relationship — Sòcrates as both fictional supplement and psychosexual complement — is at a basic bio-bibliographical level a further stage in the author's creative re-working of, and response to, his readings in psychoanalysis from the 1970s onwards. At the same time, the publication of *Carles* in 1994 also coincides with what Rosalind Krauss has referred to as the 'insistent spread of "abjection" as an expressive mode' (1996: 89) in contemporary artistic production, naming Gilbert & George as exemplars; and reminding us of abject art's[32] fixation 'not simply on sexual organs but, as well, on all bodily orifices and their secretions' (1996: 90). It is not just in terms of sexuality that Viladot disrupts the Oedipal romance, however, but also in the political, hierarchical domain. Carles' final exclusion from the system of which his father is sovereign merely confirms what he has feared from the start, that his father is responsible for his abject body and has abandoned him as waste, to waste away. Yet perhaps, following Bataille, it is possible in the case of Carles to talk about 'a paradoxical notion of castration that is just the opposite of a loss of manliness, since, as the mark of the child's challenge to the heights of the father's power, it becomes the very emblem — in all its bloody lowness — of virility' (in Krauss 1996: 99).

In Viladot's depictions of both Joana and Carles, the privileging of more salacious foreign historical reporting associated with the Black Legend (especially in *Carles*) is balanced by an imperative to retain a focus on the close, intimate, essentially human experience of each character. This is manifestly the case of Joana whose attachment to her husband's corpse is explained as a protective guardianship, and at worst (or most) as the expression of unutterable grief, and the affection for Carles (*pace* Artís) evident in Sòcrates' story. The reductive tendency of much literary journalism around the figure of Viladot belies the complex of tensions here between historical specificity, universal humanity, feminist-oriented socio-political critique, psychoanalytically-inflected aesthetics and the co-option of an excremental trope to figure the relationship between sovereignty — hegemony — and its unwanted or awkward products. Viladot was similarly located within his own cultural context, liminal, on the margins, particularly in relation to his narrative fiction, in spite of being considered one of the foremost visual poets in Spain, and recognized internationally. Around the time of *Joana* and *Carles'* composition and publication, he launched a fierce attack on the 'conservadorisme editorial i crític dels oficiants, com si, fins a cert punt, encara incidís aquell "Catalunya serà cristiana o no serà"' [conservatism of the major publishers and critics, as though to a point it were still the case that 'Catalunya will be Christian or it will not be']:

> Els domadors de la cultura escrita sembla que no han entès, ni estan disposats a entendre, que escriure constitueix una dissidència, per raó, precisament, d'aquesta llibertat personal innegociable. Des de la meva Riella [Agramunt] natal mai no m'he sentit condicionat.

> [The overseers of written culture seem not to have understood, nor are they willing to understand, that writing constitutes dissidence precisely because of this non-negotiable personal freedom. From my native Riella [Agramunt], I have never felt myself constrained.] (Viladot 1990b: 38)

The erotic and scatological are the basic expression of dissidence towards authority conceived much more broadly than Artís' historicist understanding. And while both symbolic and material articulations of the excremental are readily available in *Joana* and *Carles*, it is difficult not to read Viladot's ambivalent dynamic with the cultural establishment through the allegory of the anal-stage Freudian child negotiating the seductions of expulsive and retentive gratification: in or out?

Works Cited

ALDEA VAQUERO, QUINTÍN. 2003. 'Felipe II. Política y religión', in *La monarquía de Felipe II*, ed. by Felipe Ruiz Martín (Madrid: Real Academia de la Historia), pp. 69–110 [N.B. Vaquero is rendered erroneously as 'Navarro' on the Contents page]

ARAM, BETHANY. 2008. 'Queen Juana: Legend and History', in *Juana of Castile: History and Myth of the Mad Queen*, ed. by María A. Gómez et al. (q.v.), pp. 33–46

ARTÍS, AVEL·LÍ. 1994. 'Història d'un príncep estrafet', *Avui*, 20 October, p. 51

BONADA, LLUÍS. 1991. 'Guillem Viladot: "En el nostre país tot està passat de moda perquè les coses no es fan a fons"', *El Temps*, 7 October, p. 66

——. 1994. 'El complex de castració', *El Temps*, 8 August, p. 75

ÇAKIRLAR, CÜNEYT. 2011. 'Masculinity, Scatology, Mooning and the Queer/able Art of Gilbert & George: On the Visual Discourse of Male Ejaculation and Anal Penetration', *Paragraph*, 34.1: 86–104

CAPDEVILA, JORDI. 1991. 'Guillem Viladot publica una novel·la antihistòrica sobre la reina Joana la Boja', *Avui, Cultura*, 17 September, p. 29

CASTILLO, DAVID. 1989. 'Guillem Viladot: la literatura entesa com un acte narcisista i un compromís amb un mateix', *Avui*, 10 September, p. 65

——. 1992. 'Originalitat i fantasia', *Avui*, 22 February, p. 46

CERVERA, CÉSAR. 2015. 'La historia de don Carlos, el sádico hijo de Felipe II que la leyenda negra convirtió en un mártir', *ABC*, 22 January

CLOS, MARTA. 1997. 'La literatura en aquest país no dóna per al plat a taula', *Avui*, 4 December, p. 68

CÒNSUL, ISIDOR. 1991a. '*Lletres de Ponent* o l'art d'esbandir la boira', *Àrnica*, 6: 24–26. Reproduced at the author's request from the Generalitat's *Cultura* magazine, April 1991

——. 1991b. 'Joana de Castella: memòria d'una bogeria', *Avui, Cultura*, 2 November, p. 48

——. 1992a. 'Guillem Viladot, narrador', *Serra d'Or*, 394: 19–21

——. 1992b. '*Joana* de Guillem Viladot', *Catalan Writing*, 9: 92

——. 2000. 'Memòria de Guillem Viladot', *Serra d'Or*, 490: 48–49

DADSON, TREVOR J. 2016. Review of *España ante sus críticos: las claves de la Leyenda Negra*, *Hispanic Research Journal*, 17.6: 560–61 DOI: 10.1080/14682737.2016.1238221

DANIEL-RISACHER, NATHALIE. 1998. 'Gilbert & George: une dialectique amoureuse / Gilbert & George: An Amorous Dialectic', *Espace: Art actuel*, 45: 23–27 <http://id.erudit.org/iderudit/9625ac7>

DILLA, F. XAVIER. 1994. 'El príncep maleït', *El Temps*, 5 September, p. 72

DONAPETRY, MARÍA. 2005. 'Juana la Loca en tres siglos: de Tamayo y Baus a Aranda pasando por Orduña', *Hispanic Research Journal*, 6.2: 147–54 DOI: 10.1179/146827305X38797

DOUGLAS, MARY. 1968. 'Pollution', in *International Encyclopedia of the Social Sciences*, vol. XI, ed. by David L. Sills (New York: Macmillan and Free Press), pp. 336–41

DUNCAN, MICHAEL. 2008. 'The Human Theater of Gilbert & George', *Art in America*, October, 171–77

GARCIA, JOSEP MIQUEL. 2007. 'Viladot: la sublimació necessària', *Reduccions: revista de poesia*, 87: 96–124

GARCÍA CÁRCEL, RICARDO. 2001. 'La construcción del mito', *La aventura de la historia*, 'Dossier', 38: 1–19

GARCÍA-ESCUDERO LÓPEZ, ÁNGEL, A. ARRUZA ECHEVARRÍA, J. PADILLA NIEVA, and R. PUIG GIRÓ. 2009. 'Carlos II: del hechizo a su patalogía génito-urinaria', *Archivos Españoles de Urología*, 62.3: 179–85

GEORGE, DAVID R. 2008. 'Necrophilia, Madness, and Degeneration in Manuel Tamayo y Baus's *La locura de amor* (1855)', in *Juana of Castile: History and Myth of the Mad Queen*, ed. by María A. Gómez et al. (q.v.), pp. 61–76

GÓMEZ, MARÍA A., SANTIAGO JUAN-NAVARRO, and PHYLLIS ZATLIN (eds). 2008. *Juana of Castile: History and Myth of the Mad Queen* (Lewisburg, PA: Bucknell University Press)

GROSZ, ELIZABETH. 1994. *Volatile Bodies: Toward a Corporeal Feminism* (Bloomington and Indianapolis: Indiana University Press)

GUTIÉRREZ, MAGDA. 1994. 'Guillem Viladot: "*Carles* mostra els efectes castradors del poder sobre l'individu"', *Avui*, 1 August, p. 37

HALSEY, MARTHA. 1978–79. 'Juana La Loca in Three Dramas of Tamayo y Baus, Galdós, and Martín Recuerda', *MLS*, 9.1: 47–59 <http://www.jstor.org/stable/3194407>

JOHNSON, P. LOUISE. 2012. 'The Lyrical Taboos of Guillem Viladot', in *Barcelona: Visual Culture, Space and Power*, ed. by Helena Buffery and Carlota Caulfield (Cardiff: University of Wales Press), pp. 58–80

JONES, SAM. 2018. 'Spain Fights to Dispel Legend of Inquisition and Imperial Atrocities', *Guardian*, 29 April

JUAN-NAVARRO, SANTIAGO. 2008. 'Political Madness: Juan de Orduña's *Locura de amor* as a National Allegory', in *Juana of Castile: History and Myth of the Mad Queen*, ed. by María A. Gómez et al. (q.v.), pp. 210–27

KRAUSS, ROSALIND. 1996. '*Informe* without Conclusion', *October*, 78: 89–105 <http://www.jstor.org/stable/778907>

KRISTEVA, JULIA. 1982. *Powers of Horror: An Essay on Abjection*, trans. by Leon S. Roudiez (New York: Columbia University Press)

LABANYI, JO. 2001. 'La modernización de Juana la loca: la última obra de Galdós, *Santa Juana de Castilla* (1918), entre *La locura de amor* de Tamayo y Baus (1855) y *Locura de amor* de Orduña (1948)', in *Actas del séptimo congreso internacional de estudios galdosianos* (Las Palmas de Gran Canaria: Cabildo Insular de Gran Canaria), pp. 16–30 <http://mdc.ulpgc.es/cdm/ref/collection/galdosianos/id/977>

MORENO ESPINOSA, GERARDO. 2006. *Don Carlos: el príncipe de leyenda negra* (Madrid: Marcial Pons Historia)

PIÑOL, ROSA MARIA. 1991. 'Viladot reivindica la figura de Juana la Loca en su último libro', *La Vanguardia*, 1 October, p. 43

PONS, MARGALIDA. 2007. 'Formes i condicions de la narrativa experimental catalana (1970–1985)', in *Textualisme i subversió: formes i condicions de la narrativa experimental catalana (1970–1985)*, ed. by Margalida Pons (Barcelona: Publicacions de l'Abadia de Montserrat), pp. 7–79

POPS, MARTIN. 1982. 'The Metamorphosis of Shit', *Salmagundi*, 56: 26–61

RAVENSCROFT, JANET. 2006. 'Invisible Friends: Questioning the Representation of the Court Dwarf in Hapsburg Spain', in *Histories of the Normal and the Abnormal: Social and Cultural Histories of Norms and Normativity*, ed. by Waltraud Ernst (Abingdon: Routledge), pp. 26–52

RENDÉ, JOAN. 1982. 'Guillem Viladot, en el llenguatge divers', *Avui*, 1 August, p. 21

SALVO TORRES, RAMON. 2012. 'Guillem Viladot en el temps d'estrena de l'experimentació', *Revista de Catalunya*, 280: 88–108

SCHYFTER, SARA E. 1984. 'The Fabrication of History in Santa Juana de Castilla', *Anales Galdosianos*, 19: 53–59

SEGARRA, MARTA. 2014. *Teoría de los cuerpos agujereados* ([Santa Cruz de Tenerife]: Melusina)

SOLIÑO, MARÍA ELENA. 2008. 'Madness as Nationalistic Spectacle: Juana and the Myths of Nineteenth-Century History Painting', in *Juana of Castile: History and Myth of the Mad Queen*, ed. by María A. Gómez et al. (q.v.), pp. 175–97

STARK, WERNER. 2002 [1967]. *The Sociology of Religion: A Study of Christendom. Part Three: The Universal Church* (London: Routledge)

TASENDE, MERCEDES. 2008. 'Ramón Gómez de la Serna's Superhistory: An Original

Approach to the Life of Juana of Castile', in *Juana of Castile: History and Myth of the Mad Queen*, ed. by María A. Gómez et al. (q.v.), pp. 92–106

TORRES, ESTANISLAU. 1995. *Les tisores de la censura (El règim franquista contra l'autor i contra Manuel de Pedrolo, Pere Calders, Guillem Viladot, Montserrat Roig, Víctor Mora...)* (Lleida: Pagès)

TRIGO, XULIO RICARDO. 1991. 'Els altres camins de la novel·la històrica', *El Temps*, 18 November, p. 91

VALLEJO-NÁGERA, JUAN ANTONIO. 1977. *Locos egregios* (Madrid: Dossat)

VALLVERDÚ, JOSEP. 2000. 'Guillem Viladot al biaix', *Serra d'Or*, 490: 44–47

——. 2004. *De Morera i Galícia a Guillem Viladot* (Lleida: Edicions de la Universitat de Lleida)

VERGÉS, ORIOL. 1995. 'Guillem Viladot, *Carles*', *Catalan Writing*, 13: 83

VILADOT, GUILLEM. 1981. *La finestra induïda* (Barcelona: La Llar del Llibre)

——. 1988. 'Catàleg d'una sexualitat', *Avui*, 5 June, p. 47

——. 1990a. 'Un diccionari de la carn, la seva eficàcia i la seva utilitat', *Avui*, 3 February, p. 45

——. 1990b. 'Ponent, un paradís literari', *Serra d'Or*, 370: 37–38

——. 1991. 'Guia gnòstica o de la perversió, és a dir, de les direccions múltiples per a poetes de catalanitat provada, o sigui d'infidelitat a Verdaguer, Carner, Riba i la Universitat', *Reduccions: revista de poesia*, 52: 57–61

——. 1994. *Carles* (Barcelona: Columna)

——. 1994 [1991]. *Joana* (Barcelona: Columna)

——. 1994. *Juana la loca* (Barcelona: Apóstrofe)

——. 1995. *Carlos, hijo y víctima de Felipe II* (Barcelona: Apóstrofe)

——. 1998. 'Jo sóc també Leandre Cristòfol', *Avui*, 20 August, p. 31

——. 2000. *Ruth* (Barcelona: Columna)

VILLALON, L. J. ANDREW. 1995. 'Putting Don Carlos Together Again: Treatment of a Head Injury in Sixteenth-Century Spain', *The Sixteenth Century Journal*, 26.2: 347–65 <http:www.jstor.org/stable/2542795>

ZATLIN, PHYLLIS, and MERCEDES TASENDE. 2008. 'Jeanne de Castille at Center Stage: The Spanish Queen in Recent French Theater', in *Juana of Castile: History and Myth of the Mad Queen*, ed. by María A. Gómez et al. (q.v.), pp. 158–72

Notes to Chapter 5

1. As Viladot explains, under the regime '[e]l nom de l'Alberti era impronunciable' [one couldn't even mention Alberti] because of his Communist affiliation (Torres 1995: 48). He speaks in more detail about the incident in *El Correo Catalán*, 12 May 1977. See Guillem Viladot, 'El retorn del poeta Alberti' (1981: 47–50), and Josep Miquel Garcia (2007: 99). This act of censorship was clearly influential, but so too was Joan Triadú's *Panorama de la poesia catalana* [Panorama of Catalan Poetry] (1953): 'Uns fets polítics junt amb el rigor i la pregonesa crítics d'en Triadú em feren trobar un fitó molt important: la correcta superposició del verb i de la vida' [Certain political events together with the critical rigour and depth of Triadú led me to identify an important objective: the correct prioritization of verb and life] (Viladot cited in Vallverdú 2000: 45).

2. After 1975 Viladot contributed prolifically to the periodical press in both Castilian (e.g. *Destino*) and Catalan (e.g. *El Correo Catalán*, *Avui*). He also published thousands of articles in *La Mañana* from 1988 until days before his death (Garcia 2007: 98).

3. The dates are confirmed at the end of the novel itself (178). All textual references are to the third Catalan edition (1994). When referring to the protagonists of the novels, I adopt the Catalan Joana and Carles respectively. References to the historical figures and other fictionalized interpretations are given as Juana and Don Carlos.

4. Viladot's refusal, in his own words, to 'seguir una moda o fer-me un lloc dins del panorama cultural' [follow fashion or carve out a niche in the cultural panorama] (in Castillo 1989), negatively influenced the author's ability to find publishers. Viladot remarked sardonically that he thought the novel *Ciutadà ooooooooo01* [Citizen 00000000001] (1989), in keeping with the publication difficulties faced by Umberto Eco's *Il nome della rosa* and John Kennedy Toole's *A Confederacy of Dunces* (both 1980), would inevitably become a bestseller. The novel was eventually published by 3i4 in Valencia, having been turned down by every publisher in Barcelona (Castillo 1989; see also Vallverdú 2000: 46). Viladot is similarly consistent in maintaining that his creative discourse (in whatever medium) 'no naixia de la necessitat d'estar en sintonia amb les preferències o gustos forans, sinó que procedia del conflicte del subjecte amb el poder establert' [was not born of a necessity to be in tune with external tastes and preferences, but arose from the conflict of the subject with established power] (e.g. Viladot in Garcia 2007: 101).

5. Cònsul refers in 1992 to a novel in progress 'dedicada [...] a "El Pedrillo", bufó de Felip V [*sic*]' [centred on 'El Pedrillo', fool of Felipe V]. Since Cònsul knew of the work before its appearance and refers to 'Pedrillo', it might seem that the first version was, like *Joana*, composed in Castilian (Cònsul 1992a: 21). However, Viladot says that 'acabo de redactar per tercer cop la novel·la *Vèrtex/zero*' [I have just finished a third draft of the novel *Vèrtex/zero*], and continues wryly that he will now need to revise it significantly using the *Diccionari eròtic i sexual* (1990a).

6. In a review of *Joana*, Isidor Cònsul calls Viladot '[v]ersàtil i torrencial, heterodox i iconoclasta', 'un dels escriptors potser més originals, polivalents i injustament malconeguts de la literatura catalana actual' [versatile and torrential, heterodox and iconoclast], [one of the most original, multifaceted and unjustly neglected writers of contemporary Catalan literature]. On *Joana* specifically, he notes the characteristics that link the novel to the writer's previous work: 'Detalls com aquesta barreja d'odi i de seducció que sent Joana pel seu pare; o bé la relació amorosa de Joana amb la madrastra Germana de Foix; o bé l'atac amb efectes de possible castració vers un dels carcellers del castell' [Details such as this mixture of hatred and seduction that Joana feels for her father; or the intimate relationship between Joana and her stepmother, Germaine de Foix; or the attack on and attempted castration of one of the castle jailers]. He highlights the 'triangles de consciència edípica i [...] detalls de relació homosexual, temes, tots dos, transitadíssims de la narrativa viladotiana' [Oedipal-informed triangles and ... details of homosexual relations, both themes which are very common in Viladot's narrative]. He concludes: 'un dels mèrits més lloables de la novel·la és haver convertit el drama de la reina boja en el d'un personatge absolutament contemporani i universal' [one of the greatest merits of the novel is the transformation of the drama of the mad queen into that of a character who is absolutely contemporary and universal] (1991b: 48). Translated excerpts of this review were republished in the English-language *Catalan Writing* the following year (an indication of the desire to promote Viladot's undoubted significance further afield), together with a fragment of a review by Jaume Fabra, in which Fabra remarks on the novel's 'flashes of brilliance [...] although it falls somewhat short of its aims'. Fabra continues, 'this is nonetheless a first-class literary work, polished, brilliant and a really good read' (in Cònsul 1992b: 92). Xulio Ricardo Trigo in turn considers that '[l]'autor ha sabut interpretar una pàgina de la història des de la seva època i això és sovint el que trobem a faltar quan la literatura s'enfronta amb la història'; he concludes that *Joana* is 'una experiència engrescadora i profundament humanista' [the author has managed to interpret a page of history from his own perspective, and that is what we often find lacking when literature engages with history] [an intriguing and profoundly humanistic experience] (1991: 91).

7. In conversation with Lluís Bonada, Viladot acknowledged that *Joana* had been his best-selling work to date (Bonada 1994: 75).

8. Sam Jones demonstrates the absolutely contemporary relevance of the 'leyenda negra' [Black Legend] in Spain (2018). He explores the contrasting views of Borja Cardelús, who in 2018 was one of sixteen founding members (curiously, all male) of the Fundación Civilización Hispánica, and historian Ricardo García Cárcel. One of the Fundación's objectives is '[c]ombatir la Leyenda Negra. Dar a conocer la inmensa obra civilizadora de España y los países iberoamericanos, y su contribución a la Humanidad, tanto en los aspectos geográficos como en los materiales y culturales' [to combat the Black Legend. To make known the immense

civilizing task undertaken by Spain and Ibero-American countries, and their contribution to Humanity, in geographical as well as material and cultural senses] (civilizacionhispanica.org). García Cárcel (2001) suggests that the appearance of the Fundación cannot be uncoupled from the recent heightened tensions with and within Catalonia; Cardelús, according to Jones, 'denies there is any political dimension to the foundation's work'.

9. Viladot preferred the term 'anti-historical' (Capdevila 1991: 29; Piñol 1991: 43).

10. Werner Stark suggests that in the work of Spanish writers, as well as Covarrubias' *Tesoro de la lengua española* [Treasury of the Spanish Language], 'the undertones and overtones [of *corpus mysticum*] are sober and secular, not religious' (2002: 184–85). Joana's conception of her own position relative to this (figurative) body is external, as a daughter subjected to the changeable will of her father, and internal, as waste to be expelled (see below).

11. Trepat is credited with introducing psychoanalytic psychology to Lleida (see web publicity for her study *La necessitat d'estimar* [The Need to Love], 2012). Viladot credited her as one of his two 'mestres fonamentals' [fundamental teachers], the other being sculptor Leandre Cristòfol (1998: 31).

12. Cònsul identifies *La cendra* [Ash] (1972) as 'una peça d'aprofundiment psicològic que, analitzada en aquest sentit, encetà el corrent de discurs i recerca psicoanalítics' [a text of some psychological depth which, seen in this light, marks the first foray into psychoanalytic discourse and research] (2000: 48).

13. See, for example, Josep Miquel Garcia, who cites Viladot as follows: 'La descoberta de la psicoanàlisi com un mode de coneixement (gràcies a la psicòloga Marta Trepat) em serví per desbridar el discurs literari de tota mena de servituds als tòtems i tabús que regien (i continuen regint) la nostra societat. Dir el que era necessari de dir, com una catarsi' [The discovery of psychoanalysis as a mode of knowing (thanks to psychologist Marta Trepat) allowed me to free literary discourse from all manner of servitude to the totems and taboos that govern our society. To say what needed to be said, like a catharsis] (2007: 113).

14. Viladot makes reference to a wide range of psychoanalysts, philosophers and writers in his work, female and male, as the poem 'He bastit' [I Have Built], from *Amor físic* [Physical Love] (1983), rather curiously illustrates: '... Han quedat damunt la taula | Bataille, Foucault, Freud, Nach i, dins la faula, | Cooper, Lacan, Laing i tot un armari || de dones, com Melanie Klein, Segal, | Manoni [*sic*], Horney, Mitchel [*sic*] i Millet, | sumaris de la dona vertical' [... On the table are left | Bataille, Foucault, Freud, Nach and, in the fable, | Cooper, Lacan, Laing and a whole bureau || of women, like Melanie Klein, Segal, | Manoni [*sic*], Horney, Mitchel [*sic*] i Millet, | indexes of the vertical woman] (cited in Josep Miquel Garcia 2007: 112–13). On more than one occasion, he expresses a preference for Lacan.

15. Nevertheless, as Mercedes Tasende underlines, by the 1940s 'the historical figure had been distorted and mythologized to such a degree that most studies on the life of the queen that pretended to be "scientific" and impartial turned out to be almost as fictitious as the dramas or novels published on the same subject' (2008: 102).

16. More recent research has suggested that the origins of the Black Legend lie earlier, with the presence of 'Spaniards (or, rather, Catalans and Aragonese) [...] in southern Italy and its island possessions (Sicily and Sardinia)' (see Trevor Dadson's review of *España ante sus críticos...*, 2016).

17. 'Cabe suponer que la interpretación del papel de "Santa Juana de Castilla" por una actriz catalana, cuyos antecedentes humildes eran bien conocidos, puede haber prestado unos matices interesantes a la valoración de la representación por parte del público, puesto que desde 1917 las reivindicaciones catalanistas dominaban el panorama político, y la huelga general de 1917, aunque fracasada, había producido el espectro de una revolución proletaria que se hiciera eco de los acontecimientos en Rusia' [The fact that the role of Santa Juana de Castilla was played by a Catalan actress whose humble origins were well known, might, we imagine, have lent some interesting nuances to the public evaluation of the performance, since from 1917 Catalanist politics dominated the headlines, and the general strike of 1917, although a failure, had created the spectre of a proletarian revolution that risked echoing recent events in Russia] (Labanyi 2001: 23).

18. Giovanni Botero is credited with popularising the term in *Della ragion di stato* (1589). Juana died in 1555.

19. Joana is schooled in sexual technique by Moorish slave girls she has brought to Flanders specifically for this purpose, as she attempts to divert her husband Philip from his many mistresses.

20. Neither highlighted reference to shit is present in the Spanish version. Across the Catalan versions of both novels, there seems to be a slight but noticeable increase in the 'excremental' discourse compared with the Spanish, and Joana's mental fragility is more likely to be expressed in 'blasphemous' outbursts. The Catalan and Spanish epigraphs are different ('Només he estat un vestigi i simulacre de mi' [I have been only a vestige and simulacrum of myself], from Pessoa; and 'Castilla grado cero' [Castilla degree zero], respectively). The Spanish also incorporates a limited graphic of the family tree.

21. Martha Halsey (1978–79: 48) reminds us that Galdós, possibly following Gustav Bergenroth, presents Juana too as a follower of Erasmus. Sara E. Schyfter clarifies that Juana's 'Erasmism' in Galdós stands in place of what others see as her 'madness' (1984: 54).

22. 'Al meu peu esquerre, hi tinc sis dits, o sigui que el dit petit és doblat, vull dir que al damunt en té un altre d'igual mida i dibuix. La natura, però, que és justa i sàvia, ha fet que a la mà dreta m'hi falti el menovell i que el braç del mateix costat sigui una mica més curt, afoll que fa que el gest tingui una singularitat que tothom admira i celebra. Per si no fos prou, a més, sóc curt de talla i tinc el cos revingut i massís. L'enginy, en canvi, em surt ràpid, brillant, i en són senyal els meus ulls espavilats. La meva cara no és, ni de molt, una bellesa, però es fa mirar pels seus llavis gruixuts, els pòmuls prominents i el nas xato. Per una altra banda, la meva parla és àgil i, si em ve de gust, parlo com un cavaller encara que pensi com un serf' [I have six toes on my left foot, that is, a double little toe, with one toe of the same size and shape on top of the other. Nature, however, which is just and wise, has given me a right hand missing a little finger, and a right arm that is slightly shorter, a deformity that gives my gestures a singularity admired and celebrated by everyone. If that were not sufficient, I'm also short in stature and my body is stocky and compact. My wit, however, is quick and brilliant, as my lively eyes attest. My face is by no means beautiful, but its interest is in its thick lips, prominent cheekbones and flattish nose. Moreover, I'm an agile speaker and, if the mood takes me, I can speak like a gentleman even while I think like a serf] (*Carles*: 9).

23. The myth surrounding Don Carlos, and specifically that part of it that attributes his death directly to his father, Felipe II, seems to have been popularised first in a work by César Vichard de Saint-Réal, *Dom Carlos, nouvelle historique* [Don Carlos, Historical Novella] (Amsterdam, 1672), which became the source for Friedrich von Schiller's tragedy *Don Karlos, Infant von Spanien* (first performed in 1787). This in turn inspired Giuseppe Verdi's *Don Carlo*. See also Villalon (1995).

24. The epigraph to the Spanish edition, 'Cierto que te escucharán si lo que dices les gusta' [They will surely listen to you if they like what you have to say], is signed 'Sócrates', from Plato's dialogue *Euthyphro*. The name 'Pedrillo' is after the character's father, Pedro, but also recalls 'Lazarillo' [de Tormes], and indeed the Pedrillo of Byron's *Don Juan*, the protagonist's tutor, who is dined upon rather than cannibalistic himself (Canto II). We can only speculate as to the motivation behind the change of name: it seems clear that in the Catalan Sòcrates is intended to denote wit, wisdom and physical ugliness. The choice of Pedrillo, in turn, seems more conventional than strategic.

25. '[N]o voy a divulgar ni sus nombres ni sus obras, dado que no impera en mi ánimo la menor predisposición a la polémica ni interés en personificar sus vituperios' [I will not divulge either their names or their works, since I am not at all given to polemic or to singling people out for their insults] (Moreno Espinosa, loc. 226).

26. Note that the family tree reproduced in *Carlos* omits Felipe's first wife, Maria Manuela of Portugal.

27. In an interview with Estanislau Torres, Viladot explains his profound dislike of the Church ('Déu[,] l'han desprestigiat les esglésies' [churches have tarnished God]) on account of its 'realitat històrica' [historical reality], but describes himself as a believer (Torres 1995: 47). His portrayal of Carles' attitudes seems very close to his own, although a later interview (Clos 1997: 68) suggests he could be better termed agnostic, or even atheist.

28. Cüneyt Çakirlar writes: 'In [...] *The Fundamental Pictures* (1996), other bodily fluids enter the scene. The microscopic images of dried crystallized liquids — cracks in blood, flower-like patterns in piss, sweat and semen, bubbles in spit — serves [*sic*] an avant-gardist reappropriation of abject as readymade' (2011: 97).

29. The article is published in French, with an English translation by Janet Logan.

30. See, amongst others, Villalon (1995: 350), who suggests that the 'racier' version of this incident was disseminated by the ambassadors of France, England and Venice, while Spanish accounts merely mention the fall.

31. Here Viladot's reworking is significantly different from established historical and mythical accounts. According to Villalon (1995), the trepanation was not in the end carried out fully, but this nuance is absent from the novel. In Viladot, Vesalius (the foreigner) is given an elevated status as the figure who drains the abscesses, whereas as Villalon recalls, contemporaneous accounts mention 'doctors' and one 'Pedro de Torres'. Similarly, and entirely in keeping with Viladot's portrayal of Carles and his own anti-clericalism, the author debunks the miraculous myth that grew up around the canonization of Fra Diego de Alcalá: it is said that the remains of the Franciscan were brought to Carlos' bed-chamber and laid alongside him in bed. Carlos, unable to see because of the abscesses beneath his eyes, touched the remains before touching the abscesses, and was cured. In Viladot, a violently fevered Carles kicks the mummified remains out of his bed, onto the floor, where they crumple in a disordered heap of bones and dust (*Carles*: 92).

32. This is Kristeva's term.

CHAPTER 6

Atopia and Irishmen in the Early Novels of Albert Sánchez Piñol

Dominic Keown

Fitzwilliam College, University of Cambridge

With its origins no doubt in patriotic concern arising from periods of historical adversity, there has been a tendency discernible in Catalan culture to present the country in a defensive, almost apologetic manner. The trope is characterized by an affective diminution in status. Espriu's evocation of the 'petita pàtria' [small homeland] would be exemplary of this tendency which finds echo in the 'petit país' [small country] of Josep Pla or Pere Quart's 'pàtria tan petita | que la somnio completa' [homeland so small | I dream of it whole]; not forgetting, of course, Lluís Llach's 'País petit': 'tan petit que sempre cap dintre del cor' [so small it fits forever in my heart]. Despite the sentimentality aroused by such evocation, however, the strategy is not without its shortcomings. Such protective downsizing runs the risk of engendering a notion of isolation and introspection; or the accompanying peril of complacency, a danger that the ever-vigilant Espriu was keen to expose from his earliest writing onwards.[1]

In rhetorical terms, of course, the pathos resulting from this device of reduction may well have more to do with the *captatio benevolentiae* carried implicitly by the diminutive. To this might be added the emotive possibilities of the *topoi* of *locus amoenus* and Paradise Lost which were exploited to such great effect by the bard of Sinera. As such, it is difficult not to conclude that this vision inclines towards the subtractive and peripheral, sitting uneasily with the profile of a country which has more speakers of the vernacular than Denmark or Finland, three million more inhabitants than the Republic of Ireland, and whose presence dwarfs the national minnows of Wales, Iceland, Malta *i un llarg etcètera*.

Happily, however, though a constant, the formula is rarely employed to excess and is accompanied elsewhere in the world of domestic letters by an extrovert and much more robust, international orientation. The global receptiveness evident in recent prose fiction is much more in keeping with the abrasive cultural xenophilia exemplified by the Modernist experience of the previous century and characteristic of the nation's creativity as a whole. Just over a decade ago, for example, Àlex Broch remarked on the growing interest amongst Catalan writers for America

— and Cuba in particular — which, for the critic, constituted 'un nuevo registro temático' [a new thematic register]: an outgoing and externally engaged selection of content and theme (2004: 63). Similarly, for Galina Bakhtiarova this transatlantic fascination betrayed antithetically an edificatory desire to represent Catalonia not as diminutive but 'como una nación con lugar propio en la empresa colonial e imperial europea' [as a nation with its own place within the European imperial and colonial enterprise] (2007: 39).

It might be said that the best examples of this tendency engage both positively and censoriously with such imperial involvement — a critical attitude to be valued, in fact, when compared to historiography which has been inclined to display an unhealthy reticence in this area. The point has been duly underlined by Víctor Yustres who, in his denouncement of Catalan participation in the slave trade, considers it a subject through which local historians

> sempre han passat de puntetes malgrat [...] el pes notable [...] que la burgesia catalana va tenir en el tràfic d'esclaus a les Antilles. Els indians [...] van amassar grans fortunes, que van ser transferides i invertides al llarg del segle XIX a Catalunya, especialment a Barcelona. Aquest va ser un dels factors clau del creixement econòmic i la industrialització de la capital catalana durant aquella època.

> [have always tip-toed reluctantly despite the notable involvement of the Catalan bourgeoisie in the slave trade to the Antilles. Catalan nabobs amassed huge fortunes which were then transferred and invested in Catalonia, throughout the twentieth century, especially in Barcelona. This was one of the key factors in the Catalan capital's economic growth and industrialization during the period.] (Yustres 2015) [All online references accessed 31 July 2016.]

Indeed, Bakhtiarova has remarked how participation in this execrable trade was the norm rather than the exception in the social hierarchy of Catalonia: 'En el siglo XIX, la trata de esclavos se veía como una transacción comercial normal y los matrimonios concertados en beneficio de la capitalización constituían una práctica socioeconómica aceptada en la creciente sociedad capitalista catalana' [In the nineteenth century, trading in slaves was considered a normal commercial enterprise and marriages arranged with the aim of increasing capital were an accepted socio-economic practice in the capitalist society of Catalonia] (2007: 44).

Interestingly, in her novel of 2000 *Cap al cel obert* [Heading for the Open Sky], Carme Riera — perhaps the most significant representative of this group of whistle-blowers — is heavily censorious of Catalan involvement in this whole sad business. More specifically, as Rosalía Cornejo Parriego reveals, this author is equally scathing about what it is tempting to call the *pacto del olvido* [pact of forgetting] surrounding the issue in domestic historiography:

> La propia Riera afirma que '[e]l proceso de industrialización de Cataluña viene de Cuba. Muchos de los que allí hicieron grandes fortunas contribuyeron luego aquí a hacer la Cataluña moderna', y en su 'Nota' final alude a la 'absoluta desmemoria' del presente que quiere contrarrestar con una novela que enfatice precisamente la relación entre la esclavitud y la riqueza catalana y vasca: 'No hace tanto que fuimos emigrantes y también negreros. La Cataluña "rica i

plena" y el industrializado País Vasco, por ejemplo, se levantaron, en gran parte, con capital proveniente de los ingenios esclavistas, y aunque no nos guste, quizá el hecho de reconocerlo nos permitiría ser más generosos y tolerantes con los inmigrantes, con cuantos son diferentes o, simplemente, no piensan lo mismo que nosotros.'

[Riera herself affirms that 'Catalonia's process of industrialization comes from Cuba. Many of those who made huge fortunes there contributed later to the modernization of Catalonia', and in her final 'Note' she alludes to the 'complete lack of memory' of the present time which she wants to counterbalance with a novel which emphasizes precisely the relationship between slavery and Catalan and Basque wealth. 'Not so long ago we were emigrants and slave-traders. Catalonia "rich and whole" and the industrialized Basque country, for example, rose up in great part through capital raised by entrepreneurs from the slave trade and, even though we don't like it, recognition of this fact might allow us to be more generous and tolerant towards immigrants, towards those who are different or, simply, towards those who do not share our opinions.'] (Cornejo Parriego 2011: 9)

Albert Sánchez Piñol has been likewise direct in his denunciation of the colonial enterprise. With the sardonic eye of the attentive anthropologist, his socio-political satire of 2000, *Pallassos i monstres* [Clowns and Monsters], was to censure the imperial adventure and its consequences in Central Africa. And his subsequent novels, *La pell freda* [Cold Skin] (2002) and *Pandora al Congo* [Pandora in the Congo] (2005) address the same issue albeit from the more creative and imaginative perspective offered by fiction.

Perhaps the most innovative feature of this author's re-examination of the inhumanity of colonialism is that, unlike his domestic contemporaries, focus is removed from the Hispanic context and relocated within the alien but more global configuration of British expansionism. The strategy is hugely enriching, avoiding the pitfalls of introspection in two ways. Firstly, the less restrictive perspective internationalizes the speculation in geopolitical terms. More interestingly — and as will be seen in the second half of this essay —, it also facilitates an intertextual dialogue on the subject, outside the Hispanic context, with the most popular and influential writers of world literature. Significantly, Deerie Sariols has concocted a pertinent register of the authors whose imprint looms large in this dialectic and who are adjudged to fall into two separate camps (2007: 475). On the one hand are exponents of what Joan Ramon Resina refers to as 'literatura del imperialismo caliente' [hot imperial literature] as exemplified by Jules Verne, Wells, Kipling, Rice Burroughs, Rider Haggard and Defoe (2008: 130). On the other, figure the more sceptical and disconcerting essays of Conrad, Jack London, William Golding, Bioy Casares and even Shakespeare's *Tempest*.

The fiery exoticism and adventure of the first group of hot colonial yarns — massively popular in their day both in print and later on screen — conveyed, in their content and the character of their heroes and villains, the ravenous appetite of empire and its capitalist dynamic for expansion, domination and enterprise. More insidiously, the narration of these escapades coerced, in turn, an avid readership into embracing and perpetuating the values of empire and subordination. As

Suvendrini Perera has elucidated, the Victorian novel 'produced empire' which was then 'processed' and 'naturalised' by this genre: 'Certain fictional practices — the ordering of empire in fiction — prepared for, or made possible a climate for receiving and accommodating empire' (1991: 2, 7). With its mass appeal, as evinced in *Pandora* by the legion of ghost writers involved in the composition and mass production of Luther Flag's tales of adventure and empire, the genre functioned in the fashion of what Althusser (1970) would describe as an Ideological State Apparatus. And the coercive involvement of the literary media as an agent for the 'interpellation' of establishment values will receive further scrutiny in due course.

The selection of the geographical environment for the swashbuckling romance described is, however, problematic. The fiery exoticism of the Raj furnished Kipling with a perfect backdrop to cement the link between personal adventure and the excitement and dynamism of imperial expansion in the subcontinent. On the other hand, the freezing insecurity of the polar regions and the unpredictable menace of the high seas, whose challenge is epitomized by Conrad, provided a different perspective altogether. Siobhan Carroll has referred to these inhospitable or mutable regions as *atopia* and, following a familiar line in the deliberation about space which runs from Lefebvre (1974) to Augé (1992), depicts their threat in this type of literature as:

> 'real' natural regions falling within the theoretical scope of contemporary human mobility, which, because of their intangibility, inhospitality, or inaccessibility, cannot be converted into the locations of affective habitation known as 'place.' As spaces presumed to lie at or beyond the fringes of everyday life, atopias dialectically construct the inhabited places of home and community, providing a contrast to the familiarity, stability and security implied by idealized sites of dwelling. Unlike the wilderness of Turner's frontier, the unsettling nature of atopias is imagined as a permanent affair: They await neither improvement, nor inevitable wide-scale settlement, nor seamless incorporation into the domestic space of the nation. (2015: 6)

Accordingly, the existence of an uncolonizable *terra nullius* constitutes — and what follows is a summary of Carroll's fascinating insight — an implicit threat to the imperial geo-imaginary. The 'marvellous unknowns' of oceans, polar regions and inner earth resist, through their inhospitable climate or uninviting natural condition, anything but 'the most temporary of dwellings', posing thus a challenge to territorial appropriation and state control. In this way, atopia implied a negation of Britannia's self-congratulatory assurance of 'ruling the waves'. All of which explains, of course, the empire's historic obsession with 'the domestication of such areas' as evinced by epic projects of exploration to these most hostile of regions — like the North West Passage or South Pole — the majority of which were to end in tragedy or disaster, casting further aspersions on any boastful imperial claims at control (2015: 6–8).[2]

As a result, the warning against polar exploration in *Pell freda* maintains the dissenting anti-imperialist line, communicating the menace of the frozen wastes as registered earlier in Coleridge's 'Ancient Mariner' (1798) and Lovecraft's chilling *At the Mountains of Madness* (1936). It is no accident, for example, that close to the shore in *Pell freda* lies the visible, half-submerged wreck of a Portuguese freighter as a persistent reminder of the commercial failure of colonial trade in these indomitable polar latitudes.

An identical line is followed in *Pandora*, whose opening sentence establishes the significance of the self-same atopian challenge: 'El Congo. Imaginem-nos una superfície tan gran com Anglaterra, França i Espanya juntes. Imaginem-nos, ara, tota aquesta superfície coberta d'arbres entre sis i seixanta metres d'alçada. I, sota els arbres, no res' [The Congo. Imagine a surface area as great as England, France and Spain put together. Now imagine all this area covered by trees between twenty and two hundred feet in height. And beneath the trees, nothing] (2005: 7). It is not fortuitous, of course, that the major empires of Western Europe should be juxtaposed here with this *terra nullius*, and its relevance echoed by the risk implicit in the marine metaphor of the last phrases of the work: 'El Congo. Un oceà verd. I, sota els arbres, no res' [The Congo. An ocean of green. And beneath the trees, nothing] (2005: 592).

In fact, the motif of no-man's-land pervades the novel, and its prevalence is crystallized by the frenzied scramble for gold of the aptly named Craver brothers in the heart of Africa. As with the Conradian prototype, the inevitable intrusion of the capitalist dynamic goes hand in hand with the 'horror' of the inhumanity which is carried in this system, as epitomized by the brutal treatment of the black slaves. Appropriately, here once again — and in keeping with its literary predecessor — the urge to acquire wealth wields the germ of its own destruction.

The shaft which is sunk to extract the precious minerals and diamonds constitutes a further atopia which, quite literally, undermines the security of official discourse which is universally present on the surface. As Carroll points out, the extension of 'a communicative web of tellurian passageways' offers an alternative tale of extraordinary and chilling events which taps into a reservoir of 'histories that evade, challenge or subvert narratives of the world above', becoming a 'synecdoche for alternative and suppressed perspectives on the history of the nation state' (2015: 151).

In a manner reminiscent of Lovecraft's Antarctic terrors, Carroll's 'lost alien cultural meanings' (2015: 150) break out menacingly onto the surface, as witnessed in the form of the Tectons, the monsters from deep under the earth and relatives of the aquatic Citauca of *Pell freda*. Their appearance upsets the established order, inspiring insurrection in the slaves and virtually exterminating those involved in the prospecting. Indeed, the menace supposed by the underground lives up to its name to such an extent that, in a neat Cervantine move, the episode of alien intrusion actually makes the narrator's head start to spin as it is recounted to him, eventually causing him to faint, thus arresting development of the plot after a fashion analogous to the challenge presented by the *terra nullius* to the hegemony of official discourse (2005: 309).

It is in the journey to the Tecton city where the white explorers, now no longer masters but in bondage to their subterranean foe, are acquainted physically with the full threat of the Underworld. And the literary quality of the expression merits close consideration:

Al cap d'uns dies, el coll perillós va desembocar en una vall sense obstacles, un mar de magma sòlid. Marcus va intuir un infinit horitzontal, una planura sense límits on ni les llums verdes de les llanternes podien sobreposar-se al color carmesí d'un sòl rigurós, encrespat, amb formes de caprici, com si onades de coure haguessin cobert una horda de crustacis. Pertot arreu emergien milions de closques esmolades com ganivets, esculls que causarien suplicis medievals en els peus despullats. No podien allunyar-se d'una estreta llengua plana que travessava la planura. 'Aquí les pedres mosseguen', va dir Marcus [...]

En aquell desert bufava un vent mut i violent que bufetejava la cara dels intrusos com si el guiés una animadversió personal [...] Dormien enmig del no res i en despertar-se, la seva pell torturada estava coberta d'una mena de rosada compacta.

Marcus va batejar aquella vall com la mar de les Senyoretes, perquè aquí i allà, resseguint el camí, apareixien unes columnes sumptuoses amb la cintura prima, com si els la comprimís una cotilla molt ajustada.

[After a few days, the dangerous col opened out into an unhindered valley, a sea of solid magma. Marcus intuited an infinite horizon, a plain without limits where not even the green lights of the lanterns could impose themselves on the crimson colour of the rigorous topsoil, raised high with whimsical forms, as if waves of copper had covered a horde of crustaceans. From everywhere emerged millions of shells, honed as sharp as knives, reefs that would inflict medieval torture on unshod feet. They could not stray from a narrow, flat tongue of a path which crossed the plain. 'Here the stones have teeth', Marcus said. [...]

In that desert blew a mute and violent wind which slapped the face of the intruders as if guided by personal animosity. [...] They slept in the middle of nowhere and, on awakening, their tortured skin was covered by a type of compact dew.

Marcus christened that valley the sea of the Young Ladies, for here and there, along the way, appeared sumptuous columns which were slim round the waist, as if constricted by a tightly fastened corset.] (2005: 378–79)

For Carroll, the stasis of the tellurian landscape — its 'stubborn fixity and omnipresent darkness' — offers features which 'retard rather than enable mobility' (2015: 152). Unlike the Trade Winds whose dynamism fostered the vigorous, communicative interchange of commerce, the tellurian landscape instils a threateningly lapidary inertia throughout. There is yet more to be feared from a Lovecraftian perspective wherein, despite its geo-static fixity, the subterranean environment holds in abeyance lethal hazards, liable at any moment to erupt into sudden violent motion (*emergien milions de closques esmolades com ganivets*; *les pedres mosseguen*) from behind the pervasive oceanic latency (*mar de magma sòlid*).

Indeed, the potential metamorphosis of the environment poses a threat to the security of both status quo and capitalist enterprise. In a limitless hence unchartered — and unchartable — context (*un infinit horitzontal, una planura sense límits*), columns turn seductively into tightly corseted maidens as the threat of mutation becomes seared with violence. Precious metals (*onades de coure*) whetting the entrepreneurial lust for exploitation conceal enemy hordes of crustaceans which lie in wait. Razor sharp shells similarly wreak painful havoc, like menacing reefs to transportation, on the vulnerable carriage of bare feet which conduct the voyagers on their sojourn.

What is more, the extended metaphorical dyad morphing humanity with the geological/meteorological (*coll; llengua; vent mut i violent que bufetejava [...] com si el guiés una animadversió personal*) underlines a combination which evokes the ontological threat of dehumanization posed by capitalism as denounced by Marx and his followers. In this way, the process of petrification, pervasive throughout the journey, is analogous to the effect of commodification: the conversion of human beings into produce whose labour is to be bought and sold like the materials of the earth.

It is precisely after this fashion that Sánchez Piñol crafts his denunciation of the universality of capitalist reification. Here, slaves of Africa are, as chattel, brutalized, beaten and murdered by their greed-driven masters. The narrative juxtaposes their condition with that of their northern counterparts, the European proletariat, conscripted into military bondage to defend the economic interests and expansionist aspirations of the great powers of the continent. These wage slaves, cannon fodder in the Great War concurrent with the adventure, are driven similarly underground to their trenches and bunkers, to be slaughtered in their millions in defence of that same relentless, possessive urge of imperial interests. The pronounced staccato rhythm, the diction and the inevitable continuity of the narrative — pushing forever onwards — capture the brutal persistence of the acquisitional impulse, whose violence is enhanced by the phonic vitality of crescendo and cadence, and the searing quality of the insistent sibilance.

A similar environment is described in *La pell freda* which again hints at the perils which extreme latitudes suppose for global trade and human involvement in this enterprise. The first sight of the island inspires a vision of frozen stasis for the aspiring meteorologist, crystallized by a reflection on his destiny in this outpost which is located 'al llindar d'una frontera gèlida que mai no traspassaria' [at the threshold of a frozen frontier which would never be crossed] (2002: 8). The immovable and indomitable nature of the geography is exemplified in similarly lapidary terms by the lighthouse which boasted a 'consistència megalítica' [megalithic consistency] (2002: 8). As with the valley of the Senyoretes, communication is compromised by the reefs which surrounded the island; and the reification exacted upon humanity involved in the colonial project is conveyed, not by the geological metamorphosis of *Pandora*, but by a figurative regression to a primeval state whose indumentary atavism is imposed by the environment and its climate:

> Els mariners escocesos es protegien amb manyoples que pujaven fins al colze. Duien pells tan contundents que feien pensar en cossos de morsa. Per als senegalesos aquelles latituds fredes eren un suplici, i el capità tolerava que fessin servir greix de patata com a maquillatge protector, a les galtes i al front.

> [The Scottish seamen protected themselves with mittens which reached up to their elbows. They wore skins which were so bulky they had the shape of walruses. For the Senegalese these cold latitudes were sheer torture and the captain allowed them to use potato grease smeared onto their cheeks and foreheads as protective make-up.] (2002: 7)

The anti-imperialist intention which drives such atopic evocation is further enhanced by the appearance of an Irish cast of characters who promote similar resistance to empire in their support for the advancement of national liberation. The historical parallel which unites Ireland and Catalonia, of course, affords the author an implicit comparison with his own homeland in the context of the colonial world, and it might prove useful to underline certain key elements of historical coincidence.

Both nations have been secular victims of the imperial sway of a neighbouring big brother, one determined to eliminate difference through the imposition of an exclusively homogenous political configuration. Dissidence in the face of the centralist impulse, however, has been a constant in both communities since the Early Modern period, culminating in a series of critical moments which have brought the unitarian state to the verge of fracture. To this effect, we need only reflect on the War of Nine Years (1594–1603), the Revolt of the Catalans (1640) during the War of Thirty Years and the War of Spanish Succession (1701–14), the Croppy Rebellion (1798), and the three Carlist Wars of the nineteenth century.

In more recent times, the belligerence ensuing from the recuperation of national consciousness in both cases has been equally pronounced. The partial liberation of Ireland was secured after the Easter Rising of 1916, although the recent Troubles in the north of the island (1968–98) and political fragility of subsequent years have made patent the unsatisfactory nature of partition, a problem which is reaching crisis point once again in the uncertainty regarding the border after Brexit. In Catalonia, social disruption of a similar kind typifies the present and the recent past. Keeping the aspiration for self-government for the Principality in check was a key factor in the army insurrection leading to the carnage of the Civil War and the centralist repression of two military dictators who controlled Spain for five decades of the last century. Similarly, over the past three decades a frustrated desire for greater autonomy has fired subscription to the present movement for Catalan independence whose militant discontent continues to challenge the unity of the Spanish state, exacerbated — as in the north of Ireland — by the intransigence of an unmovable centralist mindset.

On the other hand, it is equally important to underline the complex nature of the national experiment in both countries, which has proved secularly divisive. Important sectors in these communities turned their back on the movement for self-determination and were instead happy to side with the centralist state and profit by the advantages offered by such unity. The benefit brought to Catalonia by the slave trade has already been noted. And its industrial bourgeoisie, a motor behind cultural and linguistic recovery in the early decades of the last century, was to renege in due course on the nationalist ticket and lend its full support to the centralist programme of the military dictators in exchange for the suppression of revolution and insurgence. At the other end of the social spectrum, demagogues, from Alejandro Lerroux to Inés Arrimadas, were to galvanize popular sectors, achieving notable support for the platform against independence.

Similarly, despite the power of the movement towards liberation — and the tragedies of famine and ensuing mass emigration — Ireland was by no means a disinterested party in the fortunes afforded by empire. Keith Jeffrey has illustrated the extent of the benefits reaped from the colonies by the industrial and Loyalist north in his citing of Bishop Charles D'Arcy's declaration of 1917 that '[t]he British Empire is an Irish Empire as well as a British Empire. We share in all the wealth of that grand inheritance which they, with our help, have created' (1996: 164). And, though conscious of the seismic rupture caused by the revolution of 1916, the more inclusive assessment which this historian offers, in terms of geography, religion or class, is not without relevance to the experience of the Union as a whole: 'Ireland, as a metropolitan part of empire, supplied many of its soldiers, sailors, settlers and administrators. In modern times, Irish people have both sustained and undermined the British imperial system' (1996: 1).

The pertinence of this statement to Catalonia is palpable and the same ambiguity is enshrined within the characters in both novels. The protagonist of *La pell freda* starts out in his youth as a Republican rebel in the years leading up to the Easter Rising. His punishment is to be interned in the Blacktorne School, a naval technical college established by the Crown, where he learns the trade of a maritime engineer. Subsequently, after rejecting his former colleagues and deserting the Cause in the wake of the fratricidal struggle of the Civil War, the qualifications attained at Blacktorne allow him to assume the function of a meteorologist in a lonely outpost of the British Empire.

The same drift towards orthodoxy typifies his experience on the island. Initially, in the aftermath of the destruction of the empires of central and eastern Europe, the Irishman shows himself to be progressive, educated and liberal, in keeping ideologically with the reformist nature of Wilson's Fourteen Point Plan which advocated the establishment of statehood along ethnic lines. In his anti-imperialism he is, in fact, the antithesis of his fellow human resident on the island, Batís Caffó. Reactionary, sexist and completely self-centred, the Austrian (and we note in this respect the imperial significance of the pair's countries of origin) is king of the castle, or in this case the lighthouse, and representative of the law of the jungle: 'la qüestió [...] és que sóc el més fort' [the question is [...] I am the strongest] (2002: 70). The nightly battles with the colonial other of the monsters further emphasize his primacy in a continuous rehearsal of another constant of the old order: survival of the fittest, dog eat dog or, in terms of empire and world domination, might is right.

In opposition to this caveman mentality, the Irishman is reasonable, discerning and, above all, open to change. His behaviour exhibits consistency with the rationality of scientific method and purpose; and his experience pans out as a constant journey from ignorance to enlightenment. The process is epitomized by his relationship with the Citauca. Initially, he is persuaded by Caffó to consider them as primitive, with tendencies towards cannibalism: 'Si els donem prou carronya es devoraran entre ells. [...] Amb un parell de morts n'hi ha prou perquè no s'enfilin' [If we give them enough carrion they will devour each other. [...] A couple of dead will suffice to stop them climbing up] (2002: 114). However, on closer inspection the narrator discovers the reverse to be the case. The amphibians, in fact, display a nobler, heroic trait which becomes underlined by the affirmatively human lexis, emphasizing the surprise involved in the realization:

en Batís va ferir-ne un, més aviat petit. Quatre més van córrer a auxiliar-lo. Oh, Déu meu, Déu meu. Allò que crèiem furor caníbal només era l'esforç d'uns que s'arrisquen per rescatar germans d'armes sota el foc enemic. Jo odiava especialment aquell presumpte canibalisme, aquella ànsia per devorar carronya fins i tot abans que el cos morís. Quantes vegades no havíem disparat contra individus que només volien salvar germans?

[Batís wounded one of them: a small one. Four more rushed to help it. Oh, my Lord, my Lord. What we thought was cannibalistic frenzy was really a struggle by those risking themselves to rescue their brothers in arms under enemy fire. I particularly detested that presumed cannibalism, that compulsion to devour carrion even before the body was cold. How many times had we shot at individuals who only wanted to save their brothers?] (2002: 221–22)

Indeed, the desperate sincerity of the interjections implies that the self-assured ignorance behind the pair's misinterpretation is a contributing factor to the Irishman's indignation. Prejudice, it would seem, has no place in the young man's progressive mentality. Due observation of Aneris, along anthropological lines, also allows the narrator to appreciate the higher form of life her species represent. It is precisely an awareness of her capacity for song and tears, for example, which alerts him to the emotional sophistication of the Citauca. Experimentation completes the scientific process as the protagonist is able to demonstrate, provoking laughter repeatedly through the reenactment of the clumsy episode with the firewood, the fact that the monsters possess a sense of humour: a further elevation in status, in Aristotelian terms, from the purely instinctive level of existence.

On each of these occasions — and in a manner which exemplifies rational methodology — correct analysis of data leads the Irishman to reject the accusation that the monsters are animalistic or primitive, precisely because observation confirms the opposite: that is to say, their likeness to humanity. And the outcome is significant. The rapprochement which results from this illumination leads to a period of peace, cohabitation and optimism. However, at the very moment that a positive conclusion appears to be assured, a major setback is experienced as the meteorologist regresses to that same caveman mentality previously displayed by the now deceased Batís.

If lust for acquisition and possession is the driving force behind the colonial experience, it is wholly appropriate that this reversal in mindset occurs after the Irishman has intercourse with Aneris. Amid the chaos of this pristine atopia, the primitive urge towards sexual ownership awakens, to disastrous effect, those same 'forgotten and brutal instincts' and the 'memory of gratified and monstrous passions' which had overcome Kurtz in *Heart of Darkness* (Conrad 1990: 61). The peace collapses and the Irishman, now Batís reincarnate, comes to treat with the disdain of the previous tyrannical overlord all who inhabit his domain: Aneris, the Citauca and the replacement weatherman who has been sent to relieve him.

The relevance of this change in regime to the wider history of movements of liberation from the imperial yoke is patent. Autonomy, independence and control are seen to imply qualitatively little. Here, as in former colonies, the opposition of a freedom-loving us to an oppressive and exploitative them is never superseded by a common project of collective human purpose: simply by a reorganization of the same belligerent binary. In other words, in the novel we bear witness to a neo-colonial game of musical chairs; that 'droll' lore which Conrad has an exhilarated, triumphant Marlow summarize after his elimination of Kurtz: 'that mysterious arrangement of merciless logic for a futile purpose' (1990: 65). Sánchez Piñol had described this grotesque process in *Pallassos i monstres*, his detailed study of independence in eight African colonies. It is precisely the self-same procedure that the Irishman criticized previously amongst his erstwhile colleagues in the IRA and which was the root cause of his exile:

> Els soldats enemics no passaven de ser cartutxos humans, dirigits pels interessos més foscos del planeta. Nosaltres lluitàvem amb una consciència superior de la llibertat. Per tant, l'expulsió anglesa havia de ser el pròleg d'un món diferent, més amable, més equitatiu. En canvi, els dirigents de la nova Irlanda es limitaven a reemplaçar els noms dels ocupants pels seus. Van canviar els colors de l'opressió, res més. Era un deliri obscè: els anglesos encara estaven evacuant Irlanda i el nou govern ja disparava contra els seus vells camarades.

> [Enemy soldiers were no more than human cartridges, directed by the darkest interests on the planet. We fought with a superior awareness about freedom. As such, throwing out the English had to be the prologue to a different, more loving, more equitable world. However, the leaders of the new Ireland merely replaced the name of the occupier with their own. They changed the colours of the oppression, nothing more. As delirium it was obscene: the English had not yet evacuated Ireland when the new government started firing on its old comrades.] (2002: 43)

The intrusion of the Irish and their association with duplicity in the personal and political sphere is more pronounced still in *Pandora al Congo*. The crucial figure here is a real individual who will forever be linked with the twin themes central to our deliberation, of human exploitation and national liberation. Knighted for his campaigns against slavery in Africa and South America, Roger Casement was a highly esteemed consular official and outstanding public servant of the Crown. His attempt to run guns from Germany to the Rebels in Ireland, however, made him a key figure of the Easter Rising of 1916, a crime for which he was executed by the British as a traitor later that same year.

A similar ambivalence surrounds the case of immigrant labourer MacMahon with whom the protagonist shares his digs. Initially, the Irishman expresses undying fealty and commitment to his wife, Mary. Their union was providential: 'L'estimava abans d'haver-la vist' [I loved her before I saw her]. And there could be no other woman in his life: 'vaig saber que seria la dona de la meva vida' [I realized she was the woman of my life] (2005: 201). After his spouse's death, however, the labourer wastes no time marrying his English landlady, as if without a second thought. And Hibernian duplicity surfaces again as protagonist and narrator Tommy Thomson — Tommy being the forename of the Everyman British soldier in the Great War — is rescued, significantly from no-man's-land at the front, by a regiment of nationalist Irishmen. Paradoxically, these soldiers were fighting for His Majesty as a good-will gesture in support of John Redmond's non-insurrectionary policy for Home

Rule for Ireland. And the doubt surrounding their affiliation is made explicit in the text: 'uns dies abans havia esclatat la rebel·lió irlandesa, i tothom dubtava de la fidelitat d'aquella brigada' [a few days before, the Irish uprising had taken place and everyone doubted the loyalty of that brigade] (2005: 347).

In fact, it is the condition of the Irish characters which imbues the works with further layers of meaning. They are, for example, repeatedly seen to be more accurate and perceptive in their appreciation of the intricacies of a given situation. Unlike their more conditioned English counterparts, who have been unconsciously steeped in the values of the Establishment and the primacy of empire, their assessment of a particular phenomenon is based on objective interpretation rather than any uncritical or conditioned affective response. MacMahon's scepticism after reading Garvey's fanciful version of the Craver murders is important in this respect as is made patent by his questioning regarding the security of the confinement of the slaves:

> — Saps per què als dos germans no se'ls va ocórrer això? [...]
> — Perquè eren anglesos. Jo ho sé perquè sóc irlandès. Els anglesos es pensen que dominen Irlanda perquè són més llestos que els irlandesos. No és veritat. Manen, només, perquè són més forts. Per això no es van pensar que un grapat de negres podrien concebre una maniobra evasiva tan simple. Perquè creien que els negres eren idiotes. Però no eren idiotes. Només esclaus [...]
> — Per això, per què no fugien de la mina, els negres?

> ['Do you know why the two brothers never thought of that?' [...]
> 'Because they were English. I know this because I'm Irish. The English think they rule Ireland because they are cleverer than the Irish. That's not true. They rule merely because they are stronger. It's for that reason that they never thought that a handful of slaves could conceive of such a simple evasive manoeuvre. Because they thought the blacks were idiots. But they weren't idiots. Just slaves' [...]
> 'If that's the case, why didn't the blacks just run away from the mine?'] (2005: 547)

And it is precisely the Irishman's persistent interrogation of Garvey's testimony which will lead to the *desengaño* of the denouement. The insistent logic of MacMahon's intervention obliges the narrator to realize he has been duped by the emotive power of story-telling. His attention has been diverted away from the true account of an act of murder, first attested by Casement's testimony and then reiterated by the Irish patriot in a letter before the gallows. Thomson thus ignores the obvious explanation, preferring the outlandish tale of an implausible romantic encounter between a downtrodden servant and a creature from the tellurian depths recounted — by himself as ghost-writer — in the form of a colonial adventure yarn.

In this way, the book as a whole is an illustration of the credulous assimilation of empire and its values after exposure to the coercive medium of official literature. Popular acceptance of the sensational fabrication of the murder of the Craver brothers, with the narrator's complete participation, affords an exemplum of the process of interpellation as denounced by Althusser. The insidious communication of the tendentious message — and its capacity to coerce on a massive scale — is showcased alongside the correlative peril of a lack of analytical acumen among society at large. Institutional disinformation and mass credulity are thus isolated in their historical context and posited as major contributing factors to the cataclysms of the early twentieth century. A juxtaposition which calls appropriately to mind the exaggerated but pertinent English version of Voltaire's magnificent aphorism: 'Those who can make you believe absurdities can make you commit atrocities'.[3]

The dependence on literature in these works is not merely decorative but organic. Essentially books about books, these novels — with their indulgent self-referentiality — are ideologically charged in their literary praxis. In the more obvious field of political history, the question of the interrelation between narration and nationality follows a critical line developed by such giants as Anderson (1983) and Bhabha (1990), and requires no further elucidation. However, the *Bildung* primacy afforded the topic of character development, autonomy and integrity, foregrounds in our particular case the implication of narrative in the process of social conditioning.

La pell freda begins aptly, for example, with reference to the crate-load of books that the young Irishman has taken with him for distraction during his year in the Antarctic. The centrality of precedence is flagged up immediately when, in a clear pastiche of the episode of the curate and the barber in Don Quixote's library, a long list of writers appears whose novels are burnt strategically to provide defence during the first series of attacks by the monsters. Books with their pernicious, coercive effect were, it will be remembered, the cause of the knight's descent into madness, rendering him unable to distinguish between reality and fiction. In other words, that same failing exhibited by the protagonist of *Pandora* — and extended to the general public at large — who continuously misinterprets the romance of Garvey's adventure for the actuality of events.

Similarly, in *La pell freda* — as Joan Ramon Resina (2008) and Bill Viestenz (2014) have argued — the pivotal issue is the regression of the Irish narrator from a progressive mindset associated with the superego and the inclusion of the other to the dark continent of xenophobia and primeval desire characterized by the id. As a consequence, the narrator reneges on cognitive advancement, embracing instead the uncoordinated instinctual compulsions and jealousy personified by his former neighbour and rival, Batís Caffó. Paradoxically, this vengeful xenophobe undergoes an inverse transformation suffering before his death a totally uncharacteristic attack of altruistic enlightenment:

> Batís va patir un fenomen estrany. Una feblesa interior i un llampec d'intel·ligència, que il·luminava la seva cara com un meteorit creuant l'atmosfera. Encara amb l'arma alçada, em va mirar amb la felicitat desgraciada d'aquell científic que un dia va obrir els ulls al sol fins que l'exposició li va cremar les retines, només per saber quant de temps la vista humana podia resistir la llum.
> — L'amor, l'amor — va dir.
> Va abaixar la destral amb una dolçor trista. Escoltava violins, era un home que tanca silenciosament la porta rere la qual dormen els seus fills.
> — L'amor, l'amor — va repetir, suaument, amb alguna cosa a la cara que recordava un somriure.

[Batís suffered a strange phenomenon. An inner weakness and a flash of intelligence which illuminated his face like a meteorite passing through the atmosphere. With the weapon still held high, he looked at me with the hapless bliss of that scientist who one day opened his eyes to the sun until the exposure burnt up his retinas, just to know how long human sight could stand up to sunlight.

'Love, love,' he said.

He lowered the axe with a sad sweetness. He could hear violins, he was the man who silently closes the door behind which his children lie asleep.

'Love, love,' he repeated, softly, with something in his face reminiscent of a smile.] (2002: 277)

Frailty, tenderness, insight and intelligence are human qualities more readily associated with his Irish companion, along with the philanthropy of the Austrian's last words. The interchange of roles evident in this exchange of identity again relates to literary precedence being singularly reminiscent of the Sanchification of Don Quixote and the Quixotification of Sancho which forms the basis of Cervantes's masterpiece. However, as Batís leaps to his doom amongst the monsters in mystical expiation, cosmic elements which accompany such biblical epiphanies (lightning, the trail of a meteorite, etc.) emphasize the transfigurative dimension of the self-immolation.

Quite apart from the biblical tenor of the discourse, the near-mythical demise of Batís Caffó and the mutual transformation of the protagonists recall a motif in yet another waste land — the Fisher King from the masterpiece by T. S. Eliot — whereby the neophyte, close to water and involved in the death of the old monarch, replaces his predecessor to fulfil the cycle of death and re-birth. We might also mention again, in this respect, the encounter on the banks of the Congo River in *Heart of Darkness* between the mad and ailing Kurtz and the regenerative Marlow. The accumulation of literary precedent — and the more obvious dialogic relationship of the text with *Robinson Crusoe* (1719) and *To the Lighthouse* (1927) has not even been mentioned — is so overpowering that it seems reasonable to conclude that it is precisely the danger of uncritical, affective compliance with literary precedent which is here being exposed.

Pandora al Congo deals with the same conformity in even greater detail. The narrator, Tommy Thomson, considers himself to be a lucid and informed analyst. A healthy instinct of self-preservation, for example, makes him disdain the hysterical patriotism of voluntary enlistment in 1914. He also comes to recognize that the imperial impulse for territorial domination is as responsible for the cataclysm of the Great War in Europe as it is for the execrable practice of colonialism in Africa:

Què vaig dir un dia a Marcus Garvey? 'Jo no hi hauria anat mai, al Congo.' Mentida. No era possible imaginar-se una matança general més gran que aquella guerra, i al mateix cor d'Europa. El Congo no era un lloc, el Congo érem nosaltres. El dia que vaig accedir a allistar-me em vaig convertir en el Marcus Garvey que parava la mà perquè els germans Craver li posessin cartutxos encesos. Ell llençava cartutxos d'un en un, jo dirigia canons de gran calibre cap al seu objectiu. Què era pitjor en realitat?

[What is it I said one day to Marcus Garvey? 'I would never have gone to the Congo?' A lie. It was impossible to conceive of a greater general massacre than that war, right in the heart of Europe. The Congo was not a place; we were the Congo, all of us. The day I allowed myself to be conscripted I became Marcus Garvey who held out his hands for the Craver brothers to fill with live cartridges. He threw the charges, one by one, just as I directed cannons of huge calibre towards their objective. Which was worse in reality?] (2005: 344)

Indeed, the tendentious function of literature and its interconnection with the destructive world of global capitalism is exposed quite beautifully at the start of the novel. The bibliological apology for empire — the celebration of its values and adventure (Resina's 'literatura del imperialismo caliente') — is manufactured following an industrial scheme by an assembly line of ghost writers: or, in Catalan, the *negres en cadena* of Luther Flag's production company. As has been mentioned, these wage-slave proletarians of Northern Europe, paid significantly by piece-work, are regimented, brow-beaten and exploited in the same merciless manner as the shackled African natives — the *negres en cadenes* — in bondage to the Garvey brothers in their frenzied search for gold. As in Conrad, the identity of the condition shared by the British working class and the slaves of the dark continent is evoked further by the juxtaposition of geographical coordinates. The Prime Meridian (*Secret Agent*; *Pandora*) and Equator (*Heart of Darkness*; *Pandora*) are similarly echoed in the Catalan response which also extends to the Antarctic Circle (*Pell freda*) to emphasize the global inevitability of the experience.

Despite the coherence of this exposition, however, Thomson remains so susceptible to the power of fiction and romance as constructed throughout the novel (his own creation, in the final analysis!) that, like the Manchegan knight, he loses his critical capacity to analyse the world around him and arrive at a reasonable conclusion. Unlike the Irish characters, Casement and MacMahon, his sentimentality will not allow him to see through Garvey's novelistic fabrication about the murder of the Craver brothers. What is more, in a manoeuvre reminiscent of Cervantes's nuanced layering, Thomson actually meets up with Casement and is impressed by the integrity of the anti-slavery campaigner: 'una d'aquelles persones que així que la coneixes penses: "Pagaria perquè fos amic meu"' [one of those people who, as soon as you meet him, you think: 'I'd pay money to have a friend like him'] (2005: 297). Yet, rather than accept the veracity of his testimony and the fact that Garvey is 'culpabilíssim' [guilty as hell] (2005: 298), he allows his sensibility — his susceptibility for the outlandish, heart-rending yarn which he is serializing — to blind himself to the truth of the situation.

At the end of the day, the whole sordid conduct of the Casement affair provides a spectacular parallel to the literary tergiversation which the author is keen to expose throughout. And here again, our attention is drawn to the role of fiction in the manipulation and conditioning of public opinion — the interpellation identified by Althusser and unmasked so intelligently by Sánchez Piñol.

Greatly admired for his philanthropic work in the Congo and Peru, for which he was awarded a knighthood in 1911, the anti-slavery campaigner enjoyed huge respect nationally. The esteem in which the diplomat was held was so pronounced that, once the death sentence was passed for his part in the Rebellion, the authorities were concerned that his popularity might provoke a reaction of indignation and opposition throughout the country. The threat was more pronounced still given the fact that Casement stood accused under the antiquated Treason Act of 1351 which was so arcane it was drafted in Norman French.[4]

As a consequence — and in order to silence any anticipated outcry — , the British authorities approved the selective release of what they claimed to be the accused's 'Black Diaries' to 'influential persons in both the UK and USA' (Hyde 2016, without pagination); or what Martina Devlin refers to in modern parlance as 'opinion-formers' (2016). The diaries depicted the consul as a promiscuous homosexual, anathema — as Oscar Wilde could attest — to public morality of the time. The tactic was successful and any expected protest was disarmed.

Quite apart from the irrelevance of the question of sexual persuasion and indulgence, the authenticity of the diaries remains shrouded in doubt even today. For some scholars they might be taken as fabrication, similar to the story dreamed up by Garvey to explain the murder of the Craver brothers. In this way, the whole affair — compounded by the refusal of the British authorities, a century later, to allow reliable testing with independent specialist scrutiny — leaves the process open to the accusation of fake news, employed to misinform for motives of political expediency. A fitting parallel to the interpellation effected by Althusserian Ideological State Apparatuses which is exposed so perceptively in the novel.

As such, the success of the ingenious combination of atopia and Irishmen is two-fold. Literature may, through its evocation of *terra nullius*, offer a threat to the voracious, global dynamic of imperial expansion. This by itself, however, has never managed to arrest the advance of the capitalist dynamic or official message of the state. What is also required is the elaboration of an analytical faculty among the public *en masse*, capable of isolating the tendentious message and countering the institutional dissemination of official values, in this case via the discursive medium of the written word.[5]

Finally — and to return to our point of departure — it would be unfair to understate the contribution made by Sánchez Piñol and his artistry to one other area. The dialectic conducted by this author with a plethora of classic works from the European mainstream — together with the popularity of the numerous translations of his best-sellers — involves a readjustment, from within and without, of the appreciation of the Catalan literary voice and its European relevance. Represented in this polyphonic, universal manner, the experience of the Principality, together with its literature, is no longer conveyed as peripheral or marginal, but finds itself united intricately and insistently with the international chorus. And the introspection and marginalization implied by the trope of the 'petita pàtria' can be seen to have given way to a more open and considered examination of the status of that nation within the global arena as a whole.

Works Cited

ALTHUSSER, LOUIS. 1970. 'Idéologie et appareils idéologiques d'État (Notes pour une recherche)', *La Pensée*, 151: 67–125

ANDERSON, BENEDICT. 1983. *Imagined Communities: Reflections on the Origin and Spread of Nationalism* (London: Verso)

AUGÉ, MARC. 1992. *Non-Lieux, introduction à une anthropologie de la surmodernité* (Paris: Le Seuil)

BAKHTIAROVA, GALINA. 2007. '"Americanos", indianos, mulatas y Otros', in *Memoria colonial e inmigración: la negritud en la España postfranquista*, ed. by Rosalía Cornejo Parriego (Barcelona: Bellatera), pp. 39–52

BHABHA, HOMI. 1990. *Nation and Narration* (London: Routledge)

——. 1994. *The Location of Culture* (London: Routledge)

BROCH, ÀLEX. 2004. 'Cuba en la literatura catalana contemporánea', *Cuadernos hispano-americanos*, 648: 63–71

CARROLL, SIOBHAN. 2015. *An Empire of Air and Water* (Philadelphia: University of Pennsylvania Press)

CONRAD, JOSEPH. 1990. *Heart of Darkness* (Mineola, NY: Dover Publications)

CORNEJO PARRIEGO, ROSALÍA. 2011. 'Por el cielo y más allá de Carme Riera: fluctuaciones y fijaciones raciales en un folletín colonialista', *Cincinnati Romance Review*, 30: 3–16

DEVLIN, MARTINA. 2016. 'Casement, "Black Diaries" and black arts'. *Irish Independent*, 23 April, <http://www.independent.ie/opinion/columnists/martina-devlin/casement-black-diaries-and-black-arts-34652813.html>

ESPRIU, SALVADOR. 1946. *Cementiri de Sinera* (Barcelona: La Sirena)

——. 1975. *Ariadna al laberint grotesc* (Barcelona: Edicions 62)

HYDE, PAUL. 2016. 'Lost to History: An Assessment and Review of the Casement Black Diaries'. *Breac: A Digital Journal of Irish Studies*, without pagination <https://breac.nd.edu/articles/lost-to-history-an-assessment-and-review-of-the-casement-black-diaries/>

JEFFREY, KEITH. 1996. *An Irish Empire? Aspects of Ireland and the British Empire* (Manchester: Manchester University Press)

LEFEBVRE, HENRI. 1974. *La Production de l'espace* (Paris: Anthropos)

LLACH, LLUÍS. 1980. *Verges 50* (Barcelona: Ariola)

MITCHELL, ANGUS. 2013. *16 Lives: Roger Casement* (Dublin: O'Brien Press)

PERE QUART / Joan Oliver. 1947. *Saló de tardor* (Santiago de Chile: El Pi de les Tres Branques)

PLA, JOSEP. 1958. *El meu país* (Barcelona: Selecta)

PERERA, SUVENDRINI. 1991. *Reaches of Empire: The English Novel from Edgeworth to Dickens* (New York: Columbia University Press)

RESINA, JOAN RAMON. 2008. 'Tránsito imposible: la seducción de lo abyecto en *La pell freda*, de Albert Sánchez Piñol', in *El andar tierras, deseos y memorias: homenaje a Dieter Ingenschay*, ed. by Jenny Haase et al. (Madrid: Vervuert), pp. 129–43

RIERA, CARME. 2000. *Cap al cel obert* (Barcelona: Destino)

SÁNCHEZ PIÑOL, ALBERT. 2000. *Pallassos i monstres* (Barcelona: La Campana)

——. 2002. *La pell freda* (Barcelona: La Campana)

——. 2005. *Pandora al Congo* (Barcelona: La Campana)

SARIOLS, DEERIE. 2007. 'Ombres et lumières des tropiques: Conrad et Sánchez Piñol vers un renouveau de la littérature fantastique du XXe siècle', *Revue de littérature comparée*, 324: 473–88

TORREY, NORMAN L. 1961. *Les Philosophes: The Philosophers of the Enlightenment and Modern Democracy* (New York: Capricorn Books)

VIESTENZ, WILLIAM. 2014. 'Monstrous Birth: The Evolving Neighbor in Albert Sánchez Piñol's *La pell freda*', *Hispanic Issues On Line*, 15: 179–99

YUSTRES, VÍCTOR. 2015. 'Catalunya va ser protagonista del comerç negrer amb Cuba',

Directa, 389, 31 July <https://directa.cat/catalunya-va-ser-protagonista-del-comerc-negrer-amb-cuba>

Notes to Chapter 6

1. Espriu's 'petita pàtria' is a motif in *Cementeri de Sinera* [Sinera Cemetery] (1946) and Pere Quart's version appears in 'Corrandes d'exili' [Reels of Exile], from the collection *Saló de tardor* [Autumn Parlour] (1947: 75–77). Though essentially a reflection on the Empordà, Josep Pla's 'petit país' (1958) may be taken as a synecdoche for the country as a whole, as is the case with Lluís Llach's 'País petit', a track on the album *Verges 50* (1980). For Espriu's critique of self-obsession stemming from excessive introspection and complacency, see 'El país moribund' [Moribund Country] from the short story of 1935, *Ariadna al laberint grotesc* [Ariadne in the Grotesque Labyrinth] (1975: 217–21).

2. The maritime paintings of the Dutch Golden Age bear out the ambivalence of the artistic assimilation of empire in graphic terms. If the security of trade and empire in the seventeenth century is borne out by the majestic visions of the imperial and mercantile fleet crafted by Nooms, Cuyp, Vroom, and Van de Velde (the elder), then the menace of the ocean as an uncontrollable atopia looms forebodingly in the stormy seascapes of Backhuysen and the younger Van de Velde.

3. A more accurate translation is: 'Certainly anyone who has the power to make you believe absurdities has the power to make you commit injustices' (Torrey: 1961, 277–78). Needless to say, in our age of fake news and its uncritical acceptance, the relevance of this statement to the public reaction in Britain and Spain to the 'official' reporting of the Troubles and Catalan Independence is manifest.

4. The astuteness of Sánchez Piñol is to be admired in the grotesque parallel between the trials of Casement and Garvey. The former's defence hinged on the authenticity of a text drafted in ancient French. When found guilty, the Irishman was to declare famously he had been hanged for a comma. Garvey's exoneration was dependent upon the even more questionable authenticity of a romantic adventure as ghost-written by the narrator.

5. An example of such state-sponsored mediatic laundering is the *España Global* project (<https://espanaglobal.gob.es> [accessed 16 August 2019]) whose objective, according to its webpage, is not to offer accurate information but to 'mejorar la percepción del país en el extranjero y entre los propios españoles' [improve the perception of our country both at home and abroad.]

CHAPTER 7

Caterina Albert's *Solitud*:
The Shepherd as Subject of Knowing

Jordi Larios

University of St Andrews

'Prec' [Plea], the foreword to *Drames rurals* [Rural Tales] (1902), Caterina Albert's first collection of rural stories, addressed to a 'damisel·la ciutadana' [urban damsel] and signed with the initials V[íctor].C[atalà]., begins by sketching out the author's poetics:

> [...] perdona'm, oh tu, damisel·la ciutadana!, si per encert cau en tes mans de nacre, anèmiques i gràcils, aquest llibrot feixuc; perdona'm i deixa'l de seguida, puix no s'és fet per tu: s'és fet per a altres mans més coratjoses i per gustos més rúfols. Per tu els colors que té són massa crusos, les ratlles massa negres: hi manquen mitges tintes, matisos esblaimats i corbes gracioses com espirals de fum d'un pebeter.

> [[...] please forgive me, oh urban damsel!, if by any chance this heavy book falls on your mother-of-pearl-coloured, anaemic, graceful hands; forgive me and put it aside straight away because it is not for you: it is for other, more courageous hands, for someone with a rougher taste. You would find its colours too strong, its lines too black: it lacks softer half-tones, elegant curves like smoke spiralling out of a torch.] (1951: 249)

In 'Als llegidors' [To the Readers], the preface to *Ombrívoles* [Dark Tones] (1904), her second volume of short stories, which she signed with the pseudonym Víctor Català,[1] Albert elaborates on her approach to fiction:

> El cor humà és com una casa a quatre vents: per tres hi dóna ara el sol, ara l'ombra, però el quart està reservat a l'ombra exclusivament. Els que guaiten pels primers veuen quadres alegradors sadolls de vida: no tenen taques fortes, perquè fins les notes fosques hi són assoleiades i calentes de les plenes resplendors. Mes qui se'n va a guaitar pel darrer costat, topa amb visions ombrívoles, ombrívoles d'ombra freda, verge de passats arroentaments. També n'hi ha de sol en aquestes visions, però és llunyer, darrera de tot, com el fons d'or dels mosaics bizantins, sobre la bella i planera uniformitat del qual destaquen per obscur les figures i accidents dels primers termes.
>
> Jo, quan vaig començar a guaitar a través de mon cor les coses del món, vaig ensopegar-me a fer-ho per la quarta banda; i com els mosaics de camper daurat

i brunes policromies van plaure'm per llur severitat i llur noblesa, exempta de blanes voluptats, la tirada a guaitar-los esdevingué habitud, i l'habitud... vici, segons diuen.

[The human heart is like a house exposed to the four winds: three sides are now touched by the sun, now in the shade, but the fourth is always the preserve of shadows. Those who look through the first three see joyful scenes full of life: there are no strong stains in them because even the dark notes are sunny and warm and shining. However, if you go to the fourth side and look from there, you are faced with cold, dark visions, untouched by any previous warmness. The sun is present in those visions, but it is far away, behind everything, like the golden background to Byzantine mosaics, and the darkness of figures and accidents in the foreground stands out against its beautiful, simple uniformity. When I started to look at the world through my heart, I happened to do it from this fourth side; and since I liked the nobility and severity of the mosaics with golden backgrounds and brown polychromies, free from any soft voluptuousness, the tendency to look at them became a habit, and, as they say, the habit turned into... vice.] (1951: 415)

Further on, she states:

A mi no m'espanten pas [les ombres]; molts cops asclen la meva ànima amb ses negres destrals, però la voluptat del dolor és tan real i tan corprenedora com la voluptat del gaudir; que tot són voluptats i totes les voluptats tenen el mateix encís... Quelcom encara demana en mi parlar de tristors ombrívoles [...]

[I am not scared by shadows; their dark axes often cut through my soul, but the voluptuousness of sorrow is as real and seductive as that of pleasure; there is no distinction between the one and the other, and they are equally charming... Something in me still asks to talk about gloomy sorrows [...]] (1951: 416)

In a 1926 interview, Albert explained: 'Jo estimo la vida tal com és: dolça, amarga, clara i ombrívola. Tota voldria abastar-la, però ¿quina culpa tinc si són les tintes negres les que més impressionen la meva retina? He de seguir o no la meva vocació?' [I love life as it is: bitter, sweet, light and dark. I would like to embrace all of it, but it's not my fault if the dark tones are the ones that have a major impact on my retina. Do I have to follow my vocation or not?] (quoted in Alvarado 1984: 30).

The monologue *La infanticida* [The Filicide], which was finished in 1898 but had to wait until 1967 to be premièred; the stories in *Drames rurals*, *Ombrívoles*, *Caires vius* [Life in the Raw] (1907), *Mare-Balena* (1920), *Contrallums* [Backlights] (1930), *Vida mòlta* (1950) and *Jubileu* [Jubilee] (1951); or the novel *Solitud* [Solitude] (1905), all corroborate Albert's claim that she saw the world through a dark prism. Destitution, greed, jealousy, as well as all kinds of physical and psychological violence, from assassination to rape, are the themes of those fictions. But is there a philosophical background to her 'tintes negres'? In what follows I will offer a close reading of Gaietà, one of the characters in *Solitud*, with a view to suggesting an answer to this question.

As one of the early twentieth-century novels that figure prominently in the Catalan canon, *Solitud* has been the object of several interpretations, although perhaps not as many as one would expect. After all, this is the first significant modern Catalan novel written by a woman and which has a woman as its main character, hence it can be regarded as the starting point of a line of female writers that include Mercè Rodoreda, Maria Aurèlia Capmany, Montserrat Roig, Maria-Mercè Marçal, Imma Monsó, etc.

In the prologue to its fifth edition, Albert reveals that she conceived *Solitud* as a novel to respond to those critics who had censured her tendency to 'concentrar massa l'element dramàtic, d'inquibir massa substància en poc espai' [to condense the dramatic element, to fit too much substance into little space] in *Drames rurals* (1976: 40–41). This criticism persuaded her to write 'un drama rural més, però sense limitar la volada de la fantasia, sense esquifir les descripcions, sense esquematitzar en desmesura' [another rural tale, but without setting limits to the imagination, without shortening the descriptions or schematizing too much] (Albert 1976: 40). In the words of Manuel de Montoliu, the result was 'un magne poema en prosa' or 'un gran poema en prosa' [a great prose poem] (1976: 23, 32) in which Mila, the female protagonist, finds herself between two sharply contrasting male figures: the shepherd Gaietà and Anima, the text's villain. Mila is indeed the protagonist of the novel, but there is no denying that Gaietà plays a pivotal role in it.

At the beginning of *Solitud*, upon arriving at the hermitage that they have been employed to look after, Mila and her husband, Matias, are welcomed by Gaietà, 'un homenet remirgolat amb un fauçó lluent a la mà' (1976: 60) [a small thin man with a gleaming sickle in his hand] (1992: 27). Mila takes to him straight away: 'La Mila se'n quedà emprendada. Li semblava un bon subjecte, agradós i servidor. [...] li posà uns quaranta anys' (1976: 62) [He'd won Mila's heart, this kind and helpful man. [...] Mila reckoned he must be about forty years old] (1992: 28). She considers herself lucky to have met such a decent human being in what appears to be an unfriendly, perhaps even hostile, environment. She feels comfortable in his presence: 'En la personeta del pastor hi sentia com un caliu de família, grat i retornador' (1976: 69) [That unknown shepherd lent the place a homely warmth, sweet and welcoming] (1992: 35). Her initial impression of Gaietà as a good-hearted man will be confirmed by her subsequent dealings with him. She will come to believe that he '[s]embla pare o germà de tothom' (1976: 98) [acts like everyone's father or brother] (1992: 59) by virtue of his good nature. She will admire his multiple skills (1976: 117; 1992: 74); he will become essential company to her (1976: 213; 1992: 148); and she will see him as 'l'home savi i bo' (1976: 221) [that kindly man] (1992: 154),[2] a child-like figure who gets carried away by the tales he enjoys telling (1976: 248; 1992: 174), and a serious, reflective individual who thinks twice before speaking (1976: 251; 1992: 176). After his assassination at the hands of Anima, Mila will say to herself: 'Era un savi, el pastor.... [...] Sí; era un savi i mai s'errava, com si per endavant sapigués tot lo que havia de venir...' (1976: 298) [What a wise man he was! [...] Yes, Gaietà always knew what was going to happen...] (1992: 210–11).

The shepherd takes it upon himself to show Mila round the hermitage and in the following weeks and months he will help her to adapt to her new surroundings — so much so that, according to the narrator, he 'havia fet fer a la dona son aprenentage de muntanyenca, lograr triomfar a la fi de sa naturalesa espantadissa de cervereta' (1976: 199) [guided the woman through her mountain apprenticeship, winning out at last over her timorous, fawn-like nature] (1992: 137). Up until the time of his death he will be her guide, her mentor and her protector. This is never more apparent than in those moments when the narrator draws attention to how Mila is enveloped by his affectionate gaze. In fact, Gaietà's affectionate, benevolent gaze falling upon Mila is a recurrent motif in the novel. In springtime, she undergoes a positive physical and psychological transformation that mirrors that of the mountains. Gaietà attributes her blossoming to St Pontius's miracle-working and he warns her not to badmouth the saint: 'Un dia el pastor, abrigant-la de dalt a baix amb una mirada afectuosa, li havia advertit [...]' (1976: 138).³ When the notoriously passive Matias is left speechless by the news that they have lost all their money on the festival of the roses, Mila looks first at her husband with contempt, then she seeks refuge in the eyes of the shepherd: 'Els trobà fits en ella... Aquells ulls sempre plens de fortalesa, de previsió, de serenitat, la inundaven d'una ampla mirada calda, devota, infinida...' (1976: 176) [He stared back at her, and those eyes full of strength, foresight, and serenity enveloped her in a broad, warm, devoted, infinite gaze...] (1992: 120). Shortly after this exchange, it is Gaietà's gaze that comes between her and Arnau, and stops her from giving way to desire for the young man who has just made clear that he has feelings for her:

> Uns ulls isolats, sense visatge que els enquadrés, uns ulls màgics, que no eren els de l'Arnau, abrigaren amb una ampla mirada calda, devota, infinida, la dona esblaïmada. I aquells ulls, com si tanquessin en son fons una força més serena, més dominant, més poderosa que el mateix instint de vida, feren refluir i allunyar instantàniament l'onada turbulenta. La dona es reprengué a si mateixa. (1976: 181)

> [Distant eyes, unframed by any face, enveloped the pale woman in a broad, warm, devoted, infinite gaze. And those eyes, as though embodying a force stronger than life itself, made the turbulent wave quickly recede into the distance. Mila regained her composure.] (1992: 124)⁴

Gaietà shocks Mila with the revelation that Matias is not only Anima's sidekick, but he has taken to gambling while she was ill. She looks in despair at the shepherd and is again enveloped in his protective gaze: 'son esguard clar i segur deixà anar sobre la dona una absolució amplament indulgent' (1976: 252) [those calm eyes offered her unconditional absolution] (1992: 177). Gaietà's gaze is such an important element of his characterization that the narrator will refer to his dead body as being gazeless: 'Tenia les galtes verdes i enfonsades, el front d'una blancor apagada de sèu pres, i els ulls, oberts i amb les nines entelades, careixien de mirada' (1976: 272) [His cheeks were green and sunken, his brow was dull white, like lard, and his eyes, though open, were glazed [...]] (1992: 192–93). Mila grieves for his friend, and the memory of his dead body, 'estès, desfigurat, sense moviment, sense paraula, sense mirada, sense res del que era el pastor que ella coneixia' (1976: 275) [motionless, speechless, and sightless] (1992: 194), lingers on in her mind. She cannot accept that Gaietà is dead, yet she misses his gaze, his smile and his powerful storytelling:

la idea de que el pastor no era ja d'aquest món no podia acabar de penetrar-li. Mes això no li privava a la dona de trobar a mancar aquella mirada plena de viàtics encalmadors que la socorria en els seus defalliments, aquella rialleta platxeriosa que li esvaïa les inquietuds, aquella paraula màgica que li feia veure tot lo del món bonic [...] (1976: 277)

[The fact that he was no longer in this world had not really dawned on her. But all the same, she missed his reassuring smile, his sweet laughter, his luminous stories.] (1992: 195)[5]

Gaietà's gaze is that of someone who *looks at* the world, is adept at *seeing* its beauty, and has the capacity to *convey* it to others. One morning, as he is patiently waiting for the fog to lift so that he can take his flock out, Mila mentions that watching the fog from the hermitage's terrace has saddened her. She is not a mountain person and she can't wait for the sun to come out. Gaietà laughs at her: he welcomes the fog because it helps him to think beautiful thoughts. It is in the context of this conversation that Mila gets an inkling of how he engages with the world:

— [...] M'agradi passejar-me pels cims ensoleiats amb la ramada, i veure lli enllà, sota meu, tot el món colgat per la fumera... Hi ha camins que senti veus, veus fondes, i no vegi ningú, i jo pensi en les goges que s'espitllin i que rentin la roba entorn del gorg... És una bella cosa la boira: digueu pas, ermitana! (1976: 75)

['[...] You see, I like the fog; it sets me thinking... I like to pasture my sheep up there in the sun and look down on the clouds below... On some paths I hear deep voices but you can't see a soul, so I guess the fairies must be admiring themselves in some pool while they do their laundry... The fog's pretty, don't you think, hermitess?'] (1992: 40)

During the same conversation, Gaietà notices that Mila is always looking up and he recommends that she look around: ' — Repari que vós sempre goiteu enlaire, com els ceguets... Cal escampar els uis pertot, dona...' (1976: 85) ['Why do you keep looking up like a blind man? You should look all around...'] (1992: 49). On a different occasion, Mila reminisces about her aunt and her uncle, who took her in after her mother had died: Mila's uncle was a boatman and she savours the memory of the river he used to ferry people across. She is prompted by this memory to make a general remark about the prettiness of rivers, to which Gaietà replies: ' — Tot lo del món és bonic si es mira amb bons uis, ermitana!' (1976: 201) ['Everything's pretty if you look at it right, hermitess'] (1992: 139). That Gaietà's gaze is exceptionally attuned to the beauty of the mountain becomes even more apparent when he and Mila are on their way up to Highpeak. At one point, he urges his companion to admire the spectacle of the landscape in the early morning, and the narrator describes Gaietà's gaze as he admires it himself:

— Veieu quin present de dia, ermitana. Ni un tel de boira sobre la terra ni una volva de nigulet al cel. Podíem pas atrapar mellor, com hi ha món! De dalt vorem fins a les darreres darreries... — I ullprès, encisat, passejà d'una banda a l'altra la mirada, amb la lentitud majestuosa que un rei la porpra. (1976: 224)

['See what a nice day it is? Not a speck of fog on earth or a wisp of cloud in Heaven. Lord love us, we couldn't have picked a finer morning! When we get to the top, we'll be able to see all creation...' And fascinated, he slowly gazed from side to side with the majestic serenity of a king born to the purple.] (1992: 156)

Gaietà's fascinated gaze goes hand in hand with an almost otherworldly calmness or serenity from which Mila often benefits. When troubled by the brutality of a tale he has been telling — it concerns a Moorish king who would have the young girls he disliked beheaded and her heads tossed into the Badblood Creek — 'la figura placèvola del pastor l'asserenà, semblant dir-li que no tot era terrible i dolorós en l'enclòs d'aquelles muntanyes fosques' (1976: 85) [the shepherd's cheerful face calmed her, seeming to say all was not dreadful and tragic in those dark mountains] (1992: 49).[6] Gaietà always exudes calmness. As a response to Mila's pointing out that he has multiple skills, he 'rigué tranquil·lament' (1976: 117) [he chortled] (1992: 74) and ate 'tranquil·lament' (1976: 118) [quietly] (1992: 75) in the presence of Anima.[7] The narrator reports that Mila and the shepherd 'tenien llargues i reposades hores de conversa' (1976: 199) [had long, leisurely conversations] (1992: 137) and that she is devoted to 'aquell homenet remirgolat, que a força d'enginy i bonavolença l'havia feta remuntar fins a espais serens que mai no havia conegut encara' (1976: 210) [that little man, whose ingenuity and kindness had lifted her to such heights] (1992: 146).[8] After confiding in him that she and Matias have lost all their money, Mila looks the shepherd in the eye to find that 'sos ulls verds tenien una tranquil·litat misteriosa de gorg pregon' (1976: 174).[9] She does not understand why 'un home tan serè i reposat' (1976: 189) [someone so wise and serene] (1992: 131) like Gaietà would pay attention to a brute like Anima. The narrator alludes to Gaietà's eyes, the eyes of a story teller, as 'els ulls serens del creador' (1976: 211) [[t]he creator's eyes] (1992: 147).[10] When Marieta gleefully makes him aware that Anima is casting aspersions on his motives for staying on at the hermitage, he reacts with 'una mitja rialla tranquil·la i platxeriosa' (1976: 214) [he chuckled] (1992: 148).[11] On their way up to Highpeak, Mila falls behind as he '[li] passà endavant tranquil·lament' (1976: 220) [calmly walked ahead] (1992: 153). Further on, he waits for her 'amb son aire calm i serè de costum i amb l'eterna rialleta vagant sobre sos llavis' (1976: 222) [calm as always and with a smile upon his lips] (1992: 154–55). The moment they realize that Anima is following them, 'les serenors de sa alegria' (1976: 237) [the serenity of their joy][12] vanish. On their way back down, Gaietà tells Mila the story of the Cross and she wonders if 'la serenitat del pastor' (1976: 248) [Gaietà's serenity] is somehow related to the piece of rusty metal that he always carries around as an amulet; he suggests that they have a little rest and he sits down 'tranquil·lament' (1976: 248) [calmly] (1992: 174), as is his wont. Finally, upon hearing from Mila that the people at St Pontius' Farm are giving her the cold shoulder, '[e]l pastor, sempre tan serè, es torbà lleument' (1976: 260) [the shepherd, always serene, was somewhat disturbed].

Gaietà's storytelling derives its power from the serenity of his peculiar gaze. Mila, Matias, Gaietà and the child Baldiret spend many a winter evening by the fire at the hermitage, and Baldiret is enthralled by the shepherd's 'rondalles' [fantastic tales]: 'El pastor, tot fent la seva feina, contava rondalles a En Baldiret, i sa paraula, reposada i suau, plena de l'encís foraster que havia servat dels paratges de naixença, s'aixecava en la calma roenta de la peça amb una gran majestat, senzilla i misteriosa, de ritus druídic' (1976: 124) [As the shepherd whittled, he told stories to Baldiret, and his soft voice, suffused with the lilt of his distant birthplace, filled the cozy room with its simple, druidic majesty] (1992: 79). But Baldiret is not the only one who gets hooked to Gaietà's 'rondalles'. Mila herself is transfixed by them, since they offer her a way out of her humdrum life and into 'la vida fantàstica de la muntanya' [the mountains' fantastic realm] so that 'el sentit de lo meravellós es despertà en ella com una nova consciència superior' (1976: 210) [her sense of wonder blossomed into a new and higher awareness] (1992: 146). Intrigued by his talent, one day she asks him who taught him everything he knows, all the 'rondalles' he excels at telling, and he gives the following response: ' — Unes, les més petites [...], me les contaren els avis de Sant Ponç; les atres... Nostro Senyor...' (1976: 211) ['The little ones I heard from the old folks at St. Pontius [...] and the rest... from Our Lord'] (1992: 147). Mila remains silent and he continues:

> — Con vegi un paratge nou de la muntanya, m'assegui tot solic i me'l miri bé una bella estona; i mirant-me'l, senti una escalfor en la boca del cor, i de mica en mica aqueia escalfor me se'n pugi en amunt com una fumera, i m'ompli el cap i me fa rumiar, rumiar... I com si una veu me les anés dient, me vénen totes les coses que hi deuen havere passades en aqueis paratges... I per això jo digui que me les conti Nostro Senyor, perquè, digueu: ¿pot éssere altra que la veu de Nostro Senyor aquesta que un hom sent ací dedins con rumia? (1976: 211)

> ['When I find a new spot in the mountains, I sit down all by myself and take a good look at it, and while I'm looking, I can feel my heart begin to warm, and that warmth spreads till it reaches my head... And like some voice was telling me, I think of everything that must have happened there... And that's why I say it must be Our Lord, because who else could speak inside you when you're all by yourself.'] (1992: 147)

Mila is conscious that Gaietà embellishes or idealizes reality,[13] yet he credits his storytelling with keeping her alive: ' — [...] Vós, vós sol heu fet el miracle amb les vostres falòrnies, que tot ho capgiren i ho fan veure pel cantó més bonic...' (1976: 229) ['[...] You did it with your stories, which show the good side of everything...'] (1992: 160). No wonder she will miss them so much once he is gone.

Gaietà's peculiar gaze — he looks at the world from *above*, on his own, and has the ability to tease beauty out of it — as well as his almost otherworldly calmness and powerful storytelling mean that he is above life's emotional fray.[14] His aloofness discourages Mila from talking to him about her 'ràbies somortes, estranys enartaments, decepcions de no sabia què, tremolors secrets de ventures incertes' (1976: 140) [stifled rages, strange flashes of exuberance, disappointments with she scarcely knew what, secret uncertain shudders] (1992: 92) that she experiences during springtime, and despite his affection for her and his protectiveness towards her, she is vexed by it. As they start to walk towards Highpeak, not for the first time she feels 'que mentre li estava a prop i percebia fortament la presència d'aquell home, ell, dut per les ales de pensaments misteriosos s'absentava d'ella, oblidant-la enterament'

(1976: 217) [that while she was near this man, whose presence she sensed so strongly, he was far away, oblivious, lost in his own thoughts] (1992: 151). Further up the mountain, Gaietà realizes that she has fallen behind and calls out to her. Startled by the sound of his voice, Mila 'contemplà el pastor amb l'esguard atònit amb què es guaita lo incomprensible, lo que està fora de lo natural' (1976: 222) [stared at Gaietà with the astonished gaze of one who contemplates something never seen before] (1992: 154). For a moment, in the darkness of Lightningbolt Pass, she had been afraid that he might turn against her. She soon comes to her senses, though. In fact, in a total volte-face she regrets his sexual inhibition. She has reached the provisional conclusion that he protects everybody and treats everybody the same, and there is no special place for her in his heart (1976: 222–23; 1992: 155). On more than one occasion she had wished for the two of them to be on their own, as 'sols per aquell camí arribaria potser a fondre's el gel de la indiferència o de la reserva impenetrable [de Gaietà], esdevenint sobre sa vida quelcom d'importantíssim, d'irrevocable' (1976: 228) [only thus could she breach Gaietà's reserve, forcing something important and irrevocable to occur] (1992: 159–60). That very same day she will reject her own conclusion that Gaietà has no feelings for her. Instead, she decides that she will be grateful for what she assumes to be his refusal to act on his desire:

> I ara la Mila, de nou copbatuda pel remoixell de ses impressions, variables com rufagades de tempesta, admirava xardorosament el pastor i el regraciava per lo mateix que estona abans, en el clot de Pas de Llamps, l'havia acusat: per aquella quietud de desitjos, per aquella reserva amb què cobria, com amb vel de serena castedat, la humanesa de sos sentiments. (1976: 240)

> [And now Mila, again buffeted by turbulent emotions, admired what she had cursed in Lightningbolt Pass: the reserve with which Gaietà chastely veiled his inner feelings.] (1992: 168)

Mila makes two mistakes when considering the 'quietud' of Gaietà's 'desitjos' or his 'reserve'. The first is to interpret it as a result of his age. Initially, as we have seen, she had thought that 'he must be about forty years old', but before climbing down Highpeak he reveals to her that he is approaching sixty-four. She is very disappointed with her miscalculation and angry with herself at having made it: 'Errada dolorosa, cosa repugnant, la que li havia passat!' (1976: 254) [Sixty-four! What a grotesque mistake...] (1992: 178). The second, which occurs once Gaietà is dead and Mila has been raped by Anima, is to think that what held them apart was the shepherd's respect for his late wife:

> El pastor no l'havia volguda mai a ella amb voler d'home a dona. I ara ho reparava bé; no havien estat els anys, no havia estat l'amuleta preservadora, no era una virtut o una prudència major que la dels altres homes lo que s'havia entreposat enmig d'ells, no: havia estat una memòria, una ombra, un respecte; havia estat la sola recordança de l'atra dona, de la dona seva, de l'antiga criadeta de Sant Ponç. (1976: 297)

> [Gaietà had never loved her as a man loves a woman. It was not his age, his amulet, or his virtue that stood between them. No, it had been a memory, a shadow, a respect for his beloved wife, the servant girl at St. Pontius.] (1992: 210)

Montoliu refers to Gaietà as a '[s]ímbol lluminós de la faç amable, riallera i maternal de la natura' [bright symbol of nature's kind, motherly side] (1976: 11); the 'Pastor-poeta' [Shepherd-poet] whose mental landscape is 'un món d'encanteri, en el qual el mite és la realitat' [a magical world in which the myth is the reality] (1976: 19); 'aquell home enigmàtic' [that enigmatic man] (1976: 24), so enigmatic that Mila cannot have access to his inner life; someone with a 'mentalitat deliciosament infantil i poètica' [a delightfully childish, poetic, mentality] (1976: 28); 'el geni benèfic d'aquella solitud' [the charitable genius of those mountains] (1976: 33); '[un] home primitiu' [a primitive man] (1976: 34); 'la figura dolça i misteriosa del Pastor' [the sweet, mysterious figure of the shepherd] (1976: 36); or 'la serena i misteriosa figura del Pastor, el geni d'aquelles altes solituds' [the serene, mysterious figure of the shepherd, the genius of those high mountains] (1976: 38).

In two 1967 lectures that remained unpublished until 2010, Gabriel Ferrater was adamant that '[*Solitud*] té una interpretació [...] única, coherent i inatacable' [there is only one coherent, irrefutable interpretation of *Solitud*] (2010: 57). For him, the novel is 'el relat d'una mena d'al·lucinació eròtica, per una part, de l'autora però, per altra banda, del seu personatge' [it is a tale about an erotic hallucination of the author as well as her character] (2010: 60). Mila gradually falls in love with Gaietà, a process that culminates in her decision to give herself to him, yet almost immediately comes to an end when she discovers that he is much older than she had anticipated. In Ferrater's words, 'la diferència és prou gran perquè el descobriment de l'edat real del pastor li faci fàstic i perquè reculi i renunciï al pastor' [the age gap between them is wide enough for her to feel revulsion, go back on her decision and give up on the shepherd] (2010: 61). Ferrater deftly unpicks the tapestry of sexual symbols woven into the novel, but that part of his deliberation, interesting though it is, would lead us away from the main purpose of this chapter, which is to throw light on the figure of the shepherd.

Alan Yates, who was the first to locate *Solitud* within the context of the crisis of the realist novel that unfolded at the turn of the twentieth century, suggests that Gaietà is 'l'objecte principal de la [...] sensualitat [de la Mila] que es desvetlla, i el magnetisme entre els dos arriba al paroxisme en aquell capítol "El cimalt", on la Mila s'imagina com seria lliurar-se voluntàriament al pastor' [the main object of [...] Mila's awakening sensuality, and their mutual magnetic attraction will reach its paroxysm in the chapter 'Highpeak', where Mila imagines what it would be like to give herself freely to the shepherd] (1975: 97–98). However, in Yates's reading Gaietà is not simply a conventional character in a realist novel: 'la seva presència i el seu paper a la novel·la tenen un sentit figurat' [his presence and his role in the novel have a figurative sense] in that he is 'una amalgama dels pressupòsits artístics i sentimentals del ruralisme romàntic' [an amalgamation of the artistic and sentimental premises of romantic *ruralisme*] (1975: 98). Yates views Gaità as the *bon sauvage*, a personification of 'l'esperit rousseaunià de comunitat amb la naturalesa' [Rousseau's spirit of communing with nature]: an individual who has a unique relationship with the land and its traditions, whose 'rondalles' are not just a narrative device to echo, reflect or comment upon Mila's psychological development, but 'una expressió del *volksgeist* romàntic que informa el ruralisme folklòric i costumista' [a manifestation of the romantic *volksgeist* informing folkloric *costumista* ruralism] (1975: 98).

Jordi Castellanos agrees with Montoliu's opinion that Gaietà is one of the great strengths of *Solitud* and he points out that 'la seva imatge d'home reposat i barbamec s'associa als valors morals de bondat i confiança' [Gaietà's image as a calm, clean-shaven man is associated with the moral values of goodness and trustworthiness] (1986: 612); he stresses Gaietà's 'actitud paternal, sense apetència sexual' [paternal attitude, lacking in sexual desire] (1986: 613) towards Mila; and relates the shepherd's talent as a storyteller to Joan Maragall's poetics of the 'paraula viva' [living word]: 'Sembla com si, en el pastor i allò que simbolitza, Víctor Català hi traduís la poètica maragalliana' [it looks as if Víctor Català represents Maragall's poetics through the shepherd] (1986: 614).[15]

Lola Badia takes issue with Castellanos' reading of the novel and explains Mila's situation at the hermitage as that of a woman stuck, as it were, between two rocks and a hard place: a sexually impotent husband, an old man she fantasizes about, and a thug who deserves to be put behind bars (1984: 32). Badia argues that Mila's development, her learning about the world and herself as interpreted by Castellanos, involves 'una dolorosa renúncia: la renúncia a una "normalitat sexual"' [a painful rejection: the rejection of 'sexual normality'] (1984: 33) partly brought about by her circumstances (her marriage to Matias), partly self-inflicted. She has made the 'mistake' of falling in love with Gaietà, after all, and Badia poses the question '¿quina noia que no estigui una mica malejada per una vida de frustracions pot enamorar-se d'un vellet barbamec, per molt deliciosament paternal que resulti?' [what young woman who has not been damaged by a life full of frustrations can fall in love with a clean-shaven old man, no matter how delightfully paternal he turns out to be?] (1984: 33).

As regards the male characters in the novel, Anne Charlon maintains that 'cap no és realment positiu [...] i la relació de la Mila amb ells no és satisfactòria' [none is really a positive character [...] and Mila's relationship with them is not satisfactory] (1990: 42). Charlon highlights the shepherd's protectiveness towards Mila as well as his vast knowledge of the mountain, and she understands him as a symbol of 'la saviesa popular' [popular wisdom] (1990: 42). In Charlon's view, the novel centres on Mila's growing, unfulfilled passion for Gaietà, and she considers Mila's shock upon discovering his age a 'recurs dramàtic estrany' [a strange dramatic device] (1990: 43) for which there are two possible explanations. The first is that Mila subconsciously perceives Gaietà as a father figure, and when she can no longer ignore her perception of him as such 's'esglaia davant d'una relació que pressent incestuosa' [she is terrified by a relationship she intuits as incestuous]; the second has to do with the author's own subconscious: 'és evident que [Albert] és incapaç de concebre la relació sexual entre un home i una dona d'una altra manera que no sigui com una agressió violenta de l'home contra la dona, i aquest acte li sembla incompatible amb la personalitat del pastor' [it is obvious that Albert is incapable of envisaging the sexual relationship between a man and a woman as something other than the man's violent aggression against the woman, and this seems to her to be incompatible with Gaietà's personality] (1990: 43).

Francesca Bartrina indicates that the role played by the shepherd in Mila's dream during her first night at the hermitage is that of 'pare protector' [protective father] (2001: 224) and goes along with Charlon's view that the reason for Mila's eventual rejection of him is that he is too old and she cannot contemplate what would amount to an incestuous relationship. Bartrina claims that 'la [...] característica principal [del pastor] és que està en possessió del *logos*, domina la paraula' [the shepherd's main feature is that of being in possession of the logos; he has the gift of the gab] (2001: 240). This would be the cause of Mila's attraction to him, even though she will end up by subconsciously associating him with a father figure — he protects her; he is sixty-four — and 'la ment de la Mila difícilment pot acceptar la idea d'una relació extramatrimonial, però la d'un incest, no la pot suportar de cap manera' [Mila can hardly accept the idea of an extramarital relationship, let alone an incestuous one] (2001: 242).

Brad Epps also emphasizes 'the negative presence of men' (2002: 28) in *Solitud* which includes 'the benevolent shepherd Gaietà, characterized by his love of nature and narrative' since '[he] is rendered in a less than positive light when Mila discovers that he is much older — and hence not as "naturally" or "narratively" desirable — than she had thought' (2002: 29). Like Charlon and Bartrina before him, Epps dwells on Mila's 'internalized revulsion towards the semblance of incest. For Gaietà, in stating his age, suddenly becomes a father figure to Mila, and the shape of the symbolic family that he and Mila had formed with Baldiret shifts from one of son, father, and mother to one of son, *grandfather*, and mother' (2002: 30).

Gaietà, then, has been variously described as a symbolic figure; a sweet and mysterious man; someone who is aloof and somewhat vague; the object of Mila's desire; a representation of the artistic premises underpinning 'romantic *ruralisme*'; a shepherd who is at one with the land and its traditions; a calm, principled, trustworthy figure exuding moral goodness; a father figure without any sexual appetite; an allegory of Maragall's poetics; an old man lacking in virility who is idealized by a lonely woman in the prime of her life; a symbol of the 'saviesa popular'; an individual in possession of the *logos*; and a male character whose age is of a piece with the generally 'negative presence of men' in the novel. While all these interpretations are plausible enough and complement each other, there is more to Gaietà than meets the eye. We could ask ourselves, for example, how significant his lack of 'apetència sexual' is, or why he gives Mila the impression of being aloof, or how reliable is her final assessment of Gaietà's unwillingness or inability to engage with her in a loving, sexual relationship. Indeed, why is it that Gaietà, a heterosexual man, shows no desire for an attractive young woman who is in love with him? Is it simply because he is sixty-four, as Mila initially surmises before concluding that what held them apart was the shepherd's respect for his late wife? If that were the case, I would be inclined to agree with Ferrater that '[a]quest és l'únic punt d'ingenuïtat de la senyoreta Albert, perquè si suposa que els homes de seixanta-quatre anys ja no existeixen eròticament és una mica pessimista' [this is the only sign of naïvety on Ms Albert's part, because if she supposes that sixty-four year old men do not have an erotic life, she is a bit pessimistic] (2010: 61). Was Albert *that* naive, though?

In a passage from the preface to *Caires vius* laced with Nietzschean overtones, Albert affirms:

> El geni — poder creador per excelència y principi revolucionari per excelència també — may pertany als dòcils caps de ramada, sinó als pastors que s'imposen a n'ella. Es sempre iconoclasta y ultradogmàtich; trenca tots els motlles, capgira totes les teories e imposa noves lleys, potser tan ilògiques y pernicioses com les que vulnera, però noves a la fí, es dir, desestancadores, contraries a la immovilitat, signe de mort.

> [The genius — creative power *par excellence* and revolutionary principle also *par excellence* — is never part of the docile herd; he is one of the shepherds who prevail over it. He is always iconoclastic and overdogmatic; he breaks all moulds, turns all theories upside down, and imposes new laws; they may be as illogical and harmful as the ones he disobeys, but they are nonetheless new, that is, they free one up, they go against paralysis, which is a sign of death.] (Cited in Yates 1975: 87)

Here Albert portrays the artist as 'un ésser superior (i solitari), revolucionari i messiànic' [a superior (and solitary), revolutionary and messianic being] (Yates 1975: 87). Doubtless, Gaietà is a representation of the artist, even of the *modernista* artist, but he only partially fits the profile outlined by Albert in this passage. As a shepherd, he places himself above the fray, yet we would be hard put to identify the revolutionary and the messiah in him. Significantly, the key word in the passage in question is not 'artista' [artist] or 'poeta' [poet], but 'geni', and I believe that Arthur Schopenhauer's notion of 'genius' can help us to understand aspects of Gaietà's characterization, particularly his lack of desire for Mila, that have not thus far been fully elucidated.

In *The World as Will and Representation*, Schopenhauer writes that although the 'natural function' of the human intellect is to serve the will, occasionally, and for a brief period of time, the intellect may free itself from this servitude (1969: II, 363). In such interludes, instead of knowing 'mere *relations* of things, primarily their relations to the will itself [...] the relations of things to one another', the intellect apprehends 'the purely objective nature of a phenomenon that expresses itself through all relations' (363). Freed from its servitude to the will, the intellect 'knows merely the essential' and 'has for his object the *Ideas*' that Schopenhauer, like Plato, defines as 'the permanent, unchangeable *forms*, independent of the temporal existence of individual beings [...], which really constitute the purely objective element of phenomena' (364). What is clear then is that for these ideas or forms to enter the consciousness of an individual, he has to undergo a change, to carry out an act of self-denial that involves 'knowledge turning away entirely from [his] own will', and becoming 'the pure mirror of the objective inner nature of things' (367). This amounts to achieving 'a temporary preponderance of the intellect over the will' (367). For Schopenhauer, 'we apprehend the world purely objectively, only when we no longer know that we belong to it; and all things appear the more beautiful, the more we are conscious merely of them, and the less we are conscious of ourselves' (368). Such an objective apprehension of the world requires 'a special energy and elasticity on the part of the intellect' (370) which are the defining traits of the genius. 'Genius — specifies Schopenhauer — consists precisely in the existence of a greater measure of the power of knowledge than the service of an individual will requires' (370). This surplus of the power of knowledge facilitates the apprehension of the world 'without reference to the will' (370): a disinterested, objective apprehension of the world that is necessary for the creation of the work of art. It can only take place as a result of 'a complete silencing of the will which leaves the person as pure subject of knowing' and, as Schopenhauer puts it, '[t]he aptitude for the prevalence of this state is simply genius' (371).

It is precisely such an aptitude that we see in Gaietà, the shepherd who apprehends the world objectively because in him there is 'a complete silencing of the will'. Or, in simple terms, he has no desires. Having detached himself from the world and freed his intellect from servitude to the will, his apprehension of reality is clouded by neither passion nor desire. His ability to perceive beauty in the morning fog about which Mila complains — indeed his alertness to the beauty of all things — is a direct consequence of his detachment: as Schopenhauer writes, '[e]verything is beautiful only so long as it does not concern us' (374). And Gaietà has the capacity to look at the world and come up with his 'rondalles' because '[o]nly when the will with its interests has forsaken consciousness, and the intellect freely follows its own laws, and as pure subject mirrors the objective world [...], only then do the colour and form of things stand out in their true and full significance' (373). Mila is protected by Gaietà, admires him and falls in love with him, but she does not fathom this aspect of his personality. In fact, she does not even come close to suspecting that Gaietà's lack of sexual desire has nothing to do with his age and all to do with his being a genius, not Montoliu's 'geni benèfic d'aquella solitud' or 'el geni d'aquelles altes solituds', but 'the pure mirror of the objective inner nature of things', a 'pure subject of knowing', Schopenhauer's non-desiring genius, albeit a Christianized version of it.[16]

Caterina Albert was not as naive as Gabriel Ferrater would have us believe. Irene Muñoz has brought to light a handwritten note in which the novelist set for herself the task of reading Hegel, Schopenhauer and Leopardi (see Muñoz 2016: 16). Although the note is not dated, Muñoz is confident that Albert wrote it towards the end of the nineteenth century, that is, before she started writing *Solitud*. It is my contention that Albert went on to read Schopenhauer and that, as I hope to have proven here, Gaietà is a fictionalization of his notion of 'genius' as expounded in *The World as Will and Representation*. Moreover, I would like to suggest that Schopenhauer's impact on her thinking may extend way beyond the construction of Gaietà; that her exposure to the philosopher's pessimism lies behind her 'tintes negres' — her inclination to see the world through a dark prism — which are so apparent in *Solitud*.

Works Cited

ALBERT, CATERINA/VÍCTOR CATALÀ. 1951. *Obres completes* (Barcelona: Selecta)

——. 1976 [1905]. *Solitud* (Barcelona: Selecta)

——. 1992. *Solitude*, trans. by David H. Rosenthal (Columbia, LA, and London: Readers International)

ALVARADO I ESTEVE, HELENA. 1984. 'Víctor Català/Caterina Albert o l'appasionament per l'escriptura', in Caterina Albert/Víctor Català, *La infanticida i altres textos* (Barcelona: laSal, edicions de les dones), pp. 7–35

BADIA, LOLA. 1984. '*Solitud*, novel.la', *Quaderns Crema*, 8: 27–35

BARTRINA, FRANCESCA. 2001. *Caterina Albert/Víctor Català: la voluptuositat de l'escriptura* (Vic: Eumo)

CASTELLANOS, JORDI. 1986. 'Víctor Català', in Martí de Riquer, Antoni Comas and Joaquim Molas, eds, *Història de la literatura catalana*, vol. VIII (Barcelona: Ariel), pp. 579–623

CHARLON, ANNE. 1990. *La condició de la dona en la narrativa femenina catalana* (Barcelona: Edicions 62)

EPPS, BRAD. 2002. 'Solitude in the City: Víctor Català and Mercè Rodoreda', in *Women's Narrative and Film in Twentieth-Century Spain*, ed. by Ofelia Ferrán and Kathleen M. Glenn (New York and London: Routledge), pp. 19–39

FERRATER, GABRIEL. 2010. *Tres prosistes: Joaquim Ruyra, Caterina Albert i Josep Pla* (Barcelona: Empúries)

MARAGALL, JOAN. 1978. *'Elogi de la paraula' i altres assaigs* (Barcelona: Edicions 62)

MONTOLIU, MANUEL DE. 1976. 'Valoració crítica de *Solitud*', in Caterina Albert/Víctor Català, *Solitud* (Barcelona: Selecta), pp. 9–38

MUÑOZ, IRENE. 2016. *Caterina Albert/Víctor Català (1869–1966)* (Girona: Edicions Vitel·la)

SCHOPENHAUER, ARTHUR. 1969. *The World as Will and Representation*, trans. by E. F. J. Payne, 2 vols (New York: Dover Publications)

YATES, ALAN. 1975. *Una generació sense novel·la?* (Barcelona: Edicions 62)

Notes to Chapter 7

1. On Caterina Albert's use of male pseudonyms, see Francesca Bartrina (2001: 13–39).

2. David H. Rosenthal's English version fails to register 'savi' [wise].

3. The English version condenses 'abrigant-la de dalt a baix amb una mirada afectuosa' [enveloping her in his affectionate gaze] into 'affectionately' (1992: 90).

4. The text does not specify whose eyes those are, although it is pretty obvious. In any case, whatever doubt the reader may harbour will be dispelled later on, as Mila and Gaietà are walking through the Lightningbolt Pass and she recalls the effect of his disembodied gaze on that moment of sexual tension between herself and young Arnau: 'I la Mila, estremida per un llarg calfred, reveié, en l'obagor gebrada de Pas de Llamps, aquella mirada calda, devota, infinida, que esborrà allà, en l'aixart el matí de la desfeta, la vermellor dels llavis de l'Arnau de Sant Ponç, trencant per arreu el corrent atractívol que s'havia establert entre el minyó i la dona' (1976: 221) [Mila shuddered and saw again in the darkness of that place the broad, warm, devoted, infinite gaze that had blotted out Arnau's red lips, breaking the current of attraction between them] (1992: 154).

5. The English version omits 'aquella mirada plena de viàtics encalmadors', that is, Gaietà's 'reassuring gaze'.

6. Further on in the novel, as he talks disparagingly about young, lazy shepherds, 'el rostre del pastor, sempre plaèvol, s'enserià amb una expressió tota severa' (1976: 230) [the shepherd's usually benign visage grew solemn and severe] (1992: 161). Confirmation that Anima has been following them infuriates him and 'son rostre placèvol s'enroentí d'una foguerada' (1976: 236) [his face suddenly flushed] (1992: 165). The English version has omitted 'placèvol' [placid, calm] from the last passage.

7. '[T]ranquil·lament' could easily be translated as 'calmly'.
8. '[S]erens' [serene] has been lost in translation.
9. Rosenthal mistranslates: 'her [instead of *his*] green eyes filled with the mysterious calm of a deep gorge' (1992: 118).
10. Again, 'serens' has been omitted from the English version.
11. '[T]ranquil·la' has been omitted from the English version.
12. '[T]heir happiness', in the Rosenthal's version (1992: 166).
13. As they make their way up Highpeak, she thinks: 'Potser no eren aquells llocs tot lo bells i imposadors que la paraula magnificadora de l'home li havia fet creure' (1976: 226–27) [Perhaps [those places] were not as fair and grandiose as in his stories] (1992: 158).
14. There is a distinctive Nietzschean element in the construction of this character: Gaietà is a shepherd, that is, the opposite to the 'herd' or the 'masses', which he thoroughly despises. Regarding Gaietà's contempt for the 'masses', see Albert (1976: 99, 161–62, 173; 1992: 60, 109, 117).
15. For Maragall's poetics, see his 'Elogi de la paraula' [In Praise of the Word] (1903) and 'Elogi de la poesia' [In Praise of Poetry] (1907) in Maragall (1978: 33–69).
16. Schopenhauer's is a godless universe, whereas Gaietà is convinced that Our Lord is one of the sources of his 'rondalles', the other being the old folks from St Pontius.

CHAPTER 8

Mercè Rodoreda and Maria-Mercè Marçal as 'specters granted a hospitable memory' in Mercè Ibarz's Fiction

Montserrat Lunati

Cardiff University & University of St Andrews

This essay explores the determination of some Catalan women writers to give visibility to other female writers from a recent and not so recent past, their willingness to grant them 'accommodation' and a 'hospitable memory', as Derrida (1994: 175) would put it, in the most intimate part of themselves as authors: their own work. On this occasion, I will focus on the connections that can be established between Mercè Ibarz's fiction and that of Mercè Rodoreda, and Maria-Mercè Marçal's poetry.

Elaine Showalter uses the phrase 'the happy few' to refer to those 'token' women writers in English literature who were deemed 'great' and included in anthologies, literary histories and textbooks, while many others, seen as 'minor' figures, were excluded from those canon-formation texts. This made it impossible to follow any 'continuities in women's writing [or] any reliable information about the relationships between the writers' lives and the changes in the legal, economic, and social status of women' (Showalter 1991: 7). As regards Catalan literature, what Mercè Ibarz and Maria-Mercè Marçal have done is to open lines of affective communication between the work of previous women writers and their own, and, by doing so, they have signalled how a male-dominated history of literature has kept women in a precarious position within the institution of literature. I use the phrase 'affective communication' as it is by now well accepted that emotions and affections are culturally constructed categories (Lutz 2007: 19–29), hence politically relevant.

Showalter mentions only six 'happy few' women in the history of literature in English (Jane Austen, George Eliot, the Brontës, and Virginia Woolf). In Catalan culture, a culture systematically repressed by the Spanish state since 1714, the list is even shorter: Caterina Albert/Víctor Català — 'la Víctor', as she is often called nowadays by young readers (see Ibarz 2018a) — Mercè Rodoreda and, perhaps,

Maria Antònia Salvà, Montserrat Roig, Carme Riera and Maria-Mercè Marçal. However, this is not the only problem that Catalan women writers have had to face. After Franco's death, in the crucial period of the so-called Transition (to democracy), the canon-formation agents took a restrictive view of women. As Lluïsa Julià points out,

> les universitats i altres institucions amb capacitat de lideratge, van prendre [...] una actitud extremadament restrictiva respecte els valors literaris de la pròpia tradició, en part per necessitat d'assegurar-ne uns valors indiscutibles, però amb la conseqüent menysvalorització d'aquelles veus literàries que s'apartaven de l'estètica entronitzada. Entre elles, i de forma general, la veu de les escriptores, tot i que a partir dels anys setanta una nova generació s'hi incorporava amb força.

> [universities and other leading institutions had [...] an extremely restrictive attitude vis-à-vis the literary values of their own tradition, partly due to the need to underpin some of its undisputable merits, but with the subsequent depreciation of literary voices which did not follow the dominant aesthetics. Among them, in general, the voice of women writers, even though from the 1970s onwards a new generation was becoming increasingly important.] (Julià 2007: 7)[1]

Conscious that they are within the parameters of a culture that has traditionally positioned them as outsiders, some contemporary Catalan women writers include overt references to past female authors (whether they are some of the 'happy few' or not) in their own work. Doubtless, this is a political decision which gives some authors eminence and authority. This chapter is part of a project that acknowledges the resolve of these contemporary writers not to forget previous women authors, to turn them into what Sara Ahmed would call 'happy objects', and, in the process, to become themselves 'affect aliens', that is, subjects who, against conventional mind-sets, 'refuse to put bad feelings to one side' (Ahmed 2010: 32, 50), subjects 'moved by things' who, then, 'in being moved, make things' (Ahmed 2010: 33). Indeed, Mercè Ibarz wants to remember in various explicit ways, and she relies on her own fiction to do so. My project also considers the creative power of intertextuality to open unsuspected doors of beneficial transit between writers from different and not so different eras, and to identify fascinating coincidences in their work. The Deleuzian (Deleuze and Guattari 1984) model of the rhizome may be applied here, as it proposes a transgressive freedom that overcomes the limitations of more hierarchical, arboreal relationships.[2]

I follow Foucault's interpretation of Nietzsche's concept of 'genealogy' whereby the aim of highlighting the inscription of texts of female authorship in recent works of literature by contemporary writers would have nothing to do with the pursuit of a metaphysical or essentialist search for 'origins' (Foucault 1984: 78). Rather, according to the Nietzschean and Foucauldian related concept of 'descent' (Nietzsche's *Herkunft*) (Foucault 1984: 80), it is to 'maintain passing events in their proper diversion; [...] to identify the accidents [...]; the false appraisals and the faulty calculations that gave birth to those things that continue to exist and have value for us' (Foucault 1984: 81). And, most importantly, the stress on texts from the past written by women which can be re-read and become intertextually significant in new texts is not a quest for 'erecting foundations', but to disturb 'what was previously considered immobile' (the hegemonic, canonical continuity of male literary authorship), to fragment 'what was thought unified', and to show 'the heterogeneity of what was imagined consistent with itself' (Foucault 1984: 82).

In 2007, Lluïsa Julià published a collection of essays on Catalan women's writing under the title *Tradició i orfenesa: per a una genealogia de l'escriptora catalana del segle XX*. The first two words of the title ('tradition' and 'orphanhood', the latter understood in a symbolical sense) summarize the two extremes between which women writers (and not only those putting pen to paper in Catalan) find themselves: on the one hand, the desire to belong in a (male-dominated) tradition which both fascinates and excludes them — partially, at least. On the other, the painful realization of being ignored by the very tradition they are part of, especially bearing in mind that men and women writing in Catalan share a language that has been banned during certain periods of its history. One of the purposes of my project is to respond to the tensions created by these two extremes.

Nancy Walker coined the expressions 'the disobedient writer' and 'the disobedient text' to designate those writers and works which 'reformulate [...] plot, setting, and motifs [of previous works] in order to perform their own revision of literary history' (Walker 1995: 1). Drawing on Angela Carter's assertion that 'most intellectual development depends on new readings of old texts' (cited in Walker 1995: 3), and taking into account 'women's imaginative encounters' with a problematic literary tradition that has often excluded them, what Walker proposes is 'a disobedient reading, [...] a reading that resists sexist and racist formulations and that results in a new text that attempts to overturn these formulations while remaining sufficiently referential to the original to make clear its point of origin' (Walker 1995: 3). These revisions 'not only [subvert] the traditional text', but also '[and more importantly, they lay] claim to it, entering into dialogue with [it] on an equal plane' (Walker 1995: 5).

This is what Mercè Rodoreda (2002: 79–114) does in many of the sonnets of 'Món d'Ulisses' [Ulysses' World], a poetry collection written in exile between 1947 and 1956 (Mohino 2002: 26–27). Adrienne Rich (1972: 18) sees 'writing as re-vision' as 'an act of survival for woman, [as] it is more than a search for identity, it is part of her refusal of the self-destructiveness of a male dominated society', a definition that fits Rodoreda's poetry writing, despite her self-confessed mistrust of feminism (Rhodes 1994: 163).[3] In 'Món d'Ulisses', Rodoreda creates a 'disobedient narrative [which] expose[s] [...] the paradigms of authority inherent in the [text] [she] appropriate[s]' (Walker 1995: 5): the *Odyssey*. In a sonnet entitled 'Penèlope', the poetic subject describes herself as

> Esquerpa, sola, tota fel i espina,
> faig i desfaig l'absurda teranyina,
> aranya al·lucinada del no res.
>
> [Hostile, lonely, all bile and thorn,
> I do and undo the absurd cobweb,
> A delirious, unproductive spider.]
>   (Rodoreda 2002: 84)

Here we are far from the *Odyssey*'s Penelope who, patiently waiting for her husband's return from the Trojan War, keeps her suitors at bay with the promise that she will choose a new husband when the shroud she is weaving for her father-in-law, Laërtes, is finished. She works at the loom during the day but secretly unravels the shroud at night, yet her ruse is eventually discovered. Rodoreda's Penèlope is not so patient. She is closer to the angry Penélope of Lourdes Ortiz's short story of the same title (2008) who is resentful of the time wasted, of the twenty years it has taken for her husband to return, during which they have aged, and who refuses to join in the festivities that celebrate his homecoming.[4]

With a subtle, ironic Carnerian tone, other sonnets from 'Món d'Ulisses' give voice to 'minor' characters from the epic poem: the *rentadores* [washer women], the *molineres* [female mill workers], especially one of them whose only act of rebellion is to spit in the flour even though nobody will notice (2002: 109), or the *serventes penjades* [female servants who are hanged for sleeping with their suitors] who

> Negres de sang en gleves adormida
> de puntetes entrem a l'altra vida
> amb els caps una mica decantats.
>
> [Blackened with clots of sleeping blood
> We tiptoe into the next life
> With our heads faintly tilting.]
> (Rodoreda 2002: 113)

That said, the texts I will discuss are not disobedient in the way Rodoreda revisits the *Odyssey*, or Walker understands it, or at least not entirely. Their defiance consists in becoming 'affect aliens' that behave, to some extent, like 'feminist kill-joy[s]' (Ahmed 2010: 39, 38) by refusing to follow conventional interpretations of the canon and openly acknowledging the authority of previous female voices from literary history. By bringing these voices to the fore, a discontinuous line which has traditionally been imposed upon them is unmasked and the instances of discrimination are laid bare. The act of remembering by writing about forgetfulness radically contests the exclusion of 'minor' women writers and the restrictive criteria behind the selection of the 'happy few'. Mercè Ibarz's relationship with Rodoreda's work, much like that of Maria-Mercè Marçal's poetry with Maria Antònia Salvà's, is inclusive and acknowledges the enduring literary dynamism of the older author.

I believe it would be appropriate to start a reflection of this kind by mentioning a poem by Marçal, included in her posthumous collection *Raó del cos* (2000: 29) [*The Body's Reason* (2014: 13)], whose epigraph and first line quote the ending of a poem by Maria Antònia Salvà, therefore revealing, even structurally, the link between them. Salvà's poem is about a cactus that, having been thrown away for dead, survives by clinging to the cracks and crevices of an old garden wall. That 'vell drac' [old dragon] becomes in Marçal's poem a symbol of the tenacity of women writers (Marçal 2004: 87–89) vis-à-vis their historical exclusion from language and authority, and 'their unequal access to power and agency within cultural institutions such as literature or education' (Walker 1995: 2).

D'un cactus

Com un rèptil monstruós de pell clapada,
d'entranya llefiscosa, era ajocat
al seu racó bevent la solellada.
De sobte, sa malícia desvetllada,
enrevisclant-se, va esquerdar el test.
Enllà de l'hort, que se'n perdés el quest,
dalt una paret seca fou llançat,
i al cap de temps, damunt les pedres dures,
furgant per les llivanes i juntures,
trobí el vell drac encara aferrissat.

[*About a cactus*

Like a monstrous reptile with spotted skin,
With slippery entrails, it lay
In its corner, enjoying the sunshine.
Suddenly, showing its evil nature,
Wriggling, it cracked its pot.
Beyond the garden, in an attempt to get rid of it,
It was thrown on a dried wall,
And after a while, on the hard stones,
Poking along cracks and crevices,
I found the old dragon still clinging.] (Salvà 1981 [1934])

Furgant per les llivanes i juntures,
trobí el vell drac encara aferrissat (Maria Antònia Salvà)

Furgant per les llivanes i juntures
d'aquesta paret seca; entre mac
i mac d'oblit; entre les pedres dures
de cega desmemòria que endures
et sé. I saber-te em dóna terra, arrel.
Et sé i em sé, en el mirall fidel
del teu poema, aferrissadament
clivella pedra de silenci opac
 — dona rèptil, dona monstre, dona
drac,
com el cactus, com tu, supervivent. (Marçal 2000: 29)

[*Poking along cracks and crevices,*
I found the old dragon still clinging. (Maria Antònia Salvà)

Poking along cracks and crevices
Of this dry wall; between pebble
And pebble of oblivion, among hard stones
Of blind forgetfulness you endure.
I know you. And knowing you gives me earth, root.
I know you and I know myself in the faithful mirror
Of your poem, clinging
Crevice stone of opaque silence
 — reptile woman, monster woman,
Dragon woman,
Like the cactus, like you, survivor.] (Marçal 2014: 13)

Marçal's poem, and Ibarz's works including Rodoreda and Marçal's writing, are texts that do not contest, but celebrate, the previous texts and authors they refer to so explicitly. We could also categorize Ibarz and Marçal's texts as 'melancholy', only not strictly in the way that Freud defines 'melancholia' as a pathological process in his 1917 essay 'Mourning and Melancholia' (1984: 251–68). Rather, we can regard these texts as post-Freudian in that they do not cling pathologically to the past, but maintain 'a continuous engagement with loss and its remains [...] making visible not only their social bases but also their creative, unpredictable, political aspects' (Eng and Kazanjian 2003: 3–4). As Sara Ahmed observes,

> A concern with histories that hurt is not a backward orientation: to move on, you must make this return. If anything, we might want to reread melancholic subjects, the ones who refuse to let go of suffering, who are even prepared to kill some form of joy, as an alternative model of the social good. (2010: 50)

The good news is that the literary practices of Ibarz and Marçal do not exactly kill any joy, they simply flaunt the literary spaces from which they come. Ahmed's words remind me of a passage from *No parlis de mi quan me'n vagi* [Don't Talk about Me When I'm Gone], a novel from 2010 by Ibarz that I will discuss later, in which the narrator says:

> sé que el mapa vell encara serveix. No és senzill de transitar però sí de recular. En desconec l'explicació però resulta que no és possible anar endavant, mentre que, en canvi, pots desfer el camí i, des del passat, contar. Les històries agafen aleshores un sentit viu, les contes i potser l'encertes. Apareix un urbanisme interior, un indicador de rutes interiors, un navegador de les hores i els dies.

> [I know that the old map is still useful. It is not easy to navigate, it is easier to go backwards. I don't know why but it is impossible to move forward, while, instead, you can go back on yourself and speak from the past. Stories then become meaningful, you tell them and perhaps you get it right. An inner planning appears, an indicator of inner routes, a navigator for the hours and for the days.] (Ibarz 2010: 9)[5]

Mercè Ibarz's 'Kilimanjaro' (2005)

'Kilimanjaro' is a *conte* by Mercè Ibarz from her second collection of short stories, *Febre de carrer* [Street Fever], published in 2005 (24–38). It borrows its title from *The Snows of Kilimanjaro*, a film directed by Henry King in 1952 and based on Ernest Hemingway's eponymous 1936 short story (1942: 150–75). The figure of the leopard that climbs to the eternally snow-covered African mountain, perhaps to die, is replicated in the climbing to Parc Güell, in Barcelona, of the two characters in Ibarz's *conte*: Marta Coll and a French-Catalan man whose name is never revealed but who is a second-generation exile from the Spanish Civil War and who has gone to Barcelona, specifically to Parc Güell, to keep a promise he made to his dying uncle. That uncle had left Barcelona at the end of the war and since Parc Güell was the last place he saw, he had asked his nephew to visit it on his behalf.

Unbeknown to them, these two characters are linked by family and historical ties. He is the nephew of the man who was married to Marta Coll's aunt, a woman, also called Marta, who committed suicide while in exile. The younger generation meet for the first time in Parc Güell while arguing over space on one of Gaudí's benches made of *trencadís* (little tesserae, discarded ceramic pieces put together to form another object, the iconic Gaudí mosaic: an early exercise in upcycling materials to which I ascribe a symbolical meaning that I will discuss later). Their uncle and aunt had started their love story, turned tragic by the outcome of the Civil War, arguing over a table in the Cafè de Bordeus in 1930s Barcelona. However, there is no suggestion of a repetition of the love story between the nephew and the niece. Having undergone a double mastectomy, Marta Coll, a city *flâneuse* like many other female protagonists of Ibarz's urban short stories,[6] has just left hospital. As Foucault (1984: 83) points out, '[g]enealogy, as an analysis of descent, is [...] situated within the articulation of the body and history'. Indeed, the body is a crucial element in this retrieval of previous writers' texts. Besides, Marta Coll is a character defined by a Deleuzian *intermezzo* as nothing definite is said about her chances of surviving breast cancer. She is a 'nomadic subject' who needs to 'redraft her cartographies', as Rosi Braidotti (1994: 31) would put it, the subject always being an 'embodied subject,' and the body a 'libidinal surface, a site of multiple coding [...] — a living text' (1994: 59). Marta is self-conscious of her mutilated body and the precariousness of her existence, and she feels a burning desire to walk the city's streets and parks: she has 'street fever', the *Febre de carrer* that provides the title for the whole collection.

What prompts the man to approach Marta in Parc Güell is the beautiful piece of costume jewellery she is wearing, a dove made of semi-precious stones which had belonged to her aunt and that she is using to hold her hair in place. Upon seeing it, the man identifies it as an exact replica of one that his uncle had given him. Both pieces had been commissioned by the uncle for Marta's aunt and made by a jewel-maker friend of his who ended up in the Lindemann refugee camp at Bordeaux after the Spanish Civil War. The story's intertextual and historical links are very subtle. It contains a modicum of information and lets the reader figure out the possible conversation between the characters (when the man approaches Marta in the Parc), and the rest of the coincidences between 'Kilimanjaro' and two texts by Rodoreda: *La plaça del Diamant* [In Diamond Square] (1962) and her short story 'Abans de morir' [Before I Die] (1958). Even the similarities between the characters and Rodoreda's biography are there for the reader to activate: in the 1940s, Armand Obiols, a Catalan writer and Rodoreda's partner during their exile years, spent time in the Lindemann camp.[7] As the details emerge, the connections with Rodoreda's texts become clearer for the informed reader. As Kristeva (1980: 64–91) asserts, poetic, literary language is read as double, while 'the text [effectively] becomes the intertext' (Allen 2000: 1).

First, the doves, or the pigeons, if you prefer, from *La plaça del Diamant*, are here turned into birds that cannot fly, set in stone, like petrified memories that won't go away. At one point, *La plaça del Diamant* is alluded to as a novel whose protagonists court in Parc Güell, and as 'una novel·la on una casa es transformava en colomar' [a novel where a house is transformed into a dove-cote] (Ibarz 2005: 32), an episode that persuaded the uncle to ask his friend to make a dove with semi-precious stones for Marta's aunt, the girl who in due course would become his wife — this is the jewel that after many years Marta will inherit; the other, also commissioned by the uncle but made afterwards, is the one the unnamed nephew received.

The network of connections between Ibarz's story and Rodoreda's novel is replicated in the bonds between the two characters who are the recipients of not just the twin pieces of jewellery, but also of the troubled history of their country, both in its personal and collective dimensions.

'Kilimanjaro' deals with memory on several levels. Memory is linked to specific places, such as Parc Güell, now taken over by tourists, but also a *lieu de mémoire* (Nora 1989) or, rather, in order to highlight the multiple connections, a *noeud de mémoire*, as Michael Rothberg (2010) would have it. Rothberg, and others, criticize Nora's project for 'its elision of France's long and complex colonial and postcolonial history' (Rothberg 2010: 6), and for favouring history over memory, although it is recognized that, ironically, it 'has helped stimulate a boom in the study of memory' (Rothberg 2010: 4). Rothberg suggests a new approach to remembrance that goes 'beyond the framework of the imagined community of the nation-state' (2010: 7), and requires new ways of reading and writing in a non-nationalist project in which 'multidirectional memory' favours 'encounters between diverse pasts and a conflictual present [...], but also between different agents or catalysts of memory' (2010: 9). For Rothberg (2009: 3), memory becomes the 'subject of an ongoing negotiation. Cross-referencing, and borrowing' in which the 'interaction of different historical memories illustrates the productive, intercultural dynamic' characteristic of what he terms 'multidirectional memory'.

In 'Kilimanjaro', two brands of memory related to the Spanish Civil War intersect: memories related to the forced physical exile of Catalan Republicans, and those related to the misery of life inside Spain for the 'losers' of the war, who experienced different degrees of inner exile. Parc Güell, so representative of Barcelona and, to some extent, the third character in the story, is a heavily connoted place that allows for an 'act of memory' to be performed, a complex *noeud de mémoire* rather than a site to be celebrated. It is tied to a painful recollection as the last bit of Barcelona the uncle saw before going into exile at the end of the war.

Interestingly, like Natàlia in *La plaça del Diamant*, neither of the two characters in 'Kilimanjaro' is enthusiastic about Gaudí's architecture: 'massa onades i massa punxes. Massa insistència, massa de tot. Massa història' [too many waves, too many spikes. Too much insistence, too much of everything. Too much history] (Ibarz 2005: 31). It may indeed overwhelm not just because of its aesthetics, but also because of its inevitable references to history, for being a site 'where memory crystalizes' (Nora 1989: 7).

In *La plaça del Diamant*, the imagined city that Quimet wants to impose on a young Natàlia resembles today's touristy city, 'the abstract space' of capitalism and the bourgeoisie that Henri Lefebvre talks about (1991: 85). Natàlia, however, is not keen:

en Quimet va començar a parlar del senyor Gaudí, que el seu pare l'havia
conegut el dia que el va aixafar el tramvia, que el seu pare havia estat un dels
que l'havien dut a l'hospital, pobre senyor Gaudí, tan bona persona, ves quina
mort més de misèria... I que al món no hi havia res com el Parc Güell i com la
Sagrada Família i la Pedrera. Jo li vaig dir que, tot plegat, massa ondes i massa
punxes. Em va donar un cop al genoll amb el cantell de la mà que em va fer
anar la cama enlaire de sorpresa i em va dir que si volia ser la seva dona havia
de començar per trobar bé tot el que ell trobava bé. (Rodoreda 1983: 27)

[Joe began to talk about Mr Gaudí, whom his father had met the day he was
knocked over by a tram, and how his father was one of the people who'd
taken him to hospital, poor old Mr Gaudí, such a nice man, and he'd died so
horribly... And nothing in the world could beat the Parc Güell and the Sagrada
Familia and the wavy balconies of the Pedrera. I said they were very nice but
far too many waves and sharp spikes, as far as I was concerned. He tapped my
knee with the side of his hand and he hit me so sharply my leg shot into the air
and he said if I wanted to be his wife I'd to start liking every single thing he
liked.] (Rodoreda 2013: 8)

Natàlia embarks upon a journey that is reflected in her relationship with the city
spaces: she feels uncomfortable in Parc Güell at the beginning of Quimet's courtship,
and on numerous occasions she runs carelessly through the city streets rather than
walking or strolling. It is not until the end of the novel that she finds herself more
at ease with Barcelona's urban spaces: after a period of agoraphobia, and after she lets
out a cathartic scream and writes her name on the wall of the house she had shared
with Quimet, an adult Natàlia makes her way back home looking up and down the
streets to avoid being run over by a tram, therefore initiating an easier relationship
with her own city and with herself.

In 'Kilimanjaro', Marta Coll's feelings toward the corner of the city which is the
setting of the story, also evolves. At first critical of the tourists invading Parc Güell,
she finds a way of imagining them as multicoloured tesserae, as pieces of a human
Gaudinian mosaic, a human *trencadís*:

Vistos [els turistes] tal com són ara no donen cap harmonia al lloc, ni al paisatge,
ni a la perspectiva urbana: són una mescla que més aviat fa pensar en materials
impossibles de combinar i de coordinar en un gest col·lectiu. Caldria, pensa,
una inventiva com la del vell artista. Potser així apareixeria la matèria noble de
la gent comuna, que en un lloc o un altre deu ser, de la mateixa manera que
en el trencadís de l'arquitectura habita la deixalla de l'antic material modern.

[If you look at the tourists as they are now, they do not bring any harmony
to the place, the landscape or the urban view: they are, rather, a mix that
makes you think it would be impossible to combine and coordinate them in
a collective gesture. She thinks that a creative mind like that of the old artist
would be necessary to achieve this. Perhaps the noble fibre of ordinary people,
which must be somewhere, would appear, much like the remains of the old
modern material linger in the tesserae of the new architecture.] (Ibarz 2005: 28)

In 'Kilimanjaro', both the niece and the nephew are 'postmemory subjects' in the
sense that Marianne Hirsch uses the term:

> Postmemory characterizes the experience of those who grow up dominated by narratives that preceded their birth, whose own belated stories are evacuated by the stories of the previous generation shaped by traumatic events that can be neither understood nor recreated. (Hirsch 1997: 22)

For Hirsch,

> 'Postmemory' describes the relationship that the 'generation after' bears to the personal, collective, and cultural trauma of those who came before — to experiences they 'remember' only by means of the stories, images, and behaviours among which they grew up. (2012: 5)

Indeed, we know that the man was born in exile and, for Marta Coll, the silences at home when she was growing up during Franco's dictatorship are still a powerful memory:

> Silenci, sempre el silenci. La tieta i el seu home vivien no gaire lluny de París, però ningú no els va anar mai a trobar, ni els pares de Marta Coll ho van fer quan van visitar la capital. Va ser un viatge d'amagat, una altra història familiar sense explicacions, sense alegria. [...] Un dia va arribar per correu, dins una bossa de ràfia molt ben preparada, el colom de pedreria i una carta, que ni ella ni el seu germà no van llegir. La mare, amb to greu, va donar el colom a la filla. De la germana de ton pare, va dir. No se'n va parlar més, mai més. No eren família de gaires paraules, ni l'època en volia gaires.
>
> [Silence, always silence. The auntie and her husband lived near Paris, but nobody ever went over to visit them, not even when Marta Coll's parents visited the capital. It was a clandestine trip, another family story without explanations, without joy. [...] One day the post brought a well-made raffia bag containing the dove-shaped piece of costume jewellery and a letter that neither she nor her brother ever read. Her mother, with a grave tone, gave the dove to her daughter. From your father's sister, she said. It was never talked about again. They were a family of few words, as was the period they lived in.] (Ibarz 2005: 33)

Nora writes that '[t]he quest for memory is the search for one's history' (1989: 13), and the two characters from Ibarz's story are a gripping example of the fusion of the personal and the collective dimensions of memory and history. Even though for different reasons, both have made their way to Parc Güell searching for their own complex, elusive identity, for their own troubled family and political history. Of course, the story does not offer any final answers. What matters most is the search and what the search has uncovered in an encounter that takes them (and the reader) to multiple places, literary as well as historical.

As I suggested earlier, *La plaça del Diamant* is not the only text incorporated into 'Kilimanjaro'. The name Marta Coll comes from 'Abans de morir' [Before I Die], a short story that Rodoreda wrote in the early years of her exile, when she found herself still unable to write novels, and remained unpublished until 1958. 'Abans de morir' is a narration with gothic undertones in its tragic, or rather tragicomic, set up: it strikes me as an ironic take on romance, even on melodrama, that may remind its readers of the ironist Rodoreda had been in some of her early novels such as *Sóc una dona honrada?* [Am I an Honest Woman?] (1932), *Un dia de la vida d'un home* [A Day in a Man's Life] (1934), and *Crim* [Crime] (1936), all parodies of different novel genres: the romantic novel, the psychological novel and the detective novel, respectively, as indicated by Neus Real (2005: 29), and all written before the publication of *Aloma* in 1938.[8] It is difficult to interpret literally the tragic end implied by the text, in which the protagonist and narrator, the first Marta Coll, decides to commit suicide as she cannot overcome being jealous of her secretive husband Màrius's previous lover. Màrius refuses to throw away the letters sent to him by that former lover and keeps them hidden in a briefcase. The futility of Marta's sacrifice (she hopes that by killing herself her husband will feel remorse forever after) creates a distance between text and reader usually achieved by discursive irony. At times, it sounds like a subtle parody of Daphne du Maurier's novel *Rebecca*, published in 1938 and made into a popular film by Alfred Hitchcock in 1940 — there is even a softer replica of the housekeeper, Mrs Danvers, thrown into the mix in the character of Elvira, the loyal servant to Marta's husband.

The protagonist and narrator of 'Abans de morir' meets her future husband at the Cafè dels Ocells while quarrelling over a table, an occurrence which is replicated not once but twice in 'Kilimanjaro' — through the story of the uncle and the aunt at the Cafè de Bordeus, and that of Marta and the nephew on a Parc Güell bench. A joyous, ironic tone is introduced early on through the character of Marta, with her quick, witty replies in her conversations with future husband Màrius. The first present that Màrius gives Marta is two white pigeons. Marta's response is to cook them and invite him for supper. Once they are married, Màrius gives Marta a dove made of diamonds, a piece of jewellery that she, like the Marta Coll from 'Kilimanjaro', uses to gather up her hair. Her husband also promises her that she will get another one in due course.

Pigeons are ominously present in 'Abans de morir'; they are suggestive of a nightmarish scenario that a few years later would be fully developed in *La plaça del Diamant*. Early in the story, they appear in a bad dream Marta has shortly after meeting Màrius at the Cafè dels Ocells:

> a la nit vaig tenir un malson. Viatjava i, a tot arreu, pel tren, per les cambres de l'hotel, en tots els països que visitava, em trobava amb dos coloms blancs amb les plomes del coll cobertes de sang. (Rodoreda 1979: 154)

> [I had a terrible dream that night. I was travelling, and everywhere I went — on trains, in hotels, in every country I visited — I encountered two white doves, the feathers on their necks soaked in blood.] (Rodoreda 2011: 147)

Later on, at a particularly tense moment in the story, when Marta Coll tries obsessively to meet Màrius's previous lover, the object of her jealousy, she goes to a house where, '[a]l fons del passadís hi havia una porta oberta, es veia un pati i se sentia parrupejar coloms' (Rodoreda 1979: 164) [through an open door at the end of the hall I could see a patio and hear pigeons cooing] (Rodoreda 2011: 160). As in *La plaça*, pigeons are not pleasant company, and only become acceptable when they are made of stone, something which would be incongruous in *La plaça* but it is not in 'Abans de morir'.

Illness in Rodoreda's story is a state of mind. Marta feels and looks ill as she tortures herself with jealousy: 'Em sentia com es deu sentir un convalescent després d'una malaltia llarga' (Rodoreda 1979: 161) [I felt the way a convalescent must feel after a long illness] (Rodoreda 2011: 156). This is vaguely similar to the situation in which the Marta Coll of Ibarz's story finds herself, although her illness is physical: she is convalescing from breast cancer and has gone to Parc Güell straight after being discharged from hospital.

If Rodoreda's texts provide 'Kilimanjaro' with its full semantic dimension, Maria-Mercè Marçal is the main author who can be identified in Ibarz's novel from 2010, *No parlis de mi quan me'n vagi*.

Mercè Ibarz's *No parlis de mi quan me'n vagi* (2010)

As intimated by the quotation-title from the well-known song performed by Billie Holiday, Frank Sinatra and many others, 'Please don't talk about me when I'm gone', *No parlis de mi quan me'n vagi* is a highly intertextual novel, full of literary, cinematic and musical citations. 'La música sona' [The music is playing], says the main narrator in a proleptic statement on the first page. Some of the intertexts are explicit (from Ausiàs March to Salvat-Papasseit, Thomas Bernhard or Josep Pla; from David Bowie to The Rolling Stones, Janis Joplin, Thelonious Monk or Gloria Gaynor); some are hidden and left there for the reader to activate (from Lope de Vega and Adam Zagajewski to the poetry of Jordi Larios or the cinema of Sofia Coppola), and some are alluded to in a way that will make sense only to the informed reader, Buñuel being a case in point: 'Prohibido asomarse al interior, s'havia de titular una pel·li de Buñuel' [Forbidden to Lean In, was going to be the title for a film by Buñuel] (Ibarz 2010: 142, 144).[9] Even catchphrases from adverts find a meaningful way into the linguistic fabric of the book (Ibarz 2010: 86).[10] What the title asks for, however, is not what the novel does. Instead, it explicitly talks about people after they are gone. More than that: it brings them back to life in the form of friendly ghosts.

It has been said that *No parlis de mi quan me'n vagi* depicts a generation of Catalans who as young men and women in the 1970s had fought against Franco ('la bèstia' [the beast], as he is referred to throughout the novel). Nil, an artist who draws cartoons for newspapers, and three other characters who were once friends and clandestine anti-Franco fighters are all invited to a dinner party by Valentina Morera, a freelance photographer, thirty years after going their separate ways. These three characters are *el Rat*, a corrupt socialist who had been part of Felipe González's government, Isi, a civil servant working for the Catalan autonomous government, and Nela,[11] a former ETA member. The novel may be read as a representation of urban Catalonia in the last thirty years (Ibarz 2010: 11, 38, 40–41, 50, 93, 105)[12] and it is peppered with references to the 1970s and the 1980s, such as the slogan people used to chant with a gradually louder voice to indicate that inaction as a response to totalitarianism was not an option: 'Som gent pacífica | i no ens agrada cridar' [We are peaceful people | and we don't like to shout] (Ibarz 2010: 10). Reading it as a portrait of a politically disenchanted generation may be productive but, in my view, what makes the novel truly remarkable is the presence of two ghosts, two characters who seem to live, like bats, on the rafters of Valentina's flat: 'dos morts d'upa' [two very important dead people] (Ibarz 2010: 150). Valentina tells her friends that, at the party, some of the guests will be alive and some dead (Ibarz 2010: 10). What she doesn't know is that there will be another dead guest, Nela, the former ETA member, who has died alone at home that very same afternoon. She attends the party as another ghost: 'Nela Zubiri fa una calada a la pipa, Fluxus ha acabat el seu relat, la Senyora Cogito mira des de la biga. Valentina es pren un beuratge calent' [Nela Zubiri has a puff on her pipe, Fluxus has finished his story, Mrs Cogito watches from the rafters. Valentina drinks a hot beverage] (Ibarz 2010: 192).

Valentina has a friendly relationship with the two ghosts that accompany her all the time (although, as we will see later, she is not the only character who is aware of their presence). One of the ghosts is Fluxus. When alive, he was an Argentinian who escaped from the Junta's repression and ended up in Barcelona, where he died of AIDS. He is a sweet character whose name suggests tolerance, flexibility, and the impossibility of pinning down something as fluid as identity. Significantly, his name is also that of the art group *Fluxus*:

> Founded in 1960 by the Lithuanian/American artist George Maciunas, Fluxus began as a small but international network of artists and composers, and was characterised as a shared attitude rather than a movement. Rooted in experimental music, it was named after a magazine which featured the work of musicians and artists centred around avant-garde composer John Cage. The Latin word Fluxus means flowing, in English a flux is a flowing out. Fluxus founder Maciunas said that the purpose of Fluxus was to 'promote a revolutionary flood and tide in art, promote living art, anti-art'. This has strong echoes of dada, the early twentieth-century art movement. (www.tate.org.uk/art/art-terms/f/fluxus)

The character with such an eloquent, Nietzschean name has the talent to come back from the dead not to haunt or frighten people but to help them, as he does with the foreign boy with sensual lips who offers him sex for little money in broken Spanish: 'Follo tu..., vinte iuros' [I fuck you..., twenty euros] (Ibarz 2010: 121). Later on we learn that this boy is Allal, a protégé of Nela's (a post-ETA Nela who now works for a charity helping immigrants). Fluxus gives him money without asking for anything in return: 'Fluxus és un mort [...] sabedor que els vius necessiten la companyia dels desapareguts i de vegades fins la presència i tot' [Fluxus is a dead person who knows that the living need the company of the dead, sometimes even their presence] (Ibarz 2010: 64).

The other ghost in Valentina's life is 'la Senyora Cogito', the ghost of Maria-Mercè Marçal, the poet who died of cancer in 1998 and whose poems are quoted on several occasions, thus making identification very easy for any reader acquainted with Marçal's work.[13] I will not say that Valentina is an alter ego of the author, although it is worth noticing that Marçal had been a close friend of Ibarz's and a dense network of ideas and intellectual allegiances can be easily detected here, the political and literary endeavours of two writers whose work is shaped by their gender:

la Senyora Cogito havia empeltat de fervor poemes i escrits, sobre el dolor i la passió, el calvari i el goig. Feia poemes-pregunta. De tot. Per això li diu Senyora Cogito, la Senyora que pensa. Vet aquí la benèfica Senyora Cogito, amb qui sempre pot debatre qualsevol cosa. En un racó precís de la sala, ran de terra un pic, entre les bigues un altre, hi continuen converses antigues o estroncades, converses noves.

[Mrs Cogito had instilled ardour in her poems and in her writings, dealing with pain and passion, agony and pleasure. She wrote question-poems. About anything. That is why she [the female narrator] calls her Mrs Cogito, the Lady who thinks. Here we have the benevolent Mrs Cogito, with whom she can discuss anything. In a specific corner of the drawing room, on the floor, or up in the rafters, they keep having their old or interrupted conversations, or new ones.] (Ibarz 2010: 30)

The choice of nickname is particularly interesting since Marçal is regarded rather disparagingly by certain critics as 'simply' a poet of the 'body': consciously or unconsciously, these critics espouse a hierarchical and outdated conception of the mind–body dichotomy, and associate anything corporeal with women.

Derrida's 'hauntological' approach to the recuperation of the past, whose words I have borrowed for the title of this chapter, is appropriate here as Marçal becomes a ghostly presence in Ibarz's novel. The wordplay between 'hauntology' and 'ontology' is already an indication of the links between 'being' and 'not being', as specified by Garoian and Gaudelius (2008: 114), who put forward an interpretation of Derrida's hauntological project which can be applied to Ibarz's recuperation of past female literary voices in her fiction:

For Derrida [...] hauntology is an evocative process that enables us to transgress and transform our social and historical moorings. Re-visiting, re-membering, re-conceptualising, and re-presenting knowledge from the past constitutes a critical conjuring process whereby someone or something invisible, 'beyond being', is imagined and imbued with the immanent possibility of becoming other than what we already know. (Garoian and Gaudelius 2008: 114–15)

In *Specters of Marx*, Derrida famously states:

To exorcise not in order to chase away the ghosts, but this time to grant them the right, if it means making them come back alive, as *revenants* who would no longer be *revenants*, but as other *arrivants* to whom a hospitable memory or promise must offer welcome — without certainty, ever, that they present themselves as such. Not in order to grant them the right in this sense but out of concern for *justice*. (1994: 175)

We may argue that, for some of the dead and disappeared in tragic circumstances under totalitarian regimes, the ghostly condition prevents the recognition of the physical and psychological pain that was inflicted upon them when alive. To see the dead as living and to imbue them with a ghostly existence as a way of keeping their memory alive may indeed raise a few eyebrows. However, it can also be taken to indicate an ethical resistance to closure, an uncanny example of 'impossible mourning', the type of mourning that respects the dead other's alterity and singularity (Derrida 1988: 29). Thus, it is possible to read Ibarz's novel as a narrative of loss in this Derridean sense. In it, the ghostly condition is extremely fitting. The ghosts of the dead are so alive that sometimes the living and the dead become undistinguishable:

> Fluxus no vol ser només un mort, té l'ambició i l'esperança de desplaçar-se a través d'un dia fora del temps, i com a narradora no estic lluny d'aquesta esperança seva de compartir les distintes mesures del temps, d'entrellaçar els vius i els morts que s'han estimat i els morts i els vius que es podrien haver estimat i no ho han pogut fer.

> [Fluxus doesn't want to be just dead, he has the ambition and the hope of moving outside time for a day, and as the narrator I'm not averse to his hope of sharing time on different levels, of connecting the living and the dead that loved each other, or the dead and the living that might have loved one another but couldn't.] (Ibarz 2010: 120)

As I briefly implied before, throughout the novel there is yet another ambiguous, ghostly presence: a first-person narrator about whom we know nothing except that it is definitely a 'she': a gendered voice that uses the feminine form to refer to herself, and a voice that doesn't belong to any of the female characters although she has strong links to Valentina, who, she says, has commissioned her to produce a 'true' account of the story of Valentina and her friends: 'aquest informe veraç que Valentina Morera m'ha encarregat' [this true account that Valentina Morera has asked me to produce] (Ibarz 2010: 105). The narrator feels obliged to try to be faithful to the facts, but she is also fully aware that to narrate is to construct one discourse among many possible ones: 'només fins a un cert punt la gent que contem coses podem triar, ens és dada aquesta rara fortuna, la sort impertinent de ser la secretària de l'inefable, escriure és transcriure, contar és recomptar, recontar' [those of us who tell stories are limited in our freedom to choose what to tell, we're given this rare chance, the impertinent luck of being secretary to the ineffable, as writing is transcribing, telling is checking, re-telling] (Ibarz 2010: 48).

Hers is an inquisitive voice that displays the power of an omniscient narrator, occasionally insisting that she can observe each of the characters without being seen: 'els veig, els veig, els veig' [I see them, I see them, I see them], but '[p]er ells sóc opaca. Només puc escoltar-los' [but for them I'm opaque. I can only listen to them] (Ibarz 2010: 75, 129). She is an omniscient narrator, but not like those to be found in the nineteenth-century bourgeois novel. She even chats with 'la Senyora Cogito' who, after Valentina's friends learn about Nela's sudden death, asks her: 'Pots explicar-ho, pots contar-ho?' [Could you explain, could you tell?] (Ibarz 2010: 183).[14] This narrator shows a very postmodern, metafictional self-awareness of her interventionist role in the text. She has things in common with the narrator of John Fowles's *The French Lieutenant's Woman* (1969), who, at one point, in order to underline the metafictional elements of the novel, puts on the clothes of a Victorian gentleman and gets on the train with the main male character to consider what is to be done with the character's future. In Ibarz's novel, the narrator never makes her presence felt as a full-bodied character, but, as a narrator, she is dying to interfere: 'Com a narradora hi vull dir la meva' [As a narrator, I want to have a say] (Ibarz 2010: 99), and apologizes for following the meanderings of her own memory:

> Veig que avanço i retardo situacions, que salto enrere i endavant, que barrejo el temps, que esbullo els fulls del calendari. Us en demano perdó si és que sou amants d'allò que en diuen ordre cronològic. Veureu, jo no registro fets a mesura que s'esdevenen davant dels meus ulls, sinó que evoco moments viscuts en un passat, uns passats, agavellament [sic] en el record.

> [I can see that I'm bringing forward and delaying situations, that I'm jumping backwards and forwards, that I'm mixing up time, that I'm messing up the calendar pages. I apologize if you are devoted to what is called chronological order. You see, I do not register events as they happen in front of my eyes, I rather evoke moments I've lived in the past, in many pasts, like a hoarder of memories.] (Ibarz 2010: 165–66)

The narrator is aware that memory zigzags in peculiar, yet valuable, ways: 'Narració sense ordre però amb concert' [Narration without order but with coherence'] (Ibarz 2010: 166), she says, paraphrasing a Catalan saying. However, now and then she seems to undermine her own distinctive voice, and by doing so she exposes the limitations of any narrator. She is not like those first-person voices which would never admit to being unreliable. Her first reference to herself, and there are many in the novel, is a declaration of alienation: 'Camino com si vingués d'un país estrany i no em fos possible reconèixer gran cosa entre el cel i la terra' [I walk as if I came from a foreign country and I was unable to distinguish between heaven and earth] (Ibarz 2010: 9). Later on, she states: 'no vull pas dir que ho sàpiga tot jo, i menys encara què li passa pel cap, si és que es pot dir que Nela Zubiri encara té cap' [I cannot say that I know everything, even less what goes through her head, if we can say that Nela Zubiri still has a head] (Ibarz 2010: 171). She achieves quite the opposite effect, though, and comes across as a trustworthy witness. This opinionated narrator of *No parlis de mi quan me'n vagi* has a special relationship with the ghost of 'la Senyora Cogito', or, rather, with the representation of Marçal in the novel as 'la Senyora Cogito'. She knows that Marçal is 'una afrancesada fins al moll de l'os' [a fan of French culture to the core] (Ibarz 2010: 158), an enthusiastic reader of Proust with a soft spot for Baudelaire. They converse amicably: 'la Senyora Cogito' wants to find out if the narrator feels able to relate the story of Valentina and her friends as Valentina has asked her to do. They reflect on it and conclude that it is important that she does it: 'Ens toca fer-ho, insisteix, ens toca' [We should do it, she insists, we should] (Ibarz 2010: 183). Whatever is not recorded will be lost: the way memory gets constructed is important and the interfering narrator knows it only too well. She is also aware of the significance of what remains unsaid: 'no estic aquí per narrar només el que sé i el que veig, també m'he de preocupar del que no sé. I el no saber és tan... estimulador, diguem' [I am here not only to talk about what I know and what I see, I am also concerned with what I do not know. And what I do not know is so... stimulating, shall we say] (Ibarz 2010: 133–34).

However, out of the novel's fourteen chapters, three (2, 3 and 7) are told by a third-person narrator, a voice that seems to play more effectively the role of the standard omniscient storyteller. Mercè Ibarz revealed in an interview (Serra 2010) that there are two narrators in the novel:

Hi conviuen dos narradors, l'un que utilitza la tercera persona, l'altre que parla en primera, però que no se sap quin [*sic*] és. És una mena d'espia narratiu que el lector ha de decidir qui és. I aquesta és la veu que dóna sentit al títol del llibre, perquè al final se'n va.

[There are two narrators in the novel, one who uses the third person, and another who uses the first, but you don't know who it is. It is a sort of narrative spy and the reader should decide who it is. And this is the voice that makes the book's title meaningful because in the end this narrator disappears.]

This somewhat cryptic description has been interpreted as a hint that the voice of the first-person narrator is that of an alter ego of the author herself: 'l'àgil narradora, que parla en primera persona amb tota llibertat, una cronista que no costa gaire identificar amb l'autora, que s'autoqualifica de "secretària de l'inefable", que hi és sempre i escolta, comprensiva' [the fluid narrator, who speaks in the first person with total freedom, a chronicler we can easily identify with the author, who defines herself as 'secretary of the ineffable', who is always there and listens, in an understanding manner] (Pla 2010). This view of a possible authorial voice cannot be taken at face value, though. In the 1970s, Wayne C. Booth coined the concept of the 'implied author', precisely to avoid simplistic identifications. The 'implied author' is a 'rhetorical' figure, different from the author herself and from the narrator, whose conceptual role would be to represent what the reader may infer as the set of beliefs and interests to be found in the book. The 'implied author' is, in Booth's own words, 'the ideal, literary, created version of the real man [*sic*]' (Booth 1983: 75).

As for the conflict of narratorial voices highlighted by Ibarz herself, the person (either first, second or third) who speaks is less relevant than the 'focalization' (Genette 1980: 189–94) through which the narrator speaks. In *No parlis de mi quan me'n vagi*, the focalization is similar in all chapters of the book: an *internal focalization* which occasionally abandons the first person and resorts to the third.

More Intertextual Connections

Two more links can be identified in *No parlis de mi quan me'n vagi*, this time (as in 'Kilimanjaro') with Rodoreda's *La plaça del Diamant* and her short story 'Abans de morir'. At the very end of *La plaça*, once Natàlia has gone through the cathartic experience I mentioned above, she refers to her youth as an ordeal that can be physically expelled as an abject presence of Kristevan (1982) qualities:

Un crit que devia fer molts anys que duia a dintre, i amb aquell crit, tan ample que li havia costat de passar-me pel coll, em va sortir una mica de no res, com un escarabat de saliva... i aquella mica de cosa de no res que havia viscut tant de temps tancada a dintre, era la meva joventut que fugia amb un crit que no sabia ben bé què era... abandonament? (Rodoreda 1983: 250)

[A scream I must have been carrying deep inside me for years and a little something else ran from my mouth alongside that scream that was so vast it was hard to get out of my throat, like a cockroach made from saliva, and that little something else that had been shut up inside me for so long was my youth that now rushed out screaming something or other... that I'd been forsaken?] (Rodoreda 2013: 203)

In *No parlis de mi quan me'n vagi*, when she finds out that Nela has died and the party she had planned to reunite all her friends cannot take place, Valentina throws up: 'Nil agafa Valentina i la guia cap al lavabo, li agafa el front amb la mà i l'acompanya en la vomitada que continua i continua' [Nil leads Valentina to the bathroom, holds her head with his hand and keeps her company while she vomits repeatedly] (Ibarz 2010: 190). Youth, which had lived nightmarishly in Natàlia for so long, abandons her as saliva, as something experienced bodily, organically. Valentina goes through a similar ordeal: the attempt to retrieve her youth by gathering her old friends at a dinner party has failed, at least in the way she had envisaged, and she expels it as a Kristevan abject of delusion, something that needs to be forced out of her body so that she can move on.

There is also an intertextual link between *No parlis de mi quan me'n vagi* and 'Abans de morir'. It has do to with a visual aspect of the novel and can be related to what Nancy Vosburg (1999: 72–79), who has explored the visual metaphors in Rodoreda's stories, defines as catoptric effects in 'Abans de morir', mainly the effects of mirrors or other 'implicit mirroring devices, or the dialogic self-reflections of diaries and letters' (Vosburg 1999: 65). Vosburg sees letters, diary entries, and even the nightmare Marta experiences in 'Abans de morir' as catoptric spaces for seeking self-knowledge: 'significant sign-posts for [a] narrator who is trying to make sense of her past' (1999: 72). Throughout the novel, Valentina, a professional photographer often referred to as Tina by her friends,[15] tries, not always successfully, to take photographs of them, especially of their legs and feet, a subject she is keen on:[16] 'De vegades, però, les seves fotos només tenen cames de gent pel carrer, un punt de vista insòlit que li ha valgut una certa reputació d'originalitat' [Sometimes, however, her photos only show the legs of people captured in the street, an unusual perspective that has given her a certain reputation for originality] (Ibarz 2010: 16); 'Aleshores es va centrar en les cames de la gent i només va retratar unes quantes cares, molt poques' [Then she focussed on people's legs and only photographed a few faces, very few] (Ibarz 2010: 50).

Valentina's photographs are the catoptric element in Ibarz's novel. As unreliable as Lacanian mirrors, photographs nevertheless represent an attempt to reflect subjects, objects and context and, through them, possible meanings for it all. They could, therefore, be analysed through the prism of Vosburg's observations on the catoptric elements in 'Abans de morir'.

Conclusion

Mercè Ibarz's and Maria-Mercè Marçal's willingness to acknowledge the work of older women writers in their own fiction is a serious challenge to the omission of female authors in the Catalan literary canon and suggests that things need to be done differently, more inclusively. I would like to finish this reflection with a reminder of the symbolical significance I attach to the Gaudinian *trencadís* (see Lunati 2008: 217–39). Despite the reservations that the characters in Rodoreda's and Ibarz's texts have about Gaudí's aesthetics, I see *trencadís* as a trope to describe Ibarz's own literary practice, and, above all, as a metaphor for intertextuality, especially the kind of intertextual patchwork, or upcycling, that involves the (un)conscious inclusion of other texts. This is an exercise that, read 'out of concern for justice', to quote Derrida once again, 'the justice that is their due' (Derrida 1994: 75), underlines the necessity to give female voices in literary and visual cultures the credit, respect and author-ity they deserve. Ibarz's voice, as well as Marçal's and those of others whose work we don't have time to look at on this occasion, are like the voice of 'la Senyora Cogito', '[una] veu que acull altres veus' [a voice that includes other voices] (Ibarz 2010: 34), as Valentina says, an important voice made up of the apparently irrelevant *trencadís* traditionally discarded by hegemonic discourses.

Works Cited

AHMED, SARA. 2010. 'Happy Objects', in *The Affect Reader*, ed. by Melissa Gregg and Gregory J. Seigworth (Durham, NC, and London: Duke University Press), pp. 29–51

ALLEN, GRAHAM. 2000. *Intertextuality* (London: Routledge)

BOOTH, WAYNE C. 1983. *The Rhetoric of Fiction* (Chicago, IL, and London: University of Chicago Press)

BRAIDOTTI, ROSI. 1994. *Nomadic Subjects: Embodiment and Sexual Difference in Contemporary Feminist Theory* (New York: Columbia University Press)

CATALÀ, VÍCTOR/CATERINA ALBERT. 1984 [1898]. 'La infanticida', in *La infanticida i altres textos*, ed. by Helena Alvarado (Barcelona: laSal, edicions de les dones), pp. 39–57

DELEUZE, GILLES, and FÉLIX GUATTARI. 1984 [1972]. *Anti-Oedipus: Capitalism and Schizophrenia*, trans. by R. Hurley, M. Seem, and H. R. Lane (London: The Athlone Press)

DERRIDA, JACQUES. 1988. *Mémoires: pour Paul de Man* (Paris: Galilée)

——. 1994. *Specters of Marx. The State of Debt. The Work of Mourning & The New International*, trans. by Peggy Kamuf (New York and London: Routledge)

DU MAURIER, DAPHNE. 2015 [1938]. *Rebecca* (London: Virago Press)

EDWARDS, GWYNNE. 2005. *A Companion to Luis Buñuel* (Woodbridge: Tamesis)

ENG, DAVID, and DAVID KAZANJIAN (eds). 2003. *Loss: The Politics of Mourning* (Berkeley, Los Angeles, and London: University of California Press)

FLUXUS. <www.tate.org.uk/art/art-terms/f/fluxus> [accessed 11 November 2017]

FOUCAULT, MICHEL. 1984. 'Nietzsche, Genealogy, History', in *The Foucault Reader: An Introduction to Foucault's Thought,* ed. by Paul Rabinow (London: Penguin), pp. 76–100

FOWLES, JOHN. 1998 [1969]. *The French Lieutenant's Woman* (Boston, MA: Back Bay Books)

FREUD, SIGMUND. 1984 [1917]. 'Mourning and Melancholia', in *On Metapsychology: The Theory of Psychoanalysis*, vol. IV of The Penguin Freud Library (London: Penguin), pp. 251–68

GAROIAN, CHARLES R., and YVONNE M. GAUDELIUS. 2008. *Spectacle Pedagogy: Art, Politics, and Visual Culture* (New York: State University of New York)

GENETTE, GÉRARD. 1980. *Narrative Discourse: An Essay in Method*, trans. by Jane E. Levin (Ithaca, NY: Cornell University Press)

HEMINGWAY, ERNEST. 1942 [1926]. 'The Snows of Kilimanjaro', in *The Short Stories of Ernest Hemingway: The First Forty-Nine Stories and the Play 'The Fifth Column'* (New York: The Modern Library), pp. 150–75

HIRSCH, MARIANNE. 1997. *Family Frames: Photography, Narrative and Postmemory* (Cambridge, MA, and London: Harvard University Press)

——. 2012. *The Generation of Postmemory: Writing and Visual Culture after the Holocaust* (New York: Columbia University Press)

IBARZ, MERCÈ. 2005. 'Kilimanjaro', in *Febre de carrer* (Barcelona: Quaderns Crema), pp. 24–38

——. 2010. *No parlis de mi quan me'n vagi* (Barcelona: Empúries)

——. 2018a. 'Víctor la valenta', *Vilaweb*, 24 March <https://www.vilaweb.cat/noticies/victor-la-valenta-mail-obert-opinio-merce-ibarz-victor-catala-caterina-albert/> [accessed 24 March 2018]

——. 2018b. 'La dona singular i la ciutat', *Vilaweb*, 24 April <https://www.vilaweb.cat/noticies/dona-singular-i-la-ciutat-mail-obert-opinio-article-merce-ibarz/> [accessed 24 April 2018]

JULIÀ, LLUÏSA. 2007. *Tradició i orfenesa: per a una genealogia de l'escriptora catalana del segle XX* (Palma de Mallorca: Lleonard Muntaner, Editor)

KRISTEVA, JULIA. 1980. 'Word, Dialogue and Novel', in *Desire in Language: A Semiotic Approach to Literature and Art*, ed. by L. S. Roudiez, trans. by T. Gora, A. Jardine, and L. S. Roudiez (Oxford: Basil Blackwell), pp. 64–91

——. 1982. *Powers of Horror: An Essay on Abjection*, trans. by L. S. Roudiez (New York: Columbia University Press)

LEFEBVRE, HENRI. 1991 [1974]. *The Production of Space,* trans. by D. Nicholson Smith (Oxford: Blackwell)

LUNATI, MONTSERRAT. 2008. 'Collage o trencadís: Quim Monzó, un flâneur a Barcelona', in *Poètiques de ruptura*, ed. by Maria Muntaner, Mercè Picornell, Margalida Pons, and Josep Antoni Reynés (Palma: Lleonard Muntaner, Editor), pp. 217–39

——. 2009. 'Escriptores, gènere i estudis literaris: caminant pel carrer en femení als textos urbans de Mercè Ibarz', in *Gènere i modernitat a la literatura catalana*, ed. by Enric Cassany (Barcelona: Punctum & GELCC), pp. 11–37

——. 2020. 'Memory, Mothers and Post-Freudian Melancholia in Mercè Rodoreda's "Night and Fog"', in *Discourses on the Edges of Life*, ed. by Vicent Salvador, Adéla Kot'átková, and Ignasi Clemente (Amsterdam: John Benjamins), pp. 147–68

LUTZ, CATHERINE A. 2007. 'Emotion, Thought, and Estrangement: Emotion as Cultural Category', in *The Emotions: A Cultural Reader*, ed. by Helena Wulff (Oxford and New York: Berg), pp. 19–29

MARÇAL, MARIA-MERCÈ. 2000. *Raó del cos*, ed. by Lluïsa Julià (Barcelona: Edicions 62)

——. 2004. *Sota el signe del drac: proses, 1985–1997*, ed. by Mercè Ibarz (Barcelona: Proa)

——. 2014. *The Body's Reason*, trans. by Montserrat Abelló and Noèlia Díaz-Vicedo (London: Francis Boutle Publishers)

MOHINO I BALET, ABRAHAM. 2002. 'La poesia secreta de Mercè Rodoreda', in *Mercè Rodoreda. Agonia de llum. La poesia secreta de Mercè Rodoreda* (Barcelona: Angle Editorial), pp. 11–76

NORA, PIERRE. 1989. 'Between History and Memory: Les Lieux de mémoire', *Representations*, 26: 7–24

OBIOLS, ARMAND/JOAN PRAT ESTEVE. 2004. *Bordeus 1945* (Sabadell: Fundació La Mirada)

ORTIZ, LOURDES. 2018. 'Penélope', in *Rainy Days / Días de lluvia: Short Stories by Contemporary Spanish Women Writers*, ed. with and Introduction and notes by Montserrat Lunati, trans. by Marilyn Myerscough and Charles Kelley (Liverpool: Liverpool University Press), pp. 117–43

PASCUAL, ITZIAR. 1998. *Las voces de Penélope. Marqués de Bradomín 1997: Concurso de Textos Teatrales para Jóvenes Autores* (Madrid : Instituto de la Juventud), pp. 101–35. Also available from <https://www.scribd.com/document/145548700/Las-voces-de-Penelope-Itziar-Pascual> [accessed 27 April 2018]

PLA, XAVIER. 2010. 'L'estrany sopar', *Avui*, 11 November

REAL, NEUS. 2005. *Mercè Rodoreda: l'obra de preguerra* (Barcelona: Publicacions de l'Abadia de Montserrat)

RHODES, ELIZABETH. 1994. 'The Salamander and the Butterfly', in *The Garden across the Border: Mercè Rodoreda's Fiction*, ed. by Kathleen McNerney and Nancy Vosburg

(Selinsgrove, PA: Susquehanna University Press; London and Toronto: Associated University Presses), pp. 162–87

RICH, ADRIENNE. 1972. 'When We Dead Awaken: Writing as Re-Vision', <http://www.jstor.org/stable/375215> [accessed 14 November 2015]

RODOREDA, MERCÈ. 1978 [1947]. 'Nit i boira', in *Semblava de seda i altres contes* (Barcelona: Edicions 62), pp. 41–47

——. 1979 [1958]. 'Abans de morir', in *Tots els contes* (Barcelona: Edicions 62 i La Caixa), pp. 152–70

——. 1983 [1962]. *La plaça del Diamant* (Barcelona: Club Editor)

——. 2002. *Agonia de llum. La poesia secreta de Mercè Rodoreda*, ed. by Abraham Mohino i Balet (Barcelona: Angle Editorial)

——. 2011. 'Before I Die', in *The Selected Stories of Mercè Rodoreda*, trans. by Martha Tennent (Rochester, NY: Open Letter), pp. 144–68

——. 2013. *In Diamond Square*, trans. by Peter Bush (London: Virago)

——. 2015. *Mercè Rodoreda: obra de joventut*, ed. by Joaquim Molas, Carme Arnau, and Roser Porta (Barcelona: Institut d'Estudis Catalans; Edicions 62; Fundació Mercè Rodoreda)

ROTHBERG, MICHAEL. 2009. *Multidirectional Memory: Remembering the Holocaust in the Age of Decolonization* (Stanford, CA: Stanford University Press)

——. 2010. 'Introduction: Between Memory and Memory. From *Lieux de mémoire* to *Noeuds de mémoire*', *Yale French Studies*, 118/119: 3–12

SALVÀ, MARIA ANTÒNIA. 1981 [1934]. *El retorn*, ed. by Miquel Ferrà (Palma de Mallorca: Moll)

SERRA, MONTSERRAT. 2010. 'De la transició al tripartit: Mercè Ibarz publica la seva novel·la generacional *No parlis de mi quan me'n vagi* (Empúries)', *Vilaweb*, 2 November

SHOWALTER, ELAINE. 1991 [1977]. *A Literature of Their Own: From Charlotte Brontë to Doris Lessing* (London: Virago)

SUSANNA, ÀLEX. 2010. 'Mercè Ibarz, o com novel·lar la ciutat', *El Mundo*, 15 November

VOSBURG, NANCY. 1999. 'Reflections: Spaces of Self-Knowledge in Rodoreda's Fiction', in *Voices and Visions: The Words and Works of Mercè Rodoreda*, ed. by Kathleen McNerney (Selinsgrove, PA: Susquehanna University Press; London and Toronto: Associated University Presses), pp. 63–79

WALKER, NANCY A. 1995. *The Disobedient Writer: Women and Narrative Tradition* (Austin: University of Texas Press)

Notes to Chapter 8

1. Unless otherwise stated, all translations are my own.
2. As regards the connections between Rodoreda's short story 'Nit i boira' (1947) and Maria-Mercè Marçal's poems in *Raó del cos* (2000) through the mother figure and the concept of 'desnéixer' [be unborn], see Lunati (2020).
3. 'Jo crec que el feminisme és com un xarampió. A l'època de les sufragistes tenia sentit, però a l'època actual, que tothom fa el que vol, trobo que no té sentit el feminisme [...]. Sempre he considerat que una dona té més avantatges que un home: et consideren més, fas més gràcia, tens més portes obertes [...]' [I think that feminism is like measles. It made sense when the suffragettes were active, but nowadays, when people do what they wish, I don't see any sense in feminism [...] I have always thought that a woman has more advantages than a man: people are more considerate towards you, they pay more attention to you, you find more open doors for you [...]] (Cited in Rhodes 1994: 163).
4. The figure of Penelope has been the object of many feminist revisions, one of the best being the play by Itziar Pascual *Las voces de Penélope* [Penelope's Voices] (1998), in which waiting for a loved one is not presented as a naturalized gender behaviour, but as a social and cultural imposition on women.

5. In *No parlis de mi quan me'n vagi*, the narrator also says: 'Mentre [ella] pujava els esgraons vells i amb la fusta molt gastada, sentí les petjades que l'havien precedit, com si els graons i les soles de les sabates parlessin entre ells' [While she went up the old stairs with worn wooden edges, she heard the footsteps of those who had preceded her, as though the stairs and the shoes were talking to each other] (Ibarz 2010:17). The relationship with the past is presented as far more ambiguous when it comes to the city: 'El passat desapareix i el present s'alça opac, superb i cregut de l'espectacle. Un present alliberador del farcell de la història, com una criatura que se'n va de casa' [The past disappears and the present rises up opaque, arrogant and full of its own importance. A present free from the weight of history, like a child who leaves home for good] (Ibarz 2010: 83).

6. I have examined issues of gender and urban spaces in Mercè Ibarz's short stories in Lunati (2009: 11–37).

7. During his stay in Bordeaux, Armand Obiols, the pen name of Joan Prat i Esteve (1904–1971), wrote a famous letter which circulated among the Catalan exiles and was published in 2004 as a *plaquette* under the title *Bordeus 1945*. In it, he voiced his political disagreements with the last President of the Catalan Government during the Spanish Civil War, Lluís Companys, who had been captured by the Nazis and executed by Franco in 1940.

8. Rodoreda's pre-Civil War novels are now available in Rodoreda (2015).

9. The film alluded to (and misquoted) here is *Un chien andalou*, directed in 1929 by Luis Buñuel and Salvador Dalí. As Gwynne Edwards (2005: 24) explains, their first title for this Surrealist film was *Dangereux de se pencher en dedans* [Dangerous to Lean In], 'a witty inversion of the notice to passengers beneath the windows of French railway carriages'.

10. 'Be water, my friend' is a Bruce Lee quotation used in an advert for BMW cars shown on Spanish TV around the time the novel was being written.

11. Nela is also the name of the protagonist of the 1898 dramatic monologue 'La infanticida' [The Filicide] (1984: 39–57) by Catalan writer Caterina Albert/Víctor Català.

12. *No parlis de mi quan me'n vagi* also offers a representation of the urban space of Barcelona, a recurrent feature in Ibarz's fiction. This is the main point made by Àlex Susanna in his review of the novel (2010).

13. For example: 'No dem més ales al vol de la queixa' [Let's stop moaning] (Ibarz 2010: 29); 'Amb fils d'oblit cus la memòria' [With threads of oblivion memory sews] (Ibarz 2010: 192). Sometimes a Marçal verse is paraphased: 'la memòria que cus i cus, sargidora cega' [memory sews and sews, blind darner] (Ibarz 2010: 30).

14. Fluxus also speaks with another party guest, Nil (Ibarz 2010: 192): the novel gives the dead and the living an equal ontological (or should I say hauntological?) status.

15. Would it be too far-fetched to suggest that her name is inspired by the revolutionary Italian photographer Tina Modotti (1896–1942), mentioned in the novel (Ibarz 2010: 357) as one of the famous photographers who inspire Valentina?

16. Valentina's preference for legs as the object of her photos brings to mind the kind of photos taken by Lisette Model (1906–1983), an American photographer of Austrian origin. A photograph of Lisette Model illustrates the cover of Ibarz's first collection of stories, *A la ciutat en obres* [To the City under Construction] from 2002 (see Lunati 2009). Ibarz illustrated her review of a book by Vivian Gornik (2018b) with a photograph taken by herself of the legs of an old couple sitting on a bench which is suggestive of Model's work — another way for Ibarz to inscribe the work of a previous woman artist, a photographer in this case, in her own text.

CHAPTER 9

The Magic of Money in
Narcís Oller's *La febre d'or*:
Fraudulent Representation and the
Blurring of Perception

Elisa Martí-López

Northwestern University

Most, if not all critics agree that *La febre d'or* [Gold Fever] is a great novel about the speculative market and the modernization of Barcelona. It focuses on a period of two years — from 1880 to 1882 — when the bullish stock market that started in 1876 and lasted until 1886 had the greatest impact on the city. Oller wrote about the effects of speculation and financial companies investing in the extension of the railway through the quick rise and fall of a self-made man, Gil Foix. One of the great themes in the nineteenth-century novel, Gil Foix's story allows Oller to build a narrative of modern Barcelona.[1] In Joan Ramon Resina's words, *La febre d'or* is the 'first attempt in Catalan literature to produce a bourgeois epic', a first attempt that 'falls short of its goal' (1994–95: 259).[2] This perception of *La febre d'or* as 'flawed' — its 'proportionate difficulty or distaste for the impersonal dimensions of complex society' (Resina 1994–95: 259) — has been a constant in the critical reception of the novel since its publication. As early as 1892, Jaume Brossa wrote that *La febre d'or* was an insufficient 'crónica' [chronicle], a failed social drama trapped in the minutia of domestic life (1892: 354). As Resina puts it: Josep Yxart and Jaume Brossa 'were quick to remark upon [...] the insufficiency of the social perspective and the reduction of the collective horizon to the dimension of a private drama' (1994–95: 260).[3] For Brossa, however, *La febre d'or* did not even pass the test as a domestic drama: it is, he says, a failed 'comèdia íntima' [intimate drama] unable to articulate 'la íntima estructura dels caràcters' [the characters' inner contexture] whose 'ànima' [soul] Oller 'adapta a la generalitat dels tipos creats' [adapts to the general pattern of stock types] (1892: 354). The work's 'shortcomings' are precisely the focus of my current writing on Oller. I will not argue against the flawed character of the work. I intend, however, to articulate a different way of approaching the novel in order to address both the perceived shortcomings in the author's artistry and his 'faulty' naturalism as he struggles with realism or, more precisely, with the limits of realist writing.

To address the work's 'shortcomings', I propose to consider the formal deficiencies in *La febre d'or* as the novel's participation in — and its own difficulties with — the crisis of representation (both social and artistic) that characterized the end of the nineteenth century. In my opinion, Resina's insight into the parallelism and counterpoints between the new autonomous sphere of art and that of capitalist speculation in Oller's novel sets the right tone for the discussion: 'Oller's narrative viewpoint consciously presents aesthetic autonomy and economic speculation as the departure from dependable objectivity' (1994–95: 271). It is the crisis of 'dependable objectivity' that is the novel's main theme. I would like to contend that *La febre d'or*'s formal 'insufficiencies' as social drama — the 'Barcelona improvisada' [improvised Barcelona] Josep Yxart criticized (1980 [1895]: 191), and Jaume Brossa's wish for 'un quadro més vast' [a much wider picture] (1892: 354) — as well as the novel's limitations as an intimate drama, should be read in relation to the work's exploration and struggle with the crisis of representation both in society and art that characterized the 1880s. In this sense, I agree with Jordi Castellanos that *La febre d'or*'s 'objectiu no era la ciutat sinó la riquesa i el progrés' [the objective of *La febre d'or* was not the city but wealth and progress] (1997: 150). I hope this approach contributes to our understanding of the modernity — and greatness — of *La febre d'or*. In more general terms, I hope also that my study contributes to the recognition of the particular struggle and accomplishments of late nineteenth-century Catalan authors. 'Latecomers' to realism, a mode of writing that 'does not know how to represent the Other of Europe, nor yet — which is perhaps even worse — the Other in Europe' (Moretti 1994: 103), they managed to find their own voice within the morphological 'narrow road' imposed by the new 'integrated' literary market.[4]

The crisis of dependable objectivity in *La febre d'or* is marked by the presence in the novel of numerous objects, characters, spaces, events and moments related to representation and, most particularly, framing. We find paintings, frames, portraits, painters, models, an exhibition room where art is both commented on and sold — the Sala Parés — a painter's workshop, and picture-like descriptions of domestic and urban sites. From the very moment of its publication, critics have highlighted the insistence on issues of representation and framing throughout the novel:[5] 'Oller', wrote Josep Yxart in an article published in 1895, 'posa empenyo en fixar el *color* singular que distingueix [...] eixa societat barcelonina' [makes a great effort to fix the singular *colour* which distinguishes [...] that Barcelona society] (1895: 193; italics mine).[6] Later critics have insisted on the photographic and pictorial nature of *La febre d'or*: 'Oller es el gran fotógrafo social de la Catalunya ochocentista' [Oller is the great social photographer of nineteenth-century Catalonia] (Gaziel 1930: 5);[7] it is a 'historical canvas' of the city (Resina 2008: 15); descriptions in the novel constitute 'un immens quadro' [an immense old painting] (Yates 1998: 259); it is a 'portrait' — not a 'reproduction' — of social movements (Yates 1998: 269); it is 'una esplèndida fotografia' [a splendid photograph] (Cabana 1993: 35). Similarly, critics noted the inappropriate use of visual perspectives in the novel. Yxart resorted to the word 'cosmorama' already in his 1895 review of Oller's work (193) — a word taken up by Kathleen E. Davis (1995) — and complained about Oller's choice of perspective: Barcelona, he says, would not be 'una plaça reduïda' [a restricted urban setting], 'un escenari petit' [a small stage], 'si se prenguessin les coses de més amunt' [if things were viewed from a higher point] (195), or 'd'aquestes majors dimensions, per lo alto i per lo fondo, careix fins ara la nostra novel·la' [these greater dimensions, both higher and lower, have been missing from the Catalan novel] (196). Jaume Brossa concurred: the novel, for him, lacks 'vista de conjunt' [an overall view], 'el literat no s'eleva del terre-à-terre de la vida vulgar del ciutadà' [the writer does not rise above the banalities of the citizens' vulgar lives] (1892: 356). But it is Joan Ramon Resina who has shown the full signification of metaphors of visibility and of panoramic views of the city in Oller's attempt to represent the Catalan bourgeoisie by way of its capital. According to this critic, the most important narrative strategy deployed by Oller to re-create the city in the 1880s is '[t]he issue of perspective, of the right point of view, and above all of the amplitude of the frame required in order to capture the situation at a glance' (2008: 24). All these metaphors of visibility are implicit in the titles of the two parts of the novel: 'Pujada' [ascent, rise, climb] — from where full visibility of the city is posited — and 'Cayguda' [fall, drop, downturn] — where everything is darkness — organize and summarize this story of failed social mobility. In later editions, 'Estimbada' was used instead of 'Cayguda' as the title of Part II.[8] We do not know what prompted Oller to make this change. It is significant, however, that 'estimbada' points both at the cause of the 'ups' and 'downs' in the fortune of the novel's characters' — 'timba' means both precipice and gambling house — and Oller's object of representation: the stock market's speculative years of 1880–82.[9] Again, as Jordi Castellanos has indicated, it is not Barcelona but rather the city's wealth that is the subject of *La febre d'or*. In other words, the novel is not about Barcelona, the capital city of the Catalan bourgeoisie, but rather about the capital — the speculative money — that constituted the city's modernization. From the very beginning, *La febre d'or* directs the attention of its readers to the city as capital in this latter sense.

Elsewhere I analyse a 'remarkable thing' about *La febre d'or*: 'death always makes its appearance in all [city] perspectives from above and in significant instances of street-level view' (2017: 361). Focusing on bird's-eye views narrated from the perspective of Gil Foix, the protagonist of *La febre d'or*, I hope to show how, in the city's open vistas, death — as metaphor for the processes of representation — articulates both the literary representation of Barcelona as capital — the city as constituted by money — and the crisis of dependable objectivity. I explore the two moments in Part I when the city's false visibility and Foix's false consciousness are narrated: the open vista from Giró's *torre* [villa] (in Chapter 13, Part I), and that from the top of the Montjuïc cemetery after Foix's mother-in-law's burial (last pages of Chapter 20, Part I). I contend that speculation and death subvert dependable objectivity and, in particular, the false legibility of the city in open vistas. I also point out how in *La febre d'or* Oller struggles with the 'metonymic confusion' that characterizes the bourgeois sign and threatens realist writing (Barthes 1999: 40). In this chapter, I continue my exploration of Barcelona's transformation into capital — money — in *La febre d'or* and Oller's use of metaphors of visibility to represent the crisis of realism. I analyse how the fetishism of the commodity[10] — characteristic of speculative wealth — organizes his description of the city during the gold rush focusing on the radical changes it effects on the social and spatial structure of the city, the private space of the family, and its production of fraudulent representation and false consciousness.

The Magic of Money: Libidinal Economy and the Plot of Things

At the beginning of *La febre d'or*, Josep Rodon, a politician from the provinces, arrives in a Barcelona so utterly transformed by the fetishism of commodities that the narrator, instead of describing, as the nineteenth-century novel has conditioned us to expect, the provincial's impressions of the modern city (its streets, theatres, cafés, shops), takes us directly to the source of such transfiguration, i.e., the stock market: 'Quan Josep Rodon arribà al portal de la llotja [...]' [When Josep Rodon reached the main door of the stock market [...]] (1993: I, 17), reads the beginning of *La febre d'or*.[11] The first chapter revolves around Rodon's admiration of and bewilderment at the 'força taumatúrgica' [thaumaturgic force] (I, 18) of money that has both swept away the remnant of the city's *quartier* economy and the everyday life of the 'menestrals' [artisans], and accelerated the city's deindustrialization.[12] The stock market's speculative 'fever' has metamorphosed the city into (fictitious) capital and now stands for the whole city:

> Mig esvanit per aquell garbuix, l'acalorat progressista de Vilaniu sentí per un moment l'al·lucinació que allò era una gran fàbrica de moneda [...]. En Rodon no veia ni forges, ni foc, ni manxes, ni encunys, ni diner; però el veia ressonar a sos peus, vibrant i escorredís, i a ell li bastava l'espectacle d'aquella munió cridant a la desesperada, disputant-se a l'aranya estiracabells milions i milions, per a imaginar-se la fabricació de l'or que exaltava tants d'esperits.
>
> [Staggered by all that muddle and confusion, the hot-headed radical from Vilaniu was momentarily affected by the hallucination that he was looking at an enormous money mint [...]. Rodon could see no forges, no flames, no bellows, no moulds, nor any money; but he could sense it resonating at his feet, vibrant and elusive. And all he needed was the sight of that crowd with their desperate shouting and frantic disputations over millions and millions, in order to see in his own mind the manufacture of the gold that was exciting so many spirits.] (I, 25–26)

Rodon's arrival at the stock market at the beginning of *La febre d'or* indicates the abolition of old Barcelona's indexical order and its substitution by an order of representation that is 'no longer of determination [...] based on the irreducible, immovable otherness of their component parts' (Barthes 1999: 40): 'Tothom citava noms obscurs que, enlairats de cop i volta a la categoria de potentats[,] gastaven ja molt més luxe que la noblesa, l'alta banca i el comerç antics' [Everybody was calling out strange names which, suddenly elevated to the category of potentates, could now afford and put on display much more luxury than all the nobility, big banks

and traders of old] (I, 69). Giró's new ownership of the Pedralbes *torre* — one of the
new and ephemeral financial 'wonders' — is one of the many instances in the novel
where we see property as index — the site of aristocratic, landed, money — being
transformed into sign (a commodity).[13] In the libidinal and speculative economy
of Barcelona, money 'represents' everything: 'it is an equivalent, an exchange, a
representation, a sign' (Barthes 1999: 39): 'tot era qüestió de fincar-se, d'extremar
l'ostentació' [it was all about building a grand property, taking ostentation to the
limit], insists Jordi Balanyà, Gil Foix's cousin and partner (I, 72). All classes in the
city share Rodon's enthusiasm and delight for the 'thaumaturgic force' of the stock
market and, like him, have converted with 'l'ardent fanatism of the neòfit' [the
ardent enthusiasm of the neophyte] to the 'art d'encantament' [art of enchantment]
that, spreading everywhere from the modern 'temple', was creating 'aquelles deus
de riquesa' [those sources of wealth] (I, 18).[14]

The large availability of interest-bearing money was bringing about 'com
per encantament' [as by magic] the city's general wealth and pleasure: 'Era ja
innombrable la pobrissalla que en poques setmanes s'havia enriquit' [It was
impossible to count now the number of wretchedly poor people who had in a few
weeks become wealthy] (I, 69). 'Carretades de crèdit' [Cartloads of credit] (I, 70)
have transformed Barcelona into a marketplace where consumption has substituted
for production. Barcelona's industrial neighbourhoods are quickly disappearing
from sight replaced by gaudily ornamental buildings, a city made immaterial by
speculative money, by 'un corrent invisible d'or' [an invisible flow of gold] (I, 70). In
the Barcelona of *La febre d'or*, all is surface, appearances 'one needs to acquire as signs
of what one is, or wants to be' (Brooks 2005: 28): 'Avui la gent vol una altra cosa:
es paga molt de les aparièncis' [These days people are looking for something else:
appearances count for such a lot] (I, 45), says Eladi Balanyà, Jordi Balanyà's son and
Gil Foix's unscrupulous broker. Barcelona has finally become a modern metropolis
where money no longer bears any marks of its origin in labour, and people happily
participate in the delusion created by the surface of appearances. The fetishism of
commodities has transformed the city into 'un petit París' [a little Paris] (II, 181):

> Els teatres, sempre plens, estaven enlluernadors. Les quinquilleries i ebenisteries
> anaven en orri per fer lloc al nombre creixent de grans argenteries i magatzems
> de mobles sumptuaris. Les confiteries, guanteries, rebosteries i restaurants de
> luxe es multiplicaven com per encantament. Creixia el nombre de carruatges
> particulars, començaven a avalotar carrers i places troncs fogosos com mai no
> s'havien vist a Barcelona, i, mentre minvava l'edificació en els barris industrials,
> naixien, a dreta i esquerra, cases llampants, petits hotels i palaus de debò. Un
> corrent invisible d'or arribava fins a la bossa del jornaler. El goig resplendia en
> totes les cares, la gent corria esbojarrada pels carrers, i l'alè de benestar que arreu
> es respirava empenyia el més retingut a gastar i a canviar l'or reunit a còpia de
> suors i privacions per aquells trossos de paper, gravats a mitges tintes, que el
> crèdit escampava a carretades.
>
> [The theatres, always full, were dazzling. Small hardware shops and household
> goods businesses were going to rack and ruin, being replaced by the growing
> number of big jewellers and stores selling luxurious furniture. Confectionery

stores, fashion accessory shops, delicatessens and expensive restaurants were multiplying as if by magic. The number of private carriages was increasing; phaetons drawn by excitable horses that had never been seen in Barcelona were thundering down the streets, and, while building in the industrial districts was slowing down, elsewhere on every side there were rising up spectacular houses, private hotels and authentic palaces. An invisible flow of gold reached all the way to the day-worker's bag. Delight shone in every face, people were dashing in a mad hurry along the streets, and the sense of well-being that was everywhere in the air encouraged even the most careful people to spend their money and exchange the gold coinage, earned through hard toil and sacrifice, for those pieces of faintly coloured paper which credit made available in cartloads.] (i, 69–70)

All the 'trossos de paper' and 'carretades de crèdit' [pieces of paper and cartloads of credit] circulating in the city generate the 'plot of things', i.e., 'the nexus of love, money, prostitution, furnishings, all in a marketplace that is both financial and libidinal, and whose exchanges are the source of story' (Brooks 2005: 30) that represents Barcelona's 1880–82 inflationary and libidinal economy. It is in Gil Foix's new apartment, a private space cluttered with luxurious furniture and ornamental objects, where he will rediscover his lust: he tries unsuccessfully to seduce Blanche, his daughter's paid companion, in the room she occupies in the Foix household. As importantly, the plot of things also reveals the correlation between speculative make-believe and the fraudulence of ornament in the novel. Gil Foix's new apartment, located directly across his brokerage and banking office, contains a suffocating number of very expensive and useless objects:

> Pare i noia prenien subscripcions inútils, compraven a desdir, a voltes per caritat: ell, en Foix, ho feia de cop i volta, per mer capritxo, sense gust ni pla preconcebut de dar-li col·locació, com si els diners li pesessin a la butxaca. I així anava aquella casa, omplint-se de trastos inútils, rellotges estranys muntats sobre peluix, capses de música, quadros amb vaixellets de moviment, gerros feixucs, mobles incòmodes i lletgíssims fets amb banyes de bou o baranes de ferro.

> [Father and daughter took out useless subscriptions, shopped with gay abandon, sometimes out of charity: Foix himself would do this on impulse, on a mere whim, with no discrimination or design about where the objects were to go, as if the money was burning a hole in his pocket. And that is how their household was run, getting filled with useless trappings, bizarre clocks mounted on felt, music boxes, paintings of ships in a coastal setting, big heavy vases, furniture that was both uncomfortable and very ugly with its bull-horn or iron-railing adornment.] (i, 75)

A showcase for its owner's social ambition and dreams of wealth, the fashionable furniture and ornaments that fill up his home no longer bear any mark of their origin (tradition and family) or functionality. All indexical representations of the Foix lineage are abolished to create a new and unstable social identity based on the representative value of money: 'S'havien desterrat a Vilaniu els mobles antics, guardessin o no records de família i un magatzemista, també improvisat, que tot ho endegava a estil de *boudoir de cocotte*, els havia acabat de parar aquella casa d'una manera que era un turment' [The old pieces of furniture had been sent back in exile to Vilaniu, whether or not they held any family memories, and a specialist, also plucked out of nowhere, who dressed up everything in *boudoir de cocotte* style, had put the finishing touches to the excruciating interior design] (I, 73). The 'excrutiation' inflicted on the Foix family by the chaotic accumulation of things — and later on by Gil's rediscovered lust — in the new luxurious apartment is that of a mass of heavily ornamented objects that, detached from all reference to use or real value, prevents the movement of life and, as we see later on in the novel with Gil Foix's expensive gifts to his wife and daughter, substitutes for intimacy, old family ties and responsibilities: 'La família s'ofegava, de falta d'aire, amb tants cortinatges, tapissos i catifes, i, sobretot, amb aquell excés the peluix estès per les parets, per damunt dels llits, taules i cadires' [The family was stifled for want of air, with so many drapes and curtains, tapestries and rugs, and, in particular, by that excess of felt on the walls and draped upon beds, tables and chairs] (I, 73).

Gil Foix's new apartment is not only full of useless objects, but it is also a metonymic confusion of monstrous things. The incongruous accumulation of composite objects — 'rellotges estranys muntats sobre peluix' [bizarre clocks mounted on felt], 'quadros amb vaixellets de moviments' [paintings of ships by the coast], mobles 'fets amb banyes de bou o baranes de ferro' [furniture with its bull-horn or iron-railing adornment] — are the 'wild' signs of a society whose 'order of representation' is 'no longer that of determination' (Barthes 1999: 39–40). On the contrary, the 'wild' commodities — aberrant, worthless, useless — that clutter Gil Foix's apartment are the creations of an excessive — fanciful — imagination, the expression of the endless potentiality of the desiring self and the money that represents it. Gil Foix buys 'per mer capritxo' [merely on a whim] objects that are a product of capricious minds, 'veritables cabòries d'inventors extravagants, rebuigs de taller i de botiga' [definitely broodings of extravagant inventors, cast-offs from studios and from shops] (I, 75). These products of 'broodings' are not unlike that of inventors like Gil's brother Bernat, 'mudable i somiador' [unpredictable and head-in-clouds] (I, 32), who is working on a 'cigarreta-llumí o llumí-cigarreta' [cigarette with built-in match or vice-versa] (I, 57);[15] that of speculators whose 'más o menos ingeniosas' [more or less ingenious] ideas broke 'todas las marcas mundiales en el planteamiento de negocios insensatos [...] para sacar dinero a los barceloneses contra la venta de unos papeles impresos que nunca rendirían ni un cèntimo' [every single world record in putting forward madcap business projects [...] in order to extract money from Barcelona people in exchange for printed vouchers which would never pay out a single cent] (Fontana 1961: 46); or, more to the point, that of the new modern artists whose art 'comes to reflect the intrinsic uselessness that is the condition of money's universal exchangeability, as both art and money go beyond their traditional functions and generate their specific spheres above the everyday' (Resina 1994–95: 270). Indeed, the expensive junk cluttering private and fashionable spaces, and the excess of ornament detached from all real or use value, mirror the junk stocks accumulated in Barcelona's stock market during the *febre d'or*, and stand for the deceitfulness of those who purchase them: the city's new 'potentates'. As the narrator puts it, only 'la ignorància adinerada' [ignorant well-to-do] are taken in by the fraudulent representation of these 'wild' signs (I, 75). In Oller's novel, as Resina pointed out, the 'parallelism between the essential make-believe of financial speculation and the substitution of ornament for comfort', and the 'equivalent dishonesty [...] at work in both enterprises', go hand in hand (1994–95: 271).

The fraudulent representation of a speculative economy that clutters Gil Foix's overloaded apartment is associated with scarcity of light: 'En Foix tirà cap a la sala, que amb prou feines pogué travessar, guiat només per una ratlla de llum que clarejava en un finestró, prima com un regle de vidre. A les palpentes quasi, i sense oure les pròpies petjades, que ofegava la catifa, arribà al balcó exclamant: Què redimoni! Quina mania de viure a les fosques!' [Gil Foix headed for the sitting room, which he was scarcely able to walk through, guided as he was by a thin beam of light coming in through a shutter, a beam as narrow as a glass ruler. Almost groping his way, and without hearing his own footsteps, muffled by the carpet, he finally reached the balcony exclaiming: What the devil! Talk about living in the dark!] (I, 50). The literal darkness in his cluttered apartment corresponds to the symbolic darkness of the false consciousness — 'viure a les fosques' [living in the dark] — of a city dominated by the fetishism of the commodity: 'merely to note the existence of things, whether specific objects or "the object" in general, is to ignore what things at once embody and dissimulate, namely social relations and the forms of those relations' (Lefebvre 1991: 81). Surrounded by darkness, Gil Foix contents himself with the 'mig pamet' [couple of inches] of dim light he allows into his apartment and consciousness. His shadowy apartment stands for the phantasmagoria of commodities and false consciousness: 'I, enfonsant la mà per entre sedes i malles, agafà el finestró, i amb molt de compte el badà mig pamet' [And, pushing his hand through silk drapes and wood slats, he opened the blind a couple of inches] (I, 50).[16]

The fetishism of commodity that darkens Gil Foix's cluttered apartment is what explains the absence of a secure foundation that threatens the family with collapse — and ruin — throughout the novel. It is, thus, not surprising that Gil Foix and his wife, Caterina, are constantly stumbling over the fashionable furniture that crowds and darkens their home: 'La Caterina s'entrebancava amb tants pufs, tantes tauletes i cadires, tants pedestals, posats al pas; renegava de la profusió de flors de porcelana, quadres i bibelots trencadissos, que, escampats per tot arreu, reprimien els moviments més naturals' [Caterina kept tripping over so many pouffes. So many side-tables and chairs, so many pedestals blocking the way; she cursed the profusion of porcelain flowers, pictures and fragile bibelots, which, placed here, there and everywhere, hindered all attempts at natural movement] (I, 73). At the end of the novel, and only at a great personal cost, Caterina Foix goes back to her menestral values, recovers her senses — or rather, her sight — and finds her way through the cluttered confusion of her apartment. She will try, to no avail, to take her sick husband out of the darkness of his mind — and rooms — and guide him safely — 'amb una llum a la mà' [with a light in her hand] (II, 146) — through his financial and personal breakdown: 'I, agafant-lo amorosament pel colze, la Caterina arrencà de la cadira aquell home, que, aclaparat de dolor, hagué d'agafar-se al braç de sa muller per travessar l'encortinada porta sense ensopegar' [And, taking him affectionately by the elbow, Caterina helped to lift from his chair the man, who, overwhelmed by agony, had to cling to his wife's arm in order to get past the door-blind without stumbling] (II, 149).

Smoke Haze and Perceptual Blur: Peret Foix's Spectral Presence and Blanche's Carriage Stroll

During Barcelona's gold fever, the capitalist exploitation of labour is concealed under the appearance of a relation between things, buried under the appearance of money breeding money. Shops and clerks have expelled industries and manual labourers from the city, and replaced substance with ornament: 'mentre minvava l'edificació en els barris industrials naixien, a dreta i esquerra, cases llampants, petits hotels i palaus de debò' [while construction was declining in the industrial quarters, everywhere else, on all sides, shiny new dwellings, small mansions and real palaces were springing up] (I, 69–70).[17] All the planned but never initiated projects for the urban reform of Barcelona mentioned in the novel confirm the radical disconnect between the city's speculative wealth and industrial endeavours: 'el bon Bernat' [good-hearted Bernat], points out the narrator, 'es planyia que tots els capitals preferissin les aventures de la Borsa als profits de la indústria' [complained that all the wealth favoured adventures on the stock-exchange over profits from investment in industry] (I, 63). The feigned projects of the short-lived Banc de Crèdit, an investment bank created by Giró to raise money precisely for the much-needed but never-carried-out urban reforms, are emblematic of the city's transformation into (fictitious) capital. Gil Foix's urban projects are no different from the Banc de Crèdit's spurious schemes. In the early stages of his financial success, Foix has a long list of projects for Barcelona's reform that are dear to him: a new Sant Josep market, a new hospital, a dockyard where ships would be built and repaired that would serve the entire Mediterranean. But, as he himself acknowledges to Giró at the end of the novel, when the Banc de Crèdit and Foix's own investment firm are already bankrupt, Barcelona's urban reforms will take a long while: 'Ui! Que llarg que va això!' [Oh! This will take ages!] (II, 162).

It is, thus, not surprising that Gil Foix thinks his brother Peret, a manual labourer working in a forge, a 'fantasma' [phantasm/show off]. Foix's false consciousness assigns to Peret his own condition: 'Sols aquell germà rebec, en Peret, aquell obrer orgullós que veia, en son pensament, com un fantasma, oblidat en les tenebrors de la farga, li amargava les dolçors de l'alegria' [Only that misfit brother, Peret, that proud working man who he imagined as a phantom, lost in the darkness of the forge, embittered for him the sweetness of his joy] (I, 203). Gil Foix thinks that 'pride' (I, 58) prevents Peret from accepting his employment offer and, consequently, sharing his success story, as his other brother, Bernat, does. But Peret's spectral presence in his brother's false consciousness and the city's blissful ignorance of human labour as source of value correspond to the disappearance of industrial neighbourhoods in a city dominated by the phantom-like representation of labour under the fetish of the commodity. We never meet the industrialist who owns the only factory that briefly appears in *La febre d'or*, or enter its productive spaces, and the only worker we get to know is a French overseer. The factory is located outside the city, in the neighbouring town of Sant Martí de Provençals, and it is — it feels — so far away from the city that it is perceived as almost out of reach: 'Uf!... tan lluny!... tan intrincat de trobar! Me só perduda i tot' [Gosh!... so far away!... so confusing to get to! I didn't even know where I was] (1, 256), complains Mademoiselle Blanche, the French-Catalan paid companion of Gil Foix's daughter, who, forced out of Foix's house by Gil's lasciviousness, ventures out of the city, and ends up visiting her uncle at the factory to ask for help.

The radical disconnect between the city as a space of consumption — and its false consciousness — and that of production is developed in Blanche's unwillingness to go into the factory to meet her uncle after her carriage tour — reminiscent of Emma Bovary's — through the city's commercial docks. Starting near the stock market and accompanied by Eladi Balanyà — the unscrupulous broker with whom she is in love — the ride initiates Blanche's social mobility, a rootlessness that she will not be able to escape. Her vehicle, soon engulfed by 'fileres de carros i carromatos, plens a desdir de mercaderia feixuga' [rows of carriages and covered wagons, full to the brim with bulky goods'] (1, 250), leads her directly into the urban circulation that transfigures people and things into commodities. Blind to the fraudulent intentions of her lover — he is only interested in having sexual relations with her — and totally focused on him, she does not see the 'nou món' [new world] (1, 250), the city-as-marketplace her lover has taken her into. In this new world, unknown to respectable, idle people and old money — 'per al barceloní que passa la vida engorronit per les Rambles i el passeig de Gràcia' [for the Barcelona people who spend their lives aimlessly going up and down the Rambles and the Passeig de Gràcia] (1, 250) — the anonymity and promiscuity of the marketplace is out in the open: 'el lloc era el més a propòsit per a guardar l'incògnit: ni una persona coneguda' [this was the best place to conserve anonymity: not a single familiar face] (1, 250). Things and people meet in a 'promiscuous' relation of exchange — not production — indifferent to origin, names, and identities. The commercial harbour acts out the city's libidinal economy for all to see, its metonymic confusion:

> tot un poble cridaner i bullidor d'agents de duana que s'engeguen com coets, peixeters que passen corrent a peu nu [...] la immensa panera de peix al cap regalimant aigua [...]; mariners colrats, de mirar reflexiu que caminen balancejant-se; *xufleros* cridaners [...] pillet[s] de platja, i [...] la mossa del barri que anguileja per allí fent petar les xinel·les, la gravada galta pintada, un clavell al monyo; corrues de venedors ambulants empenent carretons de taronges macades, cocos, dàtils, i altres fruites; tota una Babel de llengües amb un nexe comú, que permet promiscuar el pensament a totes les nissagues.

> [A whole rowdy mêlée of customs officers who go off like rockets, fish-sellers who run by barefooted [...] with water pouring from the huge baskets of fish on their heads [...]; sun-scorched sailors, with thoughtful eyes who sway by; rowdy chufa-nut sellers [...] rascals from the beach, and [...] the lass from the backstreets who comes and goes with clattering mules on her feet, thick make-up covering her chickenpox scars, a carnation in her hair bun; streams of street

hawkers pushing carts full of bruised oranges, coconuts, dates and other fruit; a real Babel of tongues with the one thing in common which enables them to communicate their central thought to all and sundry.] (I, 250)

Blanche, disappointed by her unfulfilled expectations of marrying Eladi, hastily gets out of the carriage and walks all the way from the city's harbour to Sant Martí de Provençals. There she asks the doorman at the factory entrance to tell her uncle to meet her outside. She needs to talk to him 'a soles' [alone] (I, 256). Blanche wants to protect her privacy from curious looks and ears, but she also needs to stay away from the space of labour exploitation which mirrors the prostitution she has been threatened with since she left Gil Foix's household, started working at Mme Leocadie's hat shop, and received Eladi in her employer's home: 'Si l'oncle no escoltava la veu del deure, si no sortia a reclamar el que era d'ella o no li posava diners a la mà per a repatriar-se, no tindria altre recurs que prostituir-se o morir de fam!' [If her uncle did not listen to the voice of duty, if he did not stand up to claim what was rightly hers, or did not put money directly into her hands so that she could go back to her own country, then she would have no alternative other than prostitution, or to starve to death!] (I, 259). The factory walls block from Blanche's — and the general — view the true material source of wealth: 'Un soroll com de pluja llunyana s'escapava sols d'aquelles parets: ni una persona pels llarguíssims caminals que deixaven entre si els interminables estenedors' [A noise like that of distant rainfall escaped from behind those walls: not a soul was to be seen in the long corridors between endless lines of drying racks] (I, 257). But the thick and filthy smog emanating from 'el bosc de xemeneies de vapor que els envoltava' [the forest of steam chimneys surrounding them] (I, 256) signals distinctively the labour exploitation hidden from view. The dark truth of abuse and helplessness saddens her: 'La noia clavà un moment la vista rumiosa en l'altíssima xemeneia, que gitava a l'aire una troca contínua de fum espès i negre. Sense saber per què, aquell espectacle acabà de contristir-la' [She looked hard for a moment at the tallest chimney belching into the air a continuous hank of thick black smoke. Without her knowing why, that view made her deeply sad] (I, 257). Blanche is trying hard to keep alive the illusion of herself — her 'dignity' — and that of marrying Eladi, avoiding the anonymity and promiscuity of the 'new world' she has so narrowly escaped. But from beyond the city limits, still in sight of the pall of smoke 'vomitant [...] per cent forats i finestres' [spewing [...] from hundreds of openings and windows] (I, 256), she understands that, in a society deluded by surface appearances, where something which is other than what it appears remains — has to remain — unknown, her fate is sealed: 'A hores d'ara, essent pura, estaria deshonrada!' [now, being pure, she would be dishonoured!] (I, 259). The filth of smog has vanished from Barcelona, and now the dazzling light of gold — money — irradiating from the stock market to the whole city creates and maintains the illusion of a surface appearance — Barcelona's deceitful wealth — that conceals the intimate relationship between labour and sexual exploitation in the city's libidinal and inflationary economy. As Pauleta Balanyà, the cynical mother of Eladi, who knows 'un reguitzell d'històries brutes de la gent de borsa' [endless dirty gossip about stockbrokers], puts it: 'són coses que els diners porten' [these are things which money brings with it] (I, 155). Consistent with her cynicism, Pauleta, who is enjoying a long-desired social status thanks to the fraudulent representation of money, does not hesitate to blame Blanche when she sees her with her (Pauleta's) son at the inauguration of the city's race tracks: 'El meu fill amb aquella desvergonyida?' [My son with that shameless hussy?] (I, 231).[18]

The fetishism of commodities that rules Barcelona's new world is captured by the narrator's impressionist 'perceptual blur' of the kind that, as Christopher Prendergast suggested, 'serves a whole social way of seeing, or rather a refusal to see significant forms of difference' (1992: 15). Indeed, 'la claror fortíssima' [the dazzling light] that illuminates the 'temple' (I, 18) — the stock market — and blinds Rodon and the city, reverberates in the harbour's 'samfaina de colors, que la boirina del sol fon i harmonitza en tintes suaus, dins d'una atmosfera de llum i vida exuberants' [blurred variegation of colours, blended in the hazy sunshine and harmonized in gentle tints, in an atmosphere of exuberant luminosity and vitality] (I, 250). The vivacious mix of light, the brightness of gold, the fever that, in Oller's novel, represents metaphorically the city's libidinal energy during those years, blinds most characters and dazzles the narrator who, similarly to impressionist painting, 'lose[s] sight of real social structures of difference and division' (Prendergast 1992: 43).[19] The absence of Peret is announced at the beginning of the novel: 'No l'esperis' [Don't expect him to come], says Gil Foix to his brother Bernat referring to Peret's refusal to attend Christmas dinner at the new nouveau riche apartment of his brother Gil (I, 58). This 'no l'esperis' should be read as a warning to the reader. The story of value made out of production and exploitation will not be told: 'N'hi ha tota una història' [There's a whole story to be told about it] (I, 58), says Gil Foix about his brother's refusal to work for him. This story is not the story told in *La febre d'or*. Oller's novel is about the phantasmagoria of speculative wealth, about the ideological transposition of material reality into a commodified world, and the spectacularizing and fetishizing bound up in looking.[20] As Blanche's uncle puts it when commenting on her niece's remarks about the factory's remoteness from the city: 'Tot un quartier d'usines. Vosatros no hi sabeu pas' [A whole district full of factories. You lot don't know what it's all about] (I, 256).

The stock market propagates like a lighthouse the brightness that creates the perceptual blur which characterizes Oller's novel. Its luminescence generates the constant circulation of signs with no referent, blinds the characters, and undermines dependable objectivity. T. J. Clark has claimed that 'the unsettling of meaning [...] was the matter of modern art, its main concern, but also the devil to handle' (1985: 72). Indeed, Oller struggled with the representation of Barcelona's libidinal and inflationary economy during the *febre d'or* years. It did undermine his search for dependable objectivity and threaten his realist writing.

Works Cited

BARTHES, ROLAND. 1999 [1970]. *S/Z*, trans. by Richard Miller (New York: The Noonday Press)

BROOKS, PETER. 2005. *Realist Vision* (New Haven, CT, and London: Yale University Press)

BROSSA, JAUME. 1892. 'Narcís Oller', *L'Avenç*, 12: 353–57

CABANA, FRANCESC. 1993. 'El balanç de *La febre d'or*', *Avui*, 1 May, p. 35

CASACUBERTA, MARGARIDA. 1999. 'Dues novel·les per a dues burgesies: notes per a una comparació entre *La febre d'or* i *L'argent*', in *El segle romàntic: actes del Col·loqui Narcís Oller*, ed. by Magí Sunyer (Valls: Cossetània), pp. 197–208

CASSANY, ENRIC. 1999. 'Narcís Oller i l'art de la novel·la', in *El segle romàntic: actes del Col·loqui Narcís Oller*, ed. by Magí Sunyer (Valls: Cossetània), pp.15–28

CASTELLANOS, JORDI. 1997. *Literatura, vides, ciutats* (Barcelona: Edicions 62)

CLARK, T. J. 1985. *The Painting of Modern Life: Paris in the Art of Manet and his Followers* (New York: Alfred A. Knopf)

DAVIS, KATHLEEN. 1995. 'The "Cosmorama" of Barcelona: Social Mobility in *La febre d'or*', *Catalan Review*, 9.1: 33–46

DOMINGO, JOSEP MARIA. 2012. 'Pròleg', in *La febre d'or* by Narcís Oller (Valls: Cossetània), pp. 9–29

FONTANA, JOSÉ. 1961. 'La vieja bolsa de Barcelona (1851–1914)', in *La bolsa de Barcelona de 1851 a 1930: líneas generales de su evolución* (Barcelona: Instituto Municipal de Historia), pp. 42–49

GAZIEL/AGUSTÍ CALVET PASCUAL. 1930. 'Un gran fotógrafo', *La Vanguardia*, 1 August, p. 5

LEFEBVRE, HENRI. 1991 [1974]. *The Production of Space*, trans. by D. Nicholson Smith (Oxford: Blackwell)

MALUQUER DE MOTES, JORDI. 2016. *Literatura i economia: la narrativa de Narcís Oller a la intersecció* (Barcelona: Reial Acadèmia de Bones Lletres de Barcelona)

MARTÍ-LÓPEZ, ELISA. 2017. 'Death and the Crisis of Representation in Narcís Oller's *La febre d'or* and Pérez Galdós's *La de Bringas*', in *The Routledge Companion to Iberian Studies*, ed. by Javier Muñoz-Basols, Laura Lonsdale, and Manuel Delgado (London: Routledge), pp. 357–67

MORETTI, FRANCO. 2005 [1983]. 'Homo Palpitans: Balzac's Novels and Urban Personality', in *Signs Taken for Wonders* (London: Verso), pp. 109–29

——. 1998. *Atlas of the European Novel, 1800–1900* (London: Verso)

——. 1994. 'Modern European Literature: A Geographical Sketch', *New Left Review*, 206: 86–109

NAVARRO, FELIP BENICI. 1879. 'Lo llibre dels Jochs Florals de Barcelona, en l'any XXI de llur restauració', *La Renaixensa*, 9.2: 508–14

OLLER, NARCÍS. 1993 [1890–1892]. *La febre d'or*, 2 vols (Barcelona: Edicions 62)

PRENDERGAST, CHRISTOPHER. 1992. *Paris in the Nineteenth Century* (Oxford: Blackwell)

RAHOLA, FREDERIC. 1893. 'La febre d'or', *La Vanguardia*, 12 January

RESINA, JOAN RAMON. 1994–95. 'The Sublimation of Wealth and the Consciousness of Modernism in Narcís Oller's *La febre d'or*', *JHR*, 3: 259–75

——. 2008. *Barcelona's Vocation of Modernity* (Stanford, CA: Stanford University Press)

SARDÀ, JOAN. 1891. 'Narciso Oller, *La febre d'or*', *La Vanguardia*, 4 May

YATES, ALAN. 1975. 'The Creation of Narcís Oller's *La febre d'or*', *Bulletin of Hispanic Studies*, 52.1: 55–77

——. 1998. *Narcís Oller: tradició i talent individual* (Barcelona: Curial)

YXART, JOSEP. 1980 [1895]. '*La febre d'or* per Narcís Oller', in *Entorn de la literatura catalana de la Restauració*, ed. by Jordi Castellanos (Barcelona: Edicions 62), pp. 191–96

Notes to Chapter 9

1. According to Franco Moretti, '[t]he dazzling rapidity of success and ruin is the great theme of the nineteenth-century novel from Balzac to Maupassant: with it the city enters modern literature and becomes, as it were, its obligatory context' (2005: 111).

2. See, among others, Josep Yxart (1980 [1895]), Jaume Brossa (1892), Margarida Casacuberta (1999), Enric Cassany (1999), Josep Maria Domingo (2012) and Alan Yates (1998).

3. Only the historian Josep Fontana considered *La febre d'or* 'una crónica fiel y documentada' [a true and well-documented account] (1961: 46).

4. 'Diffusion: the great force. One form. And an imported one [...] [I]n an integrated market — latecomers don't follow the same road of their predecessors, only later: they follow a different, a narrower, road' (Moretti 1998: 190–91).

5. Felip Benici Navarro praised Oller's talent for observation as early as 1879: 'La principal cualitat del Sr. Oller es la observació, una perspicacia especial pera acusar los objectes ab quatre trasos deixantlos fixats com una fotografia' [Mr Oller's main quality is being observant, the special perspicacity to pin down objects with a few strokes, fixing them as in a photograph] (1879: 513).

6. See also Sardà (1891) and Rahola (1893).

7. Jordi Maluquer de Motes has pointed out that the engraving on the book cover for the first edition of *Croquis del natural* [Sketches from Nature] in 1879 reproduces a camera: 'Tot i que no sabem res de cert, estic convençut que es tracta d'un disseny fet pel mateix Oller, coneguda la seva gran afició pel dibuix i per la fotografia' [Even though we don't know anything for sure, I am convinced that it is a design by Oller himself, knowing his fondness for drawing and photography] (2016: 27).

8. 'Cayguda' [fall, drop, downturn] was used only in the 1892 first edition by *Ilustració Catalana*.

9. '[T]he taste for risk had never penetrated so deeply into the very fabric of everyday life. The expression "to play the stock market" [...] originates in the nineteenth century: and the readiness with which, in Balzac's novels, the characters try to compensate for the disasters of their professional lives by gambling is indicative of the confusion between the two realms' (Moretti 2005: 121).

10. I use the notion of 'the fetishism of the commodity' to mean the concealment of the social relation of exploitation at the origin of value — represented by price — under the appearance of an exchange relation between things. In this sense, money is the supreme fetish: it disguises value even as it represents it.

11. Zola's *L'Argent* (1891) also starts with Saccard in a restaurant close to the stock market waiting for the beginning of the day's trading session.

12. In the old *quartier* economy, 'the owner was often and rightly called an "ouvrier-patron"' who 'had made his way by effort and dexterity'; the most important social and economic matters 'depended on the *quartier*'s being close-knit, separated, and intimately known' with 'its own shopkeepers and *négociants*'; and its bourgeoisie derived status and respect from their being almost as much a part of the *quartier* as the "ouvrier-patron"' (Clark 1985: 52).

13. See Martí-López (2017: 362).

14. As the narrator points out, Barcelona's stock market negotiated the 'suma fabulosa' [fabulous sum] of more than three million stock shares and moved capital of over 776 million *pesetas*, in addition to 'la més fabulosa encara de valors nacionals i estrangers que a Borsa es traficaven' [even more fabulous sum of domestic and foreign stocks that were traded in the Stock Market] (I, 69).

15. 'Tots esclafiren a riure, fins en Bernat, que, passejant-se sala amunt i sala avall, no havia dit "aquesta boca és meva", pensant en la invenció d'uns llumins "que no fossin mistos, sinó misto i cigarret, que en xuclant s'encenguessin"' [They all burst out laughing, even Bernat, who pacing up and down the hall had not said a word, as he had been thinking about the invention of some matches 'which would not be matches, but matches and cigarettes, and which would light up as you sucked on them'] (I, 57).

16. Elsewhere, we read: 'La fosca del crepuscle s'anava atapeint dins l'enfarfegada saleta, de manera que ja les interlocutores [Pauleta i Blanche] gairebé no es veien sinó com dues ombres d'indecís

perfil' [The darkness of the gloaming was taking over the crowded room, so that the speakers could barely see each other, but could just make out two shadows of uncertain profile] (I, 122).

17. Maluquer de Motes has commented on the deindustrialization of Barcelona during the last decades of the nineteenth century, and the transformation of Sant Martí de Provençals into the capital of industrial Catalonia (2016: 57–58). He has also noted the relation between the absence of Peret and the 'follia especulativa' [speculative madness] of those years (69), but he seems to find the answer to the absence of the working classes and social conflict in *La febre d'or* — the 'retret freqüent' [frequent criticism] to Oller's novel — in the limitations of the nineteenth-century novel and, specifically, the Catalan literary market. No Catalan author could afford an unnecessary or extravagant social experiment: 'Es tracta d'una observació poc atenta a la realitat de la història de la literatura, ja que ningú no havia fet mai allò que sembla exigir-se a Narcís Oller. Émile Zola fou el primer a fer entrar l'obrer a la literatura. [A successful writer in the powerful French literary market], Zola [...] es va permetre el luxe de viure una colla de mesos entre els miners per documentar-se a fons en escriure *Germinal*, quelcom d'impensable per a l'escriptor català' [This is an observation which pays little heed to the reality of the history of literature, as no one had ever done what was seemingly demanded of Narcís Oller. Émile Zola was the first to bring the working man into literature. Zola allowed himself the luxury of living a fair few months among miners to carry out in-depth research so as to write *Germinal*, something unthinkable for a Catalan writer] (68).

18. For Alan Yates, Oller rushed his characterization of Blanche. He comments on 'the unsatisfactory treatment of Blanche, particularly her reappearance and suicide in Part II' of the novel (1975: 75).

19. See Martí- López (2017: 362–65).

20. See Prendergast (1992: 34).

CHAPTER 10

Ethical and Aesthetic Revolt in
Avel·lí Artís-Gener's *Prohibida l'evasió*

Sílvia Mas i Sañé

Universitat de Vic-UCC, Campus Manresa

Avel·lí Artís-Gener/Tísner (1912–2000) has been one of the most relevant intellectuals of the twentieth-century Catalan literary landscape. Born in Barcelona, he began working as a journalist during the 1930s. When the Spanish Civil War broke out, his Republican ideals led him to become a volunteer and fight on the front line in order to defend democracy until the outcome of the conflict forced him, like so many other Republicans, into exile in February 1939. After a few months in France, in June of that same year, he and his family sailed to Mexico, where he lived for twenty-six years.

In Mexico, Artís-Gener contributed to several magazines, penned his first novel, *556 Brigada Mixta* [556 Mixed Brigade] (1945), and wrote two further works which would be published only when he returned to Catalonia, *Les dues funcions del circ* [The Two Functions of the Circus] (1966) and *Paraules d'Opòton el Vell* [The Words of Opòton the Elder] (1968), while at the same time becoming a professional in the fields of advertising, painting and stage design. Unlike many fellow exiles, he was captivated by his new home; he got to know in depth a new culture and expanded his vision of the world, as is reflected in his work.

In 1965, Tísner decided to return to Barcelona with the family he had made for himself: his return was difficult and meant beginning again, but in a few years he was fully involved in the cultural life of the city. It was after his return, when he published the novels he had written in exile, along with others that he wrote in Catalonia, such as *Prohibida l'evasió* [Evasion Prohibited] (1969) or *L'enquesta del Canal 4* [The Survey of Channel 4] (1972), that his name became known to the Catalan public. During those years he wrote essays as well as fiction, and he worked as a journalist, translator and crossword writer. His literary career culminated in the monumental memoirs *Viure i veure* [To Live and to See] (1989, 1990, 1991, 1996).

Genesis and Context of *Prohibida l'evasió*

Prohibida l'evasió gives novelistic form to the end of the author's long period of exile and represents a pivotal point between two worlds: Mexico and Catalonia. The novel was conceived and begun in Mexico but basically written in Barcelona, over a period of approximately fifteen years. Originally entitled *El cercle i la tangent* [The Circle and the Tangent], it appeared in print in 1969,[1] after winning the Prudenci Bertrana prize that same year.

The fact that Artís-Gener goes back to this novel on his return from twenty-six years of exile is essential for an understanding of the work. If exile implies trauma, returning home after so many years of being settled in another country entails yet another wrench. Tísner has to leave behind his two eldest children, his job and his house in Mexico, to return to a Barcelona ravaged by Francoism, which bears no resemblance to the city he knew almost three decades earlier and no longer has any relationship with the idealized memories formed during all those years. This change of context certainly affected the final shape given to *Prohibida l'evasió*. Although in the novel the particular historical circumstance is not explicitly thematized, we are presented there metaphorically with some alienated young people who are unable to adapt themselves to a particular place and who are constantly looking elsewhere in search of something they never find. Behind these false, passive and cowardly individuals we detect the conformism into which Catalan and Spanish society have fallen during the Franco regime. It is a society that places material comfort above political commitment.

The author articulates this critique throughout a complex and challenging literary work, along the lines of 'revolutionary art' as conceived by Walter Benjamin (2003). For the German theorist, revolution in art is to be found not only in a revolutionary message but in the transformation of established modes of communication. That is to say, engagement is achieved through the reconstruction of artistic forms and through converting the target audience into collaborators rather than simple spectators. In this same line, Theodor W. Adorno (1967) argues that art cannot be limited to simply reflecting the real world 'as it is', but must rather create an unsettling and uncomfortable effect derived from formal experimentation. Thus, elements of denunciation are found on every level of the work of art, not only in a more or less explicit message.

In *Prohibida l'evasió*, Artís-Gener launches an invective against society from the novel's structure itself, which acts as a catalyst in exposing an absurd, claustrophobic and oppressive reality. He demonstrates how a novel can be socially engaged and critical while being a complex creation in structural and technical terms. Aesthetic freedom must be the basis for denouncing moral and ethical submissiveness: it is from the very structure of the novel that the critique and denunciation of the system must arise. This is the dominant system which, from its power field (as defined by Bourdieu [1992]) influences the literary field and drives the servile art of the bourgeoisie. Artís-Gener stands at the antipodes of such an art subjected to the dominant power, to institutions and to market forces. He denounces the system in two ways: first, by launching through his characters a diatribe against the artist who submits to the market and the powers that be; and, secondly, by writing a novel which breaks from familiar, cheap conventions, and which is a complex technical construct, making no concessions and placing great demands on its readers.

This is why *Prohibida l'evasió* is a 'novel of revolt' in the sense that Joan Triadú gives to this term: 'És una revolta que consisteix a transgredir certs límits de la novel·la mantinguts en les etapes anteriors (en tècniques, en funcions, en actitud moral), i de fer-ho amb una ambició de totalitat, en un procés que recorda el de la poesia' [The revolt consists in transgressing certain limits (on techniques, on functions, on moral outlook) previously upheld, and in doing this with the aim of achieving totality, through a process reminiscent of poetry] (Triadú 1970: 41). This leads to the quest for expressive forms which can disturb and unsettle the reader, obliging them to interact with a complex text: complex because it entails a responsibility which is both ethical and aesthetic.

The formal characteristics of *Prohibida l'evasió* point back to the context of Western literature in the first half of the twentieth century — specifically interwar North American narrative, Sartrean existentialism and the *nouveau roman* — which influenced both Spanish social realism and historical realism in Catalan literature. Their shared traits are: limitation of the narrator's omniscience through a technique based on 'point of view' and on a plurality of narrative voices; spatial and temporal fragmentedness; simultaneity of action; deployment of objectivist techniques; collective protagonism and the importance of dialogue.

In Artís-Gener's preceding novel, *Les dues funcions del circ* (1966), one can discern the influence of behaviourism and the objectivist techniques of inter-war North American literature, especially the writing of John Dos Passos and Ernest Hemingway.[2] These authors were in search of a differentiated idiom that could express the contrast between the sense of castration felt by soldiers returning from war and, on the other hand, the American boom time of the 1920s, with the great technological surge of those years, the expansion and prosperity of the middle classes, the world of jazz and of the cinema, all integrated in the great system and configuration of the modern city. The new reality demanded a new language and a new technique. Despite the great difference in many aspects between Tísner's novel and *Manhattan Transfer* by John Dos Passos, both authors use similar techniques in order to express the sense of loss (in the aftermath of WWI and the Spanish Civil War) as well as the emergence and expansion of a vacuous society in which the individual feels completely isolated. These feelings of meaninglessness and alienation are given metaphorical expression through the overlapping of narrative levels, the fragmentation of perspective, typographical variations, and resorting to the 'camera eye'. We shall see that the world of the cinema has an important role, both formally and thematically, in *Prohibida l'evasió*. This key element in the novel derives no doubt from the author's direct experience in that sphere — having worked for many years in Mexico as a set-designer for both cinema and television — at least as much as from the influence of North American literature.

After the WWII the American novels of the interwar period were translated and arrived in Europe, having a powerful impact in both Italy and France. In Italy this influence would be strikingly channelled into neorealism while in France it would be absorbed by two ideologically opposing currents: initially in French existentialism and, subsequently, in the *nouveau roman*.

What existentialism sees in this new narrative mode is an assortment of innovative techniques which are perfectly matched to their message and to the intellectual climate of the time. Sartre has no hesitation in declaring his enthusiasm for the new novelistic models,[3] signifying as they do a revolution because they find an appropriate way of addressing a new historical reality which the previous models are inadequate to give expression to. Besides the aspect of formal innovation in the new techniques, Sartre is greatly interested in how they chime with his own conception of committed literature. The objectivist novel, much more than traditional narrative models, calls for an actively engaged reader because what it presents is not a finished product but a fragmentary view, accessible mainly through ellipses and heterogeneous points of view. What this abstruse mode of communication calls for, more than ever, is a collaborative reader who brings their own interpretations and endeavours to fill the gaps in the text, in line with Walter Benjamin's theoretical postulations on these processes. According to Sartre (1948), all intellectuals are inevitably bound up in, and 'engaged' with, their own times, because they cannot turn their backs on the world and the historical moment into which they were born. The creative writer's role is to function as an agent of liberation, through works which raise awareness of emancipatory values, thus providing incitement to action and to changing social reality. Tísner's novels, like the rest of his writing, conform clearly to those two principles so tightly bound into the contemporary struggle to attain for his own country basic rights and values of a free society.

During the 1950s and 1960s, in that French context, there arises a movement which, although radically opposed to existentialism in grounding and ideology, will adopt objectivist techniques under the *nouveau roman* banner (Robbe-Grillet 1961). What is paradoxical is that very similar formal resources will serve totally antagonistic causes and principles. The impact of the *nouveau roman* movement on Artís-Gener is tangential: he is interested in certain aspects like formal experimentation, objectivist techniques and, above all, the influence of cinema, but he distances himself from the *nouveau roman* with regards the functional application of the corresponding technical gearing. For Tísner, art is not a simple *divertimento* or formal game: its ultimate objective is to awaken critical consciousness with a view to transforming society.

Narrative Structure and Polyphony

Prohibida l'evasió is a 'choral' novel composed of diverse plot-lines which are not readily synthesized into a single narrative thread. The vicissitudes of a number of unhappy young people all looking for a 'way out' are narrated in eighteen chapters where we can detect five swirling movements, all closely related to space. In the first eight chapters, the main characters are scattered over three separate geographical locations: Battifredo, Paris and Mexico. What emerges from this geographical spread is a fragmentary and elliptical narrative. The second movement, Chapters 9–13, arises out of the coming together of these characters in Paris, with the result that the narration becomes more linear and chronological. This linearity is broken in the third section, Chapters 14–15, when the protagonists disperse and go three different ways: to Budapest, the Costa Brava and Genoa. They coincide again in Chapter 16, this time in a Catalan setting, specifically in S'Agaró, as the converging movement is repeated. And finally, the last chapter and the epilogue deal once more with divergence, situating us in a fictitious present time and in distant places: Chapter 18 is set in Mexico while the epilogue transports us to Paris. These movements follow one another in increasingly rapid succession and this acceleration conditions the rhythm of the novel, moving *in crescendo* as the ending comes closer. The first movement is the longest and slowest of all as it is the one which introduces each of the eight main characters, the principal settings, the techniques that are prominent throughout, and the atmosphere of strangeness and unreality which impregnates this choral novel. The unreality is generated by the way in which the narrator fractures temporal and spatial logic — spaces merge into one another: one character leaves a studio in Mexico to go into a garden in New Jersey; two separate conversations, one in Paris and the other in Mexico, are dovetailed in defiance of all logic.

Just as in Artís-Gener's two preceding novels, *Les dues funcions del circ* and *Paraules d'Opòton el Vell*, the text we are examining does not have a single narrator controlling the discourse but, rather, several narrative voices occasionally intermingling to create a polyphony that is an acquired characteristic of the twentieth-century novel. This literary artifice is used by the author in his endeavour to transmit the image of a chaotic reality, decadent and corrupt but nevertheless still containing room for hope.

Among the several narrators in the text, the first to appear, and subsequently to have a major presence, is an extraheterodiegetic voice as defined by Gérard Genette (1972). The function of this figure is to introduce the characters and to carry us through time and space, without imposing any chronological organization or control. This voice is a complex construction: it works with different focalizations which can be variously internal or at times singly focused. It is as though the narrator has no fixed angle: he might show the world through the eyes of a particular character, either through 'free, indirect' style or interior monologue, and then decide to put himself alongside the character to explain events with maximum objectivity. The reader is thus freed from a single dominant vision and given a multiplicity of points of view on events and characters. The external focalization and the objectivist descriptions of place and actions are relayed in simple language: short syncopated sentences, a uniformly sober style. In these sections of the text it is as though the narrator adopts the function of the film camera, at a far remove from any elaborate psychological introspection. This particular narrator deliberately implicates the 'receivers', sometimes addressing the narratee or, through metalepsis, interrupting the train of thought of a character with a direct, often ironic, intervention.

On occasions, objectivist experimentation leads to his presenting a scene as though it were a film script: a two-column format, with one side corresponding to the visual image, the other to the soundtrack, both with annotations pertaining to particular cinematographic details relevant to the action. This metafictional play, with the world of the cinema woven, both thematically and formally, into the text, is a constant feature of the novel. Not only are there references to specific technical features of cinematography (criss-cross, dolly in, zoom, lap dissolve), but also attempts to apply these techniques directly to the writing of the text itself.

The play with narrative voices continues with the proliferation of notes and comments which add a metafictional and metacritical dimension to the novel, converting its structure into a *mise en abyme*. This level is fundamental because, on the one hand, it reflects on fictionality, the awareness of giving rise to an imagined world, the processes of creation and reception of the literary product, while on the other hand it allows reengagement under a new light with subjects like the *theatrum mundi* already emerging in *Les dues funcions del circ*. Indeed, this element of counterpoint within the main story of *Prohibida l'evasió* is very complex,[4] creating some uncomfortable uncertainty, and not without paradox: the notes at first appear to be attributed to the film directors Jorge and Àlex, who are filming the characters belonging to the primary level of the narration; then they merge on both levels, with Jorge and Àlex becoming fictional characters who in their turn are being filmed by another director and his assistants whose voices are present only in the written notes of the latter. The importance of these notes resides in the reflection set in train from this point on regarding the function of the crew: they are the creators of the world of fiction we are reading about. In the *mise en abyme*, they are responsible for the fiction presented to us on this narrative level which we know is also fictional. This fact contributes to our seeing the characters in question as fictional entities, with neither any will power of their own nor any freedom of choice, subjected to the commands of an aleatory and absurd script which is also part of the fiction.

At the same time, this level of the text performs an essential metacritical function because the technical points being discussed and evaluated, in relation to plot development, contribute to a distanced and ironic view of the story, and implicitly of reality. This is precisely the distanciation regarding creativity and the world itself discussed by Benjamin (2003), engendering both deep reflection and critique.

We observe, though, that Artís-Gener's polyphonic playfulness does not stop here, since we encounter yet another voice that comes in at the end of the novel in the form of an epilogue: the reflections of Agnar, the chronicler of the Parisian group, that are found in his private diary. Here we have an intradiegetic narrator, a first-hand witness who supplies not only new information but also an explanation of events which we know about from another point of view. The following extract from his diary adds to the polyphony impregnating the whole novel: when this narrator offers a portrait of Viktor, the novel's one positive character, he quotes in inverted commas the Dane's words which cannot, in fact, be a literal reproduction because Agnar himself is giving a witness's evidence as a first-person narrator recalling his own memories. Thus we, as readers, have no direct access to the true source of the narrative discourse: once again reality is diffused and what we are presented with is an approximation to the truth. Agnar himself is aware of this limitation as he is putting into words Viktor's thought processes and ideas:

> He rellegit tot allò que he atribuït a en Viktor, des de "Agnar, l'única cosa acceptable..." i m'han vingut ganes d'esborrar-ho tot. No són les seves paraules ni, amb prou feines, l'essència del que em va dir. Si el pobre Viktor ho llegia em clavaria una bona puntada de peu al cul, per haver empobrit el seu llenguatge. O el seu pensament, que és pitjor. I això no obstant, a desgrat de la meva torpor, he de deixar damunt el paper allò que em va dir de l'ànima.

> [I have re-read everything I attributed to Viktor, from 'Agnar, the only acceptable thing...' and I really felt like deleting it all. Those words are not his or even the essence of what he said to me. If poor Viktor were to read it, he would give me a good kick in the arse, for having watered down his language. Or his thoughts, which is worse. Despite this, though, and despite my lassitude, I have to set down on paper what he said to me about the soul.] (Artís-Gener 1969: 235)

Agnar knows that his version of events is only an approximation, and that it can in no way communicate to us the essential truth. This reflection on writing brings to mind *Paraules d'Opòton el Vell* where the old Aztec gets frustrated by the difficulty of putting events into words and he becomes aware of the particularities of the writing process, drafting over and over again the same fragments, in pursuit of the impossible goal: to give linguistic expression to the world (Mas 2008). This is one of the recurrent elements in *Prohibida l'evasió*; it is emphasized as much in the very structure of the novel, with its overlapping levels, as in the polyphony and plurality of voices which contradict one another, so that we are reminded of how language itself is beset by self-consciousness and its own limitations. From a poststructuralist perspective, we could say that we are unable to access the true centre of any discourse because of its being always affected by deferral and never completely apprehensible. The instability and elusiveness of meaning is shown in the interplay of different voices, diversely interlocking, and the implicit conception that language is not transparent. The formal experimentalism of *Prohibida l'evasió* predicates that all modes of discourse are equally fictitious and that no single one can claim superior truthfulness.

Metafictional Writing

The formal complexity of *Prohibida l'evasió* is not a mere game of technical artifice but rather an indispensable mechanism to give expression to a dense philosophical message. It is an exceptional case of form and content merging inseparably in a compact whole, since the structure of the novel is a reflection on itself, on reality and on our relationship with the world. Artís-Gener uses metafiction in order to awaken the readers' consciousness, confronting them with such major themes as failure of communication, alienation and freedom. Patricia Waugh defines metafiction thus:

> 'Metafiction' is a term given to fictional writing which self-consciously and systematically draws attention to its status as an artefact in order to pose

questions about the relationship between fiction and reality. In providing a critique of their own methods of construction, such writings not only examine the fundamental structures of narrative fiction, they also explore the possible fictionality of the world outside the literary fictional text. (1984: 2)

Waugh's definition highlights the two fundamental aspects of metafictional discourse: on the one hand, awareness of its own artificiality and status as a fictional construct; on the other, its ability, through this self-awareness, to provide a reflection not only on the text itself but also on reality, hence to query whether the world around us can be viewed in any way objectively or as a constructed phenomenon shaped by specific conventions. By consciously 'confusing' reality and fiction, the boundaries between them become diluted or effaced, so that our sense of contrast between the two levels is made much less stable than it might have been.

Consequently, metafictional writing has embedded in it a critical reflection which, as well as creating an ironic distancing, situates the text in an ambiguous position: 'metafiction as a borderline discourse, as a kind of writing which places itself on the border between fiction and criticism, and which takes that border as its subject' (Currie 1995: 2). That is to say, the text addresses issues which loom large in literary criticism, like the role of the reader in the process of interpretation, or the relationship between art and life. When such issues are foregrounded, the creative work is situated in an intermediate zone, between fiction and criticism, with the result of making this distinction subjected to questioning, and also of showing that the distinction itself is by no means diaphanous.

Prohibida l'evasió is an exercise in metafiction because it is a fiction which, self-consciously, refers not only to other fictions but also to itself as a linguistic construction. From a poststructuralist perspective, the work's structure, with its different narrative levels, the multiplicity of points of view and different — sometimes overlapping — narrators prevents us from having access to a fixed centre of meaning or to a single reliable interpretation incorporating all the elements in the text. What we find in *Prohibida l'evasió*, by contrast, is a fragmentary discourse, often contradictory, which leaves us in an uncomfortable position because we cannot easily determine what is fiction and what is reality. And it is precisely this uncertainty that leads us to question our own reality and to conceive of it as being as artificial and as fabricated as fiction itself. The expressive metalevels we encounter in the novel reflect this awareness of social and cultural construction, inseparable from — while also raising questions about — language's important function in shaping and maintaining our sense of reality.

The objectives of *Prohibida l'evasió*, unlike those of many other metafictional works, go beyond the established generic limits within which fiction is discussed. That is to say, we are not surprised to find references to theatre in theatre, to novels in a novel, or to poetry in poetry, but *Prohibida l'evasió* is a different case: there is a fusion of cinema and novel, much more complex than it seems at first sight. This is a novel that deals with cinematic themes but which is itself imbued with cinematographical content and form: what happens in *Prohibida l'evasió* is the material of a cinematographic production, with all the filming directions incorporated in it. We have noted already that in this novel-cum-film there is a reflection on the work's process of creation and its reception, a reflection which is just as attributable to the viewers of the possible film as to the novel's readers. Artís-Gener thus utilizes artistic interdisciplinarity in order to fuse these two spheres and to make us engage in a reflection on fictionality and reality. This interdisciplinary fusion is made possible thanks to the elements which narrative fiction and the cinema have in common, and thanks also to their mutual influence (Magny 1948).

The complexity of *Prohibida l'evasió* is due in large measure to the confusion between what is 'real' and what is 'fictional' within it. Let us consider why this is so. If we imagine the novel as a conjoining of different levels of fictionality, we find in the first stage the references to productions being filmed by Àlex, Willie and Jorge. These characters, situated at the level of reality in the framework of the novel, are film directors and producers. This means that we encounter both comments and analysis concerning their own work coming from them and from the narrator, and we encounter also theatrical digressions on cinema as art form. Sometimes it is the characters themselves who reflect on the language of cinema:

> — El cinema és l'art del suggeriment — pontificava en Willie — . L'espectador ha de discernir i interpretar amb el pensament el que veu a la pantalla. Cal establir el que n'hauríem de dir militància de l'espectador. És una tècnica antiquada adreçar-se al públic com qui ensenya les beceroles, presentant unes seqüències mastegades i digerides, perquè a l'espectador li fuig tot l'interès: l'única cosa que pot fer pel seu compte és vomitar-les o defecar-les. El director ha d'anar a mitges amb el públic. Cinquanta per cent per a cadascú.

> ['Cinema is the art of suggestion', pontificated Willie. 'The spectator has to discern and interpret with their mind what they see on the screen. We have to establish what we might call the militancy of the spectator. It is an outdated technique to address the audience as if they are children, presenting them with sequences that have been pre-chewed and digested, because the spectator loses all interest: the only thing they can do on their own is vomit or defecate them. The director has to go halves with the audience.'] (Artís-Gener 1969: 95–96)

Willie, in line with Sartre, is calling for an active viewer, one who participates in the work, which must be complex enough to capture their interest. A similar objective is proposed by the narrator himself:

> I, encara (per si tot l'anterior no era prou), hi ha l'obligació de reeixir quan un gos de color verd damunt un fons de roques i un salt d'aigua simbolitza que l'Odette Farkot ha fet el més extraordinari descobriment dins si mateixa. Que és un símbol obscur? El cinema té un llenguatge-balbuç suggeridor i el suggeriment funciona en relació amb la receptivitat de cadascú. És interpretatiu com una pintura de Kandinsky.

> [And furthermore (as if what was going wasn't enough), there is a duty to succeed when a green dog against a backdrop of rocks and a waterfall represents that Odette Farkot has made a most extraordinary discovery within herself. This is an obscure symbol? Cinema has a suggestive babbling-language and the suggestion works better or worse depending on the receptiveness of each person. It's as open to interpretation as a Kandinsky painting.] (Artís-Gener 1969: 208)

What is being defended here is a symbolic and suggestive cinema which obliges the viewer to interpret what they see on the screen in the same way they would react in looking at a contemporary work of art. As in a Kandinsky painting, there is not one single valid interpretation: what matters is the picture's capacity to suggest different feelings in each and every viewer. It turns out that this theory applies to the novel we are reading, becoming thus a metaliterary commentary. *Prohibida l'evasió* is also symbolic and suggestive in this way, requiring an active reader to make sense of it. As in looking at the Kandinsky picture, the receptor must supply the fifty per cent required by the novel.

Àlex's and Jorge's productions are both reportage or documentaries as well as fictional films in which the *fiction* itself is emphasized. Cinematic scenography creates the illusion of reality, taking in the viewers and making them believe something which is unreal, so that what prevails is the spectator's interpretation, even though it might be false.[5]

We have indicated that this first filmic level is presented as being fictional, and even if we are able to accept this, the second stage on this same scale is more uncomfortable for us: Àlex, Willie and Jorge are also filming what we have been considering until now to be the 'reality' level of the novel: Andy, the Battifredo scenes, or Odette and the Paris circle. This is paradoxical because it goes against our logic, being about characters who belong on the same level, and the fact of it being filmed means that we inevitably situate some characters on a level superior to that of others. This supposition is questioned, though, when the author makes all of them coincide and become acquainted in Paris, now as characters on the same level. Unlike those Pirandellian characters in search of an author to give them life, here we find cinema producers and directors coinciding on the same level with their characters. And it is precisely this encounter, with the producers themselves being filmed, that raises questions about the 'reality' of the whole situation. The three cinema experts are immersed in a motion-picture production which draws them all into it and which, definitively now, makes it impossible to distinguish what is fictional from what is not. By the same token, the film props are integrated into reality and we cannot discern to which category they belong: 'El parc, més artificial que natural, fètid dipòsit d'escombraries fins al Segon Imperi, va enlluernar l'Andy, incapaç com era de distingir entre les roques de l'illa les reals i les d'escenografia' [The park, more artificial than natural, a foetid dumping ground for refuse since the Second Empire, dazzled Andy, incapable as he was of distinguishing between the rocks of the island, the real ones and those in the film set] (Artís-Gener 1969: 137). Just like Andy, we too are unable to discern the real landscape from the film scenography because the characters' behaviour converts each and every space into a grand film set and thus makes life itself one great theatre. Filming reduplicates all their actions on two levels: one of them real and the other being filmed, but this is done in such a manner that it is impossible to see the two planes separately. This effect is accentuated by the intercalated notes which resemble a film-maker's directions used by him during shooting. Bearing in mind that what is filmed here is the entire narrative, the 'reality' of the novel is fictionalized and treated like a film before it goes to the cutting room.

We have also indicated how Àlex and Willie made their films and gave their instructions: now we see this applied at a higher level. The notes which interrupt the narrator's discourse have a very important metacritical function: they serve to guide us in the set-up of the final scene and so we are given an explanation of how the fragmentary 'takes' previously narrated are to be combined. This interpretation or 'gloss' on the text itself behaves like the Choir in Greek tragedy, showing once again the same self-consciousness and self-reflection regarding the act of creation.

In this to-and-fro movement between levels, Artís-Gener is alerting us to the fictionality or falseness of them all: not one of them evades the deceit of appearance and of reality-as-illusion. All the characters are alike: they are all constrained and must act according to a script, looking at the camera and playing a role assigned to them, conscious that they are performing a part, but their drama is that they cannot break free from it. Indeed, Artís-Gener goes even further in his *mise en abyme* when he includes in it us readers and the narrator himself. Not even the latter is free to create and control the fiction and to decide the future of the characters. What controls the course of events is the script, and the role assigned to the narrator is to comment on these events without having any power over, or influence on, them. We too are affected by this overriding function: we are readers trapped inside the fiction just like the spectators watching a film. Our reaction is accounted for in the composition of the all-controlling script itself. We too are watching some characters in action who, in playing their parts, draw us into the *dramatis personae*: we have our roles as spectators and, as such, we form part of the performance. This is made clear by the narrator's statement to the effect that 'tots hi som', we are all in this together, characters and spectators forming a part of life's great stage-show:

> Tothom està — tots hi som — dins l'enreixat. Algú es fa il·lusions una vegada i altra que n'és fora, que potser passa a frec de la reixa però part de fora, cal insistir. Com si de la magna funció teatral solament en fos un espectador, enteneu? Però ja ho anirem veient amb calma: tenim de coll una llarga jornada per examinar l'enreixat, tots els qui hi són dins i els qui es pensen que mai no hi han posat els peus.

> [Everybody — each and every one of us — forms part of the grille. Somebody might have the illusion time and again that they are outside it, that they might brush against it but on the outside, definitely. As though they were just a spectator at the great theatrical performance, you know? But we shall see, we shall see, all in good time: we have a long day ahead of us to be able to examine what fences us in, everybody inside and all those who think they have never set foot in there.] (Artís-Gener 1969:16–17)

The vertigo evoked here, with this structural *mise en abyme*, may refer to the socio-political context of Spain in the 1960s. We are captives in the text just as the characters are trapped in their distressing reality, just like the intellectuals in a country deprived of its liberty, where evasion is prohibited. That is how the author succeeds in communicating the claustrophobia and the feeling of imprisonment suffered by so many during the years of Franco's dictatorship.

Omnipresence of the Camera Eye

The metafictional reflection of *Prohibida l'evasió* is intrinsically related to the themes which vertebrate the novel: failure of communication, individual alienation, the theatre of life, freedom. These are subjects with which Artís-Gener had already engaged in his narrative prior to *Prohibida l'evasió* (and with which he would continue to engage subsequently). They fit in perfectly with the existentialist current so prominent in those years. In an unpublished interview with Artís-Gener that took place in the winter of 1996, in response to one of my questions, he referred to the influence on him of existentialism during his years of exile:

> Vaig ser un fan de Sartre i de l'Existencialisme. Hi vaig creure molt però després vaig veure que s'anava desmuntant progressivament, que no aguantava segons quines anàlisis, que no era prou sòlid. [...] A *Prohibida l'evasió* hi ha trets existencialistes sense dir-ho, implícitament. La vaig escriure quan era sartrià fins al moll de l'os.

> [I was a fan of Sartre and of Existentialism. I believed strongly in it, but later I could see that it was unravelling, that it could not withstand certain lines of analysis, that it lacked solidity. In *Prohibida l'evasió* there are some implicit existentialist traits, although they are not declared as such. I wrote the novel when I was steeped in Sartrean ideas.]

In his novel, Artís-Gener weaves an existentialist message, with just a glimmer of optimism, working with the imaginative possibilities offered by the camera counterpoint, that omnipresent eye which continuously registers the characters' actions. He declared: 'A mi em sembla que és un invent feliç, des del punt de vista del novel·lista, aquesta càmera que sempre és present a la narració i que no és sinó la consciència col·lectiva' [I think it is a felicitous invention, from the novelist's point of view, this camera which is always present in the narration and which is simply the collective consciousness] (Fuster 1996: 24). His suggestion that the camera can be interpreted as the consciousness of society is fully justified in the novel as a whole, enabling us to link it to other associated themes, as we have observed earlier. Underlying this understanding of things is the notion that there is not just one single reality, since 'reality' is a social construct and as such is variable.

In *The Social Construction of Reality* (1966), the theoreticians Berger and Luckmann postulate that everyday life — which we apprehend as something partly ordered through language and social norms — naturalizes social conventions in such a way that they appear 'objectivized' so that we do not perceive their artificiality. By means of the power of institutions, certain schemata and modes of behaviour strike us as natural even though they are not, as is demonstrated in the fact that they are altered as the social context changes. Institutions undertake to typify these attitudes which become roles accepted and shared by the community. In line with this theory, individuals do not act freely as autonomous subjects: rather they absorb and assume internally a specific role which adjusts their behaviour to the specific social context. This approach makes possible a comparison with acting: we all perform a role which is socially recognized, it being the case that how others see us is more important than how we really are. In the 'being'/'seeming' dichotomy, the scales tip towards the second term of the binomial. Role-playing means that appearance prevails over authenticity, an idea which runs through the whole of *Prohibida l'evasió*.

The characters are aware of the presence of a film camera recording continuously all their movements and actions. This conditions everything they do, since they are concerned more about the image they will project than about the genuineness of their attitudes. In this sense, meaning is given to the author's proposed aim of identifying this camera with the consciousness of society. What the camera registers is their social projection, the view which other people have of an individual, and this is the major preoccupation of the characters: they do not seek their own identity or try to discover their true self, but rather to make others believe that they are what they make themselves out to be, when all the time this is nothing but a disguise which is conventionally marked by society itself. This attitude leads to the individuals' alienation and to self-deception, because they surround themselves with objects expected to overcome their anxiety of nothingness and to construct for themselves a particular image, even though the more the individuals rely on *things* in order to define themselves, the more they are separated from their true self. Karl Jaspers (1967) talks about losing oneself in objectivity when the individual submits to a present of factual things. In *Prohibida l'evasió* we find many characters who submit to this and for whom 'having' is more important than 'being'. Gingin, for example, would like to buy a Mercedes, even though he cannot drive and never leaves Battifredo, just because the car would look good parked outside his house. According to Zygmunt Bauman, in this consumer society 'labels, logos and brands are key terms in the language of recognition' (Bauman 2008: 23). They are what enables us to obtain and to keep a particular social level, but only if everybody else recognizes them. Material progress signifies for the characters their triumph in the eyes of society, but it is a mere façade with nothing behind to sustain it: a false illusion of security. This is social hypocrisy, putting on appearances, which nonetheless seems to work in this overall representation of life. In Tísner's novel, this hypocrisy is criticized through characters who never for a moment cease to look straight at the camera. Sometimes they are aware of playing a role to impress others, but even when unaware of this, they do not stop acting. Thus, action (free or faked) and representation become inseparable. Andy is the character who best illustrates this hypocrisy and conventionalism, the vacuity and narcissism of postmodern man (Lipovetsky 1983).

The novel's characters, even if at times they are aware of playing a role, do not have the strength to reject it. The tragedy of Lois, for example, is to see herself acting out some familiar scenes which she recognizes as being socially stereotyped, but which she cannot free herself from. Moreover, Tísner often uses metafictional devices whereby his characters recognize themselves in literary models, or they feel that they are participating in a fictional work. Jorge, in his relationship with Aurora, feels as though he is the protagonist in a cheap sentimental novel, overacting like all the other characters in it, mouthing predictable and meaningless clichés. As in *Les dues funcions del circ*, the characters look for a proper setting for their pronouncements, and the place itself becomes a stage for their contrived and mannered performance.

We have come back to the 'play within a play' which uncovers a false situation: if Jorge is aware of his own performance and feels like a character in a novel, it is because he is neither sincere with Aurora nor true to his own words.

Sometimes the narrator himself is responsible for establishing cinematographic connections. Gioia has taken on board and internalized the canons of beauty popularized by the cinema, and she projects an image which conforms to the model derived from the world of the motion picture.[6] Every movement of hers is studied and imitated, conforming to a model which has come straight from the screen. Filmed images are conspicuous in the novel: if Gioia seeks escape into the world of cinema, Jorge looks for it in screenings of his own work. This Mexican director, before he became successful, began by making low-budget films about everyday life: he had pointed the camera at everything and those images were more important for him than reality itself. Thus, when filming Aurora in a swimsuit on the beach, he cannot wait for the take to be completed in order to relive the experience when it is projected on to a screen. Jorge also evades reality; he escapes the present and prefers to live through memories provided by filmed images. Distance always lends enchantment, allowing momentary experience to be recreated and manipulated to one's taste: Jorge will artificially create a mood of yearning in order to convince himself that he does love his fiancée. Therefore, the image, the representation, the imitation is more important than reality itself. Jorge's is a clear case of reality being reinvented in film images, creating an artificial and false realm of experience which prevails over the real-life one. This is the society of spectacle: as Guy Debord proposes in *La Société du spectacle* (1967), the spectacle supplies fragments or images of reality, but they do not add up to anything like total reality. This idea refers us back to the moving camera in *Prohibida l'evasió*, filming aleatory and partial fragments of real life which are served up as an entertainment. As the French theorist says, the spectacle is an objectivized vision of the world, offering social reality through a prism of unreality. Representation becomes what is real, the image assumes priority status and appearance triumphs over a true vision of society: herein lies contemporary man's great alienation.

This representation and the distance it establishes brings to mind the plays of Brecht and his theory of the alienation effect. Like the playwright's characters, those in *Prohibida l'evasió* are shown to be playing a role and, as we have seen, they are conscious of this. There are numerous references to acting itself, to the realization that a role is being played which need have nothing to do with the personal experience of the player. One character may perform several different roles, with different masks being put on or removed depending on different situations. Odette, for example, when beginning a new love affair, feels that she is playing a new character in the cast and that she has left her previous role behind, like a snake changing its skin:

> [Odette] es lliurava apassionada a la nova vivència de companya del pintor nord-americà Andrew Cummings, feixuc esforç per reencarnar-se en un nou paper de la llista de *dramatis personae*, perquè sabia de cert que, l'Odette Farkot anterior, havia de deixar-la arraconada damunt un prestatge d'Ambroise-Thomas, dissecada, abandonada com la pell anterior d'una serpent.

[Odette passionately assumed the new life-experience of being the partner of the North American painter Andrew Cummings, a demanding effort to be re-embodied as a new figure in the *dramatis personae*, because she knew for sure that the previous Odette Farkot needed to be left on one of Ambroise-Thomas's shelves, desiccated and abandoned like an old snake-skin.] (Artís-Gener 1969: 166)

Here we recognize the self-conscious actor's awareness that their function is always to be inside someone else's skin. Unlike Brecht's actors, though, who choose their role and are allowed critical liberty regarding their interpretation of it, the characters in *Prohibida l'evasió* have to live out this experience as a kind of punishment, since they do not choose the parts they play and this conditions how they act.

The Brechtian alienation effect is felt by us as readers: we cannot identify ourselves with Artís-Gener's characters because we see them acting, recognizing their artificial behaviour, so that rather than identifying with them we reflect on them and their behaviour. They represent attitudes that are easily recognizable in our own society, and awareness of this necessarily brings us to a critical positioning and to a proper interpretation of the denunciation articulated by Artís-Gener in these pages. To quote Barthes (1964) on Brecht, criticism is a substitute for magic, whereby we have revealed to us the artifice shaping the novel's construction and we are warned not to 'naturalize' any of its elements. Moreover, Artís-Gener shows us the mirror itself and not just what it reflects, because the idea is to highlight the whole paradox.

So far we have dwelt on how the characters in *Prohibida l'evasió* do not act freely but rather according to the role assigned to them. What must be analysed next is how this role is not chosen by them but rather imposed on them, in the same way that everything that happens in the novel is predetermined. On this, I want to refer again to the study by Berger and Luckmann on the construction of reality. After asserting that all institutionalized behaviour implies certain roles, they add: 'The institution, with its assemblage of "programmed" actions, is like the unwritten libretto of a drama. The realization of the drama depends upon the reiterated performances of its prescribed roles by living actors' (1966: 92). That is to say: the institution would behave like an unwritten play, a play which becomes a performance as the people involved take on the roles assigned to them by the institution itself. In *Prohibida l'evasió*, Artís-Gener presents to us a world in which the characters perform a role conforming to a previously written script. Most of the characters have a copy of this script which indicates to them what they must say and do all through the 'performance'. The peculiar thing about it is that, as 'the unwritten libretto of a drama', it is unfinished and it is being written as the characters are performing. The fact that the pages as yet unturned do not exist does not mean that the actors can determine the future. The characters listen to the director's voice and they are constantly revising the script. Sometimes, they are so closely identified with their role that they have no need to read from it because the words come to them spontaneously: they believe that they are the personality they represent.

This script is a complement to the film camera and it also symbolizes social consciousness: the roles adopted by the actors are typifications of contemporary society and, as members of it, they can all predict the behaviour demanded by their parts. The characters come across as actors who have learned their roles, and everything that happens seems like a work of fiction. Reality, thus, is figured as a social construction which operates rather like a play or a film. In the life lived out on the stage, individuals have no freedom of choice, once they have accepted a role. This imposes on them a specific behaviour: Andy 'es pregunta quantes coses més li farà fer el seu paper' [wonders how many more things his part will oblige him to perform] (Artís-Gener 1969: 137) and Odette is much saddened to read the next scene she has to perform in.[7] The camera in question is omnipresent and it is turned into an eye which spies on them and from which they cannot escape. This eye is the gaze of other people. In *L'Être et le Néant* (1943: 292–341), Sartre had indicated the importance of this watchful eye. When someone else looks at me, they turn me into an object. Their gaze deprives me of my freedom, but, at the same time, it enables me to see myself as I am, giving me a view of myself. This vision given back to us can create anguish. Roger Garaudy writes:

> 'Quelle angoisse de découvrir soudain le regard comme un milieu universel d'où je ne me puis évader... Celui qui me voit me fait être; je suis comme il me voit.' Je parviens, en effet, à me connaître tel que je me vois vu par autrui. Cette transformation est si profonde que je finis toujours plus ou moins par ressembler à ce que l'on attend de moi.

> ['What anxiety suddenly to discover someone else's power of sight as a universal medium I cannot escape from... Whoever sees me gives me being; I am just how they see me.' In fact, I come to know myself according to how I observe I am seen by another person. This transformation goes so deep that I end up feeling more or less like what is expected of me.] (1960: 97)

What Garaudy says here, glossing a short fragment from Sartre's *Le Sursis* [The Reprieve] (1945), picks up the importance possessed by the gaze of others in the construction of the self: we end up appearing and behaving like what society expects of us. This is the attitude of the characters in *Prohibida l'evasió*: the camera is nothing other than this outside gaze which acts as a mirror for self-contemplation, because the individual sees themselves through the view that others have of them. In line with this, we could find a certain parallelism with Sartre's play *Huis clos* [No Exit], first performed in 1944, where three characters are eternally condemned to share a closed space from which there is no escape. In this room, each of them will have to bear the watchful eyes of the other two, and this is precisely their punishment. The absence of any mirrors means they have no view of themselves except what the others offer them, to their discomfiture. Their tragedy is that they cannot change their image because life has come to an end, they are dead, and the final reckoning is being made. As Sartrean characters, they are nothing other than the sum of their previous actions and what they chose to be: a recipe for existential anguish. The view of other people, like the camera in *Prohibida l'evasió*, is there like a constant reminder of this.

In Tísner's novel, it is not Hell but a prison that is the setting. But as in Sartre's Hades the door is firmly shut and escape is prohibited, as the title makes it clear. Everybody is confined in this prison, this great theatrical performance in which they have their part to play. Artís-Gener includes all of us in this theatre of life: 'És evident de tota evidència que sempre actuem. Tots, actuem. Potser és el mateix origen de la societat humana, de la relació' [It is clear from all the evidence that we are always acting. All of us, acting. Perhaps this is the very origin of human society, and relationships] (Artís-Gener 1969: 19–20). And, as we have pointed out in discussing literary structure, within the enclosure there is the narrator himself alongside us, the readers. We cannot be simple spectators of this because we all play the role assigned to us, as though we had no power of decision. The narrator does not decide on the course of events, he can only comment on what happens in the script, and even this has gone out of his control. Our own reading is also foreseen in this complex puzzle, or trap, set for us by the author. As Joan Triadú observed:

> L'autor hi posa distància, brechtinianament, però alhora es veu obligat a admetre que 'l'escenari' comprèn també el seu paper i que l'única llibertat que es pot permetre és la del comentari, amb el qual presenta el clixé girat a l'inrevés. [...] L'evasió és prohibida perquè és impossible. També ho és per al lector, si és atent, si és capaç de llegir amb densitat.

> [The author interposes distance, in the manner of Brecht, but he is obliged at the same time to admit that the 'scenario' includes his role, and that the only liberty available to him is to comment on the action, thus incorporating the inversion of the cliché [...] Evasion is forbidden because it is impossible. The reader is also held captive, if he pays proper attention, if he is capable of reading densely.] (Triadú 1970: 41)

We too are in the prison of frustrated human relationships and of communication failure. Viktor, although he is the one person who often manages to stand outside the cell walls, is sometimes held captive there. As a social being he cannot escape completely from society and what does imprison him is, precisely, his relationship with others. Perhaps this is why Tísner decided on *Prohibida l'evasió* for his title instead of *El cercle i la tangent*. The latter makes a clear allusion to Viktor's outside position in relation to the circle: his movements only touch lightly its periphery, on the outside. The definitive title, on the other hand, is more pessimistic: it reinforces the idea of how difficult it is to escape from the prison, and it links with the quotation above to the effect that we are all held inside the penal compound, including those who think they are in another place. But, as we said at the beginning, Tísner hints at solutions, and Viktor, although not completely free from contamination, points us towards the road to freedom.

The Road to Freedom

Artís-Gener always defined *Prohibida l'evasió* as a protest against failure of communi-cation, and in fact this theme pervades all the others: artistic representation, the lack of freedom, and alienation. The place of imprisonment is constituted by failed human relationships, the breakdown of communication and lack of understanding between people. Acting a part and the constraints of conventionalism only make communication, already beset with obstacles deriving from language itself, more difficult. The idea that language is deceptive and conducive to misunderstandings is encountered in Tísner's earlier works, and here it reappears as a salient theme. Indeed, the novel's preliminary epigraph explicitly signposts this: 'Si no ens entenem per llenguatge, entenguem-nos per amor' [If we cannot achieve understanding through language, let us understand one another through love]. With this quotation from Ramon Llull's *Llibre d'Amic e Amat* [Book of the Lover and the Beloved], Artís-Gener conveys a message which is shared with the novels published before *Prohibida l'evasió*: understanding between people must be possible thanks to the common human spirit. It is not language that can achieve this but, rather, fraternity and love. That is why failure of communication hangs over the pages of the book and affects the relationships between so many characters who, lacking true affection, resort to language, which is deceptive and leads inevitably to distancing and misunderstanding. *Prohibida l'evasió* is shot through with verbal disagreements in which language, instead of serving as a vehicle for communication, makes it all the more difficult to achieve. We find examples of this in the conversations between Andy and Lois, where words themselves are unreliable, often seeming to be inappropriate in their particular contexts, with the speaker's intention being misrepresented. This kind of misunderstanding is accentuated by the fact that the characters often speak to one another in different languages (English, French, Italian and Mexican Spanish), thus further impeding communication. The characters feel themselves to be captives of language and isolated from others through this inability to be properly understood. Conversations turn into monologues because there is no true dialogue, no exchange of ideas. In the face of this breakdown of communication, all the characters attempt to run away, moving from one place to another, but there is no escape because they carry their own prison with them.

Viktor is conscious of this human limitation and he offers a very interesting digression on the social function of language and its communicative capacity. This comes about at the point where the break-up with Odette occurs. Their relationship has ended because they are starting to depend on language in order to understand one another:

> — No, Odette. No ens podem entendre.
> — Fins ara ens hem entès perfectament.
> — Mentre la nostra relació no depenia de les paraules. Ens detectàvem els pensaments sense haver de formular una frase. Però ara, l'entesa, hauríem d'afirmar-la en el llenguatge, i el llenguatge humà té una pobresa esbalaïdora.

> ['No, Odette. We cannot understand one another.'
> 'Until now we have communicated perfectly.'

'While our relationship did not depend on words. We could read each other's mind, without having to form a sentence to explain. But now we would have to affirm this understanding through language, and human language is alarmingly impoverished.'] (Artís-Gener 1969: 158)

This dialogue refers us back to the opening epigraph from Ramon Llull: while they have understood each other through love, their relationship has worked well, but it becomes impossible when love disappears and their communication has to be based on language. Viktor continues:

Tota la història universal és plena de malentesos, de males interpretacions de les paraules de l'altra gent. I mentre la relació humana depengui del llenguatge estarem perduts. La llengua, contra tot el que ha estat afirmat, no és vehicle de comprensió, sinó tot el contrari. [...] Hi ha hagut guerres espantoses perquè un capitost havia malinterpretat el pensament d'un capitost veí. Jo mateix, ara que vull explicar-te una manera de pensar meva, sento insuficient la paraula. A mesura que et dic els meus mots, tinc consciència de les llacunes d'*arrière pensée* teva que deixo en el curs de les meves paraules. [...] Hem establert tot un sistema universal a base de l'intercanvi parlat, oblidant la ineficàcia del sistema.

[The whole of universal history is filled with misunderstandings, misinter-pretations of other people's words. And for as long as human relations depend on language, we are done for. Language, whatever has been said about it, is not a vehicle for understanding, but just the opposite [...] There have been horrifying wars because one leader had misinterpreted the thinking of a neighbouring chief. Now that I want to explain to you something about how my mind works, words fail me. Even as I am saying my words to you, I am aware of the gaps containing your afterthoughts that I leave out in the flow of my words [...] We have set up an entire universal system based upon spoken exchange, overlooking how inefficient that system is.] (Artís-Gener 1969: 159)

This conception of language has many points of contact with poststructuralist approaches, which highlight the unstable nature of meaning: the sign comes from a system of differences, and of deferment, in the sense that meaning is always held back. These two characteristics of the sign would explain why the linguistic system, as Viktor says, is inefficient for communication and inevitably entails misunderstanding. The breakdown of communication is a theme which acquires its full relevance in post-war European literature, since it throws light on such a major crisis of values as has arisen.

Failure of communication, hypocrisy, social conventionalism and fake acting turn human life and society into a huge prison. The unhappy and frustrated inmates do nothing to change their situation. From an existential point of view, inertia and the lack of will-power impede decision-making and the capacity to control and change direction in life. The escape which people seek is too comfortable and facile, thus inauthentic: they choose to 'get away from it all', to travel abroad, but, as we have pointed out, the prison goes with them because they carry it inside them. 'En Jorge va sentir-se empresonat i amb un intens desfici de tornar a la capital' [Jorge felt imprisoned and beset by an anxious urge to go back to the capital] (Artís-Gener 1969: 47), in order to get away from Aurora; Luigi is tired of arguing with Margherita and he can see no solution, feeling 'un cansament tot igual al de la seva dona' [a weariness identical to his wife's] (Artís-Gener 1969: 66); Gioia dreams of escaping from Battifredo, from her father's shop and from the reality of her surroundings, but her only way out will be suicide; Àlex is obliged by his father to study a five-year degree which holds no interest for him because, as he says, there is no way out, 'Prohibida l'evasió' (Artís-Gener 1969: 99).

There is only one character in the entire novel who has not set eyes on the camera: Viktor. As we have noted, he represents individual freedom, the authentic being who acts according to his own principles because he has found his true self. He is also the character who lives on the margin of society and its conventions, which is why he does not see the camera: his behaviour is independent of prevailing social criteria. His philosophy of emancipation is synthesized by him in this statement: 'El millor per a nosaltres és el que ja portem dins i ja ho tenim i és imprescriptible. Ningú ens ho pot prendre' [The best for us is what we already carry within ourselves, what we already have and what is imprescriptible] (Artís-Gener 1969: 220).

The novelist uses Viktor to express a Sartrean notion of the free and fulfilled individual: man attains freedom when he is what he wants to be and becomes what he wanted to become. Two basic ideas of Sartre's existentialism stand out here: man is nothing other than what he makes of himself, and, to achieve this, his life-project must be based both on the capacity for negation and on a positive commitment (Sartre 1943). Viktor represents the individual who seeks his own essential self and who, on this journey of self-discovery, overcomes alienation and also manages, at many points, to be truly free. These ideas are postulated clearly by him on several occasions: 'Agnar: l'única cosa acceptable del món és un mateix, tal com hi hagi arribat, tarat o sencer. I l'única lluita que realment val la pena és la que fem per retrobar-nos a nosaltres mateixos' [Agnar, the only tolerable thing in this world is you yourself, just as you are and have become, blemished and scarred, or in one piece] (Artís-Gener 1969: 234). He is the only character who turns his back on the appeals and blandishments all around him, rejecting materialism and conventionalism, and who lives in accordance with his own principles, playing no other role than that of being himself, Viktor.

In Viktor's approach to finding fulfilment, the Sartrean influence is very strong, both in terms of his project and the thinking behind it, and also in terms of the importance of negation: self-affirmation is also founded on the ability to say no to the siren songs of the world. In order to be free, a person must make their own way through life, with all its implications: endeavour, renunciation and, above all, responsibility. All in all, this is about being happy and being true to oneself, something which is attainable through the struggle for freedom. Manuel de Pedrolo, who Tísner admired greatly, put it this way:

> la llibertat no consisteix pas a ésser lliure entre uns límits, sinó en la possibilitat de franquejar-los, en la intenció d'enderrocar-los. [...] És la llibertat el que instaura l'ordre, un ordre, i no pas l'ordre el que desencadena o permet l'exercici de la llibertat. El nostre ordre, l'ordre humà, més enllà de tota contingència de caràcter social o polític, consisteix en el nostre projecte; per dir-ho en termes sartrians, en aquest 'ésser alguna cosa que es llança cap al futur i que és

conscient de projectar-se cap al futur.' Una consciència que només podem tenir en la mesura en què escollim i escollim, doncs, els altres en aquest acte de fer ús de la nostra llibertat.

[freedom does not consist of being free within certain limits, but in the possibility of breaking through them. [...] Freedom is what installs order, a particular order, and it is not order that prompts or legitimates the exercise of freedom. Our order, human order beyond all social or political contingency, constitutes our project: to put it in Sartrean terms, it is 'being something which is projected towards the future and which is conscious of being projected towards the future.' This is a consciousness which we can have only to the extent that we make the choice; choosing, then, others to share in this act of making full use of our liberty.] (Pedrolo 1980: 37)

Viktor represents the individual who is capable of breaking with established order in the name of freedom, which is why he lives on the edge of society, with the result that other people see him as a social misfit. Nevertheless, he is the character who awakens the conscience of the others: towards the end of the novel, Jorge, following Viktor's example, begins to devise his own project which will enable him to get out of prison. He is still unaware what the key to emancipation might be, but the important thing is that he outlines a scheme of private non-conformism which is indispensable for personal self-fulfilment:

— [...] També sóc dins la presó, la presó d'evasió prohibida. Però m'aguanta la convicció que algun dia en sortiré, alliberat del tot. Per quin camí? No el conec pas. Potser el cinema mateix, o la poesia. No ho sé. Però l'afany de sortir-ne, el tinc cada dia més arrelat i almenys ara ja comprenc què volia dir en Viktor amb allò de la posició exterior.

['[...] Here I am in prison, no way out. But I am sustained by the conviction that one day I shall leave it, a completely free man. Which way? I certainly do not know. Perhaps through film-making itself, or through poetry. I don't know. But to get out of here is something ever more deeply rooted inside me, and at least I know now what Viktor meant when he talked about taking an outside position.'] (Artís-Gener 1969: 225)

Here as in the rest of his output of novels, despite criticism and disappointment, Artís-Gener leaves ajar for us the doorway to hope, because he believes in humanity, and that social regeneration must be possible. But, in order to achieve this, like Tísner himself, we cannot evade our own responsibility, the commitment to the world and the country in which we live. A challenge like this can only be made through a work which is complex and demanding, experimentally complex in its verbal engineering, which draws our attention and our appropriate responses from the first line to the last.

Works Cited

ADORNO, THEODOR W. 1967. *Prisms*, trans. by Samuel and Shierry Weber (London: Neville Spearman)

ARTÍS-GENER, AVEL·lí /TÍSNER. 1945. *556 Brigada Mixta* (Mexico: Col·lecció Catalònia)

———. 1966. *Les dues funcions del circ* (Barcelona: Proa)

———. 1968. *Paraules d'Opòton el Vell* (Barcelona: Cadí)

———. 1969. *Prohibida l'evasió* (Barcelona: Edicions 62)

———. 1972. *L'enquesta del Canal 4* (Barcelona: Aymà)

———. 1989. *Viure i veure/1* (Barcelona: Pòrtic)

———. 1990. *Viure i veure/2* (Barcelona: Pòrtic)

———. 1991. *Viure i veure/3* (Barcelona: Pòrtic)

———. 1996. *Viure i veure/4* (Barcelona: Pòrtic)

BARTHES, ROLAND. 1964. *Éssais critiques* (Paris: Seuil)

BAUMAN, ZYGMUNT. 2008. *The Art of Life* (Cambridge: Polity Press)

BENJAMIN, WALTER. 2003. *Understanding Brecht*, trans. by Anna Bostock (London and New York: Verso)

BERGER, PETER L., and THOMAS LUCKMANN. 1966 [repr. 1991]. *The Social Construction of Reality* (London: Penguin Books)

BOURDIEU, PIERRE. 1992. *Les Règles de l'art: genèse et structure du champ littéraire* (Paris: Seuil)

CURRIE, MARK (ed.). 1995. *Metafiction* (New York: Longman)

DEBORD, GUY. 1967 [repr. 1996]. *La Société du spectacle* (Paris: Folio)

FUSTER, JAUME. 1992. 'Introducció a les novel·les d'Avel·lí Artís-Gener', in *Obres Completes de Tísner*, I (Barcelona: Pòrtic), pp. 7–18

———. 1996. 'Avel·lí Artís-Gener, un home del renaixement', in *Tísner: miscel·lània d'homenatge*, ed. by Isidor Cònsul (Barcelona: Publicacions de l'Abadia de Montserrat), pp. 21–30

GARAUDY, ROGER. 1960. *Perspectives de l'homme: existentialisme, pensé catholique, Marxisme* (Paris: Presses Universitaires de France)

GENETTE, GÉRARD. 1972. *Figures III* (Paris: Seuil)

JASPERS, KARL. 1967. *Philosophical Faith and Revelation* (London: Collins)

LIPOVETSKY, GILLES. 1983. *L'Ère du vide: essais sur l'individualisme contemporain* (Paris: Gallimard)

MAGNY, CLAUDE-EDMONDE. 1948. *L'Âge du roman américain* (Paris: Seuil)

MAS, SÍLVIA. 2008. *Les novel·les d'exili d'Avel·lí Artís-Gener* (Barcelona: Publicacions de l'Abadia de Montserrat)

PEDROLO, MANUEL DE. 1980. 'Ésser lliure', in *Els elefants són contagiosos. Articles (1967–72)* (Barcelona: Edicions 62), pp. 35–41

ROBBE-GRILLET, ALAIN. 1961. *Pour un nouveau roman* (Paris: Les Éditions de Minuit)

ROMAGUERA RAMIÓ, JOAQUIM. 1995. *Tísner l'escenògraf* (Barcelona: Pòrtic)

SÁNCHEZ NORIEGA, JOSÉ LUIS. 2000. *De la literatura al cine: teoría y análisis de la adaptación* (Barcelona: Paidós)

SARTRE, JEAN-PAUL. 1943. *L'Être et le Néant* (Paris: Gallimard)

———. 1948. *Qu'est-ce que la littérature?* (Paris: Gallimard)

TORRE, GUILLERMO DE. 1968. *Ultraísmo, existencialismo y objetivismo en literatura* (Madrid: Guadarrama)

TRIADÚ, JOAN. 1970. 'Panorama de la novel·la catalana, entre la mitificació i la revolta', *Serra d'Or*, 131: 41–43

WAUGH, PATRICIA. 1984. *Metafiction: The Theory and Practice of Self-conscious Fiction* (London and New York: Routledge)

Notes to Chapter 10

1. *Prohibida l'evasió* was subsequently published in 1985 and 1992. All quotations are from the first edition.

2. Jaume Fuster asserts that *Prohibida l'evasió* 'entronca [...] amb les novel·les d'influència cinematogràfica, tan conreades a la literatura nord-americana des del *Manhattan Transfer* de John Dos Passos' [chimes in with the wave of cinematically influenced novels that, after *Manhattan Transfer* by John Dos Passos, were so widely cultivated in North American literature] (1992: 14–15).

3. On Sartre's 1938 contributions to *La Nouvelle Revue Française*, see Guillermo de Torre (1968: 188–94).

4. The counterpoint technique is a constant feature in Tísner's novels: in *Les dues funcions del circ* the circus is the basic motif, while in *Paraules d'Opòton el Vell* it is the set of critical notes accompanying the Aztec chronicle. See, on this topic, Sílvia Mas (2008).

5. According to Artís-Gener, '[e]l cinema, tot, de començament a final, és una trampa, una trampa fabulosa encaminada a enganyar la càmera, que és molt càndida, s'ho creu tot si està ben fet [...] mai no saps on comença la mentida i on la veritat, i si el color que s'ha aconseguit aquí és el mateix de l'altra tonalitat, la trampa és total, perfecta, no hi ha ningú que pugui discernir entre l'autenticitat i la simulació. Això és una veritat autèntica en cinematografia i té un pes enorme, és absolutament primordial' [All cinema, from beginning to end, is a trick, a fabulous trick designed to deceive the camera, the very candid camera which takes everything in if it is well presented [...] you never know where deception or truth begins, and whether the colour used here is the same as the other hue, the deception is total, perfect, no-one at all can discriminate between authenticity and simulation. That is an incontrovertible truth in cinematography, it carries a lot of weight, it is absolutely primordial] (quoted in Romaguera Ramió 1995: 130–31).

6. 'El cine aparece como espacio mítico capaz de identificaciones y proyecciones del sujeto que encuentra en tipos cinematográficos modelos de héroes o de deidades que satisfagan deseos más o menos subconscientes, lugar de evasión frente a una realidad provinciana y triste o a una situación insoportable' [Cinema appears as a mythical space in which the subject is capable of identifying themselves with heroes or deities that satisfy desires which are more or less unconscious, a place which provides evasion from provincial reality or from a situation which is unbearable] (Sánchez Noriega 2000: 35).

7. 'En la divisió esquerra del guió, la correponent a la imatge, va veure borrosament tot el tros que seguia. Era la trista escena de quan en Viktor es quedava sol i entaforava les seves andròmines en el sac de U.S. Navy. [....] L'Odette va enretirar el cendrer i va tancar el guió. La continuació, per altra banda, se la sabia de memòria. Era acudir a corre-cuita a la segona cita concertada amb l'Andy' [On the left-hand page of the script, the side with the visual illustrations on it, she saw a vague outline of the following section. It was the sad scene about Viktor being left on his own and stuffing his kit into the U.S. Navy bag [...]. Odette moved the ash-tray and closed the script. She knew by heart, in any case, what came next. She had to rush to the second meeting arranged with Andy] (Artís-Gener 1969: 162).

CHAPTER 11

Laughing on the Other Side:
Humour in the Exile Narrative of
Avel·lí Artís-Gener, *Tísner*[I]

Rhiannon McGlade

University of Cambridge

El humor y la ironía forman parte de una visión de la realidad, a la que siempre he sido fiel [...] Es mucho más divertido tomar las cosas por el ángulo ingenioso, que por el trágico.

[Humour and irony form part of a perception of reality to which I have always remained faithful. It is much more fun to see the lighter, rather than the tragic, side of things.]

Avel·lí Artís-Gener (in Piñol 1994: 41)

Having previously expressed a 'special kinship' with the Second Spanish Republic, President Lázaro Cárdenas opened Mexico's doors to refugees from the Peninsula, with some 6,000 making the trans-Atlantic journey between April and August 1939 (Schuler 1998: 56; Faber 2002: 171; Villarroya 2000: 42). Among this initial wave of émigrés was the humourist Avel·lí Artís-Gener (1912–2012), who, under the moniker Tísner, had earned particular notoriety for his cartoon and editorial work in the Catalan satirical press of the time. Undeterred by exilic displacement, Tísner soon became part of the nascent diasporic Catalan press and was one of very few foreign cartoonists to break into the Mexican satirical market (McGlade 2016: 52–54). Meanwhile, his fascination with the humorous manipulation of language — a trademark of his cartoons — provided the crossover to a lesser-known literary coming of age that developed over a 26-year period of exile and continued well into his return to Barcelona. For Sílvia Mas (2008: 13), it is the author's renown as a comic figure that has caused his work to be overlooked by the Catalan canon. However, I would go further by suggesting that this lack of critical attention is also closely tied to the classification of the works themselves as humorous. Indeed, as Cristina Larkin maintains, 'irrespective of their success within their genre, [humorous works] are not generally considered to qualify as "good" literature, but are classified [...] as light by-products of the far more weighty novelistic genre'

(2000: 104). Of course, this tendency ignores the fact that narrative humour is a highly complex, multifaceted form, underpinned by a biphasal process that can be mapped to Stuart Hall's (2000) concept of encoding and decoding.[2] With a view to foregrounding the value of Tísner's literary work, this chapter will discuss the author's use of humour in his exile narrative, comprising: *556 Brigada Mixta* [556 Mixed Brigade] (1945); *Les dues funcions del circ* [The Two Functions of the Circus] (1966) and *Paraules d'Opòton el Vell* [The Words of Opòton the Elder] (1968).[3]

A key facet of exilic satire is the expression of solidarity and in-group identity, since decoding the humour often relies on the existence of a shared system of historical, social, linguistic and/or aesthetic references. Here, as elsewhere, in 'getting' the joke contextual appreciation is a necessary tool for recognizing cultural and period-specific codes. We must additionally account for instances where 'certain codes may be so widely distributed in a specific language, community or culture [...] that they appear not to be constructed' and rather are 'profoundly naturalised' (Hall 2000: 55). This in turn enables us to examine the role of humour in any given culture or period in order to gain unique access to the shared views and values of extant societies. Indeed, Charles Knight has observed that the complexities of satire produced in exile enable us to look beyond the surface of history, offering the opportunity to 'closer examine the hidden or repressed values that affirm dissent and proclaim the urgency of change' (2004: 115). For Knight, this must be viewed within a context where the 'shifting identity of the homeland corresponds to the multiple perspectives of the satiric exile, whose task becomes the discovery of cultural and political forces that control or transcend historical change' (2004: 109). Exiles typically acquire a permanent status of temporary residence: being 'both *from* a country and *in* a country, but not *of* a country' (Knight 2004: 81 [original emphasis]), and are thereby never fully integrated into their adopted context. This instability is reflected in the anxiety related to return, as Tísner himself explained: 'El fet és que, en el llarg període d'exili, hom detura el temps respecte al país d'origen. Aquí [...] la vida pot continuar el seu curs. Aquí. Allà, no: enllà de l'oceà [...] tot s'ha paralitzat. Res no es mourà fins que hi tornis' [The fact is that during the long period of exile, time stands still in relation to our countries of origin. Here [...] life can go on. Here. Not there: across the ocean, everything has become paralyzed. Nothing moves until you return] (Artís-Gener 1972: 21).

With the aim of exploring the role of humour in response to the situation of exile within Tísner's narrative, I will adopt a two-pronged approach that encompasses self-contained occurrences of humour as well as the existence of an overarching humorous tone. At the local level of events within the text, this will draw on what Larkin (2000: 100) has termed 'internal' and 'external' incongruity, where internal refers to the intradiegetic level and 'those elements in a story which deviate from the reader's expectations as created within the context of the novelistic discourse itself', and external relates to 'elements [...] which clash with the reader's encyclopaedic knowledge of the everyday world outside the novel'. Although Larkin is expressly concerned with a singular type of humour (incongruity and its resolution), this chapter proposes that such an approach can be usefully expanded to consider examples of the Superiority and Release-relief theories of humour. To that end, some basic introductions seem appropriate here.

Humour Theory[4]

Superiority theory focuses on the nature and function of humour based on ridicule. Drawing upon Platonic and Aristotelian observations on humour, Thomas Hobbes in *Leviathan* (1968 [1651]: 5) described laughter as the expression of 'a sudden glory arising from some conception of some eminency in ourselves'. According to this view, a major condition for humour is tethered to our sense of superiority over another in a certain situation.[5] Closely tied to superiority as a condition for humour is its function in the relationship with identity. Holmes and Marra (2002: 393) maintain that 'humour can contribute to the on-going construction and reinforcement of inter-group boundaries by providing an acceptable means of objectifying or distancing the "other" group'. This supports Knight's observations that 'simple nationalistic satire stresses the distinction of one's own country from others by exaggerating [the latter's] negative qualities' (2004: 59). As will be suggested here in relation to Tísner's work, we can often see humour as a tool for, and a product of, 'othering' for the purposes of creating or reinforcing in-group identity.

In *Jokes and their Relation to the Unconscious* (2001 [1905]), Sigmund Freud discusses humour both as a means of relieving aggression resulting from social control and as a tool of aggression in itself. For Freud, the function of humour is akin to a release valve, with laughter as the physical by-product, since 'a joke will allow us to exploit something ridiculous in our enemy [... and] represents a rebellion against that authority, a liberation from its pressure' (2001 [1905]: 103–05). Although much of Freud's writing on humour has been refuted — since his observations are the product of specific social conditioning and do not account for other forms of non-humorous energy beyond laughter — some basic Freudian humour principles remain appropriate in the present context. In particular, humour as a legitimate form of release in the face of accumulated aggression is highly pertinent to our understanding of the often-traumatic experience of war, post-war and exile.

Lastly, Incongruity theory describes humour's biphasality — present in the set-up and punchline of jokes — and draws upon the Ciceronian notion that the root of laughter lies with disappointed expectation.[6] Adapting this approach for a modern audience, Henri Bergson explains: 'a situation is invariably comic when it belongs simultaneously to two altogether independent series of events and is capable of being interpreted in two entirely different meanings at the same time' (2008 [1900]: 48). Incongruity, then, is a key component of puns and has become integral to linguistic deconstructions of jokes.[7]

It should be noted that far from competing over the different aspects of humour with which they engage, the Superiority, Release-relief and Incongruity theories often complement one another at times of overlap. In what remains, this chapter will expand Larkin's incongruity-focused model to discuss the role of all three primary humour theories in both self-contained episodes and sustained tones across the diegetic levels in Tísner's exilic novels.

The Three Novels

556 Brigada Mixta

First published in Mexico in 1945 as part of Col·lecció Catalònia,[8] *556 Brigada Mixta* (BM) tells the day-to-day experiences of an anonymous soldier during the Spanish Civil War. This hybrid of generic convention combines fiction, autobiography and news reportage to produce a striking first-hand account of the conflict, buttressed by Tísner's signature irony. In the first instance, post-war narratives produced in Spain were primarily the concern of the victors, dominated by accounts of patriotic bravery and the barbarism of the 'red terror'.[9] Catalan literature was largely forced underground or into exile and explicit treatment of the war was rare — with the notable exception of Joan Sales's *Incerta glòria* [Uncertain Glory] (1956) — although the marks of its impact could be readily observed in later works by authors such as Mercè Rodoreda and Maria Aurèlia Capmany. Far from the pathos that came to typify the way in which many post-war authors of Republican leaning engaged with the conflict,[10] Tísner's 'parodic satire' — as Hutcheon (1985: 62) would have it — uses humorous interjections to create a bathetic reflection of the daily experiences of an average Republican soldier on the front. Although less lyrical in its tone than the author's subsequent novels, within BM lie the foundations of a literary style characterized by subtle sophistication, attention to detail, and a proclivity for seeking moments of mirth in unlikely places. This incongruous approach to the tragedy of conflict in turn triggers the reader's sense of relief and release. The novel favours anecdotal, seemingly banal, details over protracted, epic battle scenes or a succession of heroic accounts, and avoids both frivolity and melodrama. Nevertheless, Tísner successfully retains a sense of action through the rapid narration of events, with a style that has elicited cinematic comparisons (Guarner 1945: 9–14).

Tísner's overt antimilitarism is reflected in the sustained leitmotiv of the lack of professionalism and incompetence in the higher echelons of the military and is typically manifest in those humorous episodes created through superior–inferior role reversal. This is particularly discernible in the persistent mockery of the group's commanding officer, Quiñones. On the one hand, this is due to his many ineptitudes: 'hi vam anar a cavall, amb una lentitud exasperada, imposada per la poca pràctica del comandant en les coses d'equitació' [we went there on horseback, at an exasperatingly slow pace due to commandant's lack of experience in all things equine] (1945: 179). On the other hand, the derision stems from Quiñones' infuriating leadership, seen in the tongue-in-cheek statement, 'això és napoleònic. Potser som davant un geni i no ens n'adonem!' [that's Napoleonic. Perhaps we're in the presence of a genius and we just don't know it!'] (1945: 168). Thus, the resulting group identity distinction is between Republican rank-and-file soldiers and their superiors rather than the two combatant sides. Indeed, references to encounters with the Nationalists are kept to a minimum and, where they do appear, favour generalized observations over detailed descriptions of individuals. The effect is one that underlines the detachment of those at the front from the political causes of the war, which in turn contributes to the author's portrayal of the youthful naivety of the Republican soldiers. Moreover, the space created by this approach supports the sustained presence of a humorous tone in the otherwise sober theme of war.

Through an alternating narrative, Tísner deftly controls the pace of the piece. The first person conveys the more reflective, at times tender, moments, while the collective 'we' enables the author to present a shared experience that goes beyond the fictional characters and tends towards a more playful, ironic tone. In the portrayal of what is ostensibly a serious subject, the author uses self-contained jokes, typically injected as a counterpoint to offer momentary comic relief, while at the same time contributing to the pervasive humorous tone. In the songs from the trenches, for example, Tísner reproduces verses taken from the Republican war-time song, *Si me quieres escribir* [If You Wish to Write to Me], combining them with additional variants, such as *Los emboscados* [The Ambushes], and other adaptations that he attributes to members of the 556 Brigade.[11] Before each verse, the narrator offers a summative sentence, moving without reflection from one to the next:

Una melopea, persistent com un tam-tam africà, parlava d'una fonda establerta a la línia enemiga i dels plats que s'hi servien:

> El primer plato que dan
> son granadas rompedoras
> y el segundo, de metralla
> para refrescar la memoria.

La cançó, després, se n'anava cap a la rereguarda:

> Al llegar a la retaguardia
> lo primero que se ve
> son milicianos de pega
> sentados en el café.

Després tornava al front, nostàlgica dels permisos que mai no arribaven:

> En la sierra de Alcubierre
> hay un farol encendido
> con un letrero que dice:
> "El permiso se ha jodido".

[A persistent melopoeia, like an African tam-tam, told of an inn set up behind enemy lines and the types of dishes that were served there:

> The first course they serve
> is grenades
> and the second, is shrapnel
> to refresh the memory.

The song then went on to talk about the rear-guard:

> Upon arriving at the rear-guard
> the first thing you see

> are militiamen
> sat in a café.

Later, it focused again on the front, nostalgic for the long-awaited permits that
never arrived:

> In the mountains of Alcubierre
> a streetlight shines
> with a sign saying:
> 'Furlough has been screwed'.]
>   (1945: 97–98)

Tísner's inclusion of the chosen verses maintains the pace of the narrative and
introduces a deliberate variation of humorous forms, while retaining the verisimilitude on which this semi-autobiography relies. The recognizable songs also
have the function of creating group identification for readers of Republican leaning.
In particular, the addition of the code-switched summative sentences effects a
distance between the narrator and those singing the song, drawing attention to the
inclusion of Castilian within the text and thereby encouraging the reader through
marked language use to identify with the Catalan in-group.

Again, we observe the sustained theme of the troops' dissatisfaction with the lack
of professionalism in the ranks. The depiction of the already-settled militiamen sat
in cafés avoiding combat brings about a temporary inferiorization of those with
assumed superior status through ridicule, while also providing relief in the derision
of the inherent hypocrisy. The use of humour to this effect is closely connected
to Freud's belief that the aggression of a joke is bound to its rebellious nature
whereby it facilitates the expression of criticism outside of accepted boundaries.
Furthermore, the incongruous image of plates of armaments instead of food and an
official poster using profanity to describe the frustration at the persistent delaying of
permission for leave are highly illustrative of the gallows-style humour throughout
BM. In its technical construction, the situation set-up relies on Incongruity; in its
content, it draws on Relief-release to produce a humour based on the discharge of
tension in the face of repression and/or war.

Tísner's multifaceted use of humour can also be seen in the episode of the Dia de
Sant Joan bombing. Here, the description of the attack maintains a distance between
the soldiers — presented like actors on a stage — and the reader *qua* audience. The
piece is dotted with humorous jabs that eventually lead to the grotesque with the
death of Bori, the only redheaded soldier in the group, who is identified by the
discovery of ginger hair on a piece of skull stuck to the wall. The macabre nature
of this observation, which is contrasted with the chaos of the bombing, elicits a
brief moment of reflection and is one of many references to the notion that war
has robbed these men of their youth. Nevertheless, Tísner is careful not to linger
and in so doing avoids labouring a sense of pathos. Indeed, in one single paragraph
he moves from describing the long hours spent burying dead bodies, to the act of
removing Bori's skull fragment from the wall with a fork, followed by the image
of dead frogs stuck to the belfry and the collapsed houses in the village (1945:
110). Each element is delivered with the same detached tone, producing a sense of

incongruity since the sight of the dead frogs and the burying of dead soldiers are met with the same emotional response. This, in turn, acts as relief in the wake of the numerous lifeless bodies of soldiers and the death of a close comrade. In this way, Tísner exposes the general plight as well as the personal experience of war on the Republican side.

References to the scarcity of food and resources often underpin the light-hearted account of the Republican soldiers' daily experiences. The author creates an entire scene that hinges upon the incongruous use of opera glasses for binoculars. With the idea that the glasses could belong to 'una dama d'opulent sina, pecaminosament escotada' [a woman with an opulent chest and a scandalously low-cut neckline] (1945: 68), the narrator playfully subverts stereotypical gender roles to mock his superior, Palau. The incongruous opera glasses in a military setting reappear during battle. Here, Tísner generates a sense of exaggerated excitement, comparing the soldier's reports to that of a football commentator: 'Hem tocat la Casa Gran. Ara tot salta enlaire; ells corren; l'hem escapçada de meitat per amunt' [We've hit the Big House. Now everything's flying in the air; they're running; we've taken the top off] (1945: 119). This connection with sport is a comment on the naïve conceptions of war and emphasizes the incongruous quotidian nature of traumatic experience.

Freudian humour takes on another form in the build-up of tension leading to the action. This is initially presented through the impatience of a youthful and exuberant group of soldiers, keen to realize their idealized images of war but frustrated by the reality of an endless sense of waiting: for the postman; for orders; to go to the front; and for battle. This anticipation reaches an amusing climax through the image of the constantly ringing telephone that 'mai no era el que esperàvem' [was never who we were waiting for] (1945: 122). This comical frustrated expectation echoes the anxious wait Tísner describes in relation to the anticipated return from exile, which will be discussed below. The asinine aspects of war are also the subject of the author's ironic observations regarding the posters used to advertise literacy classes to those who, naturally, could not read them (1945: 39).

While BM might not be a narrative of unrelenting laughter, all three branches of humour introduced at the beginning of this chapter facilitate an interpretation of the text that serves to elucidate its unique engagement with the recent conflict. Not only is Tísner confronting the repression of post-war dictatorship that has forced him to write this work in exile, but he is also using BM to challenge — in Freudian terms — a social taboo by treating with humour a war whose trauma would have been a likely painful experience for his intended readers. In addition to the relief it provides, Tísner's own view was that his humorous treatment of the subject was a way of disarming the conflict of its power, attempting to raise hope:

> La presència de la ironia, d'aquest sarcasme, és un mecanisme defensiu. Fins ara no ho havia dit mai però es troba implícit als meus llibres; la ironia no és per provocar, ni per fer més digestiu un passatge sinó que té una finalitat molt concreta, de contrapunt, de balança. És explicar que no tot és negatiu, que sempre hi ha una porta oberta a l'esperança. En aquest sentit el meu missatge és forçosament optimista.

[The presence of irony, of this kind of sarcasm, is a defence mechanism. I haven't said it until now but it's implicit in my books; irony is not for provocation, nor to make a passage easier to digest, rather it has a very specific purpose, that of counterpoint, of balance. It's a way of explaining that not everything is negative, that there is always an open door to hope. In this sense, my message is unavoidably optimistic.] (in Poch and Jaén 1993: n.p.)

The novel's publication outside of Spain, as well as a small print run, minimized its initial exposure, although it was subsequently reissued several times.[12] Despite its rejection by the author later in life,[13] in the immediate aftermath of Spain's conflict and in the context of exile, Tísner was able to deliver in BM a distinctive version of the Civil War experience by infusing the tragic with the comic. The variation of pace and voice combine humorous episodes with a sense of reflective humanism, which expose his antimilitaristic stance and question the justification for war, its wasting of young lives as well as of youth itself.

Les dues funcions del circ

Unlike many of his peers, Tísner refused to restrict himself to taking part in the affluent and thriving Catalan community in Mexico and became enamoured of pre-Colombian culture. Nonetheless, he remained committed to a return home: 'vaig tenir consciència clara que l'exili es deteriorava i arriscava de convertir-se en emigració convencional' [I realized that the situation of exile was at risk of deteriorating into a state of conventional emigration] (in Oliver 1989: 12). Although written during his time in Mexico, the second novel under discussion, *Les dues funcions del circ* (DFC), was not published until 1966, shortly after Tísner's return to Barcelona.

For DFC, exile is not only the creative context, but also a central component of the narrative and its structure. The autobiographical events of Tísner's original voyage to Mexico inspired his use of DFC as a metaphor for the varied experiences of exile.[14] The novel tells the story of the Catalan Borrell brothers, stranded on the island of Martinique after their migrant vessel is forced to interrupt its transatlantic voyage for repairs. Jaume goes ashore seeking treatment for his brother Gabriel's tuberculosis and soon makes a place for himself in society. Helped by the influential Doctor d'Anretar — a Republican sympathizer — they gradually adapt to island culture, befriending the physician's nieces.[15] Despite this help to assimilate, the brothers — and by extension the reader — are repeatedly reminded of the distinct group identities of islanders and 'békés' [whites]. The Borrells become ensconced in island life and find themselves inadvertently embroiled in the black-market dealings of a Dutchman with a criminal past. Ultimately, the only escape is death, which for Mas (2008: 124) is in keeping with the failure trope common in Catalan exilic novels.

In DFC, Tísner tackles the concept of culture shock, with the protagonists trapped between their real context of exile and the memory and desire for an idealized Barcelona, frozen in time. The dreamlike interpolation of a narrative chronicling the activities of a circus reinforces the notion of escape from reality, as well as evoking images of past lives. Thus, the author uses the novel to engage with the renewed complexities of the exilic predicament following the end of the Second World War, after which the lack of Allied intervention in Spain led many refugees to understand their exile as a more permanent situation. When he began writing the novel in 1961, Tísner's memories of his own visit to Martinique in July 1939 had begun to fade. He therefore determined to return and spent days absorbing the culture of the island so as to be sure to do it justice in his fictional rendering. This commitment to research is still more apparent in his subsequent novel, *Paraules d'Opòton el Vell*, the final text examined in this chapter.

While the topics of exile and cultural clash were explored by a number of writers at the time,[16] as in the case of BM, what is noteworthy in Tísner's engagement with them is his skilled manipulation of the narrative structure. DFC is constructed across a series of binaries: the two distinct personalities of the brothers; locals and outsiders; natives split along racial lines; urban and rural; land and sea; and the real versus the imagined. Each dichotomy contributes to an overall metaphor within the novel for the duality of exilic identity. In his portrayal of the Borrell brothers, Tísner uses the interpolation of the narrative voices, at times creating ambiguity regarding the identity of the speaker. Injected like a series of jab-lines,[17] this is one of several subtle hints throughout the novel that one of the brothers is simply the alter ego of the other. The reader learns that these exchanges are actually the product of Gabriel's delirious dreams, a fact that the author reveals like a punch-line to provoke relief in resolving the sustained incongruity. Tísner has accounted for this toying with the narrative structure as part of a deep fascination with Freudian psychoanalytical thinking on the subconscious, and the creative possibilities afforded by dreams.[18] A split personality of frustrated expectation is manifested in Jaume as the embodiment of all of Gabriel's unfulfilled aspirations and is a clear metaphor for the challenging exilic experience and the longing for home. In DFC, this notion is not only portrayed in terms of the more patent themes of culture clash and otherness, but also through the framing image of a man within touching distance of land and yet confined by illness to a boat offshore.

The majority of the humorous interjections found in DFC are used to construct a sense of otherness on the island and frequently draw upon the Superiority approach and its role in the construction of group identity. This is brought to the fore in the incongruous situation of the protagonist brothers who are considered by the islanders as part of an out-group with which the Catalans themselves do not identify: 'els francesos blancs ens discriminen sense distinció, a nosaltres i els negres' [the white Frenchmen discriminate against us, without distinguishing us from the blacks] (1966: 28). In this way, the derogatory references throughout such as 'aquests francesos són una colla de bèsties' [those French are a bunch of beasts] (1966: 33), are an attempt to establish that it is this group, not the brothers, that is 'other'. This in turn heightens the humour since their failure to convince anyone of this point evokes the in/out-group identity paradigm through the use of Superiority humour.

The author's humour recourse in DFC characteristically appears in the dialogue, an approach which favours the use of self-contained jokes. The result is that while these comedic interruptions provide relief and/or moments of independent wit, they do not sustain an overall humorous tone in the same way as BM. Nevertheless, the humour is a key tool for the way Tísner articulates his binaries. Indeed, when the brothers compare the abundance of mangoes on the island with their high cost at home, Tísner does not miss the opportunity afforded by *trepitjar* [trip/tread] for wordplay:

> — Aquí van regalats.
> — I els trepitgen.
> — Ah sí? Que en fan vi?
> — Ase!
>
> ['Here they give them out freely.'
> 'And they tread on them.'
> 'Oh yeah? Do they make wine from them?'
> 'Ass!'] (1966: 21)

The syllepsis used to juxtapose the meanings of tripping over and the vinification process, is highly characteristic of the author's injection of gag-humour. In this exchange, it serves the purpose of distinguishing between the playful and serious personalities of the brothers, while breaking up the wistful exchanges about the home they have left behind.

Counterpoint and contrast also underpin the sustained dichotomy of the imagined and the real via the aforementioned interpolated visual accounts of the circus. Ironically, this usually fantastical realm plays the very specific role of a return to reality from the world of fiction within the novel, with the influence of Chaplin's cinematic style discernible in the final scenes where the circus packs up and boards the boat. However, the relevance of these seemingly self-contained circus episodes, and the fact that the characters within were designed to represent daily life, was broadly lost on Tísner's readers and critics. When interviewed on the motivation behind the circus elements, he explained:

> 'No són dues performances de cap circ, sinó les dues funcions del circ, de funcionament: l'una, que el circ té la missió de donar coherència a la invenció del germà, tot creant la contrafigura [*sic*], un ambient i uns personatges. L'altra gran funció del circ en la novel·la és la de ruptura.'
>
> [It is not about two performances of a particular circus, but the two functions of a circus: one, that the circus has the task of making the brother's invention coherent, also creating a counterpoint, an atmosphere and characters. The other major function of the circus in the novel is that of rupture.] (Serra 1992: 13)

As with the wordplay in the dialogue, there is a sense of relief — in Freudian terms — since the circus scenes act as a break from the mounting tension in the events of the plot. The escapism provided by these episodes ties in to an exoticization of the Americas, often present in Catalan exile narrative.[19] In the case of DFC, Mas (2008: 124) argues that the fault does not lie with the adopted land, but rather the culture and tradition internalized by the exiles themselves, which undermines the possibility of fully adapting to the new environment. Thus, Tísner reflects the emotional oscillation of the exilic predicament through overlapping storylines, which speaks to the dual paradigm of relief through escape alongside a longing to return. In its final pages, like the proverbial Ouroboros, the narrative reverts to the beginning, as if time has stood still, a representation of Tísner's notion that for the exile time freezes in the country of origin until the point of return. The island itself becomes a metaphor for exile through a growing sense of isolation — both temporal and geographical.

The complex emotional experience of exile lies at the novel's heart as it grapples with questions of belonging and identity. The humorous interjections, though never far from the surface, do not undermine the sober issues which the author wishes to tackle. Rather, Tísner's comic interludes are judiciously inserted to frame group identity and character development, while providing light relief through their controlled handling as a tool for balance and contrast. DFC is structured around incongruity set-up and resolution, with jab-lines that hint at the deciphering of ambiguity via alternating narrative voices. The relief in the final reveal is two-fold: first, acting like a punch-line to resolve the incongruity, and second, releasing the built-up tension developed by the interpolated fictional finale, with the parodic use of the oneiric trope to draw the narrative to a close.

Paraules d'Opòton el Vell

Experimentation with generic form is again at the heart of Tísner's best-known literary work, *Paraules d'Opòton el Vell* (POV) (1968). Inspired by the author's affinity for Mexico, POV is an elaborate and audacious depiction of conquest that challenges the typically Eurocentric discourse of 'discovery' and stands as a creative eulogy to the country that had been his home-away-from-home for over twenty years. Full of humour, yet permeated by a tone of serious commentary, this rich and detailed novel tackles a range of social questions including alterity (Mas 2008), cultural clash — as in DFC — and the global importance of language. At a time when the Mexican government had shown relatively little interest in revisiting its Aztec heritage (Eberenz 1986: 217), POV offers an itemized recreation of the Aztec worldview that engages the theme of oppression through a comic exercise in cultural relativism.

The novel charts the journey of fictional Aztec explorers who — a few years prior to Columbus's journey West — inadvertently stumble upon the Galician shores of Spain, having been sent out in search of the deity Quetzalcoatl. Just as historically the Tlacalteca formed an alliance with Hernán Cortés against Moctezuma II, the Galicians in POV decide to join the expedition in a bid to rid themselves of Castilian oppression. As the Aztecs make their way through Asturias, Castile and the Basque Country, the clash of cultures between the visitors and the local populations is playfully depicted through a series of misunderstandings that encourage a reading based on Incongruity and Superiority theories of humour.

The narrative structure of POV incorporates multiple levels, which can be mapped to Gérard Genette's (1983) narratological poetics. At the extradiegetic level, we are presented with a Catalan who is interested in learning Nahuatl with the help of a young autochthonous speaker. The reader is subsequently introduced to the intradiegetic narrator when the young man delivers an old manuscript written by a certain Opòton the Elder. In translating the sixteenth-century writings of Opòton, the Catalan is keen to highlight the shared plight of the Nahua and his own people, subjugated by Castilian dominance.

In the artificial exoticization of everyday, long-established Spanish customs and religious practices, Tísner demonstrates his proclivity for contrast. Taking the opportunity to create mock wonder, the use of chairs and dining tables is discussed extensively and repeatedly to emphasize a sense of incongruous incredulity:

> Però ells no seuen a terra, a la gatzoneta, ans en cadires de moltes menes, com els Senyors de casa nostra, però ells hi seuen encara que no siguin senyors. Tots, pobres o rics, tenen icpal·lís. I les menges tampoc no les posen damunt una estora, ans en fustes altes dites taules [...] I així queda dit, posat que és cosa certa.

> [But they don't sit on the ground, crouching, but on all manner of chairs, like the Masters back home do, although these people sit on them despite the fact that they are not themselves Masters. All of them, rich or poor, have *equipales*.[20] Nor do they put their food on the carpet, but rather on tall wood called 'tables'. [...] And I am telling you this, because it is true.] (1992a: 119)

This use of descriptive irony based on external incongruity — in Larkin's terms — can also be seen in the accounts of clothing and appearance: 'la gent galega [sic], en llur obstinació, no pot entendre que nosaltres no hàgim d'anar malfardats com ells' [the Galician people, in their obstinacy, do not understand that we do not have to be dishevelled like them] (1992a: 122), and '[Dona Ximena] tenia el cos ben format, amb totes aquelles coses que la dona ha de tenir i ella les tenia de bona mida i al seu lloc i ho vam poder comprovar tantost va vestir-se com nosaltres' [Dona Ximena had a good figure, with all of those bits that women should have, and she had them in good proportion and in their place and we were able to attest to this as soon as she dressed like us] (1992a: 113).

In choosing Nahuatl as the original language of Opòton's text, Tísner draws direct comparisons with the officially repressed status of Catalan at the time of writing (Mas 2008: 164). This connection is made throughout the novel, for example when Opòton explains the warm welcome by the local population: 'As Espanhas do Máis Alá és terra poblada per moltes tribus diverses, dominades per un Gran Senyor dit Tantomontamontatanto el qual amb la seva Senyora, els tenia tots ben dominats' ['Spain of Over There' is a land of many different tribes, ruled by the Great 'Equal-Opposites-In-Balance' who, with his wife, had them all subjugated] (1992a: 186).

The playful choice of the name, Tantomontamontatanto, is a compound form of the motto commonly associated with the Spanish royals Isabella and Ferdinand II, active supporters of the conquests of the Americas.[21] However, beyond an exercise in historical accuracy for the sake of verisimilitude, Tísner's reference to these particular figures is part of a critical, anti-Francoist theme that pervades the novel. The Franco regime extolled the virtues of the 'Catholic Monarchs', sharing the commitment to unify Spain and ensure the linguistic and cultural dominance of Castile through the suppression of minority identities in the Basque Country and Catalonia (Edwards 2013: ix). As a result, any initial surface-humour in the role-reversal implied by the derision of Tantomontamontatanto and the subsequent establishment of group identity boundaries between rulers and ruled, is buttressed — in Relief-release terms — by the additional covert criticism of the Franco dictatorship. This further supports the potential of extending Larkin's internal/external framework to include Freudian humour principles.

Throughout POV, Tísner foregrounds the irony in the worship of Christian saints and offers a tongue-in-cheek portrayal of the *autos de fe*, drawing parallels with the Aztecs' own practices of idolatry and human sacrifice. These are some of a plethora of instances that deride the hypocrisy of the Conquistadors' depiction of Latin America as a land of uncivilized barbarians, since it is now the arriving Aztecs who are the self-proclaimed cream of the crop. By highlighting the inferiority of the conquistadors *qua* Franco's Spain through a combination of Superiority and Relief-release approaches, Tísner uses humour to reinforce group-identity distinction between the Catalan diasporic in-group and its modern-day oppressor.

In addition to the story-within-a-story approach, Tísner employs, through Opòton, a narrative full of technical Nahuatl as well as frequent apologies for his own artistic and linguistic lapses, in a style reminiscent of Bernal Díaz del Castillo's sixteenth-century memoirs of the Spanish conquests, *Historia verdadera de la conquista de la Nueva España* [The Real History of the Conquest of New Spain]. Moreover, there are parodic echoes of Cervantes's *Don Quixote* in the distinction between the diegetic levels. With the narratorial interjection, 'sempre he cregut que aquest passatge era fantasia d'Opòton' [I always thought that this passage was another of Opòton's fantasies] (1992a: 165), Tísner attempts to assert the non-fictional — and therefore incontrovertible — status of the text.[22] As part of this approach, the author also indulges his love of language and wordplay, peppering Opòton's narrative with archaisms and colloquialisms, meanwhile employing the narrator to explain that these phrases are necessarily preserved in his translation, since they are key to a true reproduction of the Aztec text.

The result of the measured injection of 'foreign' language — Tísner also maintains Galician and Castilian in its original where it appears — is a sustained verbal incongruity providing individual instances of humour, while at the same time contributing to the underlying comic tone of the text. Here, as elsewhere, the author is rarely able to resist the opportunity for wordplay. When a group of local Galician women hear a sneeze, they respond with the customary 'Susús' [bless you], not being initially aware of the explorers' presence. Upon noticing the men — naked, as was their custom — an amusing scene is described as the women flee shrieking. We are then told that, 'els vam dir Sususes puix, si no criden o xisclen, solen dir susús, oi més quan algú esternuda' [we called them 'Blessyous', since if they weren't shouting or whistling, they were always saying 'bless you', especially if someone sneezed] (1992a: 96). The humour is bolstered by the use of dramatic irony, which appears here in its common application as a tool for imbuing the omniscient audience or reader with superiority over the less-informed protagonists.

The Susús scene is preceded by an extended, distracted, rambling text and the unanticipated inclusion of the action and chaos is a welcome variation in pace in such an extensive novel. Tísner resorts to his characteristic approach of counterpoint and contrast to heighten the build-up of tension, and thereby — after Freud — the subsequent humorous effect at the moment of release. In POV, this is also achieved through the continuous insertion of paratext, supposedly added by the manuscript's owner, as well as the hidden presence of his cousin as literary critic. The footnotes, like the inclusion of the bibliography at the end, lend the piece a sense of pseudo-authenticity, and, most importantly, offer a necessary break from the long passages delivered by a narrator's unfettered stream of consciousness until he loses his train of thought and the novel ends.

The stylistic strokes, intertextuality, narrative structure and historical frame of the novel are constructed with such meticulous precision that the reader is soon lulled into following it as an accurate history of events.[23] Beyond this successful narrative crafting, POV conveys the deep influence of exile on Tísner's life via the portrayal of a narrator in the role of 'other' which, according to Mas (2008: 14), provides us with a unique and unfamiliar view of ourselves. The loyalty he felt for his adoptive home was reaffirmed when the author subsequently published his translation of the text in 1992, stating unequivocally that this was not a translation into Spanish but into Mexican.[24]

By way of conclusion, while often performing very different literary functions, the works in question reflect the evolution of Tísner's career as an author and of his relationship with the exilic experience. Through the humour of the day-to-day life of the soldiers in BM, Tísner achieves a tangible verisimilitude to reflect the realities of war beyond accounts of heroic battles and epic scenes. The mundanity, as well as the humour with which it is delivered, presents an incongruous account of the tragedy. Nevertheless, far from undermining the conflict's penetrating effects, Freudian humour theory can be used to understand BM's portrayal of the mourning of a lost youth in both macabre and light-hearted episodes. The emotional challenges of exile are treated with a similar playfulness in DFC and the stylistic combination of binaries, contrast and counterpoint across the narrative levels draws on each of the approaches to humour in blend and isolation. Yet, these episodes of humour also form part of serious reflections relating to cultural shock, alterity, frustration and loss as part of the exilic experience. Finally, Tísner's historical account of counter-conquest is not as detached from the painful experiences of exile as it would initially seem. Cast through the lens of the Superiority and Freudian approaches, we can elucidate that, like BM before it, POV champions the cause of the forgotten, using derisive humour to denounce the repressive forces behind the author's exile.

In its treatment of war, exile and conquest, Tísner's early narrative engages themes not typically associated with the humour genre. Nevertheless, his humorous interjections as part of — and in addition to — a subsidiary, yet sustained, comical tone produce a multitude of effects beyond stylistic entertainment. Reflecting Hall's (2000: 55) concept of 'profoundly naturalised' codes, in all three novels Tísner employs humour to introduce cultural allusions and motifs in the portrayal of recognizable quotidian events, based on assumed in-group familiarity. In addition to the decision to write in Catalan — thereby sacrificing a potentially numerous and lucrative Spanish-speaking readership — Tísner's cathartic-while-humorous rendering has the effect of reinforcing a collective linguistic and cultural identity with his intended readers. Although he continued to publish novels following his return to Barcelona, he remained a minor figure in literary circles and soon re-joined the world of the popular press with which he had remained strongly connected. In part, it is perhaps this decision to refocus his talents that has reinforced Tísner's relative anonymity within the narrative field. However, his commitment to exploring the Catalan exilic experience through creative combinations of the tragic and the comic, at a time when linguistic and cultural repression threatened the entire future of the literary tradition, demands that his work be recognized for its significant contribution to twentieth-century Catalan writing.

Works Cited

ARTÍS-GENER, AVEL·LÍ/TISNER. 1945. *556 Brigada Mixta* (Mexico City: Col·lecció Catalònia)

——. 1966. *Les dues funcions del circ* (Barcelona: Proa)

——. 1972. *Al cap de 26 anys* (Barcelona: Pòrtic)

——. 1991. *Viure i veure*, vol. 3, 2nd ed. (Barcelona: Pòrtic)

——. 1992a. *Paraules d'Opòton el Vell*, in *Obres completes de Tísner*, II: *Novel·les, 2* (Barcelona: Pòrtic), pp. 7–292

——. 1992b. *Viure i veure*, vol. 1, 6th edn (Barcelona: Pòrtic)

ATTARDO, SALVATORE, and VICTOR RASKIN. 1991. 'Script Theory Revis(it)ed: Joke Similarity and Joke Representation Model', *Humor*, 4: 293–347

BAREA, ARTURO. 1946. *The Forging of a Rebel* (London: Granta Books)

——. 1951. *La forja de un rebelde* (Buenos Aires: Losada)

BARGALLÓ, JOSEP. 2010. 'México, territorio de la literatura catalana', in *Cataluña en México*, ed. by J. M. Figueres and J. M. Murià (Mexico City: Instituto Nacional de Antropología e Historia)

BERGSON, HENRI. 2008 [1900]. *Laughter: An Essay on the Meaning of Comic*, trans. by Cloudesley Brereton and Fred Rothwell (London: Wildside Press)

BORRÁS, TOMÁS. 2016 [1939]. *Checas de Madrid*, ed. by Álvaro López Fernández and Emilio Peral Vega (Madrid: Escolar y Mayo Editores)

CALDERS, PERE. 1964. *L'ombra de l'atzavara* (Barcelona: Edicions 62)

CAMPILLO, MARIA. 2005. 'Els escriptors catalans exiliats i "l'Amèrica furienta"', in *Narrativa catalana de l'exili*, ed. by Julià Guillamon (Barcelona: Galàxia Gutenberg), pp. 27–29

CICERO. 1942. *De Oratore/On the Orator*, trans. by E. Sutton and H. Rackham, Book II, ch. 63, Loeb Classical Library, 348 (Cambridge, MA: Harvard University Press)

CÒNSUL, ISIDOR. 1993. 'Actualitat de la novel·lística de Tísner', *Avui, Cultura*, 14 February, p. 81

EBERENZ, ROLF. (1986). 'México reflejado en la narrativa catalana del exilio', in *Actas del IX Congreso de la Asociación Internacional de Hispanistas* (Centro Virtual Cervantes), pp. 211–19

EDWARDS, JOHN. 2013. *Ferdinand and Isabella* (Abingdon: Routledge)

FABER, SEBASTIAN. 2002. 'Contradictions of Left-wing Hispanismo: The Case of the Spanish Republicans in Exile', *Journal of Spanish Cultural Studies*, 3.2: 165–85

FREUD, SIGMUND. 2001 [1905]. *Jokes and their Relation to the Unconscious*, vol. VIII of the Standard Edition of the Complete Psychological Works of Sigmund Freud (London: Vintage)

GARCÍA SERRANO, RAFAEL. 1943. *La fiel infantería* (Madrid: Editorial Nacional)

GENETTE, GÉRARD. 1983. *Narrative Discourse: An Essay in Method*, trans. by Jane E. Levin (Ithaca, NY: Cornell University Press)

GUARNER, VICENÇ. 1945. 'Pròleg', in *556 Brigada Mixta*, by Avel·lí Artís-Gener (Mexico City: Col·lecció Catalònia), pp. 9–14

HALL, STUART. 2000. 'Encoding/decoding', in *Media Studies: A Reader*, ed. by Paul Marris and Sue Thornam (New York: New York Press), pp. 52–90

HOBBES, THOMAS. 1968 [1651]. *Leviathan* (Harmondsworth: Penguin)

HOLMES, JANET, and MEREDITH MARRA. 2002. 'Humour as a Discursive Boundary Marker in Social Interaction', in *Us and Others: Social Identities across Languages, Discourses and Cultures*, ed. by Anna Duszak (Philadelphia, PA: John Benjamins), pp. 377–400

HUTCHEON, LINDA. 1985. *A Theory of Parody: The Teachings of Twentieth-Century Art Forms* (New York and London: Methuen)

KNIGHT, CHARLES. 2004. *The Literature of Satire* (Cambridge: Cambridge University Press)

LARKIN GALIÑANES, CRISTINA. 2000. 'Relevance Theory, Humour, and the Narrative Structure of Humorous Novels', *Revista Alicantina de Estudios Ingleses*, 13: 95–106

LYTTLE, JIM. 2001. 'The Effectiveness of Humor in Persuasion: The Case of Business Ethics Training', *The Journal of General Psychology*, 128.2: 206–16

MAS I SAÑÉ, SÍLVIA. 2008. *Les novel·les d'exili d'Avel·lí Artís-Gener* (Barcelona: Abadia de Montserrat)

MCGLADE, RHIANNON. 2016. *Catalan Cartoons: A Cultural and Political History* (Cardiff: University of Wales Press)

MORREALL, JOHN. 2009. *Comic Relief: A Comprehensive Philosophy of Humor* (Oxford: Wiley-Blackwell)

OLIVER, MARIA ANTÒNIA. 1989. 'Avel·lí Artís-Gener, Tísner', *Serra d'Or*, 359: 10–15

PIÑOL, ROSA MARIA. 1994. ' "Es importante saber reírse de la propia sombra", dice Tísner', *La Vanguardia*, 12 May, p. 41

POCH, CESC, and MARTA JAÉN. 1993. 'Entrevista a en Tísner', *La Llançadora*, 2

SCHULER, FRIEDERICH. E. 1998. *Mexico between Hitler and Roosevelt: Mexican Foreign Relations in the Age of Lázaro Cárdenas, 1934–1940* (Albuquerque: University of New Mexico Press)

SERRA, MÀRIUS. 1992. 'La ena de Tísner', *Cultura*, 37: 12–19

VILLARROYA FONT, JOAN. 2000. *1939: derrota i exili* (Barcelona: Generalitat de Catalunya)

Notes to Chapter 11

1. The author gratefully acknowledges the support of the AHRC in the preparation of this chapter, which was funded as part of the research project, 'Multilingualism: Empowering Individuals, Transforming Societies', under the Open World Research Initiative.

2. For Hall, recognizing the influence of 'technical infrastructure', 'relations of production' and 'frameworks of knowledge' are key to understanding the way in which meaning is communicated and interpreted.

3. Here, 'exile narrative' encompasses the act of producing narrative in exile, narrative by someone who is experiencing exile, and a situation whereby the work itself can be considered to be in exile.

4. For a more detailed exposition of the primary humour theories, see, for example, Morreal (2009).

5. Expanding upon Lyttle (2001), I have previously nuanced this argument to suggest that it is the foregrounding of the inferiority of another, rather than our own superiority, that typically underpins this type of humour (McGlade 2016).

6. Cicero discussed humour and laughter at length in his treatise 'De Oratore' [On the Orator] (1942).

7. See, for example, Attardo and Raskin's (1991) pioneering work describing semantic and verbal theories of humour.

8. Col·lecció Catalònia was a not-for-profit initiative established by Tísner's father, Avel·lí Artís Balaguer, with the aim of bolstering the Catalan canon in the face of Francoist repression.

9. See, for example, Tomás Borrás's *Checas de Madrid* [Checas of Madrid] (1940) and Rafael García Serrano's *La fiel infantería* [The Faithful Infantry] (1943).

10. See, for example, Arturo Barea's *La forja de un rebelde* [*The Forging of a Rebel*] (1941–44), originally published in English during his exile in Britain.

11. *Si me quieres escribir* was also known as *Ya sabes mi paradero* [You Already Know My Whereabouts] and *El frente de Gandesa* [The Gandesa Front].

12. In the second edition, published in 1969 by Pòrtic, Tísner replaced the original prologue, which praised the author not only as a soldier but for the importance of his work to studies of historical memory, with a note announcing tweaks to expression and spelling in the text. In fact, he actually removed significant content, such as references to the Republicans holding prisoners, citing censorial pressure. In 1984, Pòrtic republished BM in its original form.

13. Tísner revealed a kind of disdain for the text remarking that his memoirs, *Viure i veure* [Living and Seeing], would be an authentic account of what happened to supersede BM, which he labelled 'falsejador' [fake], 'frívol' [frivolous] and 'intranscendent' [trivial] (1991: 14).

14. During unanticipated problems with his passenger ship, the *Ipanema*, Tísner temporarily disembarked at Martinique in order to seek medical assistance for his ailing brother, Arcadi.

15. In his memoirs, Tísner explains that the actual doctor in question — Lefranc de Touré — was highly influential and a keen supporter of the Spanish Republic, but this is where the autobiographical connection ends (Artís Gener 1992b: 92).

16. See, for example, Pere Calders's *L'ombra de l'atzavara* [The Shadow of the Agave] (1964).

17. 'Jab-lines differ from punch-lines in that they can be found anywhere in a text but the end (the position occupied exclusively by the punch- line). The two also differ in function: a punch-line serves to disrupt the narrative flow, while jab-lines are fully integrated in it' (McGlade 2016: 67; n. 33).

18. References to Freudian theory are made both in the novel itself (1966: 81) and in *Viure i veure* (1992b: 511).

19. See, for example, Campillo (2005).

20. An *equipal* (or *ycpal*) was a type of ground-level throne used by the Aztecs.

21. The saying became more familiar in its expanded form 'tanto monta, monta tanto, Isabel como Fernando' [Ferdinand and Isabella amount to the same].

22. See the depictions of Cide Hamete Benengeli in Cervantes's *Don Quixote Part I*.

23. The success of this verisimilitude achieved by Tísner in POV can be attested by its official reception. Taking at face value the claim in the book that the manuscript was presented to the Museo de Culturas Prehispánicas de México — an entirely fictitious institution —, the appointed censor wrote a letter of complaint stating that rather it should have been directed to Seville's Archivo General de Indias (Bargalló 2010).

24. A previous translation into Spanish by the poet Angelina Gatell in 1977 was subject to criticism from the right-wing newspaper *El Alcázar*, which declared it an anti-Spanish abomination.

CHAPTER 12

Catalan *Noucentisme* and Narrative: From Discursive Analogy to Moral Anagogy

Josep Murgades

Universitat de Barcelona

Littera gesta docet, quid credas allegoria,
moralis quid agas, quo tendas anagogia.[1]

Terminological Preliminary: *Noucentisme*

On other occasions I have taken the opportunity to offer a synthetic overview of
a movement which was headed politically by Prat de la Riba with a programme
whose ideological thrust was given verbal consistency by Eugeni d'Ors: two
dimensions compressed in the equation 'El Noucentisme: a l'anagogia per l'analogia'
[*Noucentisme*: to anagogy via analogy] (Murgades 2014: 315; 2018).

The underlying first principle is the assumption, duly explicated, that 'analogy'
is to be understood, in this case and in general, as the discourse of myth, that is to
say, as the deliberately literary fashioning of language. The second principle is that
by 'anagogy' we are to understand the ambition of influencing and transforming,
from above, the values and behavioural patterns of a particular society as a whole:
specifically, in the historical context of Catalan *Noucentisme*, the values and
behaviour of those sectors directly implicated in the 'bourgeois revolution' driven
by political Catalanism against the Spanish state in the first decades of the twentieth
century.

In the case of *Noucentisme*, then, there was a deep-seated conviction regarding
the efficacy of words, of the arts and of culture in general — of everything that,
in Marxist terminology, we could still call 'superstructures' — for the purpose of
bringing about certain fundamental changes: in social behaviour, in labour relations,
in the means of production. This was bourgeois idealism, then, obviously. But none
the less operative for all that — always at the superstructural level — when it came
to: a) creating awareness of a specific sense of nationhood; b) rescuing a language
from a tokenism which was confined to the levels of high culture or of dialectalism

with a folkloric justification, thus ensuring the status of Catalan as a fully-fledged language proper; c) bringing literary and artistic activity into line with the most advanced Europe-wide currents.

The Narrative and Poetic Principles of *Noucentisme*

The notes which follow are an attempt to trace briefly that dialectical process leading towards a certain measure of fulfilment (anagogy) through artistic creativity (analogy) in one specific sphere of literature: that of narrative prose.[2] And I shall limit myself even further here by focusing exclusively on the short narrative forms.[3] The reason for this is that the field of the novel in that period is still relatively unmapped and, at present, less explored than some people think or, in their supine ignorance, would have it.[4]

The point is that narrative *lato sensu* is quite evidently one genus — compared with others like poetry, the essay, even oratory — which does not have a clearly elevated standing in the theoretical hierarchy of the *noucentista* movement. Nor is it a modality earnestly or assiduously cultivated in the movement's literary practice. It is, nevertheless, a category of creative writing which does have a presence in that specific repertoire. And it is no less significant there, in fact, than some of the most representative aspects of *noucentista* poetic theory and practice.

This is a poetics which, as both a reflection and focus of irradiation — for interests and expectations, for aspirations and of needs — stands at the antipodes of any poetics of extravagance and hyperbole, of the manifesto or of denunciation, of the animosity inherent in παρρησία. In this sphere *Noucentisme* affirms itself, rather, as a poetics of attenuation and litotes,[5] of strict conformity and social sanction (both ironically focused),[6] of the programmatic insistence on παροιμία.[7]

Framing this are the particular premises of a post-symbolism which lends itself more readily to the imaginative possibilities of figurative expression than to the straight lines of explicitness. And this can be as applicable to prose production as it is to poetry especially. Thus, we can understand how and why the development of *noucentista* narrative is marked by the postulation — and the exercising — of containment and renunciation, elusion and metalepsis, limitation and ellipsis. Implied in this are intellectualism and difficulty put in the way of simple reading, so as to strengthen both transmission and reception of meaning aimed at making anagogy possible. And the overcoming of stumbling blocks in the quest for improvement in every sense must, obviously, be something which will begin on high and will be projected from above.

The Parable as Narrative Subgenre

In line with this postulation, and if for brevity's sake we needed to equate the whole narrative corpus of *Noucentisme* with a single dominant literary procedure, that of parable would be the most appropriate. Parable is the analogical discourse par excellence (Dupont 1980 and 1981). Its main tendency, rather than towards direct moralizing, is to give expression to types of behaviour which exemplify, through emulation or contrast, models of praxis to be imitated or avoided. The referents are not expressed through abstract ideas but, rather, clothed in concrete images. Parable, then, still in line with Dupont's analysis, is a means of overcoming disjunction: between reality and the ideal, between lived experience and aspiration, between established modes of behaviour and alternative ones aspired to.[8]

In one of his sporadic incursions into narrative, Carles Riba showed himself to be well aware of this dimension. In the delightful 'Intenció de l'autor' [Declaration of intent] (Riba 1924: 7–12) with which he prefaced *L'ingenu amor* [Ingenuous Love], the author goes into the subject of courtship (not something which makes much sense to present-day generations) and he also categorizes the four pieces which make up the collection as 'històries, o si es vol paràboles' [stories, or if you will, parables] (1924: 11).

Certainly. His *parables* enable Riba to illustrate a certain concept of love, based on the 'esperit de renunciament' [spirit of renunciation], on something thus very different from being 'una passió engolidora i violenta' [a consuming and violent passion] (1924: 11), exactly as befitted the behavioural model (not to say the *Weltanschauung*) of *Noucentisme*. And this is how the subject is representatively given shape in 'La donzella que s'afaiçonà un estimat' [The Young Lady Who Made a Lover for Herself] in *L'ingenu amor*, a parabolic replaying in folk-tale key of the story's central precept: 'darrera el llindar de l'admiració devota i del desig gentil, comença encara un llarg camí de renunciament dolorós; i hom no abasta la perfecció d'amor fins que no n'ha petjat una per una totes les espines de sofrença' [beyond the threshold of devout admiration and courteous desire, there lies ahead a long road of painful renunciation; and perfection in love is not achieved until all the sharp thorns of suffering have pierced the soles of one's feet] (1924: 64).[9]

La Ben Plantada[10] by Eugeni d'Ors

Thus, we subscribe to the convention of considering *La Ben Plantada* (1911) by Eugeni d'Ors as the cornerstone of *noucentista* narrative. We do not mean the paradigmatic *novel* of *Noucentisme* (a very scant repertoire, at least in comparison with the immediately preceding phase of the *modernista* novel), since this work has been looked on, rather (and with a distinctly dismissive attitude), as an 'anti-novel'.[11] And *La Ben Plantada* is too long to be classified in the short-story corpus of *Noucentisme*, being made up of a gathering of the etherealized and sublimated *gloses*, highly condensed sketches which d'Ors published regularly in the daily newspaper *La Veu de Catalunya*.

What we do have in *La Ben Plantada* is the cornerstone of something else: of the model *überhaupt* of narrative for *Noucentisme*; that is to say, of that discursive *analogy*, more or less disguised in parable form, which is aligned with, and aspires to, anagogical efficaciousness — or transcendental sublimation — in one way or another.

This is accordingly a work where one can detect some of the elements — both of thematic recurrence and of formal treatment — that sit more easily in *Noucentisme*'s scheme of poetic values. Where a narrative element is incorporated there — we must emphasize this again — it is in the form of analogical (that is, fictionalized) recounting of conflicts which have their resolution through the key of litotes (i.e. attenuation), designed to express moral anagogy (i.e. refinement of behaviour). In this light, it is quite clear that *La Ben Plantada*, as an aesthetic sublimation of *noucentista* ethics (Murgades 1987b: 72–73), stands out as a paradigmatic reference point.

Present *in nuce* within *La Ben Plantada* are numerous motifs and formal procedures which would later become habitual in many narrative products clearly affiliated with *Noucentisme*, regardless of the variations and individual characteristics of particular works and their authors. Definitive traits in d'Ors's text are: neutralization, through aesthetic transcendence, of any kind of serious conflict; the hypostatic idealization of the Mediterranean scenery and spirit; enthusiastic reverence for established conventions (or, more truly, conventions in the process of becoming established); exaltation of a disciplinary ethic based on work and duty; the allegorical (parabolic) formulation of this whole scheme of values, with its cataphoric plot resolution — leaving aside the scandal it produced at the time —[12] recreating literally, on the biblical precedent, the great anagogy represented by the 'ascension' of Teresa, *la Ben Plantada*, and by the lesson she preached.

Treatment of the Matter of Conflict in *noucentista* Narrative

As a bourgeois movement with the corresponding values of a middle class fearful of losing its status or, at best, of not feeling sufficiently steady and legitimated in that status, *Noucentisme* cannot for this reason wholly turn its back on reality, on what it perceives as reality in the terms of those specific values and of that particular social position.

What it can do, however, is to cut out the thorniest aspects of the contemporary status quo by reducing them to more superficial and ultimately more assimilable manifestations. This is done, of course, with the firm hope of being able through such a procedure to have an influence on the underlying social reality. So we can consider now some examples of this neutralization — generated in the narrative aims and ambitions of *Noucentisme* — of various types of conflict.

First and foremost, we have basic social tensions. The class struggle unleashed in the years immediately following the Great War figures in these stories by J. M. López Picó: 'Les primeres bones festes' [The First Happy Christmases], 'La supervivència' [Survival], and 'Les confidències del locaut' [Confidences from the Lockout] (López-Picó 1922: 27–32, 33–38, 39–45). In the first of these, the violent trauma caused by bombs is minimized as the word for 'bomb' appears here not in its usual sense but in a way that makes *bomba* synonymous with its derivative *barrabomba*, defined in the dictionary as a 'fanal gros i rodó de paper' [large round paper lantern], thus recreating literarily a sugary sentimental version of a would-be *Barcelona felix*. In the second story, the disturbing repercussions of the great strike at *La Canadenca* generating station in February–March 1919 (events merely alluded to in the text) are equated simply with changes in habitual routines, something which causes inconvenience for 'our good man', the protagonist. The third story beatifically extols the sweet-sounding water of a drinking fountain, the music coming from a barrel organ, and being able still to make regular visits, even if surreptitious, to the local café: things which enable good citizens to overcome irksome consequences of an industrial lockout. If in reading tales of this kind we can suspend disbelief, as Coleridge preached, not just generally but also (mighty hard though it is) about their historical veracity, then we can agree that, as an exercise in trivializing the real world — or, more to the point, turning it inside-out — the *noucentista* political blueprint, via López-Picó in this case, is extremely effective...

Then we can consider linguistic/cultural, ultimately political, conflict. In the short stories and satirical sketches of *La creació d'Eva i altres contes* [The Creation of Eve and Other Stories] (1922) we have Josep Carner assaulting a Spain which is Castilian-dominated in terms of outlook, behavioural reflexes, attitudes — diametrically opposed, then, to the Catalan temper (or to what it is implied the latter ought to be). 'El castellà en el tren o l'amistat' [The Castilian on the Train or Friendship] (Carner 1922: 41–45) shows 'la raça privilegiada i abassegadora' [the privileged, voracious race] (45) flaunting its presumption, its swagger and self-interested familiarity. Or we have the parable — unambiguous in formulation and in intent — of 'Les dues vies' [The Two Ways] (Carner 1922: 129–34) where a Catalan and a Castilian, members of a religious order, react in quite different ways to the same possibility of gustatory delight: the former with restraint and anagogical delectation, the latter with catagogical fatalism.

But where the irreducible differentiation between the Two Spains is without doubt to be found is in 'La guerra' [War] (Carner 1922: 145–50), because of the objective gravity of the historical setting and because of the comic-pathetic critique Carner applies to it. This is a devastating censure of the Spanish government's policy in its Moroccan war centred simply on contrasting it starkly, in a kind of anticipation of *Forrest Gump*, with the reaction of an enlisted infantryman, 'un pobre minyó mancat de [...] seny' [a poor lad [...] a bit on the dim side] (147), horrified at the prospect of firing at and harming the men in the opposing trenches. Due to its simplicity, the litotic attenuation deliberately applied here by Carner could not be more effective as a scathingly ironic assault on the pompous and grandiloquent emphasis of flag-waving Spanish patriotism.

Another scenario of conflict in the period is the contrast between northern and southern Europe and their respective developmental 'speeds' (as it is euphemistically put nowadays). The explanation given by the South in this context is well known to everybody: self-affirmation in the supposed continuity of the Latin peoples and their perpetuation of the classical inheritance; ontological communion with the notional eternal essences of Mediterranean culture, etc. Indeed, a version composed in narrative terms of this mammoth ideological construct is to be found in the 'Rondalla moderna del cotxer i de la bondat de Barcelona' [A Modern Tale about the Cabdriver and the Excellence of Barcelona] (López-Picó 1922: 5–25). One bright sunny day a hired coach-man refuses to take a young English client to where he wants to go — a dive of ill repute — and insists instead on driving him around the brightly lit smart districts of Barcelona. The ensuing dispute turns into a distorted one-act farce that nearly becomes a diplomatic incident. But the cabdriver has his way, and he is able to extol the beauty and salubriousness of 'el cel i el sol' [the sky and the sun] (23) of Spain, a Spain archetypically represented here by the Catalan capital (with tacit allusion to the mephitic mists and pervasive greyness conventionally associated with hyperborean Europe, its wealth notwithstanding).

Carner's 'El gelat de xocolata' [The Chocolate Ice-cream] (1922: 165–71), contrasting a villa on the Italian Riviera with a Scottish castle and their respective lady owners, is focused on the delicacy enshrined in the title. To no avail are the perfectionism applied or the quality of the ingredients used in preparing the dessert according to 'els principis de la civilització britànica' [the principles of British civilization] (171). The only ice-cream which turns out as it should is the one resulting from typically meridional hybridization and legerdemain.

In a prose piece which functions similarly as a parable, although with inserted reflections of Homeric characters (Nausicaä) and of magical elements derived from folk tales, Josep Sureda Blanes's *La princesa que tenia el rellotge aturat* [The Princess Whose Watch Had Stopped] (2005 [1930]) stretches credibility to the limit. Ellipsis is exploited here to the maximum in narrating how a Catalan banker well established professionally in Paris also shines brilliantly in the social life of the capital, thanks to 'la suprema elegància parisina, aviat assimilada' [the supreme Parisian elegance quickly assimilated] of his wife who is of rural Majorcan stock but endowed, for this very reason, with 'la serena i honesta grandesa patrícia de la nostra pagesia' [the serene and impeccable patrician grandeur of our peasant folk] (Sureda Blanes 2005: 53).

Religion can be seen as another constant sphere of conflict potential in this period. In 'El rector de Valldaura' [The Priest of Valldaura] by Carles Soldevila (1929: 79–97), however, this subject is not addressed in relation to transcendental concerns. The story deals, rather, with the conflict of points of view between a young parish priest (temperamentally very different from his aged predecessor in the incumbency) and his bishop. While the young cleric's outlook entails a social commitment to his flock as a whole (not very different from the stance of the worker-priests we knew in the 1960s), the bishop's views are sectarian and ultraconservative. The resulting clash between the two, added to the latter's threat to formally ostracize his rebellious subordinate, is resolved by the voluntary entry of the young priest into the Franciscan order — the only option open to him if he wants to persevere at least in practical evangelism, albeit on the margins of the established ecclesiastical jurisdiction. There is, thus, no real breaking of the traditional order, nor any confrontation between the characters involved. The outcome entails renunciation and ulterior accommodation to a satisfactory compromise, Franciscan in spirit, with the *aurea mediocritas* which *Noucentisme* adopted from its origins in Horace.

No one can deny, though, that an extreme case of conflict lived internally is the one in which an individual is led to the determination to end his/her own life. The repertoire of *noucentista* narrative supplies two instances of such a situation — 'Pensar-hi bé' [Second Thoughts] (López-Picó 1922: 113) and 'El miracle' [The

Miracle] (Soldevila 1926: 69–72) — each of which is resolved by the potential suicide being dissuaded from the act. In the first of these, an extremely brief piece which comes close to being a pure apothegm, the character who changes his mind is a young man who listens to the advice of a venerable sage about undressing before throwing himself into the river: the ritual itself of taking off his clothes and folding them carefully is sufficient to make him change his mind.

The second story is a considerably fuller and more subtle narrative composition about a man with the surname of Catarineu, an irreparable failure in life, on the verge of ending it all, who desists from that criminal act when in the street he comes across an individual, even more destitute and helpless than himself, 'un gos que regira un munt d'escombraries' [a dog scavenging in a pile of garbage] (Soldevila 1926: 72). In a narrative twist, which owes as much to the generic form of the apologue as to the Franciscan spirit, this dog opens his mouth just to proffer a gentle, drawn out 'Bona nit, senyor Catarineu' [Good night, *senyor* Catarineu] (72). The empathy produced by the greeting is enough to restore, anagogically, the will to live in the unfortunate protagonist.

Our horizon broadens if we consider at this point the relationship between the bourgeoisie and the intellectuals, between economically productive and culturally creative activity, which was a significant zone of conflict in the period under discussion here and also, now seen in historical perspective, a watershed line in the respective dynamics of Catalan *Modernisme* and *Noucentisme*. This subject had been addressed in *Cigales i formigues* [Crickets and Ants] (1901) and in *L'auca del senyor Esteve* [The Amusing Story of Mr. Esteve] (1951 [1907]) by the *modernista* painter and prolific author Santiago Rusiñol. Two writers with such unequivocally *noucentista* credentials as López-Picó and Carner give their own slant on the same sociocultural tensions, in terms which have become distinctly conciliatory.

The former does this in a brief 'moralitat' [morality] — 'De les formigues i les cigales' [On Ants and Crickets] (López-Picó 1922: 89) — in which the ants complain about having to work 'sense una mica de cançó que ens ajudi' [without a bit of song to help us], the crickets having fallen silent because, it is implied, present times 'no estan per cantúries' [are not right for singing]. Carner's perspective in 'L'artista d'un sol quadro' [The Artist with One Painting to his Name] (1922: 103–07) has a fuller narrative framework and is more subtle. Here the author combines in a single character the vocations of haberdasher and painter for whom the contradiction would be more or less bearable except that, unlike his work in the shop, his efforts at painting never attain fulfilment. This is due to the fact that the 'camp de blat' [field of corn] which he aspires to paint is always changing, always elusive because of its constantly varying aspect. So the lesson here is clear: a suggestion of compatibility between the two vocations — one lucrative, the other ludic — but with the implied pre-eminence of the one which proves to be considerably more complex and transcendental than the other. It is, at bottom, one of so very many illustrative versions of the old Hippocratic aphorism: *ars longa, vita brevis*.

The *noucentista* Angle on the 'Dark Side'

It is certainly true that *Noucentisme* favours the 'blacking out', by exclusion, of aspects of reality deemed to be impure or indecent (Murgades 1987a: 55). However, when we do very occasionally encounter just the opposite (which by literal antinomy might be called 'blacking in'), such as a case of violent death, the subject is given a narrative treatment which stays in line with the requirements of attenuation and fastidiousness that characterize the movement's poetics.

Thus, in Carner's 'La vella polida' [The Refined Old Lady] (1922: 47–53), all the circumstantial evidence has pointed to the old lady of the title as the culprit of a robbery which resulted in the murder of the man she worked for. She is not convicted, presumably absolved, though the end of the story is deliberately ambiguous and relativistic regarding the responsibility for the crime and the circumstances in which it was committed, the personality of the 'old lady' who was under suspicion, and the professionalism of the jury.

Two stories by Joan Sacs, each recounting a murder, are composed in a key which is anti-sentimental and certainly no less amoral than the preceding example. (We observe in passing that this author's writing is a clear manifestation of a certain tendency in *Noucentisme* towards a primary emphasis on an eminently formal and 'dehumanized' art — in line with Ortega y Gasset's well-known denomination — which is characteristic of the avant-garde.)

'En Sidret, paleta i serafí' [Sidret, Bricklayer and Seraphim] (Sacs 1929: 15–22) sets up a contrast between the candour of a young working man and the cold-hearted wickedness of some professional criminals, unperturbed by their having wrongly identified and murdered him. This is black humour, hard and devoid of emotion, as a kind of litotic antidote to the extreme violence directed during that period against workers' movements by paid agents of the employers. Then, in 'Repensament' [Second Thoughts] (Sacs 1929: 35–52), the author deliberately parodies some clichés from the 'pulp fiction' of the time (the husband who throttles his wife, after discovering her in bed with a lover who had been hiding in the wardrobe). The cliché is contrasted with an alternative which, rather than anything like *passionel*, is one hundred per cent cerebral: the husband's self-restraint (his 'second thoughts'), on being released from prison, about vengefully murdering a previous lover of his wife. Contrary to what could be expected in the story-line of 'les novel·les de pa sucat amb oli' [clichéd sentimental pot-boilers] (Sacs 1929: 51), the option is taken to renounce all impulsiveness and, ultimately, to accept the ambivalence inherent in human life.

Another angle on this is found in Martínez Ferrando's 'El petit Rovira' [Young Rovira] (1930: 109–65). The character in the title was guilty of deliberately causing the death of his partner in their circus double-act. But his culpability is morally diluted by the dangers involved in what they were performing, by the lenient sentence imposed by the court, and by his quick return to the circus to figure again in the same sort of act where risk is inherent equally in the working conditions and in the gratuitousness of the conventions of all 'entertainment'. Then, in the case of 'El suïcidi d'en Rafael Galiana' [The Suicide of Rafael Galiana] by the same author (1924: 151–63),[13] it is not the act of suicide itself which stands out but what it signifies as a settling of intellectual scores with the victim on the part of a mediatized narrator, in his retrospective account of the facts coloured by a variety of literary and philosophical associations.

Ironic Awareness of One's own Limitations

Noucentisme was an ironic movement *par excellence* and was, thus, not averse to allowing intellectual commitment to its own cause to be incomplete,[14] with the result that some of its short narrative pieces effectively define an awareness of limitations in the *noucentista* project itself.

A veritable parable of this is Duran Reynals's 'Les falzies del palau del bisbe' [The Maidenhair Ferns at the Bishop's Palace] (1918: 7–17). A 'jove i ardent' [young and ardent] (8) new bishop commissions a project designed to cure permanently the poor drainage in his garden, the cause of a rampant proliferation of the ferns. The drawback is that the landscaping works create problems even more serious than sodden ground, including in particular that of cutting off the water supply to the whole neighbourhood. The moral is that one must be resigned to the impracticability of wanting always to make things better than they are, in order to avoid even more serious disadvantages. Furthermore, although future improvement and progress might be possible, it is necessary to take into account the negative consequences that will be entailed equally in any reform of the status quo.

So too, in 'La cadireta' [The Little Chair], Carner (1922: 157–64) effectively emphasizes the limits of enlightened projects ('No pot haver-hi cosa més cruel que una tirania de mestres d'estudi' [There can be nothing more cruel than a tyranny imposed by schoolmasters] [163]). In the frame of a typical group of regular customers in a café, this view is applied to the Bolshevik revolution that was taking place at the time, and Carner exemplifies it, parabolically, through an anecdote regarding alterations made to the cathedral in Palma de Mallorca by 'un arquitecte genial [a genius of an architect] (164), tacitly but quite obviously referring to Gaudí. The 'noble visió desempallegada' [noble and now uncluttered vision] (164) resulting from the demolition of the choir stalls is nevertheless disconcerting for an old lady who, feeling stranded in the great open space that the nave has become, is so disorientated that she does not know where to position her own little chair on which she liked to sit to say her prayers.

Less collective and monumental in scope, more focused on intellectual attitudes, are two comparable pieces, analogous with the last one in terms of story-line and reflection on the risks and shortcomings of enlightened rationalism translated into actual measures for social improvement. The stories in question are 'Homes i esperits' [Men and Spirits] by Duran Reynals (1918: 77–122) and Carner's 'La casa chic' [The chic House] (1922: 151–56).

The first of these centres on the clash of character between an optimistic, rather scatter-brained tobacconist and a pessimistic, empirical pharmacist. The conflict between these two is mediated by a watchmaker, conciliatory by nature, the third member of the group that meets every day to talk over a coffee or a drink. Symptomatically, it is he who has to pick up the pieces of an episode in which both a technical, material dimension and a mysterious, transcendent one are in play, in equal measure. In the end it is the pharmacist who is finally driven mad — 'un boig digne' [a worthy madman], it is firmly pointed out — because he stayed 'fidel a la seva trista veritat' [faithful to his own sad version of the truth] (Duran Reynals 1918: 121). This exemplifies the kind of balancing act that the *noucentista* mindset resorts to in order to reconcile reason — always *ma non troppo* — with impulses that belong more to the realm of the subconscious.

In Carner's story, considerably more perplexing than the last, it is the secondary character — in this case 'una minyona cepada, lletja, escarràs, renegaire com un oriol, meravellosa cuinera' [a tough young maid, ugly, hardworking, foulmouthed, a marvellous cook] (1922: 153) — who, doggedly resistant to adopting new ways of working and new modes of behaviour, refuses to accept the job offered to her by an attractive young French woman married to a man with 'idees socialistes' [socialist ideas] (154), despite the lure of much improved working and general living conditions they propose. What is the point in undertaking an ambitious social transformation if those who would most benefit from it are the ones who put up most resistance? This is the awkward question posed as the text's bitter-sweet conclusion.

Still in this discussion of the self-critical and, ultimately, self-ironizing facet of *Noucentisme* directed against some of its most cherished principles, we should incorporate here Carner's 'El viatge ingràvid' [The Weightless Journey] (1922: 135–43): a burlesque account of a journey to Barcelona made by an individual who is inclined to self-harm, '[un] estiracordetes de si mateix' [his own worst enemy] (137). He is extremely respectful of social conventions — the very ones so exalted by *Noucentisme* — to the extent that he ends up starving to death as a result of observing them.

In the same vein, Manuel Brunet's novella *El meravellós desembarcament dels grecs a Empúries* [The Amazing Disembarcation of the Greeks at Empúries] (1925) was quite appropriately categorized in its day as a 'paròdia poemàtica' [poematic parody].[15] The label refers to the central current of *Noucentisme*'s classicizing and Mediterranean-focused aesthetics, while from our present-day perspective we could designate the text itself quite simply as '*gentle* parody', imbued much more with moderated reprobation than with sarcastic mordacity.

Narrating *déclassement*

The theme of rising up (or falling down) the social ladder — *déclassement* in one direction or the other — is present, with varying degrees of prominence, in the narrative repertoire of *Noucentisme*. But manifestations of the subject tend to be predominantly in terms of failure to go up, or of distinct regression, in social standing, rather than of any profound conviction about real opportunities for upwards mobility. Regarding the first of these two types, one can detect that the anagogical impulse functions in contrast with the aversion caused by cases of immobility or of flagrant 'catagogy' that are dealt with.

Thus we have: a) immobility — stagnation — or the simple impossibility of looking forward to a future in a higher social position for the son of a worthy and clean-living ragman and his wife (Duran Reynals, 'Les il·lusions de l'Angelina' [Angelina's Wishful Thinking] [1918: 51–75]); b) failure to gain promotion in his career as a musician for a person who cannot shake off personal shortcomings on every level (Duran Reynals, 'Història d'un plaga' [The Tale of a Bright Spark] [1918: 19–49]); c) sullying regression into anarchoid primitivism of a couple who can easily be seen as caricatures of values and attitudes so dear to certain elements in *modernista* bohemianism (Carner, 'El cim' [The Summit][16] [1922: 183–90]).

In the second category, where upward mobility is in the frame, the story-lines generally move towards a *deus ex machina*. Pure ellipsis. The objective is not to reconstruct in literary form the various stages which can credibly lead to a favourable change of fortune. The possibility of such individual 'progress' is used as a strategy: a) to show the pathetic drift into kitsch — or simply the moral degradation — of a working-class family who rise in status thanks to the favourable economic climate created by Spanish neutrality in the Great War of 1914–1918 (Soldevila, 'La fortuna dels Molines' [The Fortune of the Molina Family] [1917: 171–88]);[17] b) to set forth the lethal dangers of confusing art and life, real life and art(ificiality), which can lead to dilution of the correct relationship between naturalness and artifice, or vice-versa (Plana, 'Vida d'un actor' [An Actor's Life] [1923: 93–134]); c) to weigh up the positive benefits of grafting Mediterranean virtues on to the aspiration to make an impression at a certain level in 'high society' (Sureda i Blanes, 'La princesa que tenia el rellotge aturat' [The Princess Whose Watch Had Stopped] [2005: 33–53]).

'Sota el nivell dels homes' [Below the Human Level] by Martínez Ferrando (1930: 167–86) presents a singular case which, if it is not really one of *déclassement*, is at least of a character's managing to maintain, at some cost, his status within the precarious stratum of a particular intellectual subproletariat. This is certainly one of the most authentic and most emotively charged pieces of narrative in the whole repertoire of *Noucentisme*. A modest and solitary humanities teacher, having been dismissed from his place of work, manages to survive on the meagre income he gets from looking after another man's dog. The situation lasts until the poor animal dies, of starvation, unbeknown to his real master. The 'cruelty' of this tale does not lie mainly in the gently dispassionate way it unfolds, nor in the soft-pedal effect of its final outcome.[18] Its true impact is basically in the temptation the reader is inclined to feel towards interpreting it as a parable about literary professionalization and its problems in a society like that of Catalonia, at least at the time when it was written.

The Ethics of Endeavour and of Professionalism

Another value by which *Noucentisme* sets great store can be detected in the story by Martínez Ferrando just examined: the ethic of study. It applies there as a variant of an analogous principle which operates on a more general level: the work ethic. This is given thorough literary treatment, in *noucentista* terms obviously, by Carles Soldevila in two salient texts.

One of these is a brief dialogue, more dramatic than narrative in format, but always included in the short-story section of Soldevila's production: with the title of 'El pretendent' [The Suitor], in *El senyoret Lluís* [Young Mr Lluís] (1926: 137–44), and as 'Una altra Ventafocs' [Another Cinderella] in *Històries barcelonines* [Barcelona Stories] (1950: 133–38). This is an inverted reworking of the Gospel story of Martha and Mary (St Luke, 10. 38–42), in a key adjusted to bourgeois pragmatism and flavoured with a corresponding dose of frivolity: Soldevila's version has as the chosen one not the lazy and contemplative Maria/Elena but her diligent and hard-working sister Marta/Isabel.

The other story, one of this author's several masterpieces in miniature, is 'Paradís perdut' [Paradise Lost] (Soldevila 1950: 197–210). What better way to exalt the work ethic — something clearly associated of course with the reality principle — than to set it up in competition with regular opportunities for sexual satisfaction: that is, with the pleasure principle *par excellence*? Who better to personify this conflict of interests than an ageing and austere gynaecologist who, either on the initiative of an attractive midwife or set up by his medical colleagues, is provided with the opportunity for a quick bit of professional misconduct? An emergency call to another case, together with gratifying anticipation of the sense of fulfilment in store there, is more than sufficient to compensate the good doctor for missing the chance on offer of a piece of 'paradise lost', for declining the earlier 'autèntica invitació al vals...' [genuine invitation to the dance...][19] (1950: 209).

The Procedures of *noucentista* Narrative

Three major procedures that are characteristic (though not exclusively so) of *noucentista* narrative enable us to exemplify the movement's appropriately called 'arbitrary' poetics. In specifically rhetorical terms, these are metalepsis, ellipsis and cataphora. All three are deployed in the service of an ironic, distanced or even facetious intention (*eutrapelia*). A few samples will suffice.

Metalepsis, a generally broader and more sustained 'displacement' than simple metonymy, which is centred on a single word: so 'L'armari' [The Cupboard] (Carner 1922: 33–40) is the piece of furniture on to which is directed, chastely, the conjugal voluptuousness in principle more inherent in 'bedroom'.

The eponymous protagonist of 'El dentista apassionat' [The Passionate Dentist] (Carner 1922: 65–72), on account of his profession, transfers the typical anxious lover's behaviour of pulling the petals from a daisy to the job of extracting one after another the teeth of an unsuspecting patient, one of the first to visit his surgery.

The 'guests at the monastery' ('Els hostes del convent' [Carner 1922: 97–102]) are an unsavoury group of thieves who abuse the hospitality of a community of pious monks to the point that the latter eventually are in danger, almost, of having to resort to similar scrounging in order to stay alive. This tale can be read as an allusive, parabolic comparison directed against the behaviour of concert-goers whose sole intention is to meet up with the opposite sex and bring down to their own uncouth level the people who simply want to listen to the music. Still with Carner, 'El secret' [The Secret] (1922: 109–15) puts the case for eyeing up, not the young lady that one wishes to attract and win over, but the other young lady she is with. (It is hard to think of a more concrete representation of Freud's *Verschiebung*, or of a sharper illustration of how effective in practice this 'displacement' of the libido can be.)

In this same line, 'La sospitosa voluptat' [Suspicious Sensuality] by Carles Soldevila (1917: 139–51) seems at first to be about the monthly trips made by a shepherd to the town of Granollers, to go to the brothel. This is what the other characters in the story believe, and the reader is also drawn into the same plausible interpretation until such speculation is dissolved in the disclosure that the man goes to town to visit the barber's shop, for the ecstatic delight of having his head brushed with an implement 'que sembla un corró' [a bit like a rolling pin] (1917: 151).

Ellipsis, or the suppression of any detail or superfluous information deemed irrelevant for plot development: stories which function thanks to — or in spite of — all sorts of jumps, empty spaces, omissions, words which translate into colloquial language the Greek concept of ἔλλειψις. Among many examples in this category are Duran Reynals's 'Història d'un plaga' (1918: 19–49), 'Vida d'un actor' by Alexandre Plana (1923: 93–134), and 'El petit Rovira' by Martínez Ferrando (1930: 109–65), all three considered above in the section on *déclassement*.

However, the most salient exponent of plot-development through ellipsis is without doubt Joan Sacs, whose reputation as writer of short stories remains even less prominent than his standing as a cartoonist (under the pseudonym of 'Apa') or as a painter (who signed with his true name of Feliu Elias). In his literary guise he purposefully cultivated a caustic outlook and manner which puts him more in line with the avant-garde sensibility displayed by the Sabadell Group[20] than with the simple, ironic anti-sentimentalism beloved of *Noucentisme*. And he is very adept at administering the movement's very particular *arbitrarietat*, as defined by Xènius/Ors, which frees narrative composition from the imperatives of nineteenth-century Romantic *costumisme*, of positivist Naturalism and of general cause-and-effect linearity in exposition.

Cataphora, or unexpected resolution (the 'twist in the tail/tale', English has an advantage here) which encourages the reader to return to the beginning of the story and re-read it afresh. 'El tresor dels fantasiosos' [Treasure for the Fanciful] (Soldevila 1926: 145–50) subtly unmasks a professional cock-and-bull specialist whose grand display of megalomania persuades his indulgent interlocutor to give him just enough money for a steak and chips supper.

'L'home que agafà una estrella' [The Man who Caught a Star] (Sacs 1929: 23–33) homes in on the sheer will-power — parodically taken to an extreme level of hyperbole — of a pathetic individual (always designated as the poor 'quidam') who can literally snatch from the firmament and keep hold of a star. His apparent success in achieving this marvellous feat conflicts with the confusion and amusing *capitis deminutio* experienced by an extremely learned professional astronomer who is called on to testify about the phenomenon.

Carner's 'Idil·li en tramvia' [Idyll on the Tram] (1922: 123–27) is one of the most vivid examples of cataphoric plot resolution, from the pen of an author who is as outstanding an exponent of this particular strategy as of so many others in the *noucentista* narrative stock-in-trade. The autodiegetic main character imagines himself, with increasing conviction, to have fallen for a young woman on the same tram as him, after just a couple of glances exchanged. When she stands up to alight, it becomes clear that she is 'coixeta' [lame, poor thing] (127). The ironic self-deflation, with its distinctly anaphrodisiac note, is a fine example of rhetorical chleuasm.

An additional attraction of the previous story derives from the parallelism that can be made with another one which is very different and which appeared considerably later last century, but with an amusingly similar resolution: 'La cadella' [The Young Bitch] (Dracs 1980: 11–19). We hear first the lewd propositioning made by a young prostitute (the 'bitch') to a potential client who never opens his mouth, and then it is revealed that she is disabled, driving a specially adapted car and needing a crutch.

The reader may well conclude, anyway, comparing Carner's text and that of the Ofèlia Dracs collective (written perhaps by Quim Monzó?), that nowadays the genre of the *idyll* is obsolete, and has been for a long time. The literary phenomenon to which the word corresponds has quite simply disappeared, like the traditional folk tale or the epic.

Final Note

The foregoing survey falls well short of what ultimately is needed: an interpretation, however schematic, of the whole body of narrative writing that can be associated broadly, for one reason or another, with the phenomenon of Catalan *Noucentisme*. We have essayed some soundings which might serve as initial hypotheses centred both on some specific ideological positions and on certain formal procedures typical of the movement. And it is hoped that these pages can be a contribution to the full and proper examination of the subject.

Basically, the narrative corpus addressed here can be clearly seen as a reflection, a concretion and amplification of values and attitudes which the *catalanista* middle classes of the early twentieth century aspired to, and endeavoured to put into practice. In this they were behaving like their counterparts across Europe as a whole.

What stands out are: the suppression of instinctiveness in any context; attenuation of conflict in every situation where it might arise; ironic relativization of the great imponderables of human existence, be they at the individual or the collective level.

Preference for analogical formulation in all spheres — deemed more effective than deductive logic, even though the two processes are complementary — encourages the shunning of deictic expression in favour of the parabolic alternative. And, in the framework of *Noucentisme*'s standards of rigour and discipline, the procedures deployed serve — whether in prose or in poetry, either deliberately or unknowingly — to substantiate anew the venerable maxim of Ramon Llull: 'on pus escura és la semblança, pus altament entén l'enteniment qui aquella semblança entén', which could be paraphrased as 'the more obscure the image, the greater is the understanding derived by the person who properly interprets it' (Llull 1989: 72). This is a demanding prescription both for writers and for readers. It arises from and also tends to induce deliberate anagogy. In other words, rather than being an old-fashioned mode of instructive moralizing, what is entailed is a strategy to produce a more transcendental intellectual and behavioural renovation, even if this is conceived of, or simply just intuited, only for the long term. That 'long-term' ambition about which, from its progressively secular millennialism, Catalan national affirmation has always been and remains anxiously concerned. This is a constant which has been duly acknowledged in the historiographical perspective referring to ideological and political realities;[21] but it remains as something still to be properly explored through work centred on literature and the corpus of literary criticism. Poetry will stand to the fore, no doubt;[22] the essay and the pamphlet will nevertheless have to be taken properly into account, and this applies even more to the attention called for by narrative.

Works Cited

ALONSO, VICENT. 1992. *Entre la poesia en prosa i el conte literari (sobre la literatura d'E. Martínez Ferrando)* (Barcelona: Institut Universitari de Filologia Valenciana and Publicacions de l'Abadia de Montserrat)

BARBAL, MARIA. 2013. 'Prudenci Bertrana: el desig de crear', in *Llibres, monstres i catedrals: 'Josafat' de Prudenci Bertrana*, ed. by Xavier Pla (Girona: Documenta Universitària), pp. 17–33

BRUNET, MANUEL. 2014 [1925/1943]. *El meravellós desembarcament dels grecs a Empúries. L'Empordà i els empordanesos*, ed. by Francesc Montero (Girona: Diputació de Girona)

CAMPILLO, MARIA. 1983. *El conte de 1911 a 1939* (Barcelona: Edicions 62)

CARNER, JOSEP. 1922. *La creació d'Eva i altres contes* (Barcelona: Editorial Catalana)

——. 1925. 'La granota alegre i la trista (Conte per a les hores de depressió)', *La Veu de Catalunya*, 1 January, p. 1

——. 1928. 'Elogi de la lítote', *La Veu de Catalunya*, 21 July, p. 1

——. 1930. 'De la ironia, encara', *La Publicitat*, 22 January, p. 1

——. 1992 [1957]. *Poesia*, ed. by Jaume Coll (Barcelona: Quaderns Crema)

DRACS, OFÈLIA [col·lective pseudonym]. 1980. *Deu pometes té el pomer* (Barcelona: Tusquets Editors)

DUPONT, JACQUES. 1980. 'El mètode parabòlic de Jesús, avui', *Qüestions de vida cristiana*, 104: 7–24

——. 1981. *Per què en paràboles?* (Montserrat: Publicacions de l'Abadia de Montserrat)

DURAN REYNALS, EUDALD. 1918. *Quatre històries* (Barcelona: Publicacions de «La Revista»)

——. 1952. *Proses completes* (Barcelona: Editorial Selecta)

ECO, UMBERTO. 1987. *Dels miralls* (Barcelona: Destino)

LLULL, RAMON. 1989. *Fèlix o el Libre de meravelles*, in *Obres selectes de Ramon Llull*, vol. II, ed. by Antoni Bonner (Mallorca: Editorial Moll)

LÓPEZ-PICÓ, J[OSEP] M[ARIA]. 1922. *Lleures barcelonins* (Barcelona: Editorial Catalana)

MARTÍNEZ FERRANDO, ERNEST. 1924. *Històries i fantasies* (Barcelona: Editorial Catalana)

——. 1930. *Tres històries cruels* (Badalona: Edicions Proa)

MONTERO, FRANCESC. 2014. 'Estudi introductori', in Manuel Brunet, *El meravellós des-embarcament dels grecs a Empúries. L'Empordà i els empordanesos* (Girona: Diputació de Girona), pp. 5–35

MURGADES, JOSEP. 1987a. 'El Noucentisme', in *Història de la literatura catalana*, vol. IX, ed. by Joaquim Molas (Barcelona: Editorial Ariel), pp. 9–72

——. 1987b. 'Eugeni d'Ors: verbalitzador del Noucentisme', in Various Authors, *El Noucentisme* (Barcelona: Publicacions de l'Abadia de Montserrat), pp. 59–77

——. 2014. 'Aforística adiàfora', in Various Authors, *Som per mirar (II): estudis de literatura i crítica oferts a Carles Miralles* (Barcelona: Publicacions i Edicions de la Universitat de Barcelona), pp. 295–317

——. 2018. 'El Noucentisme: a l'anagogia per l'analogia', in *El Noucentisme: un nou discurs per al segle XXI. Actes del I Simposi internacional sobre el Noucentisme 2014* (Sitges: Consorci del Patrimoni de Sitges), pp. 53–79

ORS, EUGENI D'. 1911. 'Una contribución a la filosofía', *Cataluña*, 175: 81–82

——. 2004 [1911]. *La Ben Plantada*, ed. by Xavier Pla (Barcelona: Quaderns Crema)

PLANA, ALEXANDRE. 1923. *A l'ombra de Santa Maria del Mar* (Barcelona: Editorial Catalana)

RIBA, CARLES. 1924. *L'ingenu amor*, illustrated by Josep Obiols (Barcelona: Editorial Catalana)

——. 1992. *L'ingenu amor*, in *Obres completes /5. Narrativa*, ed. by with an Introduction by Enric Sullà (Barcelona: Edicions 62), pp. 189–266

RUSIÑOL, SANTIAGO. 1901. *Cigales i formigues: quadro líric en un acte* (Barcelona: Tipografia de L'Avenç)

——. 1951 [1907] *L'auca del senyor Esteve*, with an Introduction by Carles Soldevila (Barcelona: Selecta)

SACS, JOAN/FELIU ELIAS. 1929. *Vida i mort dels barcelonins* (Sabadell: La Mirada)

——. 1970. *Vida i mort dels barcelonins* (Barcelona: Editorial Selecta)

SOLDEVILA, CARLES. 1917. *L'abrandament* (Barcelona: Editorial Catalana)

——. 1926. *El senyoret Lluís* (Barcelona: Llibreria Catalònia)

——. 1929. *Una nit a Bonrepòs* (Barcelona: Les Ales Esteses)

——. 1950. *Històries barcelonines* (Barcelona: Editorial Selecta)

SUREDA BLANES, JOSEP. 2005 [1930]. *La princesa que tenia el rellotge aturat*, in *Històries de paper*, ed. by Pere Rosselló Bover (Barcelona: Publicacions de l'Abadia de Montserrat), pp. 33–53

TASIS I MARCA, RAFAEL. 1954. *La novel·la catalana* (Barcelona: Dalmau i Jover, Editors)

TUSQUETS, JOAN. 1989. *L'imperialisme cultural d'Eugeni d'Ors* (Barcelona: Columna)

UCELAY-DA CAL, ENRIC. 2003. *El imperialismo catalán: Prat de la Riba, Cambó, D'Ors y la conquista moral de España* (Barcelona: Edhasa)

YATES, ALAN. 1975. *Una generació sense novel·la?* (Barcelona: Edicions 62)

Notes to Chapter 12

1. The couplet is attributed to Nicholas of Lyra or to Augustine of Dacia, quoted by Umberto Eco in 'L'espístola XIII, l'al·legorisme medieval, el simbolisme modern' (Eco 1987: 288).

2. Forty years after the publication of the book by Alan Yates (1975), it is lamentable that there has been no other general study on the Catalan novel and other narrative forms between the late nineteenth and early twentieth centuries, to fill out the panorama and provide more up-to-date interpretation.

3. On this aspect there is still barely anything more helpful than Campillo (1983).

4. In a chapter from a book with a strange Gothic title, from the pen of a creative (and how!) personality one can read the following atrocity: 'l'època noucentista, que havia renegat de la novel·la i de la moral burgesa [!], que no s'interessava per la Literatura [!!] i, en general, per la cultura [!!!] [...]' [the epoch of *Noucentisme*, which had renounced novel-writing and bourgeois morality [!], showing no interest in Literature [!!] and, in general, for culture [!!!] [...]' (Barbal 2013: 20). This is how a certain kind of illustrious intellect interprets and pronounces on the history of the country.

5. 'Lítote [...] aquesta modèstia graciosa i tota intencionada que sembla esveltir el pensament mateix [...] no hi ha fina civilització sense eufemismes, ni bell estil sense lítotes' [Litotes [...] that charming, quite deliberate modesty which seems to make thought itself more slender and agile [...] there is no refined civilization without euphemisms, nor any elegant style without litotes' (Carner 1928).

6. '[La ironia,] aquella higiènica virtut intel·lectual, defensa púdica de l'esperit, exercisi d'esveltesa contra el monstruós, l'emfàtic, el despòtic i l'estúpid' [[irony,] that hygienic intellectual virtue, modest defence of the spirit, exercise in lithe gracefulness against everything that is monstrous, emphatic despotic and stupid] (Carner 1930).

7. 'Les generacions es lliguen més amb imatges que no pas amb pensaments' [Generations are bound together more by images than by thoughts] (Carner 1925).

8. Dupont writes: 'Certament, el terreny de la paràbola encara no és el de la realitat a aconseguir; però el camí recorregut sobre el terreny parabòlic ha determinat ja el canvi d'òptica que farà veure la realitat sota el mateix angle que el parabolista' [The territory of parable is certainly not that of the reality aspired to. However, the way taken across the terrain of parable has already determined the change of perspective which makes reality visible from the same angle as that of the parable-teller] (1981: 37).

9. J. M. López Picó (1922: 111) formulated one of his 'moralitats' [moralities] along the same line pointing to postponement of immediate gratification: '*Bon consell*. Jovençà enamorat: si la donzella et somriu, ¿per què vols besar-la? ¿No saps que la teva goluderia no et deixarà contemplar més aquest somrís?' [*Good Advice*. Young man, the young lady might smile at you, but it does not mean that you must kiss her. Don't you realize that satisfying your bodily appetite will prevent you from contemplating ever again that smile?]

10. (Translator's note) The title defies adequate translation, being an allusion to feminine perfection embodied in the central character Teresa.

11. Rafael Tasis i Marca (1954: 56) used the term to disparage the whole narrative output of d'Ors.

12. There were even some voices calling for the work to be included in the *Index librorum prohibitorum*. See Tusquets (1989: 132) on this episode and on the conciliatory judgement pronounced by the Capuchin Miquel d'Esplugues to the effect that *La Ben Plantada* 'manca del rigor teològic indispensable perquè mereixi anar a l'Índex. No basta per ser heretge la pretensió de ser-ho' [lacks the theological rigour which would ensure its deserved inclusion in the Index. Pretending to be a heretic is not enough to turn a person into one].

13. Published also in Martínez Ferrando (1930: 187–203) but with the title 'El suïcidi de Jordi Ventura' [The Suicide of Jordi Ventura] and incorporating several other substantive changes.

14. Observe Eugeni d'Ors's own ironic definition of irony: 'Llamamos *ironía* [...] no a un *disimulo*, como dicen los retóricos, sino a toda *adhesión intelectual incompleta*' [We use *irony* to mean not a *dissimulation*, as the rhetoricians say, but any kind of *incomplete intellectual affiliation*] (Ors 1911: 82, n. 1).

15. For an account of the work's contemporary reception, see Montero (2014: 11–23).

16. Observe also the antiphrastic nature of the title: the two characters certainly do live at the top of a hill (*cf.* the theme of ascension as a cliché in the literature of *Modernisme*), but the story's metaphorical implication is that they behave as though they had ended up at the bottom of a well.

17. Reproduced, with the title 'Som rics' [We Are Rich], in Soldevila (1950: 86–102).

18. The cruelty is more than relative, despite the title *Tres històries cruels* [Three Cruel Stories] of the collection in which this piece was published. Vicent Alonso (1992: 72) rightly stressed '[el] tractament comprensiu i tendre dels personatges i de les situacions' [the sympathetic and tender treatment of the characters and situations] in all three stories.

19. Is it too far-fetched to read into this formulation a euphemistic *noucentista* periphrasis for 'incitement to coitus'?

20. It is significant that this author's collection of stories, *Vida i mort dels barcelonins* [Life and Death of the Barcelonans] (1970 [1929]), came out under the imprint of La Mirada, the publishing house identified with the Sabadell Group.

21. According to Enric Ucelay-da Cal, 'todas las corrientes ideológicas de la Cataluña contemporánea

(sean carlismo, republicanismo anticlerical, catalanismo o libertarismo militante) han sido quiliásticas, de uno u otro modo ancladas en la convicción de que era inminente la parusía, el fin del tiempo con la llegada del reinado milenario en la tierra' [all of the ideological currents in contemporary Catalonia (be they Carlism, anticlerical republicanism, militant Catalanism or libertarianism) have been chiliastic in nature, anchored in one way or another in a conviction about the imminence of *parousia*, the end of time with the arrival of God's millennial kingdom on earth] (2003: 142).

22. A tiny but no less concrete instance of this excited anticipation of *parousia* is to be found in the final stanza of Josep Carner's 'Cançonetes del «Déu-nos-do»' [Songs of Would to God that...] (in *Bella terra, bella gent* [Fine Country, Fine People] [Carner 1992: 136–41]): 'Però mentre l'Enyorada | viu secreta i viu gement, | Déu nos do fer-li seguici, | cor ardit, braç amatent, | una pedra a la bassetja, | la bassetja dins el vent' [But while ever the Lady of our hearts and our longing | Lives sequestered and moaning, | Would to God we can stay in her retinue, | With hearts afire and with eager arms, | Each with a stone in our sling, | And our sling whirling in the breeze].

CHAPTER 13

The Colour of the Heavens: Vision and Death in Five Twentieth-Century Catalan Authors

Joan Ramon Resina

Stanford University

In the essays written as a young man that he published in 1938 with the title *Noces*, Albert Camus ascribed to the inhabitants of the Mediterranean countries an intrinsic incapacity for discussing death and colours ('De la mort et des couleurs, nous ne savons pas discuter' [We don't know how to talk about colours and death] [1950: 37]). It is striking to observe in such talkative peoples a natural taciturnity regarding two essential facts of their respective cultures. The *pied noir* Camus, of Minorcan extraction on his mother's side, synthesized in a concise formula the relationship between death and vision, and that between these two factors and language. This specific concomitance is also to be found in such major authors of twentieth-century Catalan literature as Joan Maragall, Salvador Espriu, Josep Pla, Pere Quart and Mercè Rodoreda.

Camus was surprised by the fact that Mediterranean man, garrulous by nature, always ready to speak on any topic whatever, has extremely impoverished ideas about death. This, he thought, demonstrated that we really cannot cope with anything really simple: 'Qu'est-ce que le bleu et que penser du bleu? C'est la même difficulté pour la mort' [What is blueness and how can we think about blueness? Death poses the same problem] (1950: 37). Blueness, Death: the infinite depth of perception, its ultimate, definitive stalling. This constellation of ideas points us towards the most famous lines of Maragall, in his *Cant espiritual* [Song of my Soul]:

> Amb quins altres sentits me'l fareu veure
> Aquest cel blau damunt de les muntanyes,
> I el mar immens, i el sol que pertot brilla?
> Deu-me en aquests sentits l'eterna pau
> I no voldré més cel que aquest cel blau.
>
> [Through which other senses could you reveal
> That blue heaven over the mountain tops,
> The immense sea and the sun shining all around?
> Give me in these senses peace eternal
> And I'll seek no other heaven than this blue sky.] (1929: 176)

These lines raise a question, followed by a plea which is almost an offer, as though Maragall were negotiating with God to limit his aspiration for 'peace eternal' in exchange for the continued assuagement of his senses. As far as I know, no one has noticed that the last two lines answer the question formulated in the preceding three: 'Through which other senses...?' is the question. And the reply: 'through these that you have now, in this life; there are no other ones'. Blueness is an effect of light filtered through the earth's atmosphere, the impression in the human brain of radiation in a spectrum compatible with the retina. The blue of the sky and man's senses are one and the same thing. This is why the poet offers to limit desire to his capacity for pure perception of colour. He is asking for a blueness that endures forever. This is the Faustian moment of Mediterranean man. In Goethe's poem, Faust wishes that time would stand still. He is Nordic man, all activity and movement, reining in his impulses when his life is slipping towards its end. For such a person, perception of beauty is one step away from death. On the other hand, if we are to believe Camus, Mediterranean man revels in his senses while they are still strong, but when he feels that his body is in decline he accepts death as a natural fatality. The lucidity which shines in his eyes bonds him with ancient man, who, when the end was near, did not cling to metaphysical illusions.

> Et je ne sais pourquoi, devant ce cri de pierre lugubre et solennel, Djémila, inhumaine dans la chute du soleil, devant cette mort de l'espoir et des couleurs, j'étais sûr qu'arrivés à la fin d'une vie, les hommes dignes de ce nom doivent retrouver ce tête-à-tête, renier les quelques idées qui furent les leurs et recouvrer l'innocence et la vérité qui luit dans le regard des hommes antiques en face de leur destin. Ils regagnent leur jeunesse, mais c'est en étreignant la mort.

> [Facing this murky and solemn vociferation in stone — Djémila, inhuman in the sunset — facing this death of hope and of colours, I do not know why I was certain that at life's end men worthy of this name must encounter again this one-on-one, renounce the few ideas they had and recover the innocence and truth which shines in the eyes of ancient men when they face up to their destiny. They recover their youth, but it is when they are embracing death.]
> (1950: 36)

There was a good deal of Nietzsche in the affirmation of the senses against a parallel world of ideas. The same Nietzsche who said of Plato that he was the finest plant of Antiquity, blaming him for inventing the notion of pure spirit and the dangerous error of the good in itself (1995: 566).

Maragall too felt the influence of Nietzsche. In a letter written in 1893, he said that he was excited by the German philosopher's 'aristocràcia dels forts, dels que viuen la vida forta i tenen major receptivitat que la majoria pel goig de viure' [aristocracy of the strong, of those who live aggressively and surpass the majority of humans in receptivity to the joy of being alive] (quoted in Corredor 1960: 65). Such vitalism seems rather unusual in a bourgeois Catholic poet, and as J. M. Corredor pointed out in the conservative *Diario de Barcelona*: 'El fet que Nietzsche hagi estat introduït a Catalunya per un diari conservador, portaveu d'una burgesia sense inquietuds intel·lectuals, és una prova més del confusionisme que regnava en aquell temps' [The fact that Nietzsche was introduced to Catalonia through a conservative newspaper, the mouthpiece of a bourgeoisie bereft of intellectual preoccupations, is one more sign of the intellectual confusion dominant at that time] (1960: 66). But as a Mediterranean, Maragall admired the classical world and rejected transcendence. Only a few days after the birth of his first child, baptized Helena with intended classical echoes, he wrote to Josep Soler i Miquel: 'Tots els nostres optimismes són malaltissos; són resignacions o són merament transcendentals. La vida contemplada per sobre i en total és hermosa: la vida viscuda és trista...' [There is something unhealthy about our manifestations of optimism: they are either a form of resignation or they are merely transcendental. Life contemplated superficially and in its totality is beautiful: living is sad...] (quoted in Corredor 1960: 64). And what makes life sad — as the immediately preceding passage affirms — is the inevitability of death.

Half a century after Maragall's death in 1911, Pere Quart responded in *Vacances pagades* [Paid Holidays]:

> Els sentits, els sentits!
> En darrer cas acceptaríem
> la mort com una renaixença
> de l'esperit, però amb els accessoris
> i tot el parament d'home mortal,
> perfets, consolidats per sempre.
> Crec en la resurrecció de la carn.
> Dic de la carn!
> Em sents, botxí?

> [The senses, the senses!
> At the end of the day we'd accept
> death as a kind of rebirth
> of the spirit, but with the accessories
> and all the trappings of mortal man,
> perfectly saved, consolidated for ever.
> I believe in the resurrection of the flesh.
> And I mean the flesh!
> Can you hear me, executioner?] (1981: 93–94)

This is pre-Christian man, again. He would not know how to respond to the offer of an afterlife and haggles with God over the terms and conditions of death. Twenty years on from this poem, with only five more to live, Pere Quart once again squared up to Maragall in his *Cant d'un home* [Song of a Man], using as an epigraph the opening words of Maragall's *Cant espiritual*: 'Si el món ja és tan formós [...]' [If the world is already so beauteous [...]]. Pere Quart adjusts this idea as follows:

> Em puny el cor aquesta visió
> d'un món formós i monstruós alhora!
> Sempre per a la mort, per a la mort
> tantes naixences, tantes renaixences!

> [My heart is riven by this view
> of a world both lovely and monstrous!
> Always for death, for death alone
> so many births and rebirths.] (1981: 55)

Pere Quart is exasperated by the 'greater birth' that Maragall expected from death. So many births and rebirths serve only to exaggerate the importance of death, and he desires not a blue sky but rather diffuse light, the gradual extinction of life. The 'eternal peace' that Maragall in his euphoric celebration of the senses wanted to merge with the intense blueness of the sky was a contradiction in terms. Resting in peace requires dimmed light and silence:

> Fora tan bo que la Natura entera,
> éssers vivents i forces en renou,
> tot aquest Tot, Senyor, distant o pròxim
> a poc a poc tendissin al repòs
> i, encara més — parlo per mi — , al silenci
> i a la llum indirecta, com de llimbs!

> [I would like the whole of Nature,
> living beings and agitated forces,
> the whole of this Oneness, Lord, near or far,
> to slowly decline into repose
> and, even more — speaking for myself —, into silence
> and indirect light, as in Limbo!] (1981: 54)

Once again, transcendence gives way to a lucidity that refuses comforting narratives. What has a Creator got to do with an incomprehensible reality and a nothingness that is even more incomprehensible? Life and death are part of the wheel that must stop turning if the word 'eternity' is to mean anything at all:

> La fe en un Cel ulterior em falla
> i el No-res — res de res! — no el puc concebre.
> Doncs si és així, deixeu-me que us invoqui:
> Senyor ¿per què, afligit o decebut,
> no suspeneu el vol de l'Aventura?
> Esbravat ja l'orgull de Creador
> ¿encara us plau sentir-vos responsable
> d'una funesta Realitat sotmesa
> a les estultes regles de l'Atzar?
> Atureu la carrera, el curs, el Temps,
> occiu la Mort i no acreixeu la Vida!
> Eternitat és goig en quietud,
> és bellesa perfecta, imperfectible!

> Us parla un cuc raríssim, ja ho sabeu,
> i que es pensa que pensa...

> Senyor, misericòrdia!

> [Faith in any ulterior Heaven fails me
> and Nothingness — absolute nothingness —
> I cannot conceive.
> So let me invoke you directly:
> Lord, in your distress or disappointment,
> why do you not interrupt the flight of the Adventure?
> Now that pride in your Creation has subsided,
> do you still enjoy feeling responsible

> for a baneful Reality subjected
> to the senseless rules of Chance?
> Stop the race, the course, Time,
> kill Death and do not foster Life!
> Eternity is delight in quiet,
> it is perfect beauty, unenhanceable!
>
> An odd worm is talking, as you know,
> one that thinks he's thinking...
>
> Lord, have mercy!] (1981: 55–56)

Once the binomial colour/death is broken, the sky is no longer blue but an indeterminate colour, ambiguous like death and indescribable like nothingness. Nothingness — which Mediterranean man, his retina filled with images, cannot imagine — is as inaccessible as the blueness of the ulterior Heaven that Maragall struggles to conceive. The Catalans' Mediterranean legacy protects them from metaphysical vertigo and disinclines them to ask 'Why should there be *anything*, instead of *nothingness*?' This aversion to the void, the spontaneous cleaving to impressions, explains the limited metaphysical concern of Catalan writers. Pere Quart, whose *Poesia empírica* [Empirical Poetry] enshrines this reluctance in the title, says of himself: 'Les inquietuds de naturalesa diguem-ne transcendent, qui les pot vèncer? Amb tot, durant llargs períodes de la seva existència [el poeta] les ha oblidades' [Who can overcome so-called transcendental preoccupations? Nonetheless, for long periods of his existence [this poet] has ignored them] (1981: 14).

The disinclination to engage in speculative thought is summed up by Pere Quart in a sentence expressing a view frequent among Catalans: 'en definitiva, és més urgent viure que filosofar' [ultimately, it is more important to live than to philosophize]' (1981: 14). In fact, the opposition 'to live/to think' is in itself metaphysical, because it conceives philosophy as a variant of nothingness, insofar as it relates to the non-existing or to an 'after-life'. Catalan semantics show that aversion to transcendentalism is ethnologically based. Catalan uses the same word, 'res', to denominate 'some*thing*' or its absence, so that the positive concept — the some*thing* — coexists with its negation, no*thing*, just as the electron and the proton coexist in an electromagnetic field.

It is also true that the ancient Greeks themselves were incapable of imagining nothingness, which is why they filled the void with a substance — tenuous and invisible but still material — which they called 'ether'. They needed it in order to explain the transmission of forces such as light and how the planets keep their places in space. But it also enabled them to get round the paradox of the denial of existence. We must remember that the Greek numerical system did not admit the concept of zero, not to mention negative numbers, values less than nothing. This same paradox led Maragall to accept the hypothesis of God's existence. Agnosticism about the possibility of capturing reality through incorporeal senses and scepticism regarding the idealist foundations of knowledge compensated him for the inability to conceive of non-existence. What daunted Maragall was not so much non-existence as the possibility of 'non-sentience'. For him the senses are the root of consciousness and the arbiters of existence. A Romantic pantheist, Maragall sees the universe impregnated with divinity, in the same way that the Greeks saw it pervaded by the ether. God is the force spanning the emptiness. Thus, spurning the body amounts to denying the creation, and Maragall imagines death as a calming of the senses in the permanence of colour. As subtle as ether, blueness is the metaphor for whatever positivity divides death from nothingness.

While in his first collection of poems, *Vacances pagades*, Pere Quart had insisted on the continuity of material reality, in the poem written in old age — in a manner he qualifies as empirical — his vision is radically altered and he asks God to put a stop to time, that is, to one of the two essential components of human reality. The poet views life and death as a game of chance which defies logic and disqualifies justification according to some providential plan. Randomness negates the architecture of the cosmos and the moral organization of life. If a throw of the dice abolishes destiny, the only possible salvation is to sneak between the Scylla of life and the Charybdis of death; to stop everything and, leaving joy and fear behind, rest in the quiet beauty of the unchangeable. The mercy for which Pere Quart beseeches God is that He should disown His creation, resolving it into something different. Man merely pretends to reason. Pere Quart sees him as a bizarre annelid that believes it is made of the same substance as the angels.

When he writes that terrible '[s]empre per a la mort, per a la mort' [always for death, for death alone] one has the feeling that Pere Quart has in mind not only Maragall but also the Salvador Espriu of *Llibre de Sinera* [Book of Sinera] (1963). Indeed, Espriu opens that collection by evoking Death as a relentless power:

> Remor de cops d'aixada, no la sents?
> Rera les altes tanques de paret.
> Sense repòs, però molt lentament,
> enllà de la cleda contínua del temps.

> [The sound of the mattock scraping, don't you hear it?
> Behind the high enclosing walls.
> Without resting, but very slowly,
> beyond time's continuous enclosure.] (1977: 405)

At the boundary of time all that can be heard are the unremitting strokes of the mattock excavating death and circumscribing a progressively empty domain. This ephemeral location, within which poetry becomes possible as a reflection on transience and the limit of life, is the same 'homeland' that Espriu had already mentioned in the second poem of *Cementiri de Sinera* [Sinera Cemetery] (1946): a geography centred on the black hole of death, the great void which dynamizes life. This austere setting is not only a 'petita pàtria' [small homeland]; it is the only conceivable home: 'Aquesta mar, Sinera, / turons de pins i vinya, /pols de rials […]' [This sea, Sinera,/ hillsides of pine trees and vines, / dusty stream-beds […]] (1977: 151). The poet goes on immediately to affirm: 'No estimo / res més' [I love / nothing else] (1977: 151). Here the verb 'to love' has an ontological meaning as well as an estimative function. (Espriu's affirmation of the things that define his being at home in the world amounts to the same *horror vacui* as Pere Quart's confession: 'i el

No-res […] no el puc concebre' [I cannot comprehend Nothingness].) In this same tenor Espriu adds, among the things worthy of the same subjective attachment, 'l'ombra / viatgera d'un núvol' [the passing shadow of a cloud] (1977: 151) — impalpability, instability: *not* the blue sky but the insinuation upon the earth of an insubstantial shape which momentarily breaks the sky's uniformity. This shadow is an image of time, perceptible against the background of eternity, in the same way that movement is perceptible only in relation to something static.

A sentence from Saint Paul (II Corinthians 7. 10) provides the epigraph to *Llibre de Sinera*: 'The sorrow of the world worketh death'. And Espriu's world is certainly a sad one, with life sequestered by the certainty of death. What is surprising, though, is the Pauline inversion of the relationship between emotion and occurrence, because we generally think of sorrow, a subjective emotion, as an effect rather than a cause of death. Saint Paul's logic connects sorrow with sinfulness, and sin — corruption — is the antechamber of death. However, in Espriu sin is displaced by consciousness. The world is a sad place because awareness of death is one of the human faculties. Thus, 'Hi ha tristesa / darrera les paraules' [Sadness lies / behind words] (1977: 234), as he had written earlier in a collection entitled precisely *Mrs Death* (1952). Without ontological grounding, the sky cannot be colour specific:

> No hi ha llum per tota la buidor del cel.
> Només uns cops d'aixada al fons del fred.
>
> [There is no light all through the sky's emptiness.
> Just the strokes of a mattock deep within the cold.] (1977: 405)

While Saint Paul sees spiritual sadness as the antithesis of the joy of salvation, for Espriu it is the subjective aspect of living in a world bounded by death. 'Damunt la terra bona s'estenia l'erm' [All over the good earth the waste land spread], we read in the second stanza of the first poem in *Llibre de Sinera* (1977: 405). This is not an image of the beauty that Maragall was sorry to leave behind, but a terrifying vision of the slow, unrelenting destruction of the human milieu. The strokes of the mattock behind the cemetery walls have turned into the noisy squads of labourers digging away in darkness. Death has penetrated to the heart of the everyday, overwhelming history and nature alike. The leafless vines are the landscape's skeleton, what remains of a world wasted by the ebbing of life. Overlooking the sea, Sinera cemetery — like Valéry's at Sète — anchors the poet's existential anguish; it is his 'small homeland'. Robert Harrison concludes from Einstein's theory of the space–time continuum that our perception of space is temporal, adding that it is also mortal in nature. We have already encountered this sentiment in Espriu. The landscape that he loves and the 'small homeland' centred on the cemetery are one and the same thing: a space grasped through the intuition of death. We love only what we know we can lose.

As one of the earliest instances of architecture, the cemetery suggests that the primordial motive for building must have been to shelter from time. In Mediterranean antiquity, the burial ground was the space on which history was founded. The rise of Mycenaean culture is associated with the excavation of two tomb circles from different epochs: the older from around 1600 BC, the newer from a century later. These circles were clearly bounded. They were a 'small homeland' with a cultural significance superior to that of the residential city, of which no remains of stone-built settlements, palaces or fortifications have been found. Made of stone, the burial sites were built with a different idea of temporality. Long duration was associated with death, as demonstrated by the circular form, an image of eternity, and by the fact that articles of value were deposited there: gold leaves, decorative objects, swords and other appurtenances of warfare (Finley 1983: 61–63). Burial alongside valuable belongings of the deceased suggests belief in the continuity of the individual's role after death. These tombs denote power and hierarchy, as do modern bourgeois cemeteries, where families rival in ostentation in death as much as in life.

In the course of his travels through the Mediterranean, Josep Pla was interested in funerary cultures. In 'Còrsega, l'illa dels castanyers' [Corsica, the Island of Chestnut Trees], an expanded version of a text first published in 1927 in *Revista de Catalunya*, Pla observes: 'Per a la gent de Còrsega, el fet més essencial de la vida humana sembla ésser la mort. Sobre la mort hi ha, a l'illa, un tresor amagat, recòndit, vivíssim, de poesia voluptuosa i esqueixada' [For the people of Corsica the most essential thing about human life seems to be death. The island contains a secret, secluded, yet extremely lively treasure of voluptuous if crude poetry] (1970: 239). Death is the defining fact of human existence. Heidegger described *Dasein*, the human existent, as a being-toward-death. Death 'limits and determines', he writes in *Being and Time* (1962: 277), not only in the sense of curtailing the possibilities of life but, above all, of creating the basic conditions of cognition. We can know only that which is limited and determinate, that which admits of a precise description in words. Pla insisted on the need to localize observation and on the superiority of description, the disciplined delineation of the outlines of things.

We have already identified limitation and determinateness in Espriu's 'small homeland' and in the poet's estimation of the essential elements of his surroundings, an austere equivalent of Maragall's 'beauteous world'. But death — which for Heidegger is an exclusively human experience — can be either authentic or inauthentic. Heidegger designates inauthentic death as 'expiration', relating it to the idea of a simple ending, the full stop of living. Authentic death, on the other hand, is an inalienable condition of *Dasein* (1962: 284), which defines the space within which *Dasein* can have authentic being.

In Corsica, Pla records some very ancient manifestations of mourning, the *lamenti* and the *voceri*. These are orally transmitted poetic forms of lamentation. As their name implies, the *lamenti* are songs of grieving. Pla explains that 'quan el cadàver ha estat produït per mort violenta els *lamenti* esdevenen delirants, indescriptiblement dramàtics' [when the cause of death was violent, the *lamenti* become delirious, indescribably dramatic] (1970: 239). Most interesting is the almost physical idea of the other world as an enduring replica of this one. There the dead person will find relatives and acquaintances, and conversations about memories and tales involving the community that he has left behind will be struck up. In this tradition death is a wicked person who is addressed most familiarly and abused like a villainous puppet (Pla 1970: 241–42). It is the equivalent of the executioner from whom Pere Quart demanded the resurrection of his body, as resurrection has been imagined by all Mediterranean peoples since antiquity. For the ancient Greeks, Hades was populated by shadows, like that of Anticlea, mother of Odysseus, who appears among the crowd of dead passing before the hero's eyes. Virgil too, in the corresponding episode in the *Aeneid*, shows Aeneas trying to embrace his father Anchises and grasping at thin air. But Virgil was a patrician influenced by the Greeks, who did not believe in resurrection. The idea of material continuity between this life and the next seems to have survived among the lower populace of the Italian Peninsula and its islands. The homely familiarity with the afterlife which Pla found in Corsica would later reappear in his down-to-earth version of Maragall's hymn. Pla asks God for permission to contemplate eternity at first hand, but only if he is allowed to leave now and then to go to the café to chat with his friends (1974: 435).

Pla's jocularity has some basis in history. In his book on the subject of death, Philippe Ariès observes that the medieval cemetery, together with the adjoining church, was the centre of social life. 'It took the place of the forum', he says (1981: 62). Imagining a conversation among the dead was only a short step away. (That step had already been taken by Dante in the *Divine Comedy*, but the topic would eventually receive the tone of down-to-earth neighbourliness in Juan Rulfo's novel *Pedro Páramo* [1955].) The word *cimeterium* had meant also a space of sanctuary in the immediacy of a church. It was the place where individuals could take refuge from earthly authorities, just like the corpses in the ground. This aspect is taken up by Espriu in *Cementiri de Sinera*, with the particularity that the graveyard has become a sanctuary of memory, the background to recollections of a life beset by death.

What most impressed Pla in Sicily was the importance of funeral customs: 'El tracte i la situació que els morts tenen en aquesta illa són tan aparatosos, tan afectuosos, tan considerables, que forçosament s'ha de reconèixer que a Sicília hi ha una conspiració permanent contra la mort, una negació de la mort, una impossibilitat de comprendre el que la mort és en realitat' [The treatment and the status accorded to the dead on this island are so ostentatious, so affectionate, so grand, that one is obliged to recognize that in Sicily there is a permanent conspiracy against death, a denial of death, an impossibility of understanding what death really is] (1970: 342). The idea of mortality dominant there, and generally in the Mediterranean, is the prolongation of life:

> un trànsit a un altre món caracteritzat pel fet d'ésser un món igual que aquest, que té, però, la particularitat que hom hi viu sense fer res, com si sempre fos festa, portant la millor roba, el barret nou i les sabates sense pols, els signes externs dels honors, si és que hom en té, els símbols del poder si és que hom en disposa. Només hi ha una diferència: és que els morts són morts.

> [a passage to another world characterized by the fact of it being a world just like this one, but with the peculiarity that its inhabitants live without lifting a finger, as though participating in perpetual revelry, dressed in their best clothes, with a new hat on and no dust on their shoes — the outward signs of status, if one has any, the symbols of power if one wields it. There is only one difference: the dead are well and truly dead.] (1970: 343)

Such *mise-en-scène* of death as a transition which changes nothing but fixes a person's social dimension permanently is a relic of the paganism that Pla questions in the same essay on Sicily.

> Sospito que el paganisme, el que als països del nord s'entén per paganisme, no ha existit ni en l'antiguitat, ni ara, ni mai. Aquesta concepció ideal del món antic és una disposició de l'esperit. En aquest sentit, el paganisme és, més que una cosa històrica, passada, un resultat possible [...], una concepció a imposar, a través del temps.

> [I suspect that paganism, what people understand by paganism in northern countries, never really existed in antiquity, nor does it exist nowadays, or ever. This ideal conception of the ancient world is simply a state of mind. Accordingly, rather than a feature of history, something belonging to the past, paganism is a possible outcome [...], a conception to be imposed in the course of time.] (1970: 339)

Interestingly, a few years after Pla's 'Còrsega, l'illa dels castanyers' appeared, the Italian anthropologist Ernesto de Martino published *Morte e pianto rituale* (1958), a book on funeral laments in southern Italy with many examples of this tradition. From this book, Robert Harrison (2003: 57) takes the idea that the objective of such ceremonies is to formalize and thus mitigate crises of grief. The rituals could well have this effect, but it seems to me that their main function, more than therapeutic or consolatory, is to socialize grief and depersonalize death, extending the sense of loss to the entire community. Socialization is the link between the rituals Martino observed and Mediterranean antiquity, specifically the impersonality of Mycenaean burial sites, which suggest collective rather than individual mourning.

Ceremonial lamentations and orchestrated manifestations of grief go back to the earliest times. Christianity attempted to banish them. Saint Paul saw in collective keening for the dead an expression of the natural despair of pagan man (1 Thessalonians 4. 13–14, quoted in Harrison 2003: 119). And Saint Augustine, in his *Confessions* (9. 12), asserts that he refrained from weeping at the death of his mother, Monica, '[f]or we did not think it right that a funeral such as hers should be celebrated with tears and groans and lamentations. These are ways in which people grieve for an utter wretchedness in death or a kind of total extinction' (quoted in Harrison 2003: 120).

Pla points out that in Corsica the public 'staging' of grief has moderated over the years. He considers it recessive and in the process of disappearing. The dwindling of the theatrical aspect of the leave-taking coincides with the privatization of death and the paring away of ceremonial which Ariès saw spreading throughout the area of Latin culture after the First World War. Until that time, an individual's death had disturbed the whole community. It was a public occasion. John Donne's poem, which Hemingway used as epigraph in *For Whom the Bell Tolls* (1940), had precisely this significance: 'Any man's death diminishes me, | Because I am involved in mankind'. Bereavement was communal, as was grieving. Recollecting his student years in Barcelona, Pla writes at considerable length about the burial services he witnessed there. These ceremonies constituted veritable public performances:

A mesura que l'enterrament caminava carrer avall, entre el borrissol d'arbres de les voreres, sortien als balcons els habitants dels pisos, senyores i senyors, amb els seus nens i nenes — i si els amos aquella tarda eren fora, les criades del servei. [...] Hi estan tan acostumats, que disposen d'una cara feta expressa per a sortir als balcons quan passen els enterraments.

[As the funeral proceeded down the street, through the foliage of the trees lining the pavement one could see the residents of the apartments on their balconies, women and their menfolk with all their children — and if the family was out that afternoon, the maids. [...] They are so used to it that they have a special face for standing on the balcony when funerals go by.] (1966: 316)

In the course of the twentieth century a new approach to death emerged, which, according to Ariès, was the opposite of everything that had gone before. Society has banished death, and routines go on without concern for the loss of a life or awareness that something important has happened. Exceptions are few and far between: people in powerful positions and statesmen are still objects of ceremonial mourning. For the rest, society manages 'disappearance', often in the custody of a hospital. If death occurs at home, funeral services relieve the family of any unwanted distress. Converted into an exclusively visual entity, the corpse is staged behind a glass in a funeral parlour before it is transported to the cemetery or the crematorium in a vehicle indistinguishable from the others. Thus is the *thing*, the object of embarrassment, evacuated. In the words of Ariès: 'A new image of death is forming: the ugly and hidden death' (1981: 569).

Mercè Rodoreda addressed the 'hidden away' death in *La mort i la primavera* [Death in Spring] with the motif of a woodcutter who carves his own coffin in a tree trunk and shuts himself in it to die unseen. A psychoanalytical perspective on the story opens up when this act is observed by the woodcutter's son from behind a hedge. Rodoreda inverts the primal scene: the child is not witnessing life's prelude but its equally obscene conclusion. The scene is oneiric, like most in this novel. Trees, says the narrator, seemed 'd'aquells que només veus quan estàs adormit' [like those that you only see when you are asleep] (1997: 247). This is the forest of the dead. People go there to die just when the springtime sun and sky conspire to give the ambience a colour reminiscent of Maragall's sky.

That this is an Oedipal scenario is confirmed by the mother's habit of hitting children and her bawling and shouting under the windows of couples on their wedding night. She is clearly obsessed with castration, a mania the novel associates with maternity. All the womenfolk in her family had displayed the same behaviour. In Rodoreda's world, castration is often a female prerogative. In *La plaça del Diamant* it is incumbent upon *senyora* Enriqueta, the neighbour who substitutes for the mother in Natàlia's sexual education and terrifies the young woman with her matriarchal lore. In Rodoreda's last novel, sexuality and death blossom in spring, the procreative season for plants and animals. It is the time of the year when the male protagonist is entranced by 'la pols de sofre que fa el casament de les flors' [the sulphurous dust produced by the marriage of flowers] (1997: 246).

Rodoreda contrasts Nature's cyclical time with historical time, a time of desolation and emptiness, pure uninterrupted duration. The village where the novel is set straddles a river, the classical image of linear time. With its foundations so precariously located, the place is beset with anxiety lest the houses be washed away by the torrent. This worry has given rise to an extraordinary ritual: each year a man goes into the river to check if the water has carried away the footing stones, and he is dragged by the current under the village, sometimes emerging with his face ripped off (1997: 244). Could this be an image of time erasing the personality? A rite of passage, like a baptism which dissolves what has gone before? An alchemical transformation? The destruction of facial features after ritual immersion signifies the price paid for, and the effect of, an extension of knowledge, since the submerged man is the only one who knows the hidden face of the village. In other words: finding out the secret foundations of the collective life demands the sacrifice of the personality. After undergoing the ritual, the protagonist reflects: 'potser la meva cara desfeta era la meva cara de debò, la que havia d'haver tingut sempre' [perhaps my disfigured face was the real one, the face I should always have had] (1997: 411). Beneath temporary accidents there is a permanent truth. This is why those who become faceless live separately and are at ease with themselves, 'perquè havien vist la veritat molt de la vora, com si haguessin tornat a néixer sense l'embranzida i l'embogiment de la primera vegada' [because they had seen the truth from very close quarters, as though they were reborn with none of the frenzy and the madness of the first time] (1997: 264). To be born, to be born again, as Pere Quart exclaimed, seeing in death nothing more than a quirk of Nature.

After settling in Romanyà de la Selva, Rodoreda read Pierre Teilhard de Chardin, the proponent of an evolutive theology according to which cosmic matter has evolved into forms of life in a process leading to a final point of absolute consciousness called the Omega point, which is the teleological motor of evolution. The goal is the unification of consciousness, humanity always tending towards a single psychic unit. Teilhard de Chardin thought that Christ is the organizing principle of the universe, its unifying centre. The body of Christ is, thus, cosmic. Not only does it spread throughout the whole universe, but it is an entirety that is being constantly created (Lyons 1982: 154–55). For Teilhard, the cross is an active force, a kind of alchemical chalice which transforms matter into spirit. 'La creu de l'arbre bullia, l'arbre anava paint' [The cross of the tree was boiling, the tree was digesting], says Rodoreda's protagonist about the cross that his father had carved in the bark of his tree before entombing himself in it (1997: 264). Death is a digestion and transformation of matter into a different state.

But what is interesting here is the Spinozan aspect of Teilhard's thought, the equilibrium between orthodoxy and pantheism, which earned him an admonition from the Holy Office in 1962. In this devout pantheism we encounter again the Maragall of the 'Cant espiritual' and the idea of human senses which do not die but evolve to contemplate the totality, the Omega point of the cosmic consciousness. Similarly but from an atheistic perspective, Camus affirms that 'le vrai, le seul progrès de la civilisation, celui auquel de temps en temps un homme s'attache, c'est de créer des morts conscientes' [the true, the only progress of civilization, the one to which a man clings from time to time, is the creation of conscious dead] (1950: 36).

Snatched by the torrential water, the protagonist of *La mort i la primavera* loses his eyes and his whole forehead, but afterwards, when he comes round, the first thing he notices is being dazzled. When he opens his eyes again, they have been strangely renewed, and looking at the river he sees the face of his father. This can be understood as the overcoming of narcissism, the moment when self-idolatry is transcended. Identifying himself with the reflected image of his father, the protagonist moves up the evolutive chain, as the preceding generation is relieved. At this point he becomes conscious of death:

> I a punta de dia vaig veure la mort. La mort era jo a dintre de l'aigua amb la cara d'un mort... I no sabia prou per què hi pensava... i em deia, on començava la mort?... Venia de damunt de la pell o sortia a sota? Era a la punta dels dits o al mig del ventre quan s'hi fa el patir del viure o en un colze o al mig d'un genoll?... On començava a matar? On vivia la mort de cada persona? en la son o en el despertar?

> [And at day-break I saw death. Death was me in the water with the face of a corpse... And I wasn't sure why I was thinking about it... and I said to myself, where did death begin?... Did it come from above the skin or did it erupt underneath? Was it at the fingertips or deep in the stomach, where the anguish of being alive seethes, or in an elbow or on a knee-cap?... Where did it start to kill? Where did each person's death live? In sleep or in waking up?] (1997: 413–14)

For Rodoreda, death is a life process. It is something active, a chrysalis working its way out of its previous body. As the central character is approaching the tree he has chosen to carve his own cross into its bark, he observes a great number of butterflies flittering above his head. The word for butterfly in Greek is *psyche*, which is also the word the ancient Greeks used for 'soul'. When death leaves the body, life is closed. Every point on its spherical surface is equidistant from its centre, like a soap bubble, and the narrator can begin his story from any place. Time has ceased to exist and the protagonist has created his own eternity, that condition in which Maragall hoped to find peace, Pere Quart anticipated perfect beauty, and Pla unbearable boredom. In the last line of the novel, however, Rodoreda gives an unexpected twist to the idea of death: 'La mort va fugir pel cor i quan ja no vaig tenir la mort a dintre em vaig morir...' [Death made its way out through my heart, and when death was no longer inside me I died...] (1997: 427). In this author's evolutive vision, death is an active principle, the biological force responsible for the psyche's metamorphosis, and to die is to be abandoned by death. When death exits the body, life is rounded off, isolated and hardened like a glass ball, which nothing can penetrate. Life — or rather, the memory of it — can then be turned into narrative. Whereas the mortal remains of the body are scattered, the scraps of the spirit are reborn to a higher awareness, an energy which flies towards the Omega point of cosmic consciousness.

For the authors here considered, death is a defining and definitive occurrence. In their own different ways — mystical in Maragall, sceptical in Pere Quart, sarcastic in Josep Pla, existential in Espriu, and initiatic in Rodoreda — they all have in common the idea of the authority of the senses, the centrality of the body in imagining a life for which death is not a metaphysical abstraction but a presence that must be eliminated — 'Occiu la mort' [Kill death] exhorts Pere Quart (1981: 56) — or somehow perfected in order to stop time, to escape from its constraint, or to enclose it in itself like a glass ball that can be observed from any angle without its shape changing in the least. If the sphere is an image of perfection, then death as 'una major naixença' [a greater birth], as Maragall hoped (1929: 177), can be nothing but the awareness of this perfection. It is necessary to die in order to see life with equanimity, with a consciousness unattainable in time. Perhaps it is equanimity that allows the men of Djémila, in Camus's *Noces*, to become rejuvenated precisely when they are embracing death. We can ask if the shine in the eyes of the ancients, facing death without metaphysical preconceptions, is not the same one that glows in the eyes newly opened for the 'faceless' protagonist of *La mort i la primavera*. Was it not with such eyes that Maragall hoped to see heaven for ever more? That Espriu gazed at the sea, the vineyards and the stream-beds? Or the lucid Josep Pla beseeched God to let him escape, not from the clutches of time but from the walls of eternity?

The Catalan temperament responds better to the senses than to any metaphysical vocation. These men and women look upon death not as a disagreeable and increasingly redundant formality, but as an evolutive prolongation, or at least as a dignified surmounting of tangible and positive life. Some of them even look upon it as a reincarnation without additives of oriental religions. And almost all with an austere, homely sort of pantheism in the background.

Works Cited

ARIÈS, PHILIPPE. 1981. *The Hour of Our Death*, trans. by Helen Weaver (New York: Alfred A. Knopf)

CAMUS, ALBERT. 1950. *Noces* (Paris: Gallimard)

CORREDOR, JOSEP MARIA. 1960. *Joan Maragall* (Barcelona: Aedos)

ESPRIU, SALVADOR. 1977. *Obres Completes*, 3rd edn, vol. I (Barcelona: Edicions 62)

FINLEY, MOSES I. 1983. *La Grecia primitiva: edad del bronce y era arcaica*, trans. by Teresa Sempere (Barcelona: Editorial Crítica)

GOETHE, W. J. 1964. *Faust. Goethes Werke*, III (Hamburg: Christian Wegner)

HARRISON, ROBERT POGUE. 2003. *The Dominion of the Dead* (Chicago, IL: University of Chicago Press)

HEIDEGGER, MARTIN. 1962. *Being and Time*, trans. by John Macquarrie and Edward Robinson (New York: Harper and Row)

LYONS, J. A. 1982. *The Cosmic Christ in Origen and Teilhard de Chardin: A Comparative Study* (Oxford: Oxford University Press)

MARAGALL, JOAN. 1929. *Poesies. Obres Completes*, vol. I (Barcelona: Sala Parés)

NIETZSCHE, FRIEDRICH. 1955. *Jenseits von Gut und Böse: Vorspiel einer Philosophie der Zukunft. Werke in Drei Bänden*, vol. II (Munich: Carl Hanser Verlag), pp. 563–759.

PLA, JOSEP. 1966. *Primera volada. Obra Completa*, vol. III (Barcelona: Destino)

——. 1970. *Les illes. Obra Completa*, vol. XV (Barcelona: Destino)

——. 1974. *Notes per a Sílvia. Obra Completa*, vol. XXVI (Barcelona: Destino)

QUART, PERE/JOAN OLIVER. 1981 [1960]. 'Cent anys de Joan Maragall', in *Vacances pagades* (Barcelona: Proa), pp. 91–95

——. 1981. *Poesia empírica* (Barcelona: Proa)

RODOREDA, MERCÈ. 1977. *La mort i la primavera*, ed. by Carme Arnau (Barcelona: Fundació Mercè Rodoreda)

CHAPTER 14

Timely Matters in
Jaume Cabré's *Jo confesso*

Mario Santana

University of Chicago

The author of an extensive body of work that includes four collections of short stories, nine novels, one play, four books of children's or juvenile literature, three essays on the art of fiction, and several scripts for television and film, Jaume Cabré is among the most celebrated and critically respected writers in contemporary Catalan literature. His books have received numerous literary awards in Catalonia and Europe, and have been translated into more than twenty-five languages — the most translated being his two latest novels, *Les veus del Pamano* [Voices of the Pamano River] (2004) and *Jo confesso* [Confessions] (2011), into seventeen and twenty-three languages (respectively).[1] Thus it is no surprise that, over the course of the last decade, an increasing number of readers and scholars have been paying attention to his *oeuvre*.

According to one of those scholars, Jaume Aulet (2009), what makes Cabré particularly attractive, engaging and readable is his careful treatment of language, an aspect of his work recognized by the Secció Filològica [Philological Committee] of the Institut d'Estudis Catalans when it made him a member in the year 2000; his ability to construct fictional worlds that are articulated in complex but comprehensible terms to the reader; and a command of literary techniques that produce dazzling effects — with sentences that famously change focalization, grammatical subject, and spatial and temporal location with astonishing ease.

My intention here is certainly not to offer a comprehensive survey of Cabré's narrative strategies, but to focus on a couple of features that are prominent in his more recent works, features that, in my view, should be regarded as artistic interventions in debates about the understanding of history and the transmission of memory — a critical issue in contemporary art and thought.[2] In Cabré's work, we find a way of constructing fiction (a poetics) that brings to the fore the dilemmas we face in answering the ethical challenges of historical memory: Why should we care about and recognize the victims of past violence? Who is entitled to give and receive recognition? How can one recover and deal with the experience of those who have disappeared? What might be the nature of such a recovery, and what would be its mechanisms and problems? What is the role of art and imagination in that process?

These concerns are arguably present throughout his career, even in those works categorized as juvenile literature: *L'home de Sau* [The Man from Sau] (1984) deals with the need to protect the archaeological patrimony, and *La història que en Roc Pons no coneixia* [The History Roc Pons Did Not Know] (1980) with the price to be paid for ignoring the past. But it is my contention here that they have become more conspicuous in the novels and short stories Cabré has published since the turn of the century (from *Viatge d'hivern* [Winter Journey] [2000] to *Jo confesso*), and that they manifest in two ways: first, in an increasingly complex treatment of time and space at the level of both story and narrative, and, second, in what we could describe as a material turn in his mobilization and articulation of fictional worlds.

Mapping Time in Cabré's Fiction

'Tot va començar, en el fons, fa més de cinc-cents anys [...]' (Cabré 2011: 14)

[It all started, really, more than five hundred years ago [...]] (Cabré 2014a: 3)

Before the publication of *Viatge d'hivern* in 2000, Cabré's fictions tended to embed their action within concrete temporal and spatial boundaries. *Galceran, l'heroi de la guerra negra* [Galceran, the Hero of the Black War] (1978) takes place in Catalonia in the mid-nineteenth century, during the Second Carlist War. *La teranyina* [The Spider Web] (1984), *Fra Junoy o l'agonia del sons* [Brother Junoy or the Agony of Sounds] (1984), and *Llibre de preludis* [Book of Preludes] (1985) form the so-called 'cicle de Feixes' [the Feixes cycle], a series of interrelated narratives that take place in the fictional city of Feixes (based on real-life Terrassa) in the first decades of the twentieth century. *Senyoria* [Seigneury] (1991) is firmly located in Barcelona during the fall and winter of 1799. Miquel Gensana, protagonist of *L'ombra de l'eunuc* [The Eunuch's Shadow] (1996), moves between Feixes and Barcelona during the second half of the twentieth century.

In contrast, the fourteen stories in *Viatge d'hivern* shift locations and times between Amsterdam and Lodz in the early seventeenth century, Leipzig on 28 July 1750, Varsovia, Treblinka and Israel between the 1940s and 1970s, Bosnia in the 1990s, and Barcelona, Vienna, Geneva and the Vatican in the late twentieth century. *Les veus del Pamano* moves between the small village of Torena in the Pallars Sobirà, Barcelona, and other areas in Spain, as well as the Vatican and Paris, mostly from the end of the First Republic in 1874 to May 2002. In *Jo confesso*, time and space expand even more, as a story that begins in the fall of 1320 reaches into the early part of the twenty-first century and takes place in various parts of Europe, Central Africa and the Arabian Peninsula. According to Cabré himself, what lies behind this tendency to weave several plots within one larger story is the desire to represent the dynamism of history (2004: 40).

Let us consider what happens in *Jo confesso*. In its 998 pages the novel tells, among many other things, the twenty-first-century story of Adrià Ardèvol Bosch. A humanist, historian of ideas, and professor of aesthetics at the University of

Barcelona, Adrià has reached his sixties and, in fear of the ravages of Alzheimer's, decided to write the record of his life. Written as a confession addressed to the deceased Sara Voltes-Epstein, the Jewish woman who was the love his life, Adrià's tale is burdened by a sense of guilt accumulated over many decades, a guilt caused not only by his own actions, but also by the legacy of his family — particularly that of his father, an antiques dealer and collector whose fortune was built upon the plundering of victims of war. If the confession of the title (originally intended to be *Confiteor*, an idea preserved in the French translation) may suggest a quest for redemption, the impossibility of finding forgiveness is also present from the first words of the novel, which according to the author (Cabré and Aulet 2012) were the last to have been written:

> Fins ahir a la nit, caminant pels carrers molls de Vallcarca, no vaig comprendre que néixer en aquella família havia estat un error imperdonable. (Cabré 2011: 13)

> [It wasn't until last night, walking along the wet streets of Vallcarca, that I finally comprehended that being born into my family had been an unforgivable mistake.] (Cabré 2014a: 3)

Besides his search for redemption and his relationship with Sara, constants in Adrià's life are his lifelong friendship with violinist and aspiring writer Bernat Plensa; his love of languages, books and ideas; the companionship of two action figures from his childhood (Sheriff Carson and Indian Chief Black Eagle, with whom he often engages in conversation); and — last but not least — a very valuable Storioni violin kept in a safe box in his father's study. The story of this violin extends over more than two centuries and will also occupy a significant part of the novel. In a very summarized form, it goes something like this: towards the end of the fourteenth century, in an isolated monastery in the Pallars Sobirà, a monk who has been for many years a fugitive from the Inquisition is finally tracked down, executed, and buried. In his pocket he carries a bag of seeds given to him by another victim of the Inquisition in Girona, and those seeds grow into a tree. Three hundred years later the tree is cut down by another fugitive, this time from the Italian Trentino, who takes the wood to the city of Cremona, and in 1764 a luthier there named Laurentius Storioni uses it to make a violin that, in Auschwitz, in 1944, will be stolen from a Jewish prisoner by a Nazi guard. After the war, Adrià's father will take possession of the violin, and it is an object that will play a pivotal role in the dissemination of guilt throughout the novel.

Distant locations and moments overlap here in ways that create for the reader not simply a sense of temporal density or thickness, but — more importantly — an impression of simultaneity. The reader is exposed to the fluidity of narrative time very early in the novel, as the young Adrià (the episode takes place in Barcelona in the 1950s) observes a visitor coming into his father's antiques shop. This prompts first a preliminary view of the shop's contents, and then an unexpected shift to events taking place three hundred years earlier in northern Italy:

> — Tenen instruments musicals? [...]
> — No gaire cosa, però si em vol seguir...

La no gaire cosa dels instruments que hi havia a la botiga eren un parell de violins i una viola que no sonaven gaire bé però que tenien cordes de tripa que miraculosament no s'havien trencat. I, també, una tuba abonyegada, dos fiscorns magnífics i una trompeta que l'agutzil de la vall feia sonar desesperadament per advertir a la gent de les altres valls que el bosc de Paneveggio s'estava cremant i els de Pardàc demanaven ajuda a Siròr, a San Martino i fins i tot a Welschnofen, que ho havien patit feia poc, i a Moena i a Soraga, que potser ja rebien l'olor alarmant d'aquell desastre de l'any del Senyor de 1690, quan la terra era rodona per a quasi tothom [...] (2011: 17–18)

['Do you have musical instruments?' [...]
'Not many, but if you'll follow me...'
The not many instruments at the shop were a couple of violins and a viola that didn't sound very good but had gut strings that were miraculously unbroken. And a dented tuba, two magnificent flugelhorns and a trumpet, which the valley's governor had sounded desperately to warn the people in the other valleys that the Paneveggio forest was burning. Those in Pardàc asked for help from Siròr, San Martino and even from Welschnofen, which had suffered its own flames not long before, and from Moena and Soraga, where they had perhaps noticed the alarming odour of that disaster in the Year of Our Lord 1690, when the earth was round for almost everyone [...]] (2014a: 6)

These evocations of past events are not flashbacks, at least not as that device is traditionally used to provide background information to the present events in the narrative. The temporal and spatial displacement that occurs in the passage is not designed to explain the history of the trumpet in the antiques shop. Far from simply pointing to the past to establish or trace back a human story existing in the present — to give an impression of the *pastness* of the present, so to speak — what these alterations in the chronological order of events show is precisely the *presentness* of the past, the fact that history, and especially the crimes of history, do not disappear or fade away. In this sense, Cabré's narrative practice is an exercise in what Mieke Bal has characterized as cultural memory:

Neither remnant, document, or relic of the past, nor floating in a present cut off from the past, cultural memory, for better or for worse, links the past to the present and future. [...] [W]e invoke the discourse of cultural memory to mediate and modify difficult or tabooed moments of the past — moments that nonetheless, impinge, sometimes fatally, on the present. (1999: vii)

That fire in the Paneveggio forest will lead to a plot of murder and vengeance that, even though it resonates and will indeed be connected with other instances of violence in the text, also stands on its own as one of the many stories that are being told. This complex articulation of narrative time reflects Cabré's moral perspective on History, emphasizing that the passage of time does not give closure to ethical responsibility. With regard to the temporal structure of *Les veus del Pamano*, he has said:

Vaig decidir considerar el temps com una cosa elàstica quan, després de moltes pàgines i anys de feina, vaig adonar-me de la imprescribilitat de la responsabilitat moral de l'individu. Tu ets responsable dels teus actes per més que hagin passat cinquanta anys. Per tant, el temps compta poc, en el terreny moral. En conseqüència, podia comptar poc en l'àmbit narratiu: sempre és present, a la novel·la.

[I decided to think of time as something malleable when, after many pages and many years of work, I realized that the moral responsibility of an individual never ends. You are responsible for your actions even if fifty years have passed. Thus, time does not count in the moral sphere — and consequently it should not count in the narrative realm either: in the novel, everything is always in the present.] (n.d.: 13)[3]

'El temps és el de menys' [time is irrelevant], states Cabré in another interview and, apropos of the narrative style of *Les veus del Pamano*, he adds:

el que interessa és la responsabilitat moral dels actes, tant se val que hagin passat cinquanta anys; la Tina, al segle XXI, i l'Oriol Fontelles, als anys quaranta, estan cara a cara i els actes de l'una i de l'altre sembla que tinguin connexió perquè el temps és el de menys i, per tant, una frase pot començar l'any 1944 i acabar el 2001, o a la inversa, perquè tot plegat té una certa connexió.

[What interests me is moral responsibility, and it does not matter that fifty years have gone by; Tina, in the twenty-first century, and Oriol Fontelles, in the 1940s, stand face to face and their respective actions seem to be connected because time is of no concern, and thus a sentence can start in 1944 and end in 2001, or vice versa, because everything is somehow connected.] (Cabré 2004: 40)

Literary critic Joan Josep Isern (2011) applies these statements to *Jo confesso*, understanding them to indicate that the novel's central idea is that the existence of evil is not restricted to a particular place, ideology, or period in history. And it is important to note that the manuscript of Adrià's confessions is being written on the back of another manuscript of his, a philosophical essay on 'the problem of evil' (Cabré 2011: 278). I want to argue here, however, that the key to the novel is not the ubiquity of evil, but rather its *imprescriptibility*, the fact that the crimes of history cannot be written out of the record, and that in this respect the narrative construction of Cabré's fiction is consistent with practices found in other forms of contemporary art that deal with cultural memory. Analysing the works of Miroslav Balka (from Poland), Ilja Kabakow (Russia), Rachel Whiteread (England), Vivan Sundaram (India), and Doris Salcedo (Colombia), Andreas Huyssen claims that they are all engaged in 'memory sculpture':

a kind of sculpture that is not centered on spatial configuration alone, but that powerfully inscribes a dimension of localizable, even corporeal memory into the work [...]. [These sculptures] perform a kind of memory work that activates body, space, and temporality, matter and imagination, presence and absence in a complex relationship with their beholder. [...] In these works, the material object is never just installation or sculpture in the traditional sense, but it is worked in such a way that it articulates memory as a displacing of past into present, offering a trace of a past that can be experienced and read by the viewer. [...] This kind of work [...] fears not only the erasure of a specific (personal or political) past that may, of course, vary from artist to artist; it rather works against the erasure of pastness itself, which, in its projects, remains indissolubly linked to the materiality of things and bodies in time and space. (2003: 110–11)

Art historian Miguel Ángel Hernández-Navarro, following Mieke Bal, has argued similarly that many contemporary artists are performing 'acts of memory':

> una reinscripción del pasado en el presente, aunque no exactamente una representación, sino una manera de hacer que el pasado vuelva al presente por medio de una especie de eco de lo sucedido, presentado a través de una lectura desde el presente. [...] La cuestión es explorar los modos en los que la historia aparece como una especie de eco o reverberación en el presente, como si aún pudiera escucharse el sonido del pasado y los tiempos se solapasen y llegaran a acoplarse.

> [a reinscription of the past in the present, although not exactly a representation, but a way of making the past return to the present by means of a sort of echo of that which occurred, presented in a reading performed from the present. [...] The point is to explore the ways in which history appears like an echo or reverberation in the present, as if one could still hear the sounds of the past and different temporalities came to overlap and fit into each other.] (2012: 24, 89)

In Cabré, this mobilization of the past in the present forces the reader to (or places the reader in a position where she can) experience two temporalities as simultaneous. Hernández-Navarro sees a cognate effect in Galician photographer Jorge Barbi's 2008 project *El final aquí* [The End Here], a collection of photographs of apparently ordinary landscapes that upon closer examination are revealed as the locations of mass executions during the Spanish Civil War (2012: 89–90). In the same way as these images force the viewer to imagine the violence of the past through the vision of the present, in Cabré's fiction the narrative constantly breaks up the present to transport the reader to the scenarios of the past: a past where the victims of historical violence are not simply *dead*, but are still *dying and being killed*.

This interconnection between past and present — indeed, the washing away of the split between past and present — serves a clear moral purpose. Cabré has expressed his fascination with the idea that two individuals, such as Nicolau Eimeric (1316–1399), Inquisitor of Girona, and Rudolf Höss (1900–1947), commandant of the Auschwitz concentration camp, could through narrative effect become *the same character* (see Cabré 2015: 14). Here is the beginning of Chapter 24 of *Jo confesso*, which closely follows a short story written by Cabré in 2003 whose title ('Palimpsestus') is also that of the section of *Jo confesso* where Chapter 24 is found:

> Fa molt de temps, quan la Terra era plana i els viatgers temeraris, en arribar a la fi del món, topaven contra la boira freda o s'estimbaven cingle fosc avall, hi havia un sant baró que va decidir consagrar la seva vida a Déu Nostro Senyor. Es deia Nicolau Eimeric, era de nació catalana i va arribar a ser un reputat professor de Sagrada Teologia de l'ordre dels predicadors al convent de Girona. El seu zel religiós el portà a capitanejar amb mà ferma la Inquisició contra la malícia herètica per les terres de Catalunya i dels regnes de València. Nicolau Eimeric havia nascut a Baden-Baden el 25 de novembre de 1900; havia estat promocionat a SS Obersturmbannführer amb certa celeritat i, després d'una

gloriosa primera etapa com a Oberlagerführer d'Auschwitz, el 1944 va tornar a
dirigir-ne les regnes per donar solució al problema hongarès. (2011: 369)

[Long ago, when the earth was flat and those reckless travellers who reached the
end of the world hit up against the cold fog or hurled themselves off a dark cliff,
there was a holy man who decided to devote his life to the Lord Our God. He
was a Catalan named Nicolau Eimeric, and he became a well-known professor
of Sacred Theology of the Order of Preachers at the monastery of Girona. His
religious zeal led him to firmly command the Inquisition against evil heresy in
the lands of Catalonia and the kingdoms of Valencia. Nicolau Eimeric had been
born in Baden-Baden on 25 November, 1900; he had been promoted rapidly to
SS Obersturmbannführer and, after a glorious first period as Oberlagerführer
of Auschwitz, in 1944 he again took up the reins of the Hungarian problem.]
(2014a: 271)

The past here intermingles with the present, and the present with the past, both in
Cabré's temporal understanding simultaneously coexistent. This ethical perspective
on the nature of time is consistent not only with Albert Einstein's conceptualization
of space-time (as physicist Brian Greene explains in *The Fabric of the Cosmos: Space,
Time, and the Texture of Reality*)[4] but, more importantly for the purposes of my
reading of Cabré, with Walter Benjamin's conception of materialist history. In
Cabré, as in Benjamin, the past not only predates the present but manages to linger
on there as a presence, which opens up the possibility of recurrent condemnation:
the violence of the past can be neither forgotten nor forgiven, because it keeps being
inflicted on its victims. There is also the possibility of redemption, though: the
historical past — its record of violence, but also the promise of everything that has
been suppressed by that violence — remains, and it is up to the historian (in this
case, the novelist) to activate it in the present.

In *Jo confesso*, Adrià writes a book entitled *La voluntat estètica* [The Aesthetic Will],
and he discusses with Bernat what can be seen as the central thesis of that fictive
book as well as of *Jo confesso*: 'no em puc estar de fer una referència a allò de no
hi pot haver poesia després d'Auschwitz' ['I can't help but refer to that bit about
how there can be no poetry after Auschwitz'], says Adrià. Bernat agrees, but Adrià
insists:

> — No. Després d'Auschwitz, després dels nombrosos pogroms, després de
> l'extermini dels càtars, que no en van deixar ni un, després de les matances de
> totes les èpoques i de tot arreu... Fa tants segles que la crueltat és present que la
> història de la humanitat seria la història de la impossibilitat de la poesia 'després
> de'. I en canvi no ha estat així, perquè precisament, qui pot explicar Auschwitz?
> — Els que l'han viscut. Els que l'han creat. Els estudiosos.
> — Sí. Tot això constarà; i han fet museus per recordar-ho. Però faltarà una
> cosa: la veritat de l'experiència viscuda: això no es pot transmetre amb un
> estudi.
>   En Bernat va tancar els fulls lligats i va mirar el seu amic i va dir i?
> — Només es pot transmetre a través de l'art; de l'artifici literari, que és el més
> proper a l'experiència viscuda.
> — Collons.
> — Sí. La poesia cal més que mai després d'Auschwitz. (2011: 658–59)

['No. After Auschwitz, after the many pogroms, after the extermination of the Cathars, of whom not one remains, after the massacres in every period, everywhere around the world... Cruelty has been present for so many centuries that the history of humanity would be the history of the impossibility of poetry "after". And yet it hasn't been that, because who can explain Auschwitz?'

'Those who have lived through it. Those who created it. Scholars.'

'Yes. All that will be evidence; and they've made museums to remember it. But something is missing: the truth of the lived experience. That cannot be conveyed in a scholarly work.'

Bernat closed the bound pages and looked at his friend and said and?

'It can only be conveyed through art; literary artifice, which is the closest thing to lived experience.'

'Bloody hell.'

'Yes. Poetry is needed after Auschwitz more than ever.'] (2014a: 482–83)

The Material Turn: Redeeming Objects

'No era pudor, sinó el pes de la història que carregaven els objectes que formaven part de la col·lecció [...]' (Cabré 2011: 141)

['It wasn't a smell, it was the weight of the history the objects in the collection were laden with [...]'] (2014a: 98)

If the tensions between history and memory — the present and the past, fiction and truth — have been a central motif in Cabré's literary production, another thread that is increasingly present in his latest works is a clear concern for the materiality of the past. This 'material turn' manifests in the importance of objects, which are given an agency usually reserved for human characters. Cabré's stories do not ignore the experience of human individuals, but they are constructed around the presence and mediation of material realities that visualize the historical processes and events that transcend the life of their characters. In *Jo confesso*, it is through the intervention of objects and the connections between them and human subjects — whether it is a matter of the latter crafting or destroying the former, giving or stealing them, or developing the ability to listen to them — that the ethical debates of the novel are played out for the reader.

Cabré's use of objects serves to ground his ethical commitment to the material traces of the forgotten victims of violence. As several art scholars have noted, including Huyssen and Hernández-Navarro, the recovery and mobilization of objects and images of the past is a major trend in contemporary art, and again one that aims to respond to Benjamin's proposal of a kind of history that will work against the closing of the past and for its preservation in the present. I believe that in his use of objects Cabré is engaged in a similar materialization of history.

As we have seen, *Jo confesso* is among other things the story of a violin. In a recent essay on the art of fiction, *Les incerteses* [The Uncertainties], which post-dates *Jo confesso,* Cabré explains that his interest in objects arises from a musical sensibility that conditions the composition of his literary work:

La vida narrativa dels objectes em fascina. Aquella sabata al mig del carrer... què hi fa? El paper rebregat amb traces d'haver servit d'embolcall de menjar oliós, què embolcallava i qui s'ho ha menjat? I el guant curosament deixat damunt l'ampit d'una finestra que dóna al carrer, qui l'hi ha posat i qui el troba a faltar, ara? De vegades penso que fixar-se en els objectes, en els detalls [...] és una estratagema musical: no un tema, sinó un simple motiu, tres notes, que té un valor potser secundari. Quan el repeteixes dit per un altre instrument en un to més agut, adquireix més valor perquè el relacionem amb la primera vegada que ha sortit. I quan el sents tocat pels contrabaixos, ja és com de la família i t'està volent dir alguna cosa. L'ofici del compositor/escriptor fa calibrar el valor i l'eficàcia de la presència del motiu/objecte en el món de la simfonia/relat.

[I am fascinated with the narrative life of things. That shoe left in the middle of the street... what is it doing there? That crumpled piece of paper with traces of the greasy meal it once wrapped, what did it contain and who ate it? And that glove carefully placed on a windowsill to the street, who used to wear it and is missing it now? Sometimes I think that to pay attention to objects, to these details [...] is a musical strategy. Not a theme, but simply a motif, three notes, which may have a secondary value — but when it is repeated on another instrument, in a high-pitched form, gains more value because we can now relate it to the first time it appeared. And when we hear it again from the double bass, it has become a member of the family and is trying to tell you something. The craft of the composer/writer consists in calibrating the value and effectiveness of the presence of the motif/object in the world of the symphony/narrative.] (2015: 81)

In the imaginary world of Jaume Cabré, artefacts are very often associated with the life experiences of the various subjects with whom they have come into contact at different points in time. In *Les veus del Pamano*, for instance, over five decades of history the tombstones in the Torena cemetery are built, damaged, rebuilt and interpreted in ways that are often antagonistic, so that the stones acquire a life of their own that goes beyond each of these individual interventions. The same applies to the many objects that populate *Jo confesso*: a medallion is given to the fugitive from the Italian Trentino by his sister in 1690 and changes hands repeatedly, often in violent circumstances and in locations including Carcassone and Saudi Arabia, until it is taken in turn from Adrià late in his life in Barcelona. 'La història de qualsevol cosa explica l'estat del present de la cosa qualsevol' (2011: 418) ['The history of any thing explains the present state of that thing'] (2014a: 307), claims Adrià. And each object projects onto the person who happens to find it its own load of emotions and experiences.

This is explicitly established in the novel in a conversation between Bernat and Adrià, when they discover that the Storioni violin has a name (Vial):

> — Tots els violins són iguals [diu Bernat].
> — Creu-t'ho. Cada violí és una història. A cada violí li has de sumar, a més del lutier que el va crear, tots els violinistes que l'han tocat. [...]
> El pare m'ho havia dit un dia amb l'storioni a la mà. Me'l va oferir amb una certa recança i va dir, sense saber ben bé què deia, vés alerta, que és un objecte únic al món. L'storioni a les meves mans era com si fos viu. Em va semblar notar-hi un batec suau i íntim. I el pare, amb els ulls brillants, em deia pensa que aquest violí ha viscut històries que no sabem, ha sonat en sales i en cases que mai no coneixerem, i ha viscut totes les alegries i els dolors dels violinistes que l'han fet servir. (2011: 109)

['Violins are all the same.'

'Certainly not. Every violin has a story behind it. There's not only the luthier who created it, but every violinist who has played it.' [...]

My father had told me that, one day, with the Storioni in his hands. He offered it to me somewhat regretfully and said, without really knowing what he was saying, be very careful, because this object is unique. The Storioni in my hands felt as if it were alive. I thought I could feel a soft, inner pulse. And Father, his eyes gleaming, said imagine, this violin has been through experiences we know nothing about, it has been played in halls and homes that we will never see, and it has lived all the joys and pains of the violinists who have played it.] (2014a: 73–74)

Thus, objects serve as embodied testimony to past events: more than inert matter, they are transformed into subjects and voices that can communicate to the reader an extended series of connections of which the characters — their lives separated by time and space — are not necessarily aware. And it should be noted that these objects may not be valuable ones. In contrast to the Storioni violin, the novel also features a humble and torn piece of kitchen cloth that plays a critical role in preserving the memory of the extermination camps.

Contemporary literary production engaged in the recovery of historical memory is naturally full of evocations of the materiality of the past. Images and photographs, documents lost and found, deserted spaces — among innumerable other examples, all are elements in an iconography that draws our attention towards, and even allows us to experience, what has preceded us. In Cabré, however, these artefacts are not simply icons that stand for the past, but are in themselves victims subjected to the violence of that past — the case of the Storioni violin is stained with the blood of previous owners. Pulsing with the life of the past, his objects do not serve just as passive instruments for remembrance, but rather become *agents*, actively *demanding* our attention, and force us to acknowledge forgotten experiences and lives.

In *The Life of Things, the Love of Things*, Italian philosopher Remo Bodei develops a paradigm for relations between humans and things that is based on the practice of art and its ability to restore meaning and emotion to the material world (2015: 78–79). For Bodei, it is in the paintings of the Flemish school, and particularly in the still lifes, that we find an artistic treatment of objects that, while respecting their material condition, can turn them into things for which we are expected to be concerned:

To rescue objects from their insignificance or from their purely instrumental use means to understand better ourselves and the events in which we are engaged — since things establish synapses of meaning both between the different segments of the individual and collective story and between human civilizations and nature. (2015: 113)

It is perhaps no coincidence that painting, and specifically the most acclaimed of the Flemish masters, Rembrandt, is featured prominently in a number of Cabré's works. Rembrandt's *The Philosopher* is on the cover of the first edition of *Fra Junoy o l'agonia dels sons*. It is also one of the leitmotifs in *Viatge d'hivern*, and is even recreated on stage in one of the scenes of Cabré's play *Pluja seca* [Dry Rain]. These allusions help to emphasize how closely Cabré's treatment of material objects is akin to the effect that Bodei observes in the still lifes of the Flemish masters, transforming them into protagonists and witnesses of history.

Catalan artist Francesc Torres has argued that the recovery and preservation of the materiality of the past is a civic responsibility. In 2004, Torres participated in the excavation of a mass grave from the Spanish Civil War in Villamayor de los Montes, Burgos, an experience which led to the 2007 exhibition *Dark Is the Room Where We Sleep* at the International Center of Photography in New York. In an article written shortly after the excavation, Torres articulates the need to interrogate the material remains of the past:

> Las trincheras del Ebro, aún hoy, [...] están llenas de latas de conserva abiertas con la llave alojada en el centro de la espiral de su cubierta retorcida. A veces aparecen cucharas y tenedores corrientes con el mango curvado hacia atrás para poderlos colgar del cinto, cantimploras, suelas de alpargata, botas de cuero. Están ahí a merced del tiempo y del capricho de algún curioso. Nadie parece asociar la lata de sardinas noruega, de aluminio limpio, con el soldado desconocido que se alimentó de ella mientras defendía, en desventaja, un ideal político decente frente al fascismo más reaccionario y brutal; ni la cantimplora con la sed atroz que sació en la garganta de un brigadista internacional norteamericano, o húngaro, o checo que quizá murió en el frente o quizá esté muriendo ahora en un asilo de ancianos; ni los pies hinchados de un chaval aterrorizado antes de entrar en combate con esas botas llenas ahora de musgo y hormigas. Si nuestra clase política fuera capaz de leer la historia en una hebilla de cinturón, no quedaría una sola fosa común, civil o militar, por destapar.

> [Even today the trenches from the Battle of the Ebro [...] are full of opened food tins, with the key still attached to the coiled and twisted cover. One often finds ordinary spoons and forks, the handle bent backwards so they could be carried hanging from the belt, and canteens, espadrilles soles, leather boots. They are there at the mercy of the weather and the whim of curious people. Nobody seems to associate the aluminium Norwegian sardine tin with the unknown soldier who ate while defending, in unfavourable conditions, a decent political ideal against the most reactionary and brutal fascism; or the canteen with the unbearable thirst that it served to satiate in an American, Hungarian or Czech international brigadist who perhaps died at the front or is now dying in a nursing home; or the swollen feet of a kid terrified before combat with those boots now full of moss and ants. If our political leaders were able to read history in the buckle of a belt, there would not be a single mass grave, whether civil or military, still to be uncovered.] (2008: 88)

In Torres's photographs and Cabré's narratives alike, objects interrogate our willingness to recover the past and to acknowledge the traces of violence that remain within it, and in this respect novels such as *Jo confesso* can be understood to train the reader's sensibility and prepare her to engage with the ethical and political evocation of the forgotten histories of the past.

'Father, do not forgive them, for they know precisely what they do' (Jankélévitch 1996: 564). These words, which provide the epigraph for *Les veus del Pamano*, echo through the pages and stories in *Jo confesso* as well. As they suggest, Cabré's fiction is deeply concerned with the exercise of retributive power, with the need to denounce abusers and to restore and recognize victims: 'em surten uns personatges enfrontats a un col·lectiu, a una institució, a un poder [...] És com a perdedors que prenen coherència i es així que me'ls estimo' [I come up with characters who stand up to a collective, an institution, some sort of power [...] It is because they are losers that they gain consistency and I embrace them] (Cabré 1990: 20). On the basis of this, I would argue that the result of Cabré's experimentation with time and materiality in his fictional works is not exactly the memorialization of the past, but rather the permanent reopening of the past onto the present. His is not a poetics of forgiveness, but one of redemption.

Works Cited

AULET, JAUME. 2009. 'El valor de la totalitat en la ficció de Jaume Cabré', *Caràcters: Revista de Llibres*, 46: 27

BAL, MIEKE. 1999. 'Introduction', in *Acts of Memory: Cultural Recall in the Present*, ed. by Mieke Bal, Jonathan Crewe and Leo Spitzer (Hanover, NH, and London: Dartmouth College/University Press of New England), pp. vii–xvii

BODEI, REMO. 2015. *The Life of Things, the Love of Things*, trans. by Murtha Baca (New York: Fordham University Press)

CABRÉ, JAUME. 1990. 'Jaume Cabré o la necessitat d'explicar el món', interview with Marta Nadal, *Serra d'Or*, 364: 19–22

——. 2004. 'La meva autobiografia és en l'estil', interview with Marta Nadal, *Serra d'Or*, 538: 38–43

——. 2011. *Jo confesso* (Barcelona: Proa)

——. 2014a. *Confessions*, trans. by Mara Faye Lethem (London: Arcadia)

——. 2014b. 'Costa moltíssim que et reconeguin l'existència', interview with Mònica Terribas, 'Els matins de Catalunya Ràdio' (10 Feb) <http://www.ccma.cat/catradio/alacarta/el-mati-de-catalunya-radio/jaume-cabre-costa-moltissim-que-et-reconeguin-lexistencia/audio/790672/>

——. 2015. *Les incerteses* (Barcelona: Proa)

——. n.d. 'Una entrevista a Jaume Cabré sobre *Les veus del Pamano*'. *Dossier Jaume Cabré, Les veus del Pamano*, 13–16 <http://www.bibgirona.net/salt/sete_cel/planes/dossier7.pdf>

CABRÉ, JAUME, and JAUME AULET. 2012. 'Jaume Cabré, finalista del Premi Crexells', Ateneu Barcelonès, 5 May <https://www.youtube.com/watch?v=-TNKUwcxmGI>

GREENE, BRIAN. 2005. *The Fabric of the Cosmos: Space, Time, and the Texture of Reality* (New York: Vintage)

HERNÁNDEZ-NAVARRO, MIGUEL ÁNGEL. 2012. *Materializar el pasado: el artista como historiador (benjaminiano)* (Murcia: Micromegas)

HUYSSEN, ANDREAS. 2003. *Present Pasts: Urban Palimpsests and the Politics of Memory* (Stanford, CA: Stanford University Press)

ISERN, JOAN JOSEP. 2011. 'Jaume Cabré i *Jo confesso*', *Vilaweb*, 1 September <http://www.vilaweb.cat/noticia/3924041/20110901/jaume-cabre-jo-confesso-mal-mal-sempre-recomenca.html#>

JANKÉLÉVITCH, VLADIMIR. 1996. 'Should We Pardon Them?', trans. by Ann Hobart, *Critical Inquiry*, 22: 552–72

SANTANA, MARIO. 2015. 'Les memòries i les coses: la materialitat del passat en la narrativa de Jaume Cabré', in *Funcions del passat en la cultura catalana contemporània: institucionalització, representacions i identitat*, ed. by Josep-Anton Fernàndez and Jaume Subirana (Lleida: Punctum), pp. 145–55

TORRES, FRANCESC. 2007. *Dark Is the Room Where We Sleep/Oscura es la habitación donde dormimos* (Barcelona: Actar)

——. 2008. 'El protocolo', in *Francesc Torres: da capo* (Barcelona: Museu d'Art Contemporani de Barcelona), pp. 87–88

Notes to Chapter 14

1. As of August 2018, the following works are available in translation: *La història que en Roc Pons no coneixia* [The Story Roc Pons Did Not Know] (Spanish); *La teranyina* [The Spider Web] (French, Spanish); *Fra Junoy o l'agonia dels sons* [Brother Junoy or the Agony of Sounds] (Hungarian, Polish, Spanish); *L'home de Sau* [The Man from Sau] (Spanish); *Llibre de preludis* [Book of Preludes] (Spanish); *Senyoria* [Seigneury] (Albanian, Dutch, French, Galician, German, Hungarian, Italian, Polish, Portuguese, Romanian, Spanish); *L'ombra de l'eunuc* [The Eunuch's Shadow] (Dutch, French, German, Hungarian, Italian, Polish, Romanian, Russian, Slovenian, Spanish); *Viatge d'hivern* [Winter Journey] (English, French, Italian, Polish, Spanish); *Les veus del Pamano* (Traditional and Simplified Chinese, Croatian, Dutch, French, German, Greek, Hungarian, Italian, Norwegian, Polish, Portuguese, Romanian, Russian, Serbian, Slovenian, Spanish); *Jo confesso* (Albanian, Bulgarian, Traditional Chinese, Croatian, Czech, Danish, Dutch, English, French, German, Greek, Hungarian, Italian, Lithuanian, Norwegian, Polish, Portuguese, Russian, Slovenian, Spanish, Swedish, Turkish, Ukrainian); *Les incerteses* [The Uncertainties] (Spanish); *En Pere i el bosc* [Peter and the Forest] (Spanish); *Quan arriba la penombra* [When the Twilight Arrives] (Spanish); *La Mariona i la Menjanits* [Mariona and Menjanits] (Spanish). See https://jaumecabre.cat/ca/traduccions/. As of February 2014, and according to Cabré, a translation of *Jo confesso* into Korean was also in the works (Cabré 2014b).
2. For a preliminary version of some of the arguments presented here, see Santana (2015).
3. Unless otherwise indicated, all unpublished translations are mine.
4. 'Although the notion of *now* plays a central role in our worldview, relativity subverts our intuition once again and declares ours an egalitarian universe in which every moment is as real as any other. [...] Just as we envision all of space as *really* being out there, as *really* existing, we should also envision all of time as *really* being out there, as *really* existing, too. [...] In this way of thinking, events, regardless of when they happen from any particular perspective, just *are*. They all exist. They eternally occupy their particular point in spacetime' (Greene 2005: 132, 139).

CHAPTER 15

'In my end is my beginning...': Some Thoughts on Translating Raimon Casellas's *Els sots feréstecs*

Alan Yates

University of Sheffield

Literary translation has been, from the start, the most satisfying if not the most remunerative facet of my professional activity, the ideal complement to linguistic and literary studies. In this I was inspired always by the encouragement and example of Arthur Terry.

Els sots feréstecs/Dark Vales (1901) by Raimon Casellas is acknowledged as a powerful expression of some central preoccupations in Catalan *Modernisme* and as a pivotal work in the evolution of twentieth-century Catalan narrative. The author provides a grim parable about a parish priest, banished to the backwoods for doctrinal heterodoxy, who tries and fails to redeem himself by bringing redemption to a hostile benighted peasant flock. It can be read as an imaginative refraction of Casellas's own mission as a prophet of *Modernisme*, presenting an archetype of the modern intellectual who aspires to improve, enlighten and dignify the society in which he lives. Catastrophic failure does not negate altogether a kind of nobility which inheres in the undertaking and in the efforts made to achieve it.

For years this novel had been in my mind as a tempting translation challenge and a desideratum for the international canon, but the project of putting *Els sots feréstecs* into English always seemed too daunting, even after retirement when I had more opportunity to take on the challenge. I was stuck in a lazy conviction that the novel was 'untranslatable'. And this idea had seemed to be confirmed when I examined closely David Rosenthal's English version of Víctor Català's *Solitud* (1905), published in 1992 and still in the catalogue of the publishers Readers International. Rosenthal's translation is worthy in several respects, but it shows signs of haste in general and it fails to do justice to two key elements in the work: the intricate representation of Víctor Català's imaginary mountain landscape and the synthetic dialect of Gaietà the shepherd, two 'keys' to the full meaning of the text.

It was through the intervention of Jordi Castellanos that I was eventually persuaded to embark on translating Casellas's novel, a work that resonates so directly with *Solitud*. Sadly, Jordi did not live to see the publication of *Dark Vales* in 2014, the product of some three years of arduous but rewarding endeavour, and several disagreeable spats with my editor and the publisher. Literary translation, nevertheless, is always a privileged and supremely satisfying mode of reading, and nowhere has the essence of this been better expressed than in Josep Carner's often quoted maxim: 'Traduir una obra és la millor manera de llegir-la: és amar-hi i penar-hi, servir-la i dominar-la... Demés d'ésser la millor manera de llegir, la traducció és el millor mètode per entrenar-se a ben escriure' [To translate a work is the best way of reading it: involving love and suffering, service and domination... As well as being the best way of reading it is the best way of training yourself to write well]. I'm grateful for the opportunity to share, in that light, something of my experience of working on *Els sots feréstecs/Dark Vales*.

★   ★   ★   ★   ★

There are some outstanding modern novels which artistically convert an actual place on the map into a 'landscape of the mind' (while vice-versa the real location on the ground can be endowed with a mythical aura derived from the fictional recreation). With *Wuthering Heights* (1847) as the archetype, the category in English would include works like Bruce Chatwin's *On the Black Hill* (1982), and *Waterland* by Graham Swift (1983) among recent outstanding examples. In each case the prominence, as virtual protagonist, of a novel's setting is explicit in the title itself. *Els sots feréstecs* is a prime example from the modern Catalan repertoire.

In his youth, Casellas made several stays in the Pyrenean foothills of the parish of Montmany, some 40 kilometres northwards inland from Barcelona, where he was befriended by the local priest, Father Josep Lladó. The near-coincidence with the name of the novel's protagonist (Llàtzer) might well be deliberate, overlaid perhaps with suggestions of the popular expression 'fet un sant Llàtzer' meaning 'victimized, badly beaten up'. The author wrote later of first going in 1870 to the Uià farm, fleeing from Barcelona with his mother during an outbreak of yellow fever in the city. With its 'cultivated terraces lining the hillside like steps rising up towards the clouds', as Casellas described the place in a private letter, Uià is a consistent point of topographical reference in the narrative. This farmstead survives in use to the present day, as does the sanctuary church up on the ridge at Puiggraciós. The view down from there is towards where the now ruinous church of Sant Pau de Montmany and its priest's house stand. These principal landmarks in the novel are complemented by numerous others which are to be found on standard maps. Indeed, the author's intimate knowledge of the local terrain imbues all his descriptions of the novel's setting and strongly flavours a subjective involvement in them.

Chapter 1 of *Els sots feréstecs* provides an oblique *mise en scène* centred on the grotesque figure of *L'Aleix de les Tòfones* and his conflictive relationship with all the other inhabitants of the Dark Vales. The first paragraph consists of a single *in medias res* utterance: *¿A on reïra de bet deuen haver anat a raure els ossos corcats d'aquell jaio del dimoni?* (Casellas 1980: 51). The fact that no quotation marks enclose those opening words adds to our immediate uncertainty. 'What's all this about?' is the most likely response of any reader, and some elucidation of that very question, applied to the opening sentence and to the novel as a whole, is the objective of this chapter.

Back to that sentence and, from there, to the observation now that this is a very deliberate angling by the novelist of a snippet of direct speech: the present tense (*deuen*) and the demonstrative (*aquell*) belong clearly to this oral mode. (The 'authenticity' of the dialect need not concern us.) The effect sought is, I think, to attune the reader to the narrative strategy and the focalization through which the whole work is constructed. But, before pursuing that any further, let's examine the immediate resonances of *¿A on reïra de bet deuen haver anat a raure els ossos corcats d'aquell jaio del dimoni?*

We are talking about one of the great shibboleths of the Catalan literary tradition, as well as a worthy entry in the 'memorable first sentence test' of narrative fiction ('En un lugar de la Mancha...', 'Stately, plump Buck Mulligan...' 'Aujourd'hui, Maman est morte', etc.). I was amazed by how many Catalan friends and colleagues, on hearing about my translation project, immediately asked, with or without quoting it from memory, how I intended to handle that intriguing opening sentence *¿A on reïra de bet...?*. Problems of detail are certainly there, but once the relevance of this utterance in stylized peasant sociolect is recognized, it can in fact be rendered with a good measure of equivalence.

'Where, in the black name of the Devil, could the rotten bones of that old muckworm have gone to rest?' (Casellas 2014: 23). Leaving aside questions of cultural differences, nuances, etc., and technical details of transposition or compensation, this might plausibly have been pronounced by an uneducated rural individual in twentieth-century England. The model in the back of my mind was the speech of the old folk I used to hear as a child in rural Northamptonshire. A detail by way of illustration: '[crafty] old bugger', recalled from that same source, has for my ear just the right ring to have been used for rendering *jaio del dimoni*, but I wanted to keep in reserve that 'bugger' as a verb rather than a noun for a 'strong' translation of the Truffle Man's call (and gesture) of defiance *La figo vus fai a tuts* (1980: 54, 57, 60): whence 'Bugger the lot of you!' (2014: 27, 30, 35) which resounds three times in the opening chapter. This considered, 'old muckworm' provides adequate compensation (added earthiness) and the right sort of figurative force in the first sentence of a very carefully angled prelude to the whole text.

Peasant speech was handled consistently in this way throughout my version. Here is a sample from Chapter 10 ('Mala nissaga!'/Bad Stock), a jumble of unattributed comments with which the locals are slagging off the priest after he has restored his church and house with no help at all from them:

> — *Mira el fotxut del rector* — *deia l'un* — , *com s'ha arranjat per a fer adobar l'església!*
> — *No sé com s'ho ha fet, el gran janfúmer!*
> — *¿No us ho só dit sempre, jo, que aquest home sap a on jeuen?...*
> — *Pesta que el toc! Per mi té pacte amb el dimoni...*
> — *Això deu ésser, rellampus!, perquè fins sembla cosa de mal art...* (1980: 110)

> ['Just look at him, the bleedin' priestman,' one of them said, 'and how he's managed to get the church repaired!'
> 'I don't know how he's been able to do it, the sly old scoundrel!'

'Didn't I always tell you that this one's a crafty blighter?'
'Blast his eyes! I reckon he's in league with the Devil...'
'For sure, for bloody sure! All this has the look of black magic about it...']
(2014: 101–02)

Close attention to this particular translation issue highlighted for me the author's technical control of his linguistic medium. The sample above illustrates how he builds up tension and articulates, in stark chiaroscuro, the crescendo of conflict between an amorphous, anonymous peasant collective and the tortured individual psychology of the priest protagonist. The 'transcription' technique gathers dramatic intensity as spoken words 'overheard' (and other sounds) resonate with increasing insistence inside *mossèn* Llàtzer's head.

I had, then, a specific strategy to replicate texture in one important aspect of the original. The approach used for rendering peasant speech was allowed to affect residually the English style of the main diegesis, where I was aiming to reproduce something of the tonal quality of the particular narrative voice and, generally, the *estil mascle* [tough style] of *modernista* ruralist writing. In my mind here was a vague amalgam of canonical voices from the English tradition of ruralist/working-class fiction from the nineteenth and early twentieth centuries: Emily Brontë, Thomas Hardy, D. H. Lawrence, and even Stella Gibbons. All I can do to illustrate this is to supply a couple of fairly representative samples, both of them focused on the key figure of the itinerant prostitute *La Roda-soques*/Footloose. The first is from Chapter 12 ('La Roda-soques'/Footloose) where this character makes her first appearance, and the second is from Chapter 13 ('Déu i el Dimoni'/God and the Devil) where the head-on clash between *mossèn* Llàtzer and the whore is first presented:

> *Allò era la temptació eterna de tot Montmany. De dia, en la solitud de les ombrívoles boscúries, joves i vells no rumiaven altra cosa. De nit, en el silenci de les cambres, plenes de tenebres, tots els homes se rebolcaven pel jaç, somniant amb aquella dona. Ni un instant, per repòs, se'ls en anava del pensament l'estranya imatge de la bagassa, amb aquells cabells rojos, com aram, amb aquelles carnasses blanques com mató, amb aquella pell llantiosa com espurnada de boll daurat. Cosa de bruixes els semblava que ni el sol ni la serena haguessin colrat aquella cara, aquell coll i aquells braços, com se colren els de tohom. Però era tan estràmbola en tot, aquella dona del dimoni!... (1980: 128)*

[The whole Montmany district was now affected by the same never-ending temptation. By day, in the loneliness of the shady woods, young men and old had nothing else on their minds. At night, in silent and dark-filled bedrooms, they all tossed and turned under the blankets, dreaming or fantasising about that woman. Not a moment's rest did they enjoy, as the exotic image of the harlot preyed on their minds: the red hair like burnished copper; the abundant flesh, as creamy-white as curds; the faintest blemishes on her pale skin, like flecks of gold. To them only witchcraft could explain the fact that neither sunshine nor the cold night air had tanned that face, that neck and those arms to the same sunburned colour as all their faces, necks and arms. But then everything was so out of the ordinary about that woman, that Jezebel!...] (2014: 123)

*   *   *   *   *

Però veus aquí que, mentres estaven els bosquerols en lo més anguniós del seu desfici, perquè ja veien que el jaio anava a girar el missal... de sobte, tot de sobte, se va sentir, enmig del silenci de la missa, una remor impensada, una fressa eixeridora de faldilles, com d'una dona que entrés a l'església tot rumbejant-se el cos. Tothom va tombar el cap de correguda, i grans i xics van sentir que el cor els feia un salt.

    — Llamp de Déu! La Roda-soques! — van mormolar, glaçats, els bosquerols. Sí: era la bagassa, que es ficava església endins [...]. Després ella va passar per entre els rengles de bancs, remenant unes faldilles de roba virolada i lluint un mocadoret al cap, tan repetit, que per davant se li veia la clenxa partida i per darrera les trenes de color encès. Va tirar amunt, amunt, fins que, al ser a més de mitja església, se va aclofar a terra tota desmandada, mig badoquejant, mig somrient. Els feligresos, com si no es poguessin revenir de la sorpresa, semblaven més morts que vius; i, quan tots varen alçar-se a l'acte de girar el missal, els uns se miraven als altres, entre encuriosits i porucs, com volguent dir: 'Què succeirà? Què deurà passar? Què serà de tots nosaltres?' (1980: 136–37)

[But just when the woodlanders were feeling the sharpest pangs of their distress, as they saw that old Josep was about to turn the missal towards the participants..., all of a sudden, in the enveloping silence of the Mass, an unexpected noise was heard: the brisk, gay swish of a skirt being whirled, like the sound that might have been made by a woman coming into church deliberately swaying her body from side to side. Everyone quickly turned to look; old and young felt their hearts miss a beat.

'God almighty! It's Footloose!' muttered the stupefied parishioners.

Yes: it was the harlot who was coming into the church [...]. Then she passed between the rows of pews, her many-coloured skirt flouncing as she moved along and with a tiny scarf on her head, so tiny and daintily tied, that it revealed from the front the neat parting in her hair and, from behind, her blazing red tresses. Up the aisle she went, more than half way towards the altar, where she squatted quite provocatively, half gaping and half smiling. The parishioners, as if unable to get over the shock they felt, looked more dead than alive; and rising to their feet as the Mass book was turned in their direction, they exchanged looks among themselves, in a mood hovering between curiosity and fright, as if to say: 'What will happen now? What can come next? What will become of us all?'] (2014: 133–34)

These extracts will have to speak for themselves. What I do want to mention here is the difficulty of finding anything like a satisfactory equivalent in English for the name of this character, a grotesque caricature of the Decadent *femme fatale* with her own heavy symbolic charge in the story: the agent of the forces of Evil, and ultimately of cosmic despair. *Roda-soques* denotes in Catalan both 'vagabond' and a woodland bird (treecreeper/nuthatch). It being impossible to convey the double equivalence in a single English word, the preferred option was to prioritize the first meaning on the basis of 'footloose (and fancy free)'. The consequent translation loss (the bird allusion being sacrificed) is minimized by this strategy, with compensation from the agility it allows: 'footloose' available both as the nickname and as an adjective, shading into the 'loose woman' idea. Moreover, my version retains allusion (at least visual) to the assonance of the original.

As already mentioned, the landscape of Montmany is a virtual protagonist in the novel. This feature as enshrined in the original title also presents a major challenge of translation. For rendering the deliberate allusion to a zone which is now designated so on the *Alpina* map, *els sots feréstecs* ('wild ravines/gorges'), no better solution was found other than to replace that geographical specificity with an inference of the central motif of Death which defines the emotional/psychological atmosphere of the narrative. (The German translator, Eberhart Vogel, simply turned his back on the same problem and resorted to *Lazarus Tod/The Death of Lazarus* (1909), incurring the disapproval of Casellas himself.) *Dark Vales* as title suggests the obsessive anxiety that dominates the story from beginning to end, from an angle which readers of the original would access via familiarity with the real places on the map. I like to think that the novelist would have been sympathetic towards this solution.

Casellas put a lot of himself into his novel and its central character, but in an imaginatively distilled and creatively fashioned way: '*intensity* of feeling and of technique' had been highlighted by him as the main desideratum in an era of crisis and change across the arts. By applying this principle in *Els sots feréstecs* he pointed the way towards new modes of fiction in Catalan, to put the literature of his own country in line with contemporary counterparts in the European *fin de siècle*. As a prominent historian and critic, of the visual arts mainly but also of literature, Casellas was fully abreast of the currents which were transforming Western culture in that major cultural watershed. In his novel he articulated his own resonant creative responses to complex and profound social and cultural upheavals in the European *fin de siècle*: the vertigo of Baudelaire's 'Plonger au fond du gouffre, Enfer ou Ciel, qu'importe? | Au fond de l'Inconnu pour trouver du *nouveau!*'; the hallucination of a godless universe derived from Schopenhauer and Nietzsche; features of the decadent 'romantic agony'; ultimately, the spectre of social revolution... All these anxieties have 'nightmare' and decadent features which cannot be isolated from coincidences with contemporary developments in philosophy, and in the 'new' sciences of anthropology, sociology/criminology and psychology (Cesare Lombroso's 'criminal atavism'; Gustave Le Bon's *Psychologie des foules* [1895]; Freud on dreams).

Thus, the tortured morbidity which pervades *Dark Vales*, like so much *fin-de-siècle* creativity, expresses an effort to explore artistically the bounds of human reason, an effort which ran up against the inadequacy of language to communicate ultimate truths and the mysteries of the human condition. The frequent use of punctuation dots for pregnant pauses in the text (a favourite post-Symbolist device) is intended to show moments of crisis where reason and words begin to fail and where silence itself is supremely expressive. In a similar way, the constant reiteration throughout of key phrases and motifs is a literary application of Wagner's musical *Leitmotiven*. This feature in *Els sots feréstecs* extends beyond the stylistic level, the texture of the narrative language, into various symbolic motifs. The central one is the obsessive fear of being buried alive. I'll highlight just a couple of samples of how this is worked into the total fabric of the narrative.

The anxiety begins in Chapter 4 ('El regne de la mort'/Death's Dominion), as soon as Llàtzer and his two household companions first set eyes on the dilapidated church and their new abode:

Amb els braços penjant al llarg del cos, no feia més que moure el cap pausadament, tot contemplant el catau mig ensorrat que d'aquella hora endavant li seviria d'estada. Al pensar que allò venia a ser com una mena de sepultura a on anava a enterrar els dies de sa vellesa, abans de ficar-se per sempre més a la tomba veritable de la mort, li entrava un defalliment d'esperit que l'omplia d'esgarrifances i congoixes...

— No... no ha vingut encara l'hora de la pau... — deia com en somnis plens d'angúnia —. No... Jo me la creia a prop, a prop... ja la tocava amb la mà... i ara s'allunya, s'allunya... perquè encara no m'he esbandit bé de les cabòries de la terra... (1980: 73)

[With his arms drooping, all he could do was to shake his head slowly as he contemplated that half-ruined hideout which from then on was to be his dwelling. As he reflected that what was happening to him was a kind of burial of the last days of his old age — before he went forever more to the real grave of death itself — he was overcome by a feeling of utter helplessness that made him shudder with dread and anguish.

'No... the hour of eternal peace has not yet come,' he muttered as though from within a deeply disturbing dream. 'No... I thought that hour was so close, so close at hand... but now it is going further and further away... because I am still not fully cleansed of earthly concerns...'] (2014: 52)

Llàtzer's optimism as he began the climb with his two servants to take possession of his new abode is here beginning already to waver. It will be worn down steadily by the hostility of his parishioners and the environment until, in Chapter 15 ('Dies negres'/Dark Days), bleak depression takes over by stages:

Però, de totes les penes que passaven, la que els atordia més eren les goteres, que, com més anava, més regalaven de pertot arreu. Allò sí que era un desfici i un neguit! No hi ha pas res al món que faci tanta angúnia com sentir les goteres fent toc, tac, *entre la fosca...* (1980: 151)

[Among all the travails they were enduring, what made them most confused and anxious were the leaks, which, as time went by, were pouring ever more persistently from all the ceilings. How their nerves were tormented by this! There is nothing on earth as disturbing as hearing in the dark the sound of dripping water: *tock, tock*...] (2014: 154)

★   ★   ★   ★   ★

I aterrat, retut, amb el cap amagat entre les mans, el sacerdot rumiava, amb esgarrifances entre pell i os, que la soletat mortuòria que somiava suara encara no era tan ferotge com la que veia venir en aquell moment. Els jaios també estaven a punt d'abandonar-lo, se'ls acabaven les forces, se moririen qualsevol instant... i ell, sol i vern, desemparat, hauria d'anar sense esma, com una ombra vagarosa, pels sots dels morts... (1980: 158)

[And, as though poleaxed, quite defeated, with his head sunk in his hands and with an intensely disquieting feeling under his skin, the priest reflected that the deathly loneliness of which he had earlier dreamed a vision was nothing like as cruel as the solitude which he now knew was in store for him. He was about to be abandoned by his aged companions: their strength was at an end and they could die at any time... And he, all alone, helpless, would be left to wander without direction, like a drifting phantom, in that valley of the shadow of death.] (2014: 162)

(I remark in passing how the rendering of *els sots dels morts* as 'that valley of the shadow of death', in the last line above, resonates with the *sots feréstecs*/Dark Vales adjustment for the main title, mentioned earlier.)

Another key motif worked into the fabric of the text is that of bells chiming (or being silenced) intermittently as the story unfolds, with the particular twist given in the movement towards crisis in Chapter 17, 'Camí del Calvari'/The Road to Calvary. Here the priest's pathetic intoning of ritual formulae is parodied in the clanging echoes coming from his servant's hand bell:

> *El sacerdot, entretant, pujava a damunt de l'euga, i després entonava a mitja veu els clamorosos versículs:*
> — *¡Apiada't de mi, oh Déu, segons la teva gran misericòrdia!*
> — Ganning, gannang! Ganning, gannang! — *responia el jaio fent dringar la campana amb tota força, mentres la vella li abrigava amb una manta les espatlles per a lliurar-lo del relent de la nit.* (1980: 169)

> [The priest meanwhile mounted the mare, and then he intoned quietly the resonant line from the psalms:
> 'Have mercy on me, oh God, according to your great compassion!'
> 'Clang, clang! Clang, clang!' responded the old man, wielding the bell with all his might to make it ring out loud and clear, while his wife covered his shoulders with a rug to protect him against the damp coldness of the night.]
> (2014: 175–76)

★　★　★　★　★

> *Sols de tant en tant aixecava els ulls enlaire i es posava a cantar baixet, com si resés, un altre planyent versícul:*
> — *¡Renta'm, Senyor, de la meva iniquitat més d'un cop i més de dos, i esbandeix-me de pecat!*
> — Ganning, gannang! Ganning, gannang! — *tornava a fer el jaio, com acompanyant amb els tocs de la campana les paraules sagrades del rector.* (1980: 169)

> [Only occasionally did he look up and then begin to chant in a low voice, as though praying, another plaintive versicle:
> 'Wash me, wash me thoroughly, Lord, from my iniquity and cleanse me from my sin!'
> Clang, clang! Clang, clang! was once again the old man's response, as if the sound of the bell was the right accompaniment to the holy words of the priest.]
> (2014: 176)

The notion of 'landscape of the mind' surfaces prominently in the features of the novel briefly discussed above. And we have seen how the effects of this are also felt, complementarily, in Casellas's selective use of an earthy vocabulary and rough-edged diction (at the time a notable innovation in literary Catalan) for presenting description and action as well as the rustic characters' speech.

I have tried to illustrate some principal stylistic features of the original to which the translation aspires to be faithful. Fidelity has also been sought in rendering the subtle relationship between a landscape and the *two* minds which are central in *Dark*

Vales: that of the narrator, merging with that of the main character. Casellas was writing at a time when the conventions of nineteenth-century realism were being seriously questioned. Objectivity and the 'authority' of the omniscient, impersonal narrator were undermined by narrative modes which offered alternatives to the great social *tableaux* of earlier realism/naturalism. Less expansive perspectives were explored in order to communicate moods and subtleties experienced by the individual mind. Under the influence of Impressionist and post-Symbolist aesthetics, suggestion challenged statement, and 'aesthetic emotion' (Casellas's own term) was deemed superior to reason-based analysis and knowledge. In this way, narrative acquired its own poetics which was deemed superior to the 'objective' realism grounded in conventions which had evolved to reflect the workings of entire societies and the lives of the individuals contained in them. Like many contemporary authors in other literatures, Casellas replaced the discredited omniscient narrator of conventional realism by inserting another consciousness in the narrative as a presence operating in the text close to the level of a character's mind. This is particularly evident in the treatment of the priest-protagonist's dreams, visions and hallucinations, leading up to and then after his breakdown, from Chapter 14 onwards. Especially innovative and challenging is the exploration of his 'locked in' catatonic condition in the final chapters. The Catalan author was feeling his individual way towards a kind of psychological novel like that which had been characterized in Henry James's concept of the 'atmosphere of the mind' and which would be perfected by Virginia Woolf. (Furthermore, there are points in *Dark Vales* where the relationship between the two 'minds' comes close to breaking point and where fragmentation of traditional narrative structures and syntax seems imminent, with liberation in the form of Joycean stream of consciousness and automatic writing just over the horizon.)

Llàtzer's struggle against the hostile world around him reaches its first climax in Chapter 14 ('La Missa Blanca i la Missa Negra'/White Mass and Black Mass) when he wills himself to perform the Mass in his own empty church, having been boycotted by the parishioners. The scene of the peasants' alternative sacrilegious ceremony, in the tavern at Puiggraciós, is related in a single paragraph presenting an infernal vision which comes to the priest *[c]om si tingués el do de veure les coses llunyes i amagades* (1980: 147), 'as though he were blessed with the gift of being able to see distant and hidden things' (2014: 147). And from this point onwards the narrative focus brings ever closer together, without quite fusing them, the narrator's perspective and the consciousness of the character, creating a hallucinatory atmosphere which prevails through to the sudden black-out effect of the ambiguous final scene. Sound effects are also strongly intensified in these final chapters where the sense of a mind closing in on itself is created, and where the essentially poetic function of language drawing attention to itself is prominent, as in this segment from Chapter 16, 'Udols de la nit'/Howls in the Night:

> *Entremig de la quietud que el rodejava, s'havia avesat a distingir els sorolls més desmaiats, més febles... i aixís passava llargues hores escoltant, escoltant en les tenebres, com si volgués desxifrar el llenguatge ignorat dels milers de sers i coses que parlen o sospiren, que glapeixen o ploren mansament dins del gran silenci de la nit.*

El cruixir de les fulles seques que s'arrosseguen somogudes per les bestioletes del terrer; l'estremitud que fan les branques dels arbres, esgarrifades per l'oreig; la cantarella del reguerol, que es va escorrent de gota en gota; la fressa llunyana del ramat, que es remena de sobte dins del clos; el clam mig apagat del malalt, que es tomba dins del seu llit d'agonia... tot això plegat componia, al fons del sot, la cantúria de la nit, trista i esporuguidora com una remor de l'altre món. Escoltant, escoltant en la quietud de les tenebres, mossèn Llàtzer havia arribat a distingir les veus dels feréstecs aucellots que s'ajoquen pels relleus del cingle o per les branques de sobre els avencs. (1980: 161–62)

[In the vast stillness that surrounded him, he had become accustomed to distinguishing the faintest, most feeble sounds... and so he spent long hours listening, listening in the dark, as though he were trying to decipher the unknown language of the thousands of beings and things which speak or sigh, which yelp or weep meekly in the great silence of the night.

The rustling of dry leaves disturbed by tiny creatures on the ground; the stirring of the tree tops when the branches suddenly feel a puff of wind; the gentle trickling sound coming from an irrigation ditch; distant noises made by sheep and cows moving now and then out in the fields; the muffled cry of the invalid turning over in the bed where their life is coming to its close... these were the sounds which combined to form deep in the ravines the chorus of the night, mournful and disturbing, like a murmur coming from the other world. Father Llàtzer's ears were attuned now to identifying in the dead of night the different calls of the fearsome nocturnal birds which nest in the cracks of cliff faces or in overhanging branches above a chasm.] (2014: 166–67)

Chapter 16 supplies a longer internalized vision of peasant debauchery presided over by La Roda-soques at Puiggraciós, and it concludes with a second *tour de force* (this time of narrative suspense) based again on sound effects, the last one being a knock on the priest's door:

Hi va haver una estona de silenci... L'home devia palpar un xic fins a trobar el picaportes. Després va trucar:
Pum, pum!... (1980: 166)

[There was silence for a moment... The person must have been groping to find the door knocker. Then it was in his hand: *Bang, bang...* (2014: 172)

The approach of this visitor has been followed through Llàtzer's perception of a sequence of howls, louder and louder, from dogs at different points on the way down the mountain paths in the direction of the priest's house. This impressive chapter is the prelude to the cruel trick (set up and perpetrated, we must assume, by the 'local entertainer' Carbassot/Pumpkin Face), to torture the priest further. Chapters 17 ('Camí del calvari'/The Road to Calvary) and 18 ('Escarnots al sagrament'/Sacrilege) are devoted to narrating the episode which is Llàtzer's own 'Road to Calvary'. The slower narrative rhythm here corresponds to the strength of (deluded) optimism and renewed vigour felt now by the priest as he goes with his servant to administer the last rites to a dying man at the furthest extreme of the parish. The change of pace makes all the more powerful the psychological relapse in Llàtzer and the subsequent shock of the denouement...

The above notes outline a reading of Casellas's highly original novel which underlies the translation strategy followed. The 'academic' issues involved should not, however, distract from the immediate appeal of *Dark Vales*. This derives from the main drama of the storyline; the balanced distribution of subsidiary plot themes and of the individual chapter units (each separately subtitled like cantos of a larger poetic whole); the poetic and musical effects of linguistic patterns: the way in which all these primary elements are worked into a coherent fictional whole, the cogent and sound composition of an engaging creative product. Characterization is highly stylized, of course, conforming to the author's innovative ambition and primary artistic intention. The figure of Father Llàtzer has to bear a lot of weight, perhaps too much. This, however, is an inevitable consequence of how the story is told, with the implications that are touched upon in the previous paragraph.

The rest of the characterization merits brief comment. Presentation of the atavistic rustics as an amorphous, subhuman mass communicates a vision which poetically reworks Zola's concept of *la bête humaine* in the light of contemporary trends in the new fields of psychology, sociology and criminology. Excessive monotony of this artistically necessary feature is obviated by the presence of two minor figures who are strategically individuated to a degree, picked out of the peasant crowd and endowed with more 'character' than other members of the rustic chorus, the latter differentiated only by resemblances to certain animals: Aleix the Truffle Man, who stars in the overture that is Chapter 1 ('L'Aleix de les Tòfones'/Aleix the Truffle Man) and whose lurking figure is glimpsed at several crucial points in the story; then, feebler as a presence than Aleix, pumpkin-faced Carbassot, who figures in the interlude provided in Chapter 6 ('La gent dels llimbs'/Dwellers in Limbo). This pairing is complemented by other presences, characters at an intermediate level between the parishioners and their priest: the old couple who serve Father Llàtzer, and the local whore. The priest's household companions, Josep and Mariagna almost steal the show as a double-act Sancho Panza to Father Llàtzer's Don Quixote. Joan Maragall saw them as just 'bellas figuras de retablo' [appealing marionettes], but the inseparable pair supply an authentically human, and humane, dimension to a novel which, given the insistence of its symbolism and its prevailing bleakness of outlook, would be much the poorer, excessively 'intellectual', without them.

In conclusion, I hope that my translation-centred perspective here has served to illuminate the artistic coherence of *Els sots feréstecs* as a sophisticated narrative composition: from that deliberately challenging first sentence, through landscape 'painting', the chorus of anonymous peasant voices, stylized characterization around the central personality, through the travails of *mossèn* Llàtzer to his tragic defeat. Fragments of his catatonic interior monologue are conveyed from inside his head as he lies surrounded at the end by his gawping flock, now silenced, who have come to see him dead and buried. The last words in reported speech are strategically placed as a prelude to this final scene of Chapter 20 ('Les Absoltes'/Absolution) and they are uttered, appropriately, by the 'old bugger' Aleix the Truffle Man:

> [...] *en Pere mestre va dir, tot sorneguer:*
> — *Ara rai!... Ja podem baixar-hi sense por...*
> — *Ta full! Uidà! Murta la cuca, murt lu verí...* — *va respondre l'Aleix de les Tòfones, mig rient per sota el nas.* (1980: 189)

[[...] Pere Mestre said very sarcastically:
      'There's no problem any more... We need not be frightened now about paying him a visit...'
      'Too flaming right, 'pon my life! Dead dogs don't bite...' responded Aleix the truffle man with a snigger.] (2014: 202)

The end of *Els sots feréstecs* is indeed in its beginning, and the *Dark Vales* version marks the culmination of a fascination with the novel that goes right back to when I first read it, half a century ago.

Works Cited

CASELLAS, RAIMON. 1980 [1901]. *Els sots feréstecs* (Barcelona: Laia)
——. 2014. *Dark Vales*, trans. by Alan Yates (Sawtry, Cambs: Dedalus)

INDEX

———